Practical XView Programming

Kenneth W. Bibb and Larry Wake

John Wiley & Sons, Inc.
New York · Chichester · Brisbane · Toronto · Singapore

Library of Congress Cataloging-in-Publication Data

Bibb, Kenneth.
     Practical XView programming / Kenneth Bibb and Larry Wake.
          p.   cm.
     Includes bibliographical references and index.
     ISBN 0-471-57460-0
     1. Windows (Computer programs)   2. XView.   I. Wake Larry.
     II. Title.
     QA76.76.W56B53 1993
     005.4'3–dc20   92-30943
                                                              CIP

Printed in the United States of America

10 9 8 7 6 5 4 3 2 1

Dedications

Ken: to April Allgaier, who has always pushed me to excel, listened when I rambled, and who is generally endearing, despite her love of bats and her tendency of almost always being right:

"Not fare well, But fare forward, voyagers"

—T. S. Eliot

Larry: This effort is dedicated to my wife, Hallie, for putting up with my time away from reality during a period when our family was in the midst of its own production; to Kyrie, for being a just generally great daughter, and to Kevin, nine days old today, for waiting until after deadline to make his appearance. Having a baby is something like writing a book...

—lkw 7/8/92

Introduction

WHY THIS BOOK?

On a bright, smoggy, Southern California spring morning, Larry and Ken bemoaned the state of XView over some carne asada burritos. There should be another XView book, one filled with tips and tricks, one with practical examples, one that makes the voluminous information easier to comprehend. They both thought that this would be a Really Nice Thing ™, Larry put his sunglasses back on, and they both went back to work.

Ken, being one of those thick individuals who always tries to convert talk into work, went and laid the groundwork for this book. Larry was surprised, but enthusiastically joined.

These two wildly different individuals were fortunately able to agree on a few things (if they hadn't, you wouldn't be reading this book):

- Parts of XView needed clarifying.
- Tips and tricks were waiting to be shared.
- Extra examples would be useful.
- Practical XView programs should be available.
- Diagrams would be nice.

We hope this book has accomplished these things, and we hope that you, the reader, will have a better understanding of XView. If not, constructive criticism and enthusiastic ravings can be emailed to

Ken Bibb   `jester@crash.cts.com`
Larry Wake   `Larry.Wake@West.Sun.COM`

For the Internet-impaired, mail can be sent to the authors in care of the publisher. As always, flames to **`/dev/null`**.

WHY XVIEW?

Using XView makes life a lot easier if you're trying to write software. Much of the low-level work has already been done for you, so that using XView instead of XLib is similar to programming in Prolog instead of assembler. The biggest reason why XView makes life easier is its simple interface. XView uses six functions for most of the work. Compare this to the arcane and voluminous function list that you need when learning Windows 3.0 or its mutant offspring Motif, and XView makes sense.

XView does a lot of your work for you. Through the use of object-oriented techniques, you can reuse created objects, and you can reuse code easily and efficiently. The notifier model makes most event handling simpler. When you create an instance of an object, you are quickly rewarded with a working object that uses the many default attributes that are available.

The XView toolkit also makes it easier to create Open Look–compliant programs, which are easier for the user to learn. Some programmers find Open Look fascist at times, but a lot of effort went into its design, and it *does* work. A user who sits down to an Open Look GUI–compliant program can reuse knowledge learned from other similar programs. This reusability is one of the best features of GUIs. The fundamentals required for Open Look compliance are built into the XView toolkit, but you still have to be careful of what you do; there are certain features that you'll have to build into your program if you want it to be fully compliant.

XView also easily integrates with Remote Procedure Calls (RPC), letting you create distributed programs with an Open Look GUI in front. This allows you to take advantage of both the network and the screen.

One of the best features of XView is the free source code. With the source, you can see how various features were implemented, and you can even use the source to locate (and fix) bugs. (But there aren't any bugs, right?)

Don't get the idea that XView is capable of solving all of your interface woes. There are a number of "bad" points to XView. If you plan on writing software that can run on a large number of platforms, especially nonnative Open Look platforms, XView may not be as portable as some choices—although it *is* available on a large number of platforms, including Sun, Solbourne, Hewlett-Packard, DEC, IBM, and DOS. XView makes use of certain window decorations and underlying mechanisms that are not available in environments like Motif. If you're interested in portability, you may want to look at OLIT[1] or one of the virtual toolkits like OI or XVT instead of XView (or just avoid the neat but nonportable parts of XView).

If you're trying to port an entire *environment,* XView is a very good choice. Full source code is available with SVR4 and via anonymous FTP on machines like **export.lcs.mit.edu**. This includes source for all of the packages, **olwm** (a window manager), and some other goodies.

Because XView implements the Open Look standards, it is not as flexible as XLib (which doesn't implement anyone's standards). When you write Open Look–compliant programs, XView helps you comply. When you're trying to break those rules, XView bares its claws and fights you tooth and nail. If you want to ignore Open Look, you'd probably be better off with another toolkit.

For applications that are almost exclusively going to work with PostScript, you will probably want to use tNt (the NeWS toolkit) instead. tNt is a PostScript-based (NeWS) interface that implements the Open Look GUI. tNt is, unfortunately, not very portable. XView also provides viewable PostScript[2] capabilities in the **XVPS** object, although most of it is based on X.

Some people want to be deviant and write programs that adhere to no existing standard. Sometimes the reason for this is good (an entirely new kind of application that has no precedent). Other reasons aren't so good—the programmer likes writing user-hostile software, forcing the users into learning an arcane interface that bears no resemblance to anything they'll ever see again.

Finally, XView doesn't provide an easy-to-use graphics paradigm. There are other packages (like Slingshot) that provide graphics. Programs using graphics will also have to use XGL, XLib (XLib makes you realize why they are called graphics *primitives*), or some other package.

---

[1]OLIT may be easier to port because it is based on Xt. You will probably run into many of the same operating problems running under a Motif manager, however, since OLIT uses the same window decorations used by XView.

[2]Neither tNt nor **XVPS** provides Display PostScript. They do allow you to view normal PostScript output. The **XVPS** doesn't technically provide PostScript functionality, since it opens a NeWS connection and lets you use NeWS CPS calls into a **PSCANVAS** xid. In order for **XVPS** to work you must have an X/NeWS server.

Acknowledgments

This project involved a lot of people, and more time than either of the authors originally anticipated. The people, events, and things that shaped this book, though not always visible on the surface, are there deep within.

Ken's Acknowledgments

Thanks to Diane Cerra of John Wiley for her patience and faith in this project; Terri Hudson of John Wiley for showing me how a book goes together, general cheerleading, and for being on the Internet; and Melanie Edmonds and the rest of Publication Services for making this shine. Matt and Chris of Waterside Productions for their help, guidance, and work (the best agents, bar none).

Thanks to my reviewers: Rick "Tank" Goldstein of SunSoft's XView development team for showing me how XView programming is *really* done and for his complaints and nags ("Oh, come on! This is a matter of perspective"); Brett Doehr, for picking the nits, guidance in vision, and for moments of Monty Python madness ("Three shall be the number of the buttons"); and Frank Greco, for writing my favorite computer column ("Pink Noise") and for discussions, guidance, and complaints.

Thanks to Heather Maxion for the **troff** formatting, indexing, sanity checks, spell checks, proofreading, and the incredible handmade linguini with clam sauce that fueled me through the final hours of this project.

Special thanks to Byte & Floppy Computers for renting the SPARCstation IPC, Bernoulli 90 Workstation Transportable, DataStor 1.2G drive, and SPARC printer used in the writing of this book.

Thanks to Island Graphics for providing a copy of their excellent program, Island Write, Draw & Paint, which was used to create all of the illustrations in this book (except for the SlingShot hierarchy chart.)

Thanks to the Free Software Foundation for their excellent work on the GNU C and C++ compilers, which were used on many of the examples.

Thanks to the dreaded Internet group, who provided encouragement, suggestions, advice, and general distraction: Anthony Doan (it's done, you can shut up now! b-geek), Charles Boudlin (friend, hunter of wabbits, typer of attributes), Rachel Nolan (**rdspock** *grin* yet-another-b-geek), Amy Bouck (no squirrels here), Scott McMahon (whose only fault is liking Genesis a wee bit too much), Yvonne ("stapler obsession"—yet-another-b-geek), Fred (**nackmor**), Trent Jakobec (the Sylvian is doing fine), John Hiatt (how's the Dream Academy?), Lee Quin (to FAQ or not to FAQ . . .).

Thanks to the people of Sun: Bill Joy (for creating my favorite programs—including **vi**, which was used for the majority of the text entry, and all of my C code), Brian Warkenstein (SlingShot is one of the best things about XView), Larry Wake (my coauthor), Jeff Wheelock (database deity), Gail Matthews (graphics godess), Derek Knight (captain connectivity), Mark Christie (all-around cool computer dude), and Kemer Thompson (Kernel Kosmos).

To the NAVSEACENPAC crowd: Jim Nelms, Rick Ezneker, Sharon Butler, Arlene Nevland, Donna Russell, Rick Braithwaite, Rich Wallace, and all the rest.

Thanks to the After Hours (defunct and missed) crowd that helped me through the early stages of this project: Seth Borden (**seth**), Heather Maxion (**max**—om shanti, lizardfriend), Heather Venzie (**ninelives**—the friendly goddess), Aurilee Gamboa (**skylark**—shiny happy person), Kimberly Smith (**sonatina**—the chick with the funky blue eyes), Jayson Mondala (**vader**—programmer with an attitude), Matt Cole (**newt**—"I'm a little teapot"), David Sworder (**commodities man**—anime and futures).

The Anarchy X group, who helped me during the middle stages: Paul Ferraro (**highlander**), Brian Vogelsang (**shylock**), Jason Hough (**owilde**), Michelle Danko (**jet city woman**—goddess!), Shari Ver Berkmoes (for being such a **sprout**).

Very special thanks to Random Hold, "Avalanche"; Marillion "Script For A Jester's Tear" (HIE concert: choice); Fish, "Internal Exile"; Happy Rhodes, "Warpaint"; David Sylvian, "Weatherbox"; King Crimson, "Three Of A Perfect Pair"; Queensryche, "Operation Livecrime" (great concert); John Katchur, "Mercy Road"; and Tori Amos, "Little Earthquakes" (moving concert), for providing the soundtrack.

And thanks to these wild and varied people and events that I'll always associate with this book: my parents; Dan Gookin (you got me into this mess!); John and Doreen Russell; Rochelle Palmer–Rabeau; Marilyn White; Dave and Susan Taylor; Kay Adams (for her AP English class); TK Dunseath; P Ledden; Cynthia N. Knox ('cause I promised I would do this); the Pinkerton guards at Renaissance, for keeping me alive; Marillion, for the chat after the Los Angeles concert; and, finally, the coyotes that keep shadowing me on my nocturnal ramblings.

Larry's Acknowledgments

The most obvious and most appropriate person to ackowledge here is Ken, for getting me enmeshed in this whole thing. Writing a book is something like having a baby, and Ken did a fine job of telling me when to push.

Additional Packages

There are a couple of packages that are useful for XView programmers.

Devguide   An interactive interface builder sold by Sun, which has an option to generate XView code.

SlingShot   A package of extensions, providing a number of useful objects that can be used on **CANVAS_SHELL**s (not a **CANVAS**, but an amazing simulation of one).

GNU gcc 2.0   There is a patch which makes **gcc** 2.0 XView-literate. It will catch a number of your more blatant errors.

OLGX   Open Look Graphics for X. Handles the painting of many Open Look objects.

Further Sources

Where to Get the Code from This Book

There are a number of places where you can get the code that's used in this book. If you have anonymous FTP access, it is available at the following site:

```
export.lcs.mit.edu
```

It will probably be carried by other sites, too. Ask **archie** (**archie@cs.mcgill.ca**), which will let you know where you can find it. The file will be called **xvprac.tar.Z**.

For those of you who aren't connected to the Internet, a disk containing the source code can be purchased from Arastar Computing for $15 (California state residents please include local sales tax). Check or money order accepted.

Files are available in the following formats:

- 3.5″ **tar** format (**tar xvf /dev/rfd0a**)
- 3.5″ 1.44M DOS format (**xvprac.zip**)
- 5.25″ 360K DOS format (**xvprac.zip**)

Send disk requests to:
Arastar Computing
PO Box 12186
La Jolla, CA 92039-2186

Where to Get XView Source Code

The source code to the XView library (and **olwm**) is available via anonymous FTP from the following sites, which are listed by country and machine name. The directory containing the XView source is also given. Before downloading the XView library from one of these sites, you should probably check **archie**[3] to verify that it is still available there.

Australia:

plaza.aarnet.edu.au	(139.130.4.6)	**/X11/contrib/xview3**
sirius.ucs.adelaide.edu.au	(129.127.40.3)	**/pub/X/R4/contrib/xview3**

---

[3] If you're not familiar with the **archie** archive-listing servers, see Appendix A at the back of this book.

Canada:

iskut.ucs.ubc.ca   (137.82.27.61) `/pub/xview`

Czechoslovakia:

iamsun.unibe.ch   (130.92.64.10) `/X11/XView`

Finland:

cs.tut.fi   (130.230.4.2) `/pub/src/openwin`
nic.funet.fi   (128.214.6.100) `/pub/X11/contrib/xview3`

Germany:

rs3.hrz.th-darmstadt.de   (130.83.55.75) `/pub/X11/contrib/xview3`
rzsun2.informatik.uni-hamburg.de   (188.1.20.32) `/pub/X/xview3`
sun0.urz.uni-heidelberg.de   (129.206.100.126) `/pub/X11/contrib/xview3`
sun1.ruf.uni-freiburg.de   (132.230.1.1) `/X11/contrib/xview3`
sun8.ruf.uni-freiburg.de   (132.230.1.56) `/X11/contrib/xview3`
x11.informatik.uni-dortmund.de   (129.217.26.140) `/pub/contrib/xview3`

Japan:

skgate0.mei.co.jp   (132.182.49.2) `/free/X/toolkits/xview3`

Norway:

ugle.unit.no   (129.241.1.97) `/pub/X11/contrib/xview3`

Sweden:

kth.se   (130.237.72.201)   `/kth/Xcontrib/Toolkits`
                                              `/XView`

United Kingdom:

src.doc.ic.ac.uk   (146.169.3.7) `/graphics/X11/contrib/xview3`

United States:

export.lcs.mit.edu   (18.24.0.12) `/contrib/xview3`
ftp.uu.net   (137.39.1.9) `/packages/X/contrib/xview3`
gatekeeper.dec.com   (16.1.0.2) `/X11/contrib/xview3`
pprg.eece.unm.edu   (192.31.154.1) `/pub/dist/xview`
xview.ucdavis.edu   (128.120.1.150) `/XView/XView3.0`

Usenet Groups

If you get usenet news, and you're interested in up-to-date news on the Open Look GUI and XView, you should subscribe to the following two groups:

alt.toolkits.xview	The XView newsgroup
comp.windows.openlook	The Open Look GUI newsgroup

There is some overlap between the two groups, and many sites don't carry the **alt** hierarchy. These groups are a great source for sample programs,

Usenet access is available all across the country either free (through nixpub[4] sites) or for a fee (through UUNET, PSI, and other local sources[5]). This is a great place for quick help. If you have any questions concerning XView, you can usually have an answer from someone within a day or two if you post your question to one of these newsgroups.

If you receive both groups, you might want to crosspost between the two groups. But if you do, remember to set your Follow-up field to one group or the other (so the thread doesn't wind up going in two different directions). If your site *doesn't* carry **alt.toolkits.xview**, some administrators are willing to add it—you may want to point out that it is a low-volume group that like all **alt** newsgroups can be added without taking the entire **alt** hierarchy.

---

[4]Nixpub sites are Public Access Unix Systems. The list of them is posted monthly to **alt.bbs** and should be available from your local university or any other local site that is already on the Internet. The list is both too long and too transient to be printed here.

[5]A good source of information on usenet is *Managing UUCP and Usenet,* by O'Reilly/Todino, published by O'Reilly & Associates. The latest edition also mentions UUCP programs available on DOS and Macintosh platforms.

Abbreviations Used in this Book

Some of the abbreviations in the following list refer to books that can be considered "standard works" in the XView world. Information on these books is provided in the bibliography at the end of this book. Other useful abbreviations are also expanded.

API	Application programmer's interface
FSF	Free Software Foundation
FTP	File Transfer Protocol
GNT	Generate tNt (part of Devguide)
GNU	Gnu is not UNIX
GOLIT	Generate OLIT (part of Devguide)
GUI	Graphical User Interface
GXV	Generate XView (part of Devguide)
GXV++	Generate XView/C++ (part of Devguide)
ICCCM	*Inter-Client Communications Conventions Manual*
OL	Open Look
OLFS	Sun Microsystems, *Open Look Graphical User Interface Functional Specification*
OLGX	Open Look Graphics for X
OLIT	Open Look Intrinsics Toolkit
OLSG	Sun Microsystems, *Open Look Graphical User Interface Application Style Guide*
RPC	Remote Procedure Calls
RTFM	Read the friendly manual
RTOFM	Read the other friendly manual
tNt	the NeWS toolkit
UI	User interface
UTSL	See the appropriate XView source file (literally, "Use the Source, Luke")
XGL	X Graphics Library
XVPM	Heller, *XView Programming Manual,* 3rd ed.
XVRM	Van Raalte, *XView Reference Manual for XView Version 3*
XView	X Window-System-based Visual/Integrated Environment for Workstations

Contents

List of Figures and Tables

▮▮▮ FIGURES

TABLES

XVIEW CONCEPTS

The Basic Blocks of XView

Supervisor:	"On this next project, you're to use the XView toolkit."
Programmer:	"OK. I can learn that."
Supervisor:	"Oh, by the way, the project is due next Friday."
Programmer:	"!"

Professional programmers do not usually learn packages at their leisure. They usually learn packages under duress and deadlines, cursing the developers that made the package, the management that decided to utilize the package, and the writers who were supposed to document the package. They spill coffee on their manuals while listening to Kim Deal sing "Gigantic" on their Sun-CDs. Student programmers eat croissants, sip espresso, and complain about the way their fees are increasing while deciding between Palm Springs and London as a spring break destination. Neither group has time for theory—they aren't interested in how things work. But for those who have met the deadlines, or have returned from spring break and are looking for something to do, a little theory might be nice, no?

When it comes to XView, the "theory" is no less important than knowing the difference between a **float** and an **int**. The theory of XView is what gives you the power to use XView easily.

XView uses an *object-oriented* interface for GUI development. An object is like a chocolate—kind of a lump with something inside it, which may be sweet and sticky. XView calls facts like these attributes and uses them to describe the object. Chocolate, for instance, has a country of manufacture, a manufacturer, the type of chocolate, and a filling (sometimes). If chocolate were an XView object, you could describe two kinds of chocolate this way:

```
xv_create(NULL, CHOCOLATE,
    CHOC_MANUFACTURER, "Cadbury's",
    CHOC_COUNTRY,   "UK",
    CHOC_TYPE,   DARK,
    CHOC_FILLING,   "Almonds",
    NULL);

xv_create(NULL, CHOCOLATE,
    CHOC_MANUFACTURER, "Hershey's",
    CHOC_COUNTRY,   "US",
    CHOC_TYPE,   MILK,
    CHOC_FILLING,   NULL,
    NULL);
```

Pretty straightforward, isn't it? (It's OK to go grab some Godiva chocolates now.)

Besides attributes, you work with *packages*. A package is just Sun's way of implementing a class. In an object-oriented world, Coke and Pepsi might be in the same class but in a different class than Cheez Whiz. (They would all probably have a common parent class since all are fluid and almost entirely artificial.) In XView, a button (you know, those funky graphics things that you can click on with your mouse) is different from a font (you can't see a font except by using it to display characters), but both are represented by packages. The XView development team knows that most programmers just want to finish their projects so they can hit the beach (or their foreheads), so they gave their packages meaningful names, like **PANEL_BUTTON** (for buttons) and **FONT** (for fonts). If a package comes from the same parent as another package, you'll see common attributes that have been *inherited* from the parent. In the real world, you can inherit hair on your palms or an overwhelming desire to deep-fry all of your food; in XView, your **CANVAS** object may inherit a **WIN_BACKGROUND_COLOR** attribute.

In summary, there are three things that you need to know about XView:

- The API (functions)
- Packages (and how to make new ones)
- Attributes (and how to set/get them)

You should also remember that XView does *not* give you Open Look–compliant programs automatically. You have to work for compliance, as for most things in life. For more info on what is required for OL compliance, read the OLFS and OLSG.

If you've got a deadline to meet, and you need something *now*, use Sun's Devguide program. It lets you interactively design your interface, generating a large portion of your code for you. For those with more time, XView *can* be done by hand. Most of the programs in the book were done this way, since Ken is a stubborn, thick-headed programmer.

The XView API

XView has a small set of general-purpose functions, which you'll use all of the time. There are a few other functions, which I will ignore at this time, because you won't use them as much as these six biggies.

xv_create( )	Creates instances of objects. You can also set the attributes of the new object at the same time; you don't have to make two calls to do something that a single call could easily do.
xv_destroy( )	Destroys instances of objects. People with destructive tendencies like this function from what I hear. It's used infrequently, because C programmers like to use all available memory whenever possible.
xv_destroy_safe( )	Usually better than **xv_destroy()** because it delays the destroy action until it is "safe" to destroy the object.
xv_find( )	A super-**xv_create()** that will see whether you already created something. If the object you're creating already exists, this function will return that object's handle[1] to you instead of creating a new instance of the object. Useful with things like fonts and cursors.
xv_get( )	Reads an attribute's current setting. This is usually needed to figure out what settings another function gave the object.
xv_set( )	Sets an attribute. This can be used to change the attributes on an existing object.

That's all of them. Unlike Microsoft Windows with its (literally) hundreds of functions for creating frames and buttons, XView give you this small set. Neat. After you use them a few times, they'll make more sense than **ioctl()**.

This is so simple because XView's object-oriented. What are the benefits of objects that you hear the pundits crow about? One real-world benefit of objects is subclassing. You can make a subclass and then turn around and make as many instances of that object as your heart desires.

---

[1] A *handle* is a value that is used to reference an object.

Suppose you have to create ten popups that are all 90 percent the same. You can create a **MYPOPUP** class and make ten instances of it. Since these popups have 90 percent in common, you can make that part of them default to the values that you need. When you create each **MYPOPUP** object, you only have to set the few attributes that need to be changed for that popup.

A "template" object, which can be used for creating these subclasses, is provided later in this chapter.

CREATING OBJECTS

The **xv_create()** function is used to create an object instance. You can also change settings while you're at it. To create a button, for example, you could say

```
(void) xv_create ( panel, PANEL_BUTTON,
   PANEL_LABEL_STRING, "Push Me",
   PANEL_NOTIFY_PROC,  button_push,
   NULL );
```

The return value of **xv_create** is the button's handle. If the program will need to refer to the item, by using the handle, save it in a variable of the proper type (here **Panel_item**) like this:

```
Panel p;
Panel_item pb;

pb = (Panel_item) xv_create ( p, PANEL_BUTTON,
   PANEL_LABEL_STRING, "Push Me",
   PANEL_INACTIVE,   TRUE,
   NULL );
```

The first argument is the parent item. In this example, the parent item is p, the panel where this button is going to appear. If the object has the root window as a base (the base frame of your application, for example), you can set the parent item to **XV_NULL**. If there is no parent, and you don't want the item associated with the root window, you can use **NULL**.

The second argument is the package that you want to create (in this case **PANEL_BUTTON**). Some packages don't have visible parts (like **FONT**), though most do.

The rest of the argument list consists of attribute–value pairs. These attributes will modify the defaults, customizing the object into something useful.

Always end the **xv_create()** argument list with a **NULL**. If you forget the **NULL**, expect all sorts of weird things to happen in your program.

Alternatively, you could have created this with the following:

```
Panel p;
Panel_item pb;

pb = xv_create ( p, PANEL_BUTTON, NULL );

(void) xv_set ( pb,
   PANEL_LABEL_STRING, "Push Me",
   PANEL_NOTIFY_PROC,  button_push,
   NULL);
```

The first example is simpler than this one and is usually preferred. There are times when you'll need to change a single setting, or a group of settings, on an existing item. The **xv_set()** here is an example of how you would do that. Like **xv_create()**, the **xv_set()** must also have its argument list terminated with a **NULL**.

Finally, some objects, such as fonts and cursors, should use **xv_find()** instead of **xv_create()**. If the font is already being used by the program, **xv_find()** will reuse the existing handle. If the font does not already exist, and if the **XV_AUTO_CREATE** attribute is **TRUE**, **xv_find()** will create an instance of the object. The following example will create a basic pointer cursor if it can't find an existing one.

```
cursor = (Cursor) xv_find ( XV_NULL, CURSOR,
    XV_AUTO_CREATE, TRUE,
    CURSOR_SRC_CHAR, OLC_BASIC_PTR,
    CURSOR_MASK_CHAR, OLC_BASIC_MASK_PTR,
    NULL ) ;
```

OBJECT ATTRIBUTES

In this example, there are two attributes being set:

```
(void) xv_create ( panel, PANEL_BUTTON,
    PANEL_LABEL_STRING,  "Push Me",
    PANEL_NOTIFY_PROC,  button_push,
    NULL ) ;
```

PANEL_LABEL_STRING and **PANEL_NOTIFY_PROC** are attributes that I want to set on this button. These have the usual form for attribute–value pairs. Some attribute–value pairs have a more complex form:

```
XV_KEY_DATA,  UNIQUE_DATA_KEY,  item_to_pass,
```

This doesn't look like a pair, but it is, because the attribute consists of more than one item. (For more on this type of attribute, see the section "Attribute Keys" in Chapter 4.) A value may also consist of more than one item:

```
PANEL_CHOICE_STRINGS,    "Bretagne",
                         "Scotland",
                         "Ireland ",
                         "Wales   ",
                         NULL,
```

This attribute (**PANEL_CHOICE_STRINGS**) takes a variable number of values. Whenever you have a variable number of values, you need to end the list with a **NULL**. You'll occasionally end up with constructs like the following:

```
PANEL_CHOICE_STRINGS,    "Bretagne",
                         "Scotland",
                         "Ireland ",
                         "Wales   ",
                         NULL,
```

where you have two **NULL**s next to each other. The first **NULL** ends the variable list, and the second **NULL** terminates the list of attribute–value pairs.

You'll also need to see what the values of attributes are when you're programming. To display the **PANEL_VALUE** of a text item, for example, you could say

```
Panel_item t;

printf ( "value: %s/n", (char *) xv_get ( t, PANEL_VALUE ) );
```

The **xv_get ()** argument list is not terminated with a **NULL** pointer. It can accept only one attribute at a time. With an **XV_KEY_DATA**, attribute, the attribute also requires the name of the desired **XV_KEY_DATA** item.

```
Frame base = (Frame) xv_get ( panel_item, XV_KEY_DATA, BASE_KEY );
```

▋NHERITANCE

Objects inherit attributes. A **PANEL_BUTTON**, for instance, is subclassed from a **PANEL**, so it inherits the attributes of a **PANEL**. The **PANEL_NOTIFY_PROC** in the previous example is an example of an attribute that is inherited from a parent item. When looking for an attribute of an item, remember to check the attributes of the parent classes after looking at the attributes of the item's class. Figure 2.1 shows the hierarchy of classes. That **PANEL_BUTTON** that we have been talking about has, besides the **PANEL_BUTTON**–specific attributes, also those of the **PANEL**, **WINDOW**, **DRAWABLE**, and **GENERIC** packages.

In the following chapters, where each of the various packages is discussed, attribute diagrams will be included to show many of the package's attributes. You'll notice that some of the attributes are from these parental packages such as **WINDOW** and **XV**.

▋ESTROYING OBJECTS

Destroying an object is much easier than creating it. You pass the object's handle to **xv_destroy_safe ()** which destroys the object. No fuss, no muss. To kill the panel button **pb** created earlier, you could say

```
xv_destroy_safe ( pb ) ;
```

▋ELATING OBJECTS

You *relate* objects on a screen by making an object the parent of another one. For example, the popup shown in Figure 2.2 could be viewed as a hierarchy of objects as shown in Figure 2.3. The popup is the parent of the frame, the frame is the parent of the panel, and so on. After you create a few XView objects, you'll find that it's so easy to assign parents that you don't think about it.

▋BJECT METHODS (CALLBACKS)

In object-oriented programming lingo, the procedures related to an object are that object's methods. In XView, these are called *callbacks*. The callbacks have defined argument lists which will be mentioned as each kind of object is covered.

You'll often find in a callback that you need to access an object that isn't in the current function. To pass that information into the callback, use **XV_KEY_DATA** fields. They'll make your program easier to debug and more object-oriented. See Chapter 4 for more information on these fields.

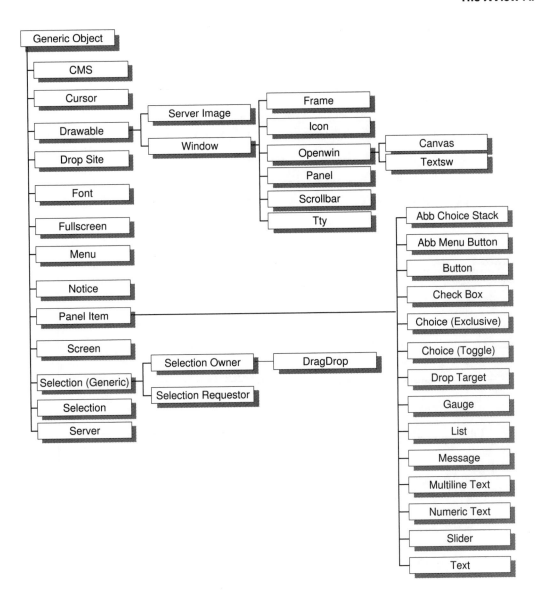

FIGURE 2.1 Object Hierarchy Chart

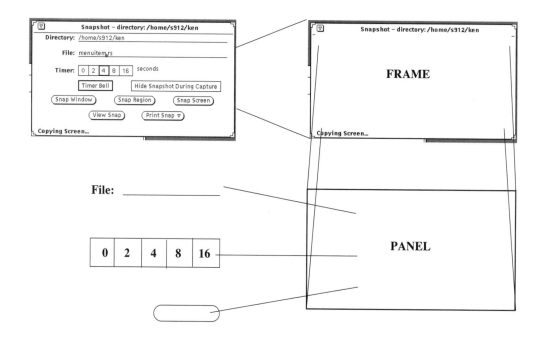

FIGURE 2.2 A Popup

PANEL ITEMS

FIGURE 2.3 Sample Popup Hierarchy

▬▬▬ **O**BJECT DEFAULTS

Many objects have default values associated with them. If this wasn't the case, you'd have to have horribly convoluted calls for creating each object, as you have in Microsoft Windows. Inherited values are taken care of whenever possible, but there are usually a couple of attributes that you *have* to set for each package. A label of some sort is usually required along with a value. You usually also want to associate a callback procedure.

Packages

Packages are used to represent your objects, so they get a lot of your attention. Many XView programmers don't consider subclassing off of existing packages to create items that they will need multiple times. This chapter contains an example of a "template" package that will make subclass creation easier.

THE TEMPLATE PACKAGE

The following are the files to create a "template" class, a dummy class that can easily be modified into whatever subclass you want. An example of a "snafu" class will follow (both the template class and the snafu class were created by Rick Goldstein).

The snafu package will show how to modify the templates into a package. To find out what you need to change in each of the template files, and to see what you should change it into, please compare the files between these two packages.

A package is made out of a collection of files. These files for a class called **TEMPLATE** would be:

`template.h`	Public header files
`template_impl.h`	Private header files
`template.c`	Methods
`template_data.c`	Package info

You'll also want to have a program for trying out the class. The **testcase.c** file listed later in the chapter is good for that.

The Public Header   The public header file is usually named after the package. It contains the attribute enumeration, defines, and other publicly available structures. The **template.h** public header looks like this:

```
/* template.h -- header file for template class
 * Author: Rick Goldstein
 */
```

11

```
#ifndef exten_template_DEFINED
#define exten_template_DEFINED

extern Xv_pkg  template_pkg;
#define TEMPLATE &template_pkg

typedef Xv_opaque Template;

#define ATTR_PKG_TEMPLATE ATTR_PKG_UNUSED_FIRST + 5/* Note: pick unique id */
#define TEMPLATE_ATTR(type, ordinal) ATTR(ATTR_PKG_TEMPLATE, type, ordinal)


typedef enum {
TEMPLATE_ATTRIBUTE = TEMPLATE_ATTR(ATTR_STRING, 1), /* dummy attribute */
} Template_attr;


typedef struct {
  Xv_generic_struct parent_data;  /* Note:  Modify for new subclass */
  Xv_opaque  private_data;
} Template_public;


#endif /* ~exten_template_DEFINED */
```

The Private Header   The name of the private header file usually is the name of the package with **_impl** appended. It contains declarations that are required by the package but not publicly available. The **template_impl.h** private header follows:

```
/* template_impl.h
 * Author: Rick Goldstein
 */

#include "template.h"


typedef struct {
Xv_opaque  public_self;
} Template_private;


#define TEMPLATE_PUBLIC(item) XV_PUBLIC(item)
#define TEMPLATE_PRIVATE(item)
                   XV_PRIVATE(Template_private, Template_public, item )
```

The Methods File   The methods file is named after the package. It contains definitions of the create, set, get, destroy, and find methods. Routines that are required by these methods should also be contained in this file. The **template.c** method file has the following format:

```
/* template.c -- methods for xv_create(), xv_get(), xv_set(), and xv_destroy()
 * (and xv_find() if you really need it)
```

```
 * Author:  Rick Goldstein
 */
#include <stdio.h>
#include <xview/xview.h>
#include <xview/panel.h>
#include "template_impl.h"



/*
 * xv_create() method
 */
Pkg_private int
template_init ( Xv_opaque owner, Template_public *public, Attr_avlist avlist)
{
  Template_private *private = xv_alloc ( Template_private );

  public->private_data = (Xv_opaque) private;
  private->public_self = (Xv_opaque) public;

 /*
  * Parse Create-Only Attributes
  *
  for (attrs=avlist; *attrs; attrs=attr_next ( attrs )) {
    switch ( (int) attrs[0] ) {
    default:
      break;


    }
  }
  */

  return XV_OK;
} /* template_init() */



/*
 * xv_set() method
 */
Pkg_private Xv_opaque
template_set ( Template public, Attr_avlist avlist )
{
  Template_private *private = TEMPLATE_PRIVATE(public);
  Attr_avlist attrs;

  for (attrs=avlist; *attrs; attrs=attr_next ( attrs )) {
    switch ( (int) attrs[0] ) {

    case XV_END_CREATE:
      break;

    default:
      xv_check_bad_attr ( TEMPLATE, attrs[0] );
      break;
    } /* switch() */
  } /* for() */

  return XV_OK;
} /* template_set() */
```

```
/*
 * xv_get() method
 */
Pkg_private Xv_opaque
template_get ( Template_public    *public,
  int                *status,
  Attr_attribute  attr,
  Attr_avlist      args
  )
{
  Template_private *private = TEMPLATE_PRIVATE(public);

  switch ( (int) attr ) {
  default :
    *status = xv_check_bad_attr ( TEMPLATE, attr );
    return (Xv_opaque) XV_OK;
  } /* switch */

} /* template_get() */




/*
 * xv_destroy() method
 */
Pkg_private int
template_destroy ( Template_public *public, Destroy_status status )
{
  Template_private *private = TEMPLATE_PRIVATE(public);

  if (status ==DESTROY_CLEANUP) {
    xv_free ( private );
  }
  return XV_OK;
} /* template_destroy() */
```

The Package Info File   The package info file is named after the package, with **_data** appended. It contains the information to fill out the **Xv_pkg** structure that represents this package. The **template_data.c** package info file looks like this:

```
/* template_data.c
 * Author: Rick Goldstein
 */

/*
 * Template package information
 */

#include <xview/xview.h>
#include "template_impl.h"

extern int    template_init();
extern Xv_opaque template_set();
extern Xv_opaque template_get();
extern int    template_destroy();

Xv_pkg template_pkg = {
  "Template",
```

```
    ATTR_PKG_TEMPLATE,
    sizeof(Template_public),
    XV_GENERIC_OBJECT, /* Note:  modify for new subclass */
    template_init,
    template_set,
    template_get,
    template_destroy,
    NULL                        /* no find */
};
```

A Test Program The following is a short program, `testcase.c`, for testing out your new package. (Since the **template** package doesn't do anything, neither does this test program.)

```
/* testcase.c -- test out our new subclass
 * Author: Rick "Tank" Goldstein
 */

#include <xview/xview.h>
#include <xview/panel.h>
#include "template.h"


int
main ( int argc, char **argv )
{
  Frame frame;
  Panel panel;

  (void) xv_init ( XV_INIT_ARGS, argc, argv, NULL );

  frame = xv_create ( NULL, FRAME, NULL );
  panel = xv_create ( frame, PANEL, NULL );

  /* what does the new subclass do? */


  window_fit ( panel );
  window_fit ( frame );
  xv_main_loop ( frame );
  return ( 0 );
}
```

▮HOW INSTANTIATION WORKS

When a method is executed, it traverses the object hierarchy, taking care of any parent classes. For example, a **CANVAS** item would follow the sequence shown in Figure 3.1.

▮THE SNAFU PACKAGE

The snafu package is implemented using the template files previously listed. The files are identified in the following list, and their listings, along with the **snafu_ui.h** listing, occupy the remainder of this chapter.

`snafu.h`	Public header
`snafu_impl.h`	Private header
`snafu.c`	Methods
`snafu_data.c`	Package info
`testcase.c`	Test the snafu package (see above)

xv_create()

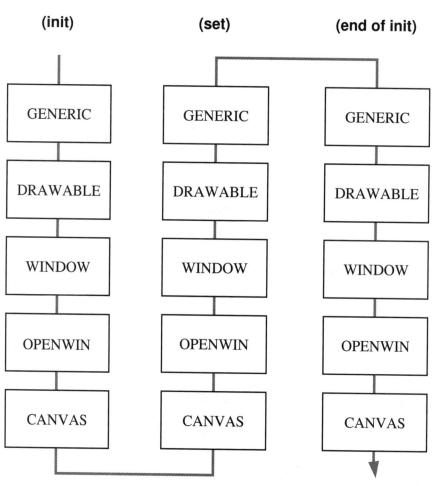

FIGURE 3.1a Instantiation Diagram (part 1)

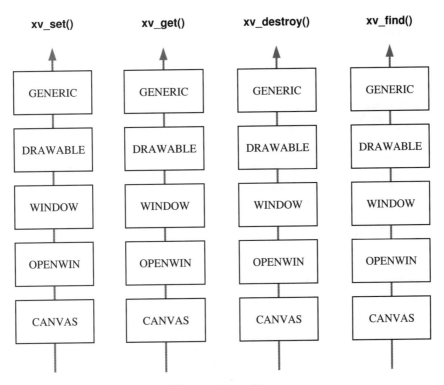

FIGURE 3.1b Instantiation Diagram (part 2)

```
/* snafu.h
 * Author: Rick Goldstein
 */

#ifndef snafu_DEFINED
#define snafu_DEFINED

#include <xview/xview.h>

extern Xv_pkg snafu_pkg;
#define SNAFU &snafu_pkg

typedef Xv_opaque Snafu;

#define ATTR_PKG_SNAFU ATTR_PKG_UNUSED_FIRST + 6
#define SNAFU_ATTR(type, ordinal) ATTR(ATTR_PKG_SNAFU, type, ordinal)


typedef enum {
  SNAFU_TYPE      = SNAFU_ATTR(ATTR_ENUM, 1),
  SNAFU_NAME      = SNAFU_ATTR(ATTR_STRING, 2),
  SNAFU_SEVERITY   = SNAFU_ATTR(ATTR_INT, 3),
  SNAFU_APPLY_PROC = SNAFU_ATTR(ATTR_FUNCTION_PTR, 4),
} Snafu_attr;

typedef enum {
  SNAFU_NUCLEAR,
```

```
        SNAFU_CHEMICAL,
        SNAFU_BIOLOGICAL,
    } Snafu_type;


    typedef struct {
      Xv_generic_struct parent_data;
      Xv_opaque  private_data;
    } Snafu_public;
    #endif /* ~snafu_DEFINED */
```

```
/* snafu_impl.h
 * Author:  Rick Goldstein
 */


#include "snafu.h"
#include "snafu_ui.h"


typedef snafu_popup_objects Snafu_ui;


/*
 * The following struct contains the stuff that is in the popup
 * when the last validation takes place (or default values on
 * creation).  This is useful for "Reset" button, or for delaying
 * creation to boost invocation performance.
 *
 * Note: There is a one-to-one correspondence between this struct
 * and the fields on the Property sheet.
 */
typedef struct {
  char name[81]; /* for simplicity, use static buf */
  int severity;
  Snafu_type type;
} Snafu_values;



typedef struct {
  Xv_opaque  public_self;
  Snafu_ui  *ui;    /* devguide stuff */
  Snafu_values *value;    /* popup's value */
  void  (*apply_proc)();
  Frame  owner;
  char label[81];   /* for simplicity, use static buf */
} Snafu_private;


#define SNAFU_PUBLIC(item) XV_PUBLIC(item)
#define SNAFU_PRIVATE(item) XV_PRIVATE(Snafu_private, Snafu_public, item)

#define SNAFU_FROM_OBJ(item)  (Snafu_private *) xv_get( (item), XV_KEY_DATA,
                                                         SNAFU_KEY );
```

```
/* snafu.c
 * Author:  Rick Goldstein
 */
```

```
#include <xview/xview.h>
#include <xview/panel.h>
#include "snafu_impl.h"

Attr_attribute INSTANCE = 0; /* may need to define this in main() */
static Attr_attribute SNAFU_KEY = 0;

static void snafu_reset_proc ( Panel_item item, Event *event );
static void snafu_apply_proc ( Panel_item item, Event *event );
static void snafu_set_value ( Snafu_values *value, Snafu_ui *ui );
static void snafu_accept_value ( Snafu_values *value, Snafu_ui *ui );
static void snafu_create_ui ( Snafu_private *private );


/*
 * xv_create() method
 */
Pkg_private int
snafu_init ( Xv_opaque owner, Snafu_public *public, Attr_avlist avlist)
{
  Snafu_private *private = xv_alloc ( Snafu_private );

  public->private_data = (Xv_opaque) private;
  private->public_self = (Xv_opaque) public;

  /*
   * setup default values and private data
   * Note:  good thing to use resources for...
   */
  private->value  = xv_alloc ( Snafu_values );
  strcpy ( private->value->name, "Unnamed Snafu" );
  private->value->severity = 50;
  private->value->type  = SNAFU_NUCLEAR;

  private->apply_proc  = (void (*)()) NULL;
  private->owner  = owner;
  strcpy ( private->label, "" );

 /*
  * Note:  to aid in invocation performance, we don't create
  * the UI objects here.  instead we wait until XV_SHOW is
  * set to TRUE.
  */

  return XV_OK;
} /* snafu_init() */




/*
 * xv_set() method
 */
Pkg_private Xv_opaque
snafu_set ( Snafu public, Attr_avlist avlist )
{
  Snafu_private *private = SNAFU_PRIVATE(public);
  Attr_avlist attrs;

  for (attrs=avlist; *attrs; attrs=attr_next ( attrs )) {
    switch ( (int) attrs[0] ) {
    case SNAFU_TYPE:
```

```
                 private->value->type = (Snafu_type) attrs[1];
                 if ( private->ui )
                   xv_set ( private->ui->type_choice, PANEL_VALUE,
                     private->value->type, NULL );
                 ATTR_CONSUME(attrs[0]);
                 break;

              case SNAFU_NAME:
                 strcpy ( private->value->name, (char *) attrs[1] );
                 if ( private->ui )
                   xv_set ( private->ui->name_text, PANEL_VALUE,
                     private->value->name, NULL );
                 ATTR_CONSUME(attrs[0]);
                 break;

              case SNAFU_SEVERITY:
                 private->value->severity = (int) attrs[1];
                 if ( private->ui )
                   xv_set ( private->ui->severity_slider, PANEL_VALUE,
                     private->ui->severity_slider, NULL );
                 ATTR_CONSUME(attrs[0]);
                 break;

              case SNAFU_APPLY_PROC:
                 private->apply_proc = (void (*)()) attrs[1];
                 ATTR_CONSUME(attrs[0]);
                 break;

              case XV_LABEL:
                 strcpy ( private->label, (char *) attrs[1] );
                 if ( private->ui )
                   xv_set ( private->ui->popup,
                     XV_LABEL, private->label, NULL );
                 ATTR_CONSUME(attrs[0]);
                 break;

              case XV_SHOW:
                 /* create UI objects when they need to be mapped! */
                 if ( ((int) attrs[1] != 0) && !private->ui )
                   snafu_create_ui ( private );
                 xv_set ( private->ui->popup, XV_SHOW, (int) attrs[1], NULL );
                 ATTR_CONSUME(attrs[0]);
                 break;

              case XV_END_CREATE:
                 break;

              default:
                 xv_check_bad_attr ( SNAFU, attrs[0] );
                 break;
           } /* switch() */
        } /* for() */

     return XV_OK;
   } /* snafu_set() */



   /*
    * xv_get() method
    */
   Pkg_private Xv_opaque
```

```
snafu_get ( Snafu_public    *public,
  int              *status,
  Attr_attribute   attr,
  Attr_avlist      args
  )
{
  Snafu_private *private = SNAFU_PRIVATE(public);

 /*
  * Note:  always "get" the validated value, not the
  * unvalidated popup contents for Snafu attributes.
  * the Panel package should do this also, but....
  */
  switch ( (int) attr ) {
  case SNAFU_TYPE:
    return (Xv_opaque) private->value->type;

  case SNAFU_NAME:
    return (Xv_opaque) private->value->name;

  case SNAFU_SEVERITY:
    return (Xv_opaque) private->value->severity;

  case SNAFU_APPLY_PROC:
    return (Xv_opaque) private->apply_proc;

  case XV_LABEL:
    return (Xv_opaque) private->label;

  case XV_OWNER:
    return (Xv_opaque) private->owner;

  case XV_SHOW:
    if ( private->ui )
      return (Xv_opaque) xv_get ( private->ui->popup, XV_SHOW );
    else
      return (Xv_opaque) FALSE;

    default :
     *status = xv_check_bad_attr ( SNAFU, attr );
     return (Xv_opaque) XV_OK;
    } /* switch */

} /* snafu_get() */


/*
 * xv_destroy() method
 */
Pkg_private int
snafu_destroy ( Snafu_public *public, Destroy_status status )
{
  Snafu_private *private = SNAFU_PRIVATE(public);

  if (status == DESTROY_CLEANUP) {
    if ( private->ui )
      xv_free ( private->ui );
      xv_free ( private->value );
      xv_free ( private );
  }
  return XV_OK;
} /* snafu_destroy() */
```

```
/**************************************************************************/


/*
 * We want to create the UI portion of the Snafu separately
 * from the rest of the object.  Because multiple calls
 * to xv_create() can be expensive, we want to delay creating
 * the UI until XV_SHOW gets set to TRUE.  Hopefully, this will
 * help invocation performance.
 */
static void
snafu_create_ui ( Snafu_private *private )
{

  /* used to attach private data to popup objects */
  if ( SNAFU_KEY == 0 )
    SNAFU_KEY = xv_unique_key();

  /* DevGuide code requires this */
  if ( INSTANCE == 0 )
    INSTANCE = xv_unique_key();

  private->ui = snafu_popup_objects_initialize ( NULL, private->owner);

  /* Post DevGuide Setup */
  xv_set ( private->ui->popup,
    XV_LABEL, private->label,
    NULL );
  xv_set ( private->ui->controls,
    PANEL_DEFAULT_ITEM, private->ui->apply_button,
    NULL );
  xv_set ( private->ui->apply_button,
    XV_KEY_DATA, SNAFU_KEY, private,
    PANEL_NOTIFY_PROC, snafu_apply_proc,
    NULL );
  xv_set ( private->ui->reset_button,
    XV_KEY_DATA, SNAFU_KEY, private,
    PANEL_NOTIFY_PROC, snafu_reset_proc,
    NULL );

  /* make sure popup reflects our default values! */
  snafu_set_value ( private->value, private->ui );

} /* snafu_create_ui() */

/*
 * Restore the popup to the state of its last validation
 * implemented as callback to "Reset" button.
 */
static void
snafu_reset_proc ( Panel_item item, Event *event )
{
  Snafu_private *private = SNAFU_FROM_OBJ(item);
  snafu_set_value ( private->value, private->ui );
} /* snafu_reset_proc() */

/*
 * Make the popup data current and notify the app
 * that the "Apply" button was pressed.
 */
static void
```

```
snafu_apply_proc ( Panel_item item, Event *event )
{
  Snafu_private *private = SNAFU_FROM_OBJ(item);

  snafu_accept_value ( private->value, private->ui );

  /* maybe pass back a structure? */
  if ( private->apply_proc )
    (private->apply_proc) ( SNAFU_PUBLIC(private), private->value->name,
                       private->value->severity, private->value->type);
} /* snafu_reset_proc() */

/*
 * set popup contents from value struct
 */
static void
snafu_set_value ( Snafu_values *value, Snafu_ui *ui )
{
  if ( !ui )
    return;

  xv_set ( ui->name_text, PANEL_VALUE, value->name, NULL );
  xv_set ( ui->severity_slider, PANEL_VALUE, value->severity, NULL );
  xv_set ( ui->type_choice, PANEL_VALUE, value->type, NULL );
} /* snafu_set_value() */

/*
 * set values struct from popup contents
 */
static void
snafu_accept_value ( Snafu_values *value, Snafu_ui *ui )
{
  if ( !ui )
    return;

  strcpy ( value->name, (char *) xv_get ( ui->name_text, PANEL_VALUE) );
  value->severity = (int) xv_get ( ui->severity_slider, PANEL_VALUE );
  value->type = (Snafu_type) xv_get ( ui->type_choice, PANEL_VALUE );
} /* snafu_accept_value() */
```

```
/* snafu_data.c
 * Author: Rick "Tank" Goldstein
 */

/*
 * Snafu package information
 */

#include "snafu_impl.h"

extern int    snafu_init();
extern Xv_opaque snafu_set();
extern Xv_opaque snafu_get();
extern int    snafu_destroy();

Xv_pkg snafu_pkg = {
  "SNAFU",
  ATTR_PKG_SNAFU,
  sizeof(Snafu_public),
  XV_GENERIC_OBJECT,
```

```
        snafu_init,
        snafu_set,
        snafu_get,
        snafu_destroy,
        NULL                            /* no find */
};
```

```
/*
 * snafu_ui.h - User interface object and function declarations.
 * This file was generated by `gxv' from `snafu.G'.
 * DO NOT EDIT BY HAND.
 */
   ifndef snafu_HEADER
   define snafu_HEADER
extern Attr_attribute   INSTANCE;

typedef struct {
        Xv_opaque    popup;
        Xv_opaque    controls;
        Xv_opaque    name_text;
        Xv_opaque    severity_slider;
        Xv_opaque    type_choice;
        Xv_opaque    apply_button;
        Xv-opaque    reset_button;
} snafu_popup_objects;

extern snafu_popup_objects
*snafu_popup_objects_initialize(snafu_popup_ojects *, Xv_opaque);

extern Xv_opaque     snafu_popup_popup_create(snafu_popup_objects *,
                                                        Xv_opaque);
extern Xv_opaque     snafu_popup_controls_create(snafu_popup_objects *,
                                                        XV_opaque);
extern Xv_opaque     snafu_popup_name_text_create(snafu_popup_objects *,
                                                        Xv-opaque);
extern Xv_opaque     snafu_popup_severity_slider_create(snafu_popup_objects *,
                                                        Xv_opaque);
extern Xv_opaque     snafu_popup_type_choice_create(snafu_popup_objects *,
                                                        Xv_opaque);
extern Xv_opaque     snafu_popup_apply_button_create(snafu_popup_objects *,
                                                        Xv_opaque);
extern Xv_opaque     snafu_popup_reset_button_create(snafu_popup_objects *,
                                                        Xv_opaque);
#endif
```

Creating a Program

The following is an example of how to write an XView program from scratch. It follows the process that I use from step to step, as follows:

- Design the program.
- Start with the XView skeleton.
- Create the base frame.
- Create the panel.
- Create panel items.
- Create callbacks.

DESIGN THE PROGRAM

For this example, I wanted a simple program that would demonstrate the **TTY** subwindow package. You can use this program like **shelltool**, with the added functionality of three buttons: one that runs the **ls** command on the subwindow, one that iconizes the frame, and one that clears the subwindow.

To do this I would need a base frame with a panel (a place to put the buttons); three buttons; and a subwindow object. Since the program is very small, that's all that was required.

XVIEW SKELETON

The XView skeleton program is as follows:

```
#include <xview/xview.h>

int main ( int argc, char **argv )
{

    Frame base;
    /* handles to other objects to be created */

    xv_init ( XV_INIT_ARGC_PTR_ARGV, &argc, argv, NULL );
    /* make global attributes unique */
```

```
base = (Frame) xv_create ( XV_NULL, FRAME, NULL );
/* any other xv_create()s */
/* any window_fit()s */

xv_main_loop ( base );
return ( 0 );
}
```

The **xv_init()** function parses the command line and handles any XView options that might be there. Next come any creates that are needed (if you don't need **xv_create()**s, you probably don't need XView). The **xv_main_loop()** routine starts event processing for the base frame.

CREATE THE BASE FRAME

The base frame is created between the **xv_init()** and the **xv_main_loop()**. In this case, it is created with the following code:

```
Frame base;

base = (Frame) xv_create ( XV_NULL, FRAME,
        FRAME_LABEL, argv[0],
        FRAME_SHOW_FOOTER, TRUE,
        XV_X, 300,
        XV_Y, 175,
        NULL );
```

Since this is the base frame, it doesn't have a parent (parent is set to **XV_NULL**). The label is set to the name of the program through the **FRAME_LABEL** attribute. It's also good to have a footer for displaying error and status messages. Finally, the location of the window is forced with **XV_X** and **XV_Y**, which are used to position the upper left corner of the object.

CREATE THE PANEL

The panel is created next, with the base frame as its parent. Nothing special needs to be set, so a very generic-looking **xv_create()** can be used:

```
Panel panel;

panel = (Panel) xv_create ( base, PANEL, NULL );
```

CREATE PANEL ITEMS

The panel items for this program are three buttons. Since the program will need to use their handles, it is necessary to define variables for them.

```
Panel_item pl, pc, pi;
```

The actual **xv_create()**s follow the creation of the panel:

```
pc = (Panel_item) xv_create ( panel, PANEL_BUTTON,
        PANEL_LABEL_STRING,     "Clear",
        PANEL_NOTIFY_PROC,      clear,
        NULL );
```

```
pl = (Panel_item) xv_create ( panel, PANEL_BUTTON,
        PANEL_LABEL_STRING,     "ls",
        PANEL_NOTIFY_PROC,      ls,
        NULL );

pi = (Panel_item) xv_create ( panel, PANEL_BUTTON,
        PANEL_LABEL_STRING,     "Iconize",
        PANEL_NOTIFY_PROC,      iconize,
        NULL );
```

For each button, the parent is the panel that the button is going to sit on. Try to make the purpose of each button clear by labeling each button with the function that it is to perform. Then, associate a notify procedure onto each button and name it after what it is to do. The workings of the callbacks will be discussed a little later.

CREATE THE TTY SUBWINDOW

The **TTY** subwindow needs to be created, and it looks a little more convoluted:

```
tty = (Tty) xv_create ( base, TTY,
        WIN_ROWS,       24,
        WIN_COLUMNS,    80,
        TTY_QUIT_ON_CHILD_DEATH, TRUE,
        NULL );
```

Here a **TTY** subwindow is created with the base frame as its parent. Then some of the attributes are set: The **TTY** subwindow is to have 80 columns and 24 rows and is to be *suicidal*—it will go away when the shell that is running inside it terminates.

ATTRIBUTE KEYS

Attribute keys are used to pass data into objects. For example, each of the panel buttons needs to modify the **TTY** subwindow when pushed, but the subwindow handle is not within defined as an attribute for a button. The **XV_KEY_DATA** feature can be used to give each button an additional attribute, whose value in this case will be the subwindow handle. (Alternatively, you can use global variables, but global variables should be avoided.) With the **XV_KEY_DATA** approach, the only global variable needed will be an identifier for the new attribute:

```
Attr_attribute TTY_KEY;
```

This global attribute identifier is set once, in the **main()** routine just after the call to **XV_init**:

```
TTY_KEY = xv_unique_key ( );
```

This assigns a unique value to the key—and the keys need unique values if there is more than one within a package.

Now the new **TTY_KEY** attribute can be used to pass the handle of the **TTY** subwindow into the buttons once they are created:

```
(void) xv_set ( pc, XV_KEY_DATA, TTY_KEY, tty, NULL );
(void) xv_set ( pl, XV_KEY_DATA, TTY_KEY, tty, NULL );
(void) xv_set ( pi, XV_KEY_DATA, TTY_KEY, tty, NULL );
```

▰F̲INISH THE MAIN FUNCTION

There are then a few miscellaneous things left. Since the panel is now complete, you should run the **window_fit ()** macro on it (in this case a **window_fit_height ()**, because we want the panel to have the same width as the window). Then we **window_fit ()** the base frame around the panel and canvas. Finally, **xv_main_loop ()** is used to "turn on" processing, and is followed by **return (0)**, which returns a status of 0.

▰C̲REATE CALLBACKS

There must be a callback routine for each of the three buttons. As previously explained, the subwindow's handle needs to be passed to the callback through **XV_KEY_DATA** .

The callback defined for the **PANEL_BUTTON** package has the following format:

```
void callback ( Panel_item button, Event *event )
{

}
```

So, for the **ls** callback, the function is set up like this:

```
void ls ( Panel_item button, Event *event )

{

        char *lsmsg = "ls\n";

        ttysw_input ( xv_get ( button,XV_KEY_DATA,TTY_KEY ), lsmsg,
                                        strlen ( lsmsg ) );

}
```

The **ttysw_input ()** function needs a handle to a TTY subwindow as the first argument. The callback gets that by using **xv_get ()** to retrieve the handle of the subwindow through **XV_KEY_DATA** . The next argument is the string that is to be input through the subwindow. In this case the string is **"ls\n"** (without the **"\n"** the screen would just display **"ls"** and wait for the user to press Enter). The final argument is the length of the string being passed to the function.

The other two functions are very similar:

```
void clear ( button, event )
Panel_item button;
Event *event;
{

        char *clmsg = "clear\n";

        ttysw_input ( xv_get ( button, XV_KEY_DATA, TTY_KEY ),
                        clmsg, strlen ( clmsg ) );
}

void iconize ( button, event)

Panel_item button;
```

```
Event *event;

{

        char *icmsg = "^[[2t";

        ttysw_output ( xv_get ( button, XV_KEY_DATA, TTY_KEY ) ,
                        icmsg, strlen ( icmsg ) );
}
```

The only thing that should be pointed out here is the **icmsg** string. This is retrieved from the bottom of the <**xview/tty.h**> file, in which a number of other escape sequences are provided for doing other things. Also, because there is an ESC embedded into the string, if you **cat** or **more** this file, the window will iconize when it hits the string. This comes in handy around April 1.

COMPILING XVIEW PROGRAMS

Now that the program is written, we need to compile it. A typical compile line looks like:

```
host% cc -g f.c -o file -L$OPENWINHOME/lib -lxview -lolgx -lX11
```

where **f.c** and **file** are replaced with the filename of the C program and the name of the executable, respectively.

Here is a **csh** script for compilation that I call **tcc**:

```
#!/bin/csh
cc -g $1.c -o $1 -L$OPENWINHOME/lib -lxview -lolgx -lX11
```

It can be used to compile a file (like **ttysw.c**) as follows:

```
host% tcc ttysw
```

which is much easier to type than the longhand method. If the program is more complicated or requires something more sophisticated, use a makefile.

Once the program compiles, run it. Try clicking on the buttons. Try using it as a shelltool. Fun, isn't it?

THE PROGRAM

Here's the whole program, put together for compilation:

```
/* ttysw.c -- Open Look tty sub window
 * Author:   Kenneth Bibb
 * April 1992 -- Arastar Consulting
 *-----------------------------------
 * Basic frame with panel and ttysw
 */

#include <xview/xview.h>
#include <xview/panel.h>
#include <xview/tty.h>
```

```
Attr_attribute TTY_KEY=NULL;


void ls ( button, event )
Panel_item button;
Event *event;
{

        char *lsmsg = "ls\n";

        ttysw_input ( xv_get ( button, XV_KEY_DATA, TTY_KEY ), lsmsg,
                                             strlen ( lsmsg ) );
}

void clear ( button, event )
Panel_item button;
Event *event;

{

        char *clmsg = "clear\n";

        ttysw_input ( xv_get ( button, XV_KEY_DATA, TTY_KEY ), clmsg,
          strlen ( clmsg ) );

}

void iconize ( button, event )
Panel_item button;
Event *event;

{

        char *icmsg = "^[2t";

        ttysw_output ( xv_get ( button, XV_KEY_DATA, TTY_KEY ), icmsg,
            strlen ( icmsg ) );

}

int main(argc, argv)
int argc;
char **argv;

{

        Frame base;
        Tty tty;
        Panel panel;
        Panel_item pc, pl, pi;

        xv_init ( XV_INIT_ARGC_PTR_ARGV, &argc, argv, NULL );
        TTY_KEY = xv_unique_key ();

        /* create the base frame */
        base = (Frame) xv_create ( NULL, FRAME,
                FRAME_LABEL,        argv[0],
                FRAME_SHOW_FOOTER,  TRUE,
                XV_X,               300,
                XV_Y,               175,
                NULL );
```

```
      /* create the panel */
      panel = (Panel) xv_create ( base, PANEL, NULL );

      /* create some buttons */
      pc = (Panel_item) xv_create ( panel, PANEL_BUTTON,
              PANEL_LABEL_STRING, "Clear",
              PANEL_NOTIFY_PROC,   clear,
              NULL );
      pl = (Panel_item) xv_create ( panel, PANEL_BUTTON,
              PANEL_LABEL_STRING, "ls",
              PANEL_NOTIFY_PROC,   ls,
              NULL );

      pi = (Panel_item) xv_create ( panel, PANEL_BUTTON,
              PANEL_LABEL_STRING, "Iconize",
              PANEL_NOTIFY_PROC,   iconize,
              NULL );
      window_fit_height ( panel );

      /* create the ttysw */
      tty = (Tty) xv_create ( base, TTY,
              WIN_ROWS,                24,
              WIN_COLUMNS,             80,
              TTY_QUIT_ON_CHILD_DEATH, TRUE,
              NULL );
      (void) xv_set ( pc, XV_KEY_DATA, TTY_KEY, tty, NULL );
      (void) xv_set ( pl, XV_KEY_DATA, TTY_KEY, tty, NULL );
      (void) xv_set ( pi, XV_KEY_DATA, TTY_KEY, tty, NULL );

      /* fit the frame around the ttysw and panel */
      window_fit ( base );

      xv_main_loop ( base );
      return ( 0 );
}
```

PART

II

XVIEW HINTS AND TIPS

The following chapters cover a number of the XView packages. Although they're set up in alphabetical order (to make it easier to look up whichever package you're interested in), you should still start with the following packages:

- General (Chapter 13)
- Miscellaneous (Chapter 18)
- Buttons (Chapter 6)
- Help (Chapter 14)
- Notifier (Chapter 21)
- Icons (Chapter 15)
- Gauges (Chapter 12)
- Cursors (Chapter 9)
- Notices (Chapter 20)

The General and Miscellaneous chapters cover some attributes and features that are useful when using the other packages. Buttons is a fairly simple package to start with, and the program used in the Buttons chapter is modified for the Help chapter. The Notifier is used in the Icons and Gauges sample programs (Icons uses it in the animated icon, and Gauges uses it for powering `dftool`). Cursors are often ignored; the program in this chapter demonstrates the OL-compliant cursors. Finally, Notices talks about proper use of notices *(don't lock the whole screen)* and has a nifty little recursive routine that will make all of an application's frames dynamically go busy.

Abbreviated Menus and Choices

W hen you have a limited amount of space to work with, abbreviated choices and menus are convenient. They are similar in many ways—for example, they both have a button that is used to invoke an item, and they both are small—but they also have some differences (otherwise, they'd be the same package). Abbreviated buttons, on the other hand, are not currently implemented as part of XView. See the OLFS, p. 102, for more info on abbreviated buttons.

ABBREVIATED CHOICE

Abbreviated choices have the attributes shown in Figure 5.1. The callback for an abbreviated choice object is as follows:

```
int

choice_notify_proc ( choice, val, event )

Panel_item choice;

int val;

Event *event;

{

}
```

The abbreviated choice callback is the same as a choice callback:

- **choice** is the handle of the **panel_choice** item.
- **val** is an integer that says which choice was selected.
- **event** is the event that called the callback.

ABBREVIATED MENU

An abbreviated menu has the attributes shown in Figure 5.2. The callback for an abbreviated menu is as follows:

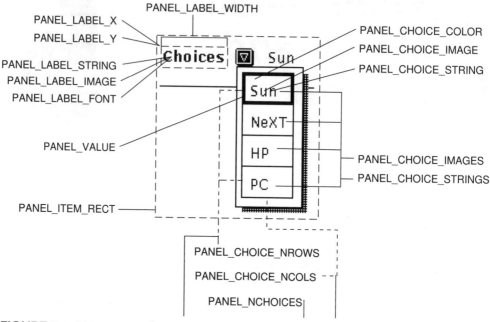

FIGURE 5.1 Abbreviated Choice Attributes

```
int abbmenu_callback ( menu, menu_item )

Menu menu;

Menu_item menu_item;

{

}
```

The abbreviated menu callback is the same as a menu callback:

- **menu** is the handle of the menu where the event happened.
- **menu_item** is the handle of the menu item that was selected.

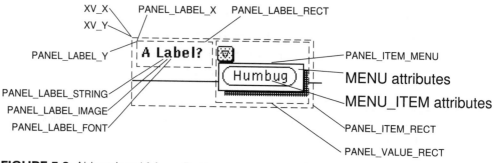

FIGURE 5.2 Abbreviated Menu Button

DIFFERENCES BETWEEN ABBREVIATED CHOICE AND ABBREVIATED MENU BUTTONS

You may have noticed that these two items are very similar in function and appearance. The main differences are the following:

- Abbreviated menu buttons use the menu package.
- Abbreviated choice buttons use the choice package.
- Open Look abbreviated menu buttons are implemented with the abbreviated choice button package.
- The abbreviated menu button package is not Open Look–compliant.

SAMPLE PROGRAM

```c
/* abb.c -- Abbreviated choices and menus
 * Author:  Kenneth Bibb
 * April 1992 -- Arastar Consulting
 *------------------------------------
 * Basic frame with abbreviated menu buttons and abbreviated choice buttons
 */

#include <xview/xview.h>
#include <xview/panel.h>

/* call back for abbreviated choice
 */
void
selected_choice ( item, value, event )
Panel_item item;
int value;
Event *event;
{
        printf ( "you selected %s\n", ( item, PANEL_CHOICE_STRING, value ) );
                    (char *) xv_get
}

/* callback for abbreviated menu
 */
void
menu_proc ( menu, menu_item )
Menu menu;
Menu_item menu_item;
{
        printf ( "you want %s\n", ( menu_item, MENU_STRING ) );
                    (char *) xv_get

}

int
main ( argc, argv )
int argc;
char **argv;
{
```

```
        Frame                           frame;
        Canvas                          canvas;
        Panel                           panel;
        Panel_item                      pcs;
        Menu                            menu;

    xv_init ( XV_INIT_ARGC_PTR_ARGV, &argc, argv, NULL );

    frame = (Frame)xv_create ( NULL, FRAME,
                FRAME_LABEL,      argv[0],
                XV_X,             300,
                XV_Y,             175,
                NULL );

    panel = (Panel) xv_create ( frame, PANEL, NULL );

    /* create the abbreviated choice
     */
    pcs = (Panel_item) xv_create ( panel, PANEL_CHOICE_STACK,
                /* PANEL_LAYOUT, PANEL_VERTICAL, */
                PANEL_LABEL_STRING,     "Systems",
                PANEL_CHOICE_STRINGS,   "Sun", "NeXT", "HP", "PC", NULL,
                PANEL_NOTIFY_PROC,      selected_choice,
                PANEL_VALUE,            0,
                NULL );

    /* a menu to attach to the abbreviated menu
     */
    menu = (Menu) xv_create ( XV_NULL, MENU,
                MENU_ITEM,

                                MENU_STRING, "Bah",
                                NULL,
                MENU_ITEM,

                                MENU_STRING, "Humbug",
                                NULL,
                MENU_NOTIFY_PROC,    menu_proc,
                NULL );

    /* create the abbreviated menu
     *------------------------------

     */
    (void) xv_create ( panel, PANEL_ABBREV_MENU_BUTTON,
                XV_Y,                       xv_get ( pcs, XV_Y ) + 4,
                PANEL_ITEM_MENU,            menu,
                PANEL_LABEL_STRING,         "Sentiments",
                NULL );

    /* fit the panel around the two abbreviated items
     */
    window_fit_height ( panel );

    /* create a canvas
     */
    canvas = (Canvas) xv_create ( frame, CANVAS,
                XV_X,                       0,
                XV_HEIGHT,                  WIN_EXTEND_TO_EDGE,
                XV_WIDTH,                   WIN_EXTEND_TO_EDGE,
```

```
                CANVAS_X_PAINT_WINDOW,          TRUE,
                NULL );
window_fit ( frame );

xv_main_loop ( frame );
return ( 0 );
}
```

Buttons

T he boring but ubiquitous button is an occasionally underrated member of the UI reper-
toire. Buttons are fairly straightforward, the primary oddity about them being the number of different Open Look GUI–defined buttons. Button notification procedures are also
straightforward. This chapter provides examples of a few of the more commonly seen
button notification procedures.

Common attributes of buttons are shown in Figure 6.1.

OL STANDARD BUTTON TYPES

The Open Look GUI defines a number of standard button types (shown in Figure 6.2):

- Menu button (pulldown)
- Menu button (pullright)
- Window button
- Highlighted button
- Default button
- Inactive button

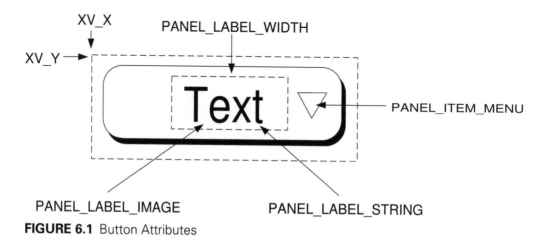

FIGURE 6.1 Button Attributes

OPEN LOOK Button	Button Name	Required Attributes
(Normal)	Normal Button	PANEL_BUTTON
(Cancel)	Default Button	PANEL_DEFAULT_ITEM, button,
(Button Window...)	Window Button	PANEL_LABEL, "Window...", PANEL_NOTIFY_PROC, window_proc,
(File ▽)	Pulldown Menu Button	PANEL_ITEM_MENU, menu,
(Menu Right ▷)	Pullright Menu Button	PANEL_LAYOUT, VERTICAL PANEL_ITEM_MENU, menu,
(Snap Region)	Busy Button	PANEL_BUSY
(Menu Right ▷)	Inactive Button	PANEL_INACTIVE
(Highlight)	Highlighted Button	(depress a button)

FIGURE 6.2 Standard Open Look Button Types

- Busy button
- Abbreviated menu button

All of these (except for the highlighted button) are implemented in XView. A button highlights when pressed, and you can force a button to highlight with synthetic events, but it isn't something that you'll normally need.

Unlike the highlighted button, you'll often use the others. Menu buttons provide an attachment point for your menus, window buttons invoke popup windows; default buttons can be set (making your package easier to use); inactive buttons can be set when the button's action is disabled for whatever reasons; busy buttons can be set when a long action is initiated; and finally, abbreviated menu buttons (described in Chapter 5) can be used when your popup has a restricted amount of space.

MENU BUTTON (PULLDOWN)

To create a standard pulldown menu button, use code like the following:

```
Panel panel;
Menu  menu;
```

```
(void) xv_create ( panel, PANEL_BUTTON,
        PANEL_LABEL_STRING, "Menu",
        PANEL_ITEM_MENU,     menu,
        NULL );
```

The parent object, **panel**, needs to be previously defined, along with the **menu** object. The **PANEL_LABEL_STRING** sets the string on the button's face. **PANEL_ITEM_MENU** ties **menu** to this button.

The **PANEL_LAYOUT** is typically **PANEL_HORIZONTAL**, so the menu is a pulldown menu. When **PANEL_LAYOUT** is changed to **PANEL_VERTICAL**, the menu becomes a pullright menu button. **PANEL_LAYOUT** is an attribute of **panel**, usually set when you create **panel** (see Chapter 22).

MENU BUTTON (PULLRIGHT)

To create a standard pullright menu button, use code like the following:

```
Panel panel;
Menu  menu;

xv_set ( panel, PANEL_LAYOUT, PANEL_VERTICAL ) ;
(void) xv_create ( panel, PANEL_BUTTON,
        PANEL_LABEL_STRING, "Menu",
        PANEL_ITEM_MENU,     menu,
        NULL );
```

Looks familiar, huh? The parent object, **panel**, needs to be previously defined, along with the **menu** object, and the **PANEL_LAYOUT** of **panel** needs to be set to **PANEL_VERTICAL** for the menu to be a pullright. If the panel's **PANEL_LAYOUT** is **PANEL_HORIZONTAL**, you'll wind up with a standard pulldown menu button. The **xv_set()** can be used to set **PANEL_LAYOUT** if **panel** has already been created.

Again, **PANEL_LABEL_STRING** sets the string on the button's face. **PANEL_ITEM_MENU** ties **menu** to this button.

WINDOW BUTTON

To create a standard window button, code similar to the following is needed:

```
Attr_attribute POPUP_WINDOW_KEY;

routine ()

{

        Frame Fsub;
        Panel panel;

        POPUP_WINDOW_KEY = xv_unique_key ();
        (void) xv_create ( panel, PANEL_BUTTON,
                PANEL_LABEL_STRING,          "Window...",
                PANEL_NOTIFY_PROC,           window,
                XV_KEY_DATA, POPUP_WINDOW_KEY,  Fsub,
                NULL );

}
```

POPUP_WINDOW_KEY is defined globally so that it can be used by **routine()** and **window()** as the key data identifier. **Fsub** is the popup's frame, whereas **panel** is the parent item. **PANEL_LABEL_STRING** sets the string on the button's face. To indicate that this button causes a window to pop up, the **PANEL_LABEL_STRING** string should end in an ellipsis (...).

   PANEL_NOTIFY_PROC makes **window()** the callback routine for this button. With **XV_KEY_DATA**, we associate the subwindow frame **Fsub** with this button so that the call-back routine will have access to it.

   The **window()** function is defined as follows:

```
void window ( Menu menu, Menu_item mitem )
{
        xv_set ( xv_get ( menu, XV_KEY_DATA, POPUP_WINDOW_KEY),
                 XV_SHOW, TRUE,
                 NULL ));
}
```

This routine displays the popup **Fsub** by setting its **XV_SHOW** attribute to **TRUE**. We retrieve the handle to **Fsub** with the **xv_get()** using the specified **XV_KEY_DATA** item.

HIGHLIGHTING A BUTTON

Creating a highlighted button is not straightforward, and although mentioned in the OLFS, it doesn't serve a purpose (except for showing that the button is being depressed). Because it is not OL GUI–compliant, I won't go into how to highlight a button. (Hint: You can probably do it with synthetic events.)

SETTING DEFAULT BUTTONS

You set default buttons on the panel that owns the button. To make a button the default button on **panel**, save its handle on creation in a **Panel_item** variable **button** and do the following:

```
Panel panel;
Panel_item button;

xv_set ( panel, PANEL_DEFAULT_ITEM, button );
```

Note: Both **panel** and **button** must previously exist before doing this.

INACTIVATING A BUTTON

When the required conditions for using a button do not exist, you should make the button inactive ("grayed out"), as follows:

```
Panel_item button;

xv_set ( button, PANEL_INACTIVE, TRUE, NULL );
```

To activate the button, you would reset the attribute:

```
xv_set ( button, PANEL_INACTIVE, FALSE, NULL );
```

◼ BUSY BUTTON

When an action is going to take an extended or unknown period of time, you should make the button that initiated the action go "busy." To make the button **button** busy, do the following:

```
Panel_item button;

xv_set ( button, PANEL_BUSY, TRUE, NULL );
```

To turn off the busy status, change the value of **PANEL_BUSY** to **FALSE**.

◼ BUTTON NOTIFICATION PROCEDURE TYPES

There are two main kinds of button procedures:

- ◼ Popup windows
- ◼ Command buttons

Popup Window Procedure   Displaying a popup window is fairly easy. Associate a callback to the button, in which set the **XV_SHOW** attribute for the window is set to TRUE. An example of this was shown previously. Once again, here is the primary code:

```
void window ( Menu menu, Menu_item mitem )

{

        xv_set ( xv_get ( menu, XV_KEY_DATA, POPUP_WINDOW_KEY ),
                    XV_SHOW, TRUE, NULL );

}
```

Remember to use key data: It makes your programs easier to debug by eliminating global variables.

Command button   Making a command button is as easy as making a popup window. Let's create two buttons on a panel, "Apply" and "Cancel."

```
Panel panel;

(void) xv_create ( panel, PANEL_BUTTON,
                    PANEL_LABEL_STRING,  "Apply",
                    PANEL_NOTIFY_PROC,   command_button,
                    NULL );

(void) xv_create ( panel, PANEL_BUTTON,
                    PANEL_LABEL_STRING,  "Cancel",
                    PANEL_NOTIFY_PROC,   command_button,
                    NULL );
```

We associate one callback to both buttons and check the **PANEL_LABEL_STRING** of the button to see which one was pushed.

```
void command_button ( Panel_item item, Event *event )

{

        if ( strcmp ( "Apply", xv_get ( item, PANEL_LABEL_STRING ) == 0 )
```

```
        apply_procedure ();

}
```

This example assumes that you only have two choices ("Apply" and "Cancel") and that the "cancel" button will dismiss the popup. This routine is designed to be the callback of both the "Apply" and "Cancel" buttons.

SAMPLE PROGRAM

The program **button.c** shows examples of the different kinds of Open Look–compliant buttons. Included are examples of a menu button ("File"), a popup window button ("Button Window ..."), a "Highlight" button (which will highlight if you hold the Select mouse button down over it), an "Inactive" button (which will inactivate all the other buttons until you Select it again), a "Busy" button (which will make all the other buttons busy until you Select it again), a "Cancel" button (which is the default—it will dismiss the popup window), and a "Menu Right" button (which will display a menu to the right of the button).

```
/* button.c -- Open Look basic button types
 * Author:  Kenneth Bibb
 * March 1992 -- Arastar Consulting
 */

#include <stdlib.h>
#include <xview/xview.h>
#include <xview/panel.h>
#include <xview/canvas.h>
#include <xview/xv_xrect.h>
#include <xview/openmenu.h>

/* set up key data variables
 */
Attr_attribute BASE_FRAME_KEY = NULL;
Attr_attribute POPUP_WINDOW_KEY = NULL;
Attr_attribute POPUP_PANEL_KEY = NULL;
Attr_attribute BUTTON_KEY = NULL;
Attr_attribute BUTTON2_KEY = NULL;


/* test menu stub
 */
void menu_stub ( menu, menu_item )
Menu menu;
Menu_item menu_item;
{
        char s[64];
        Frame frame = (Frame) xv_get ( menu, XV_KEY_DATA, BASE_FRAME_KEY,
            NULL );

        sprintf ( s,"Menu: [%s]\n", xv_get ( menu_item, MENU_STRING ) );
        (void) xv_set ( frame, FRAME_LEFT_FOOTER, s, NULL );
}

/* highlight a button
 */
```

```c
void highlight ( button, event )
Panel_item button;
Event *event;
{

}

/* inactivate all buttons except the "Inactive" button
 */
void inactive ( button, event )
Panel_item button;
Event *event;
{
        Panel Pbutton = (Panel) xv_get ( button, XV_KEY_DATA,
                POPUP_PANEL_KEY );
        Panel_item ph = (Panel_item) xv_get ( button, XV_KEY_DATA,
                BUTTON_KEY );
        Panel_item pi = (Panel_item) xv_get ( button, XV_KEY_DATA,
                BUTTON2_KEY );
        Panel_item i  = NULL;

 /* if the highlight button is inactive
  *            activate all panel items (in this case, buttons)
  * else
  *            inactivate all panel items (in this case, buttons)
  *            activate the inactivate button
  */
 if ( xv_get ( ph, PANEL_INACTIVE ) == TRUE ) {
                PANEL_EACH_ITEM(Pbutton, i)
                            xv_set ( i, PANEL_INACTIVE, FALSE, NULL );
                PANEL_END_EACH
 } else {
                PANEL_EACH_ITEM(Pbutton, i)
                            xv_set ( i, PANEL_INACTIVE, TRUE, NULL );
                PANEL_END_EACH
                xv_set ( button, PANEL_INACTIVE, FALSE, NULL );
 }

}

/* busy all buttons except the "Busy" button
 */
void busy ( button, event )
Panel_item button;
Event *event;
{
        Panel Pbutton = (Panel) xv_get ( button, XV_KEY_DATA,
                            POPUP_PANEL_KEY );
        Panel_item ph = (Panel_item) xv_get ( button, XV_KEY_DATA,
                            BUTTON_KEY );
        Panel_item i  = NULL;

        /* if the highlight button is busy
         *            turn busy off on all panel items
         * else
         *            turn busy on for all panel items
         *            turn busy off on busy button
         */
        if ( xv_get ( ph, PANEL_BUSY ) ==TRUE )
        {
```

```
                  PANEL_EACH_ITEM(Pbutton, i)
                      xv_set ( i, PANEL_BUSY, FALSE, NULL );
                  PANEL_END_EACH


    }
    else
    {
          PANEL_EACH_ITEM(Pbutton, i)
              xv_set ( i, PANEL_BUSY, TRUE, NULL );
          PANEL_END_EACH
          xv_set ( button, PANEL_BUSY, FALSE, NULL );
    }


}

/* "Button Window..." callback:  display button window
 */
void button_window ( button, event )
Panel_item button;
Event *event;
{
      xv_set ( xv_get ( button, XV_KEY_DATA, POPUP_WINDOW_KEY ),
                      XV_SHOW, TRUE, NULL );
}

/* "Cancel" button callback
 */
void cancel ( button, event )
Panel_item button;
Event *event;
{
      Frame frame = (Frame) xv_get (button, XV_KEY_DATA,
            POPUP_WINDOW_KEY);

      /* pull the pushpin (see Chapter 11) and unmap the window
       */
      (void) xv_set ( frame, FRAME_CMD_PIN_STATE, FALSE,
                      XV_SHOW,                         FALSE,
                      NULL );
}

/* display the popup window
 */
void show_it ( window, event )
Xv_Window window;
Event *event;
{
      if ( event_action ( event ) == ACTION_MENU &&
      event_is_down ( event ) ) {
              Menu m = (Menu) xv_get ( window, WIN_CLIENT_DATA );
              menu_show ( m, window, event, NULL );
      }
}

/* repaint the canvas
 */
void repaint ( canvas, win, dpy, xwin, xrect )
Canvas canvas;
Xv_Window win;
```

```
Display *dpy;
Window xwin;
Xv_xrectlist *xrect;

{
    GC gc;
    int width, height;

    gc = DefaultGC ( dpy, DefaultScreen ( dpy ) );
    width = (int) xv_get ( win, XV_WIDTH );
    height = (int) xv_get ( win, XV_HEIGHT );
}

int main ( argc, argv )
int argc;
char **argv;
{
    Frame           frame;
    Frame           Fbutton;
    Panel           Pbutton;
    Panel_item      ph, pi, pb, pc;
    Canvas          canvas;
    Panel           panel;
    Menu            m, m_undo;


/* initialization
 */
xv_init ( XV_INIT_ARGC_PTR_ARGV, &argc, argv, NULL );
BASE_FRAME_KEY   = xv_unique_key ();
POPUP_WINDOW_KEY = xv_unique_key ();
POPUP_PANEL_KEY  = xv_unique_key ();
BUTTON_KEY  = xv_unique_key ();
BUTTON2_KEY  = xv_unique_key ();

/* create base frame
 */
frame = (Frame) xv_create ( XV_NULL, FRAME,
            FRAME_LABEL,              argv[0],
            FRAME_SHOW_FOOTER,        TRUE,
            XV_X,                     300,
            XV_Y,                     175,
            NULL );

/* create button subframe
 */
Fbutton = (Frame) xv_create ( frame, FRAME_CMD,
            FRAME_LABEL,              "Button Examples",
            XV_X,                     400,
            XV_Y,                     200,
            NULL );

/* retrieve subframe's panel
 */
Pbutton = (Panel) xv_get ( Fbutton, FRAME_CMD_PANEL );
xv_set ( Pbutton, PANEL_LAYOUT, PANEL_VERTICAL, NULL );

panel = (Panel) xv_create ( frame, PANEL, NULL);

/* create file menu
```

```
    */
    m = (Menu) xv_create ( XV_NULL, MENU,
                MENU_ITEM,

                                                    MENU_STRING, "New...",
                                                    NULL,

                MENU_ITEM,

                                                    MENU_STRING, "Save...",
                                                    NULL,

                MENU_ITEM,

                                                    MENU_STRING, "Print...",
                                                    NULL,
                MENU_NOTIFY_PROC,                   menu_stub,
                XV_KEY_DATA, BASE_FRAME_KEY,        frame,
                NULL );
    (void) xv_create ( panel, PANEL_BUTTON,
                PANEL_LABEL_STRING, "File",
                PANEL_ITEM_MENU,        m,
                NULL );

    /* command window button
     * display "Button Window"
     */
    (void) xv_create ( panel, PANEL_BUTTON,
                PANEL_LABEL_STRING,                 "Button Window...",
                PANEL_NOTIFY_PROC,                  button_window,
                XV_KEY_DATA,  POPUP_WINDOW_KEY, Fbutton,
                NULL );

/*-------------B u t t o n    W i n d o w-------------------*/

    /* create the "Highlight button
     */
    ph = (Panel_item) xv_create ( Pbutton,  PANEL_BUTTON,
                PANEL_LABEL_STRING, "Highlight",
                PANEL_NOTIFY_PROC,  highlight,
                NULL );

    /* create the "Inactive" button
     */
    pi = (Panel_item) xv_create ( Pbutton,  PANEL_BUTTON,
                PANEL_LABEL_STRING,                 "Inactive",
                PANEL_NOTIFY_PROC,                  inactive,
                XV_KEY_DATA,  POPUP_PANEL_KEY,   Pbutton,
                XV_KEY_DATA,  BUTTON_KEY,        ph,
                XV_KEY_DATA,  BUTTON2_KEY,       pi,
                NULL );

    /* create the Busy signal
     */
    pb = (Panel_item) xv_create ( Pbutton,  PANEL_BUTTON,
                PANEL_LABEL_STRING,                 "Busy",
                PANEL_NOTIFY_PROC,                  busy,
                XV_KEY_DATA,  POPUP_PANEL_KEY,   Pbutton,
                XV_KEY_DATA,  BUTTON_KEY,        ph,
                NULL );

    /* create the "Cancel" button
```

```
           */
     pc = (Panel_item) xv_create ( Pbutton,  PANEL_BUTTON,
                 PANEL_LABEL_STRING,                  "Cancel",
                 PANEL_NOTIFY_PROC,                   cancel,
                 XV_KEY_DATA,   POPUP_WINDOW_KEY,  Fbutton,
                 NULL );

    /* create the "Menu Right" button
     */
    m = (Menu) xv_create ( XV_NULL, MENU,
                 MENU_STRINGS,
i                                                      "Marillion",
                                                       "Genesis",
                                                       "IQ",
                                                       "Twelfth Night",
                                                       NULL,
                 MENU_NOTIFY_PROC,                     menu_stub,
                 XV_KEY_DATA, BASE_FRAME_KEY,          frame,
                 NULL );

    (void) xv_create ( Pbutton, PANEL_BUTTON,
                 PANEL_LABEL_STRING, "Menu Right",
                 PANEL_ITEM_MENU,        m,
                 NULL );
    /* make "Cancel" the default button
     */
    (void) xv_set ( Pbutton, PANEL_DEFAULT_ITEM, pc, NULL );

    /* make everything nice
     */
    window_fit ( Pbutton );
    window_fit ( Fbutton );
    window_fit_height ( panel );

    /* set up the canvas
     */
    canvas = (Canvas) xv_create ( frame, CANVAS,
                 XV_X,                      0,
                 XV_WIDTH,                  WIN_EXTEND_TO_EDGE,
                 XV_HEIGHT,                 WIN_EXTEND_TO_EDGE,
                 CANVAS_REPAINT_PROC,       repaint,
                 CANVAS_X_PAINT_WINDOW,     TRUE,
                 NULL );
    window_fit ( frame );

    /* create the popup */
    m = (Menu) xv_create ( XV_NULL, MENU,
                 MENU_GEN_PIN_WINDOW, frame, "Popup Menu",
                 MENU_ACTION_ITEM,    "Quit", exit,
                 NULL );
    xv_set ( canvas_paint_window ( canvas ),
                 WIN_CONSUME_EVENTS, WIN_MOUSE_BUTTONS, NULL,
                 WIN_EVENT_PROC,         show_it,
                 WIN_CLIENT_DATA,        m,
                 NULL );

    xv_main_loop ( frame );
    return ( 0 );
}
```

Canvas

Many applications require displayed data. For the fullest control over this data, you can use the **CANVAS** package or, if you want to use one of the Slingshot items, a **CANVAS_SHELL**.

A **CANVAS** gives you more control over your displays, but it also requires more work. A **CANVAS_SHELL** lets you use one of the many items that are provided with Slingshot. Which is more appropriate depends on your application: If you want to write a spreadsheet, for example, a **CANVAS_SHELL** would be more appropriate. If you're writing a paint program, the **CANVAS** would probably be more appropriate.

The **CANVAS** package will be discussed in this chapter. **CANVAS_SHELL**s are discussed in the Slingshot section (Chapter 33).

A **CANVAS** object has the attributes shown in Figure 7.1.

ANATOMY OF A CANVAS

Canvases are made out of the following three windows, which appear to be a single window:

Main Subwindow   The Main Subwindow is the one that you "see." It's owned by the frame, and it owns the views.

View   The View controls which part of the paint window is shown. Views may be split, and scrollbars can be associated.

Paint   The Paint window is where you do all of your drawing. It's also where events take place, so the Paint window is very important to the programmer.

These windows are shown in Figure 7.2.

WRITING TO THE CANVAS

To draw on a canvas, you'll want to draw on the canvas's Paint window. You'll typically want the repaint procedure to do the actual drawing, since doing so ensures that you'll have a valid window to draw in before your program starts drawing. The preferred way of writing to canvases is with Xlib function calls.

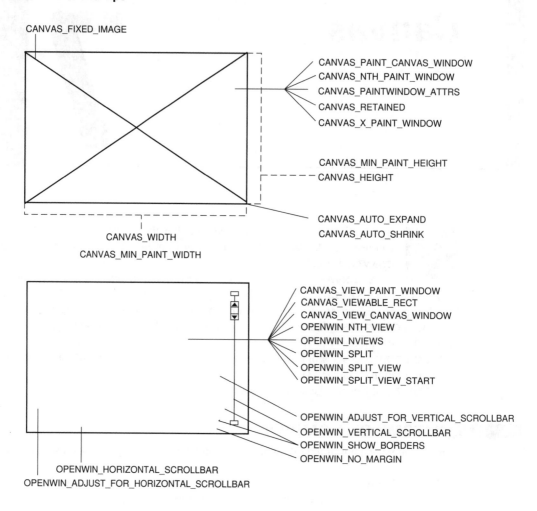

FIGURE 7.1 Canvas Attributes

ASSOCIATING A SCROLLBAR WITH THE CANVAS

Attaching a scrollbar with a canvas is fairly simple. Use the canvas as the parent of the scrollbar—the connections are done automatically. There are a number of attributes that can be set to modify the way that the scrollbar manipulates the canvas.

You should also remember that OL scrollbars are splittable. If this features creates problems, you'll want to disable it.

DIFFERENCE BETWEEN CANVAS AND TEXTSW

If you need to have a general-purpose text interface, you should use a **TEXTSW** or **TTY** subwindow. These can handle curses and text input and output. They do not give you the

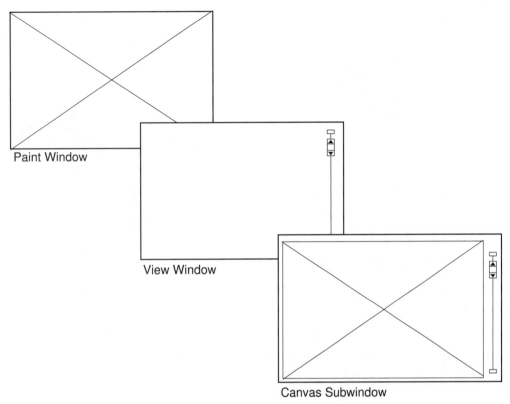

FIGURE 7.2 Anatomy of a Canvas

control necessary for desktop publishing or other similar tasks. For that you'll want to use a canvas.

If you're working with a lot of PostScript, you may want to consider the tNt library instead of XView.

SAMPLE PROGRAM

This example draws an X on the canvas so that there will be something to look at as you mess with the scrollbars. The scrollbars are splittable, use default paging, and demonstrate other features.

```
/* canvas.c -- canvas demonstration program
 * Author:   Kenneth Bibb
 */

#include <X11/Xlib.h>
#include <xview/xview.h>
#include <xview/panel.h>
#include <xview/canvas.h>
#include <xview/scrollbar.h>
#include <xview/xv_xrect.h>
```

```
void
draw_line ( canvas, paint_window, display, xwin, xrects )
Canvas canvas;
Xv_Window paint_window;
Display *display;
Window xwin;
Xv_xrectlist *xrects;
{
        GC              gc = DefaultGC ( display, DefaultScreen ( display ) );
        int             width = (int) xv_get ( paint_window, XV_WIDTH );
        int             height = (int) xv_get ( paint_window, XV_HEIGHT );

        XDrawLine ( display, xwin, gc, 0, 0, width, height );
        XDrawLine ( display, xwin, gc, 0, height, width, 0 );
}

int
main ( argc, argv )
int argc;
char **argv;
{
        Frame base;
        Canvas canvas;
        Scrollbar horiz, vert;

        xv_init ( XV_INIT_ARGC_PTR_ARGV, &argc, argv, NULL );

        base = (Frame)xv_create ( XV_NULL, FRAME,
                    FRAME_LABEL,             argv[0],
                    FRAME_SHOW_FOOTER,       TRUE,
                    XV_X,                    300,
                    XV_Y,                    175,
                    NULL );

        canvas = (Canvas) xv_create ( base, CANVAS,
                    CANVAS_AUTO_EXPAND,      FALSE,
                    CANVAS_AUTO_SHRINK,      FALSE,
                    CANVAS_WIDTH,            1000,
                    CANVAS_HEIGHT,           1000,
                    CANVAS_REPAINT_PROC,     draw_line,
                    CANVAS_X_PAINT_WINDOW,   TRUE,
                    NULL );

        horiz = (Scrollbar) xv_create ( canvas, SCROLLBAR,
                    SCROLLBAR_DIRECTION,     SCROLLBAR_HORIZONTAL,
                    SCROLLBAR_SPLITTABLE,    TRUE,
                    NULL );

        vert = (Scrollbar) xv_create ( canvas, SCROLLBAR,
                    SCROLLBAR_DIRECTION,     SCROLLBAR_VERTICAL,
                    SCROLLBAR_SPLITTABLE,    TRUE,
                    NULL );
        window_fit ( base );

        xv_main_loop ( base );
        return ( 0 );
}
```

Choices

hoice items are a familiar part of the UI world. Exclusive choice items are called *radio buttons* by other UIs, and nonexclusive choice items are called *choice buttons*.

    To tell the difference in OL between exclusive and nonexclusive buttons, look at the spacing between the buttons. Is there a space? If there *isn't* a space, you're looking at *exclusive* choice items (you can only choose one). If there *is* a space, you're looking at *nonexclusive* choice items.

The attributes for choices are shown in Figure 8.1. The buttons in choice items may be laid out horizontally, as in the figure, or vertically. This is controlled by the **PANEL_LAYOUT** attribute (see chapter 22). To stack the choice items on top of each other, use **PANEL_VERTICAL**.

CHOICE VALUES AND SETTING DEFAULT CHOICE

The **PANEL_VALUE** format for choices can be confusing. The format of your **PANEL_VALUE** depends on whether the choice is exclusive or nonexclusive.

Exclusive Choice   When working with exclusive choice buttons, the buttons are numbered from left to right, starting with zero, as shown in Figure 8.2.

    To ask the item for its value, we would use **xv_get()**:

```
int i;
Panel_item choice;

i = xv_get ( choice, PANEL_VALUE );
```

If the third button was pressed, i would be 2. If the first button had been pressed, i would be 0.

    To set a default choice, set **PANEL_VALUE** to the choice item's button. (This is supposed to be done only on menus, according to the OLFS, but it's useful.) To set the third button, we would use:

```
Panel_item choice;

(void) xv_set ( choice, PANEL_VALUE, 2, NULL );
```

The value would be 2 because the leftmost choice is 0.

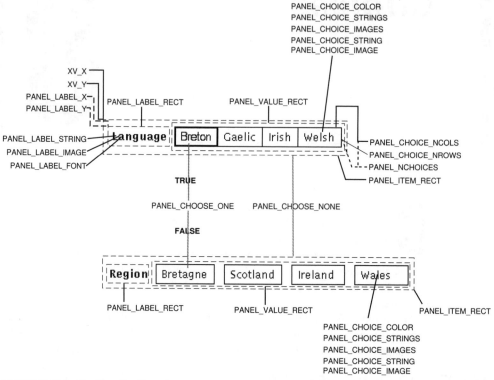

FIGURE 8.1 Choice Attributes

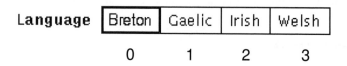

FIGURE 8.2 Exclusive Choice Values

$$Bretagne + Ireland = 0101 = 5$$
$$Scotland + Wales = 1010 = 10$$

FIGURE 8.3 Nonexclusive Choice Values

Nonexclusive Choice   Nonexclusive choice items are bit-mapped, where the leftmost button is the rightmost bit, as shown in Figure 8.3.

We can retrieve the current value in the same way in which we retrieve the value of an exclusive setting:

```
int i;

Panel_item choice;

i = xv_get ( choice, PANEL_VALUE );
```

If the first and third buttons were depressed, i would be 5 (binary 101 is decimal 5). If the first and fourth buttons were depressed, i would be 9 (binary 1001 is decimal 9).

To set a default choice, set **PANEL_VALUE** so all relevant bits are set to 1. To set the default to being the first, second, and fourth buttons, we would set **PANEL_VALUE** to 11 (binary 1011 = decimal 11).

```
Panel_item choice;

xv_set ( choice, PANEL_VALUE, 11, NULL );
```

GETTING A CHOICE STRING

Retrieving a string involves the **PANEL_VALUE**, so the same differences are encountered between exclusive and nonexclusive settings as when setting and retrieving numerical values from them. To retrieve an exclusive choice setting's string, you can do the following:

```
Panel_item choice;

(char *) xv_get ( choice, PANEL_CHOICE_STRING,
xv_get( choice, PANEL_VALUE ) );
```

We take **PANEL_CHOICE_STRING** and provide it with the index to the string (through **PANEL_VALUE**).

To retrieve a nonexclusive choice setting's string is a little more complicated, since the value is a bitmap. The following routine will display all selected choices (the unselected choices appear as empty boxes).

```
Panel_item choice;

int i,n;
```

```
n = xv_get ( choice, PANEL_CHOICE_NCOLS ) ;

for (i=0; i<n; i++)
printf ( "[%s]\t", (xv_get ( choice, PANEL_VALUE ) & (1 << i) )
                ? (char *) xv_get (choice, PANEL_CHOICE_STRING, i )
                : "        " );
                printf ( "\n" );
```

INACTIVATING A CHOICE

To make a group of choices inactive, use the following:

```
Panel_item choice;

xv_set (choice, PANEL_INACTIVE, TRUE, NULL);
```

According to the OLFS (pp. 108, 112), making a single choice inactive is not part of the Open Look GUI.

INDETERMINATE CHOICES

Indeterminate choices, though an interesting part of the Open Look GUI, are not currently supported. With a little luck, they'll be supported in a future version of XView.

SAMPLE PROGRAM

The sample program displays a popup window containing an exclusive and a nonexclusive setting. When you select an exclusive item, its value will be displayed in the footing of the base frame. When you press the "Show Choice" button, the string of the selected exclusive setting will be displayed in the footing of the base frame.

When you select a nonexclusive setting, value of the setting (in hex) will be displayed, followed by the selected string(s) in the footing of the base frame.

```
/* choice.c -- Open Look basic choice types

 * Author:  Kenneth Bibb

 * March 1992 -- Arastar Consulting

 *-----------

 * Need "show choice" button to print out the string that is chosen.

 * Need to add choice_stack

 */


#include <stdlib.h>

#include <sys/param.h>

#include <xview/xview.h>
```

```
#include <xview/panel.h>

#include <xview/canvas.h>

#include <xview/openmenu.h>

#include <xview/xv_xrect.h>


Attr_attribute  FRAME_BASE_KEY;

Attr_attribute FRAME_CHOICE_KEY;

Attr_attribute LANG_CHOICE_KEY;

Attr_attribute REGION_CHOICE_KEY;

Attr_attribute  CHOICE_BUTTON_KEY;


void
menu_stub ( m,mi )
Menu m;
Menu_item mi;
{
     char s[48];
     Frame frame = (Frame) xv_get ( m, XV_KEY_DATA, FRAME_BASE_KEY, NULL);

     sprintf ( s,"Menu: [%s]\n", xv_get ( mi,MENU_STRING ) );
     (void) xv_set ( frame, FRAME_LEFT_FOOTER, s, NULL );
}


void
show_choice ( item, event )
Panel_item item;
Event *event;
{
     char s[48];
     Frame frame = (Frame) xv_get ( item, XV_KEY_DATA, FRAME_BASE_KEY);

     Panel_item pi = (Panel_item) xv_get ( item,XV_KEY_DATA,
        LANG_CHOICE_KEY);

     sprintf ( s,"exclusive: %d-[%s]\n", xv_get ( pi,PANEL_VALUE ),
        xv_get ( pi,PANEL_CHOICE_STRING, xv_get ( pi,PANEL_VALUE ) ) );
        (void) xv_set ( frame, FRAME_LEFT_FOOTER, s, NULL );
}


void
inactive ( item, event )
Panel_item item;
Event *event;
{
     Panel_item pi = (Panel_item) xv_get ( item, XV_KEY_DATA,
        LANG_CHOICE_KEY);
     Panel_item pj = (Panel_item) xv_get ( item, XV_KEY_DATA,
        REGION_CHOICE_KEY);
     Panel_item pk = (Panel_item) xv_get ( item, XV_KEY_DATA,
        CHOICE_BUTTON_KEY);
```

```
        if ( xv_get ( pi, PANEL_INACTIVE ) == TRUE ) {
                xv_set ( pi, PANEL_INACTIVE, FALSE, NULL );
                xv_set ( pj, PANEL_INACTIVE, FALSE, NULL );
                xv_set ( pk, PANEL_INACTIVE, FALSE, NULL );
        }
        else
        {
                xv_set ( pi, PANEL_INACTIVE, TRUE, NULL );
                xv_set ( pj, PANEL_INACTIVE, TRUE, NULL );
                xv_set ( pk, PANEL_INACTIVE, TRUE, NULL );
        }

}

void
language ( item, value, event )
Panel_item item;
int       value;
Event    *event;
{
    char s[64];
    Frame frame = (Frame) xv_get ( item, XV_KEY_DATA, FRAME_BASE_KEY);
    sprintf ( s,"Value: [%d]\t", xv_get ( item, PANEL_VALUE ) );
    (void) xv_set ( frame, FRAME_LEFT_FOOTER, s, NULL );
}

void
region ( item, value, event )
Panel_item item;
unsigned int    value;
Event    *event;
{
        char s[64];
        Frame frame = (Frame) xv_get ( item, XV_KEY_DATA, FRAME_BASE_KEY);

        sprintf ( s, "hex: [%x]:[%8.8s]\t[%8.8s]\t[%8.8s]\t[%8.8s]\n",
                        xv_get ( item, PANEL_VALUE ),
                        ( xv_get ( item, PANEL_VALUE ) & ( 1 << 0 ) )
                                        ? (char *) xv_get ( item,
                                        PANEL_CHOICE_STRING, 0 )
                                        : " ",
                        ( xv_get ( item, PANEL_VALUE ) & ( 1 << 1 ) )
                        ? (char *) xv_get ( item,PANEL_CHOICE_STRING, 1 )
                        : " ",
                        ( xv_get ( item, PANEL_VALUE ) & ( 1 << 2 ) )
                                        ? (char *) xv_get ( item,
                                        PANEL_CHOICE_STRING, 2 )
                                        : " ",
                        ( xv_get ( item, PANEL_VALUE ) & ( 1 << 3 ) )
                                        ? (char *) xv_get ( item,
                                        PANEL_CHOICE_STRING, 3 )
                                        : " "
                        );
        (void) xv_set ( frame, FRAME_LEFT_FOOTER, s, NULL );
}

void
choice_window ( m, mi )
Menu m;
Menu_item mi;
```

```
{
        Frame Fchoice = (Frame) xv_get ( m, XV_KEY_DATA, FRAME_CHOICE_KEY);

        xv_set ( Fchoice, XV_SHOW, TRUE, NULL );
}


void
show_it ( window, event )
Xv_Window window;
Event *event;

{
        if ( event_action ( event ) == ACTION_MENU & event_is_down ( event) ) {
                    Menu m = (Menu) xv_get ( window, WIN_CLIENT_DATA );
                    menu_show ( m, window, event, NULL );
        }
}


void
repaint ( canvas, win, dpy, xwin, xrect )
Canvas canvas;
Xv_Window win;
Display *dpy;
Window xwin;
Xv_xrectlist *xrect;
{
        GC gc;
        int width, height;

        gc = DefaultGC ( dpy, DefaultScreen ( dpy ) );
        width = (int) xv_get ( win, XV_WIDTH );
        height = (int) xv_get ( win, XV_HEIGHT );
}


main ( argc, argv )
int argc;
char **argv;
{
        Frame                   frame;
        Frame                   Fchoice;
        Canvas                  canvas;
        Panel                   panel;
        Panel                   Pchoice;
        Menu                    m, m_undo;
        Panel_item              ph, pi, pj, pk;

        xv_init ( XV_INIT_ARGC_PTR_ARGV, &argc, argv, NULL );
        FRAME_BASE_KEY = xv_unique_key ();
        FRAME_CHOICE_KEY = xv_unique_key ();
        LANG_CHOICE_KEY = xv_unique_key ();
        REGION_CHOICE_KEY = xv_unique_key ();
        CHOICE_BUTTON_KEY = xv_unique_key ();

        frame = (Frame) xv_create ( NULL, FRAME,

    FRAME_LABEL,                argv[0],
                    FRAME_SHOW_FOOTER,      TRUE,
                    XV_X,                   300,
                    XV_Y,                   175,
                    NULL );
```

```
      Fchoice = (Frame) xv_create ( frame, FRAME_CMD,
                 FRAME_LABEL, "Choice Examples",
                 XV_X,                       325,
                 XV_Y,                       200,
                 NULL );
      Pchoice = (Panel) xv_get ( Fchoice, FRAME_CMD_PANEL );
      panel = (Panel) xv_create ( frame, PANEL, NULL);

      m = (Menu) xv_create ( NULL, MENU,
                 MENU_ACTION_ITEM,               "New...", menu_stub,
                 MENU_ACTION_ITEM,               "Save...", menu_stub,
                 MENUITEM_SPACE,                 NULL,
                 MENU_ACTION_ITEM,               "Print...", menu_stub,
                 MENU_ACTION_ITEM,               "Quit",exit,
                 XV_KEY_DATA, FRAME_BASE_KEY, frame,
                 NULL );
   (void) xv_create ( panel, PANEL_BUTTON,
                 PANEL_LABEL_STRING, "File",
                 PANEL_ITEM_MENU,     m,
                 NULL );
   (void) xv_create ( panel, PANEL_BUTTON,
                 PANEL_LABEL_STRING,         "Choice Window...",
                 PANEL_NOTIFY_PROC,          choice_window,
                 XV_KEY_DATA, FRAME_CHOICE_KEY, Fchoice,
                 NULL );

   ph = (panel-item) 1 xv_create ( Pchoice, PANEL_BUTTON,
                 PANEL_LABEL_STRING,         "Show Choice",
                 PANEL_NOTIFY_PROC,          show_choice,
                 XV_KEY_DATA, FRAME_BASE_KEY, frame,
                 NULL );
   (void) xv_set ( Pchoice, PANEL_DEFAULT_ITEM, ph, NULL );
   pk = (Panel_item) xv_create ( Pchoice, PANEL_BUTTON,
                 PANEL_LABEL_STRING,         "Inactive",
                 PANEL_NOTIFY_PROC,          inactive,
                 NULL );
   pi = (Panel_item) xv_create ( Pchoice, PANEL_CHOICE,
                 PANEL_NEXT_ROW,             -1,
                 PANEL_LABEL_STRING,         "Language",
                 PANEL_CHOICE_STRINGS,       "Breton","Gaelic","Irish",
                                                 "Welsh",NULL,
                 PANEL_NOTIFY_PROC,          language,
                 XV_KEY_DATA, FRAME_BASE_KEY, frame,
                 NULL );
   (void) xv_set ( ph, XV_KEY_DATA, LANG_CHOICE_KEY, pi, NULL );
   pj = (Panel_item) xv_create ( Pchoice, PANEL_TOGGLE,
                 PANEL_NEXT_ROW,             -1,
                 PANEL_LABEL_STRING,         "Region",
                 PANEL_CHOICE_STRINGS,       "Bretagne",
                                             "Scotland",
                                             "Ireland ",
                                             "Wales   ",
                                         NULL,
                 PANEL_NOTIFY_PROC,          region,
                 XV_KEY_DATA, FRAME_BASE_KEY, frame,
                 NULL );
   (void) xv_set ( pk,
                 XV_KEY_DATA, LANG_CHOICE_KEY,      pi,
                 XV_KEY_DATA, REGION_CHOICE_KEY,    pj,
                 XV_KEY_DATA, CHOICE_BUTTON_KEY,    ph,
                 NULL );
```

```
        window_fit ( Pchoice );
        window_fit ( Fchoice );
        window_fit_height ( panel );
        canvas = (Canvas) xv_create ( frame, CANVAS,
                    XV_X,                          0,
                    XV_WIDTH,                      WIN_EXTEND_TO_EDGE,
                    XV_HEIGHT,                     WIN_EXTEND_TO_EDGE,
                    CANVAS_REPAINT_PROC,           repaint,
                    CANVAS_X_PAINT_WINDOW,         TRUE,
                    NULL );
        window_fit ( frame );

        /* popup */
        m = (Menu) xv_create ( NULL, MENU,
                    MENU_GEN_PIN_WINDOW, frame, "Popup Menu",
                    MENU_ACTION_ITEM, "Quit", exit,
                    NULL );
        (void) xv_set ( canvas_paint_window ( canvas ),
                    WIN_CONSUME_EVENTS, WIN_MOUSE_BUTTONS, NULL,
                    WIN_EVENT_PROC,   show_it,
                    WIN_CLIENT_DATA, m,
                    NULL );
                    xv_main_loop ( frame );
}
```

Cursors

9

CHAPTER

Cursors are highly visible features of the Open Look GUI that like most parts of the GUI, are usually taken for granted by the user.

XView cursors have the attributes shown in Figure 9.1.

CHANGING CURSOR SHAPES

When certain conditions occur inside of your program, you may want to alert the user by changing the cursor to some shape other than the basic one. There are a number of standard Open Look GUI–compliant cursors available. These cursors are shown in Figure 9.2.

COLOR CURSORS

You will occasionally want to use color cursors. This is typically discouraged, since it makes the cursor harder to see, since color should have meaning, and since some users may have a monochrome display.

One use for a color cursor would be to show what color was currently chosen in a paint program (then the color would have meaning).

Cursors can have the foreground or background color changed, but are restricted to one-bit depth. The background color is used for the cursor's mask. To set the background color of the cursor use **CURSOR_BACKGROUND_COLOR**. The foreground color is used for the cursor itself. To set the foreground color of the cursor, you can use **CURSOR_FOREGROUND_COLOR**.

To create a red cursor, for example, you could do the following:

```
#include <xview/cms.h>

Xv_singlecolor fg, bg;

/* define foreground as red */
fg.red = 255;    /* 0 means off, 255 full on */
fg.green = 0;    /* 0 means off, 255 full on */
fg.blue = 0;     /* 0 means off, 255 full on */

/* define background as white */
bg.red = 255;
bg.green = 255;
bg.blue = 255;
```

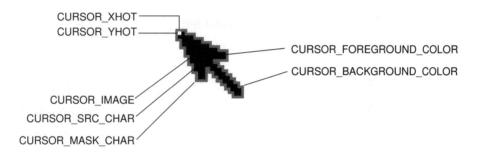

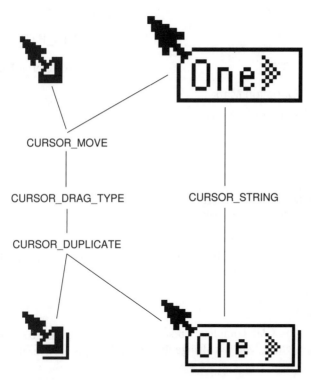

FIGURE 9.1 Cursor Attributes

POINTER	POINTER NAME	#DEFINE
	Basic	OLC_BASIC_PTR
	Move	OLC_MOVE_PTR
	Duplicate	OLC_COPY_PTR
	Move Text	OLC_TEXT_MOVE_DRAG
	Duplicate Text	
	Busy	OLC_BUSY_PTR
	Pan	OLC_PANNING_PTR
	Target	OLC_NAVIGATION_PTR
?	Question Mark	

FIGURE 9.2 Standard Open Look Cursors

```
(void) xv_set ( cursor,
        CURSOR_FOREGROUND_COLOR, &fg,
        CURSOR_BACKGROUND_COLOR, &bg,
        NULL );
```

If you try this and you end up with a gray cursor, bring up the workspace properties color chooser; it will reset the color cube, so the cursor will be red.

SAMPLE PROGRAM

To see the various Open Look GUI–compliant cursors, the demo program **cursor.c** can be used. By selecting a choice setting, you can change the cursor that appears over the canvas.

```
/* cursor.c -- cursor demo
 * Author: Rick Goldstein from an idea by Ken Bibb
 * March 1992
 *---------------------------
 * The ugly #ifdefs were inserted by Ken so this
 * would compile on both his IPC (XView 3.0) and
 * on his SLC (XView 2.0)
 */
```

```
#include <stdio.h>
#include <xview/xview.h>
#include <xview/panel.h>
#include <xview/canvas.h>
#include <xview/cursor.h>
#include <xview/svrimage.h>
#include <xview/cms.h>

/* the question mark image was generated by IconEdit
 * using the OLGUIFS description as input.
 */
static short question_image[16] = {
    0x7C00, 0xC600, 0x0600, 0x0600, 0x0C00, 0x3000,
    0x6000, 0x6000, 0x6000, 0x1000, 0x6000, 0x6000,
    0x0000, 0x0000, 0x0000, 0x0000,
};

/* handle to the cursor window
 */
Attr_attribute CURSOR_WINDOW_KEY;

/* the notify procedure for the PANEL_CHOICE item
 * in the cursor_window.  This is what changes the cursor.
 */
void
cursor_choice_callback ( item, value, event )
Panel_item item;
int value;
Event *event;
{
    Xv_Window  cursor_win = (Xv_Window) xv_get ( item, XV_KEY_DATA,
            CURSOR_WINDOW_KEY );
    Xv_cursor   cursor = (Xv_cursor) NULL;
    Xv_cursor   qcursor = (Xv_cursor) NULL;
    Xv_singlecolor fg, bg;
    Server_image qimage = (Server_image) NULL;
    int     csr_type;
    int     csr_mask;


    if ( !cursor_win )
        return;

    switch ( value ) {
    case 0:                                                 /* basic */
        csr_type = OLC_BASIC_PTR;
        csr_mask = OLC_BASIC_MASK_PTR;
        break;

    case 1:                                                 /* move */
        csr_type = OLC_MOVE_PTR;
        csr_mask = OLC_MOVE_MASK_PTR;
        break;

    case 2:                                                 /* copy */
        csr_type = OLC_COPY_PTR;
        csr_mask = OLC_COPY_MASK_PTR;
        break;
```

```
    case 3:                                                     /* busy */
        csr_type = OLC_BUSY_PTR;
        csr_mask = OLC_BUSY_MASK_PTR;
        break;

    case 4:                                                     /* text */
#ifdef OLC_TEXT_MOVE_DRAG
        csr_type = OLC_TEXT_MOVE_DRAG;
        csr_mask = OLC_TEXT_MOVE_MOVE_MASK;
               /* why isn't it OLC_TEXT_MOVE_DRAG_MASK ? */
#endif
        break;

    case 5:                                                     /* panning */
#ifdef OLC_PANNING_MASK_PTR
        csr_type = OLC_PANNING_PTR;
        csr_mask = OLC_PANNING_MASK_PTR;
#endif
        break;

    case 6:                                                     /* target */
#ifdef OLC_NAVIGATION_LEVEL_MASK_PTR
        csr_type = OLC_NAVIGATION_LEVEL_PTR;
        csr_mask = OLC_NAVIGATION_LEVEL_MASK_PTR;
#endif
        break;

    case 7:                                                     /* ? */
        /* create a server image of the '?' */
        if ( !qimage )
            qimage = xv_create ( XV_NULL, SERVER_IMAGE,
                                 XV_WIDTH,              16,
                                 XV_HEIGHT,             16,
                                 SERVER_IMAGE_BITS,     question_image,
                                 NULL );
        if ( !cursor )
            cursor = (Xv_cursor) xv_find ( XV_NULL, CURSOR,
                                 CURSOR_IMAGE,          qimage,
                                 /* should have a mask image */
                                 NULL );
        break;

    case 8:                                                     /* basic */
        csr_type = OLC_BASIC_PTR;
        csr_mask = OLC_BASIC_MASK_PTR;
        break;

    } /* switch() */


    if ( value == 8 ) {
      fg.red = 250; fg.green = 000; fg.blue = 00;
      bg.red = 255; bg.green = 255; bg.blue = 255;
    }

    /* Note:  cursors are xv_find-able so they can be shared */
    if ( !cursor )
```

```
#ifndef OLC_TEXT_MOVE_DRAG
    if ( value == 4 )
                cursor = xv_find( XV_NULL, CURSOR,
                                    CURSOR_STRING,          "Ack",
                                    NULL );

    else
#endif
  cursor = xv_find( XV_NULL, CURSOR,
                        CURSOR_SRC_CHAR,        csr_type,
                        CURSOR_MASK_CHAR,       csr_mask,
                        NULL );

   if (value == 8)
     xv_set( cursor,
                CURSOR_FOREGROUND_COLOR, &fg,
                CURSOR_BACKGROUND_COLOR, &bg,
                NULL );
   xv_set ( cursor_win,
           WIN_CURSOR, cursor,
           NULL );
} /* cursor_choice_callback() */

void
main ( argc, argv )
int argc;
char **argv;
{

    Frame               frame;
    Canvas              canvas;
    Panel               panel;
    Panel_choice_item   choice;
    Cms                 cms;

    (void) xv_init ( XV_INIT_ARGC_PTR_ARGV, &argc, argv, NULL );
    CURSOR_WINDOW_KEY = xv_unique_key ();


    frame = (Frame) xv_create ( XV_NULL, FRAME,
                            FRAME_LABEL,      argv[0],
                            NULL );

    panel = (Panel) xv_create ( frame, PANEL, NULL);

    choice = xv_create ( panel, PANEL_CHOICE,
                        PANEL_LABEL_STRING,     "Cursor:",
                        PANEL_NOTIFY_PROC,      cursor_choice_callback,
                        PANEL_CHOICE_STRINGS,
                                                "Basic",
                                                "Move",
                                                "Copy",
                                                "Busy",
                                                "Text",
                                                "Panning",
                                                "Target",
                                                "?",
                                                "Red",
                                                NULL,
```

```
                              NULL );
          window_fit_height ( panel );


          /*
           * change background color to show off cursor mask
           * note:  will share default colormap with panel, so
           * I don't need to reallocate the Control colors.
           */

          cms = xv_create ( XV_NULL, CMS,
                              CMS_SIZE,  1,
                              CMS_NAMED_COLORS,  "steel blue", NULL,
                              NULL );

          canvas = (Canvas) xv_create ( frame, CANVAS, NULL );

          xv_set ( canvas_paint_window ( canvas ),
                  WIN_CMS,                    cms,
                  WIN_BACKGROUND_COLOR,       0,
                  NULL );


          xv_set ( choice,
                  XV_KEY_DATA, CURSOR_WINDOW_KEY, canvas_paint_window (
                  canvas ), NULL );

          window_fit ( frame );
          xv_main_loop ( frame );
          exit ( 0 );
}
```

Working with Devguide

Since a program's graphical user interface is visual in nature, it makes sense to design it in a visual way. Sketching it out on paper is one way, but, hey, we've got this computer in front of us—why not use it?

The OpenWindows Developer's Guide (Devguide) lets us do this—it uses the Open Look GUI to help you design applications that themselves will have an Open Look GUI. Besides allowing you to easily create, place, and rearrange objects on the screen until you're satisfied with program layout, it will also generate code which you may merge with your own code, to create those objects.

The main visual component of Devguide is shown in Figure 10.1. Think of it as a palette of objects that you can build a window with, dropping each new piece into place as you develop your application.

You begin to build up an application by using the mouse to drag the glyph representing one of the two types of windows onto the desktop: either a base window (represented by a window corner with an abbreviated menu button) or a popup window (represented by a window corner with a pushpin). Typically, the first window of an application will be a *base window,* like the one shown in Figure 10.2.

A window will then be filled with one or more of the four basic pane types: a panel, a canvas, a TTY subwindow, or a text subwindow. You can then use Devguide to create and organize your

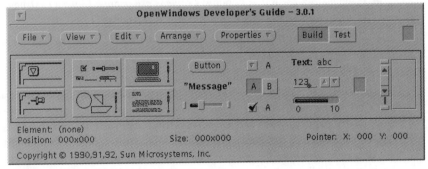

FIGURE 10.1 Devguide Main Window

71

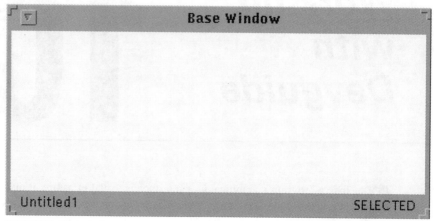

FIGURE 10.2 A Base Window

panel items and create the *hooks* necessary for attaching your working routines to the panel items.

For further information on using the Devguide interface builder, see the *OpenWindows Developer's Guide 3.0 User's Guide.* The rest of this chapter will be concerned with working with the code GXV generates.

PROGRAM ORGANIZATION OF DEVGUIDE-GENERATED CODE

The code produced by GXV (the Devguide program used in generating XView code for C) and the code produced by GXV++ (the Devguide program used to generate XView code for C++) follow several useful conventions:

- All user interface–specific routines are put in a separate file.
- Handles to a particular window's objects are grouped into a C structure or C++ class (depending on whether GXV or GXV++ is being used).
- Window creation is done in terms of "instances" of a particular window; several identical windows may be created, each considered to be a different "instance" of the same window style.

The end result of this is that your application code can treat the creation and manipulation of the window interface as calls to "black boxes," so that your code doesn't need to know, for example, what happens when **my_app_window1_objects_create()** is called; the function returns a pointer to a structure of handles of all the objects that comprise that window.

As an example, we'll create a tool to list the output of a given program on demand. To begin with, we'll hardwire the program to be the UNIX command **dmesg**. The mouse actions use the Select button except where the mouse's Menu or Adjust button is specifically mentioned.

We'll rapidly go through the steps it takes to create the interface with Devguide:

1. Drop a base window object onto the root window.

2. Double-click on this new window's pane to bring up the "Base Windows" property sheet; change the label of this window to "Dmesg Checker" by triple-clicking on the "Label:" text field and typing in the new name. Click Apply and dismiss the sheet.

3. Drop a control area near the lower left corner of our base window; use its resize points to make it cover the entire width of the window, and make it tall enough to hold a button.

4. Drop a button near the center of the control area.

5. Double-click on this button to bring up the "Buttons" property sheet; change its name to **check_button**; change its label to "Check Dmesg File." Hit Apply.

6. Click on the "Connections..." button on this sheet to bring up the Connections window.

7. This window should already have the following values:

```
Source: Buttons (Untitled :: button1)
Target: Buttons (Untitled :: button1)
When: Notify
Action: CallFunction
```

Enter the function name: **check_button_notify**. Click on the "Connect" button, and dismiss this sheet and the Buttons sheet.

8. Drop a text pane in the upper portion of the window; resize it to fill the remainder of the window not filled by the control area pane.

9. Double-click on the pane to bring up the "Text Panes" property sheet; change the "Operation" setting to Read-only; hit Apply and dismiss the sheet.

10. Save this file (using the menu for the main window's File button) as **dmesg_check.G** (Devguide requires the **.G** extension).

11. In a **shelltool** window, enter the command

```
gxv dmesg_check
```

Note: When using **gxv**, don't include the **.G** extension.

Like all descriptions of mouse-based actions, this takes much longer to describe than it does to do; the actual time it took to go from the idea of this example to completion of this part of the GUI was less than 4 minutes. For this first phase, our program looks like the code listed in Listing 10.1.

```
;GIL-3
(
(
  :type              :base-window
  :name              window1
  :owner             nil
  :width             532
  :height            288
  :background-color  ""
  :foreground-color  ""
  :label             "Dmesg Checker"
  :label-type        :string
  :initial-state     :open
  :show-footer       t
```

```
         :resizable         t
         :icon-file         ""
         :icon-label        ""
         :icon-mask-file    ""
         :event-handler     nil
         :user-data         ()
         :actions           ()
)
(
         :type              :control-area
         :name              conrtols1
         :owner             window1
         :help              ""
         :x                 0
         :y                 0
         :width             532
         :height            51
         :background-color  ""
         :foreground-color  ""
         :initial state     :visible
         :show-border       nil
         :menu              nil
         :event-handler     nil
         :user-data         ()
         :actions           ()
)
(
         :type              :button
         :name              check_button
         :owner             controls1
         :help              ""
         :x                 208
         :y                 16
         :width             126
         :height            19
         :constant-width    nil
         :button-type       :normal
         :foreground-color  ""
         :label             "Check Dmesg File"
         :label-type        :string
         :initial-state     :active
         :menu              nil
         :notify-handler    check_button_notify
         :event-handler     nil
         :user-data         ()
         :actions           (
           (
           :from            (window1 check_button)
           :when            (Notify )
           :to              (window1 check_button)
           :function_type   CallFunction
           :arg_type        ()
           :action          (check_button_notify)
           )
         )
)
(
         :type              :text-pane
         :name              textpanel
         :owner             window1
         :help              ""
```

```
            :x                   0
            :y                   51
            :width               532
            :height              237
            :background-color    ""
            :foreground-color    ""
            :initial-state       :visible]
            :show-border         t
            :read-only           t
            :event-handler       nil
            :user-data           ()
            :actions             ()
            )
       )
```

LISTING 10.1 `demsg_1.G`

One aspect of GXV code that can be unwieldy is the length of the names it assigns to variables and handles. Our example application is stored as **dmesg_check**; its main window is left with the default Devguide name of **window1**. From this, GXV will create a variable named

```
dmesg_check_window1
```

to store the pointer to the structure of handles for the window, and an initialization routine for this window named

```
dmesg_check_window1_objects_initialize() .
```

Since the function is externally defined (in the "untouchable" file **dmesg_check_ui.c**), and it only appears once in our application code, we'll leave it alone. But we'll be using the variable in every XView call we make, so let's make it something shorter: we'll use **main_ip**, as it is the instance pointer to the application's main window. We'll use this convention of *windowname_ip* for the instance pointers in all the Devguide-generated examples in this book.

Here's the **main()** routine for our **dmesg** checker. Since the window creation code, including the callback definition for the "Check" button, is hidden in the "black box" of **dmesg_check_window1_objects_initialize()**, the **main()** routine is quite small and should be mostly self-documenting:

```
void
main ( argc, argv )
int argc;
char **argv;
{
   dmesg_check_window1_objects *main_ip;
   /*
    * Initialize XView.
    */
   xv_init ( XV_INIT_ARGC_PTR_ARGV, &argc, argv, NULL );
   INSTANCE = xv_unique_key ();

   /*
    * Initialize user interface components.
```

```
               * Do NOT edit the object initializations by hand.
               */
              main_ip = dmesg_check_window1_objects_initialize ( NULL,NULL ) ;

              /*
               * Turn control over to XView.
               */
              xv_main_loop ( main_ip->window1 );
              exit ( 0 );
          }
```

Line by line: After the Devguide-generated variable declaration, we make our standard call to **xv_init()** to initialize our X environment. (The next line, initializing the variable **INSTANCE**, is not actually necessary for our application, but the code in **dmesg_check_ui.c** expects it, so we leave it in place.)

The next line creates the main window and stores the pointer to its structure of object handles in **main_ip**.

Next is our usual call to **xv_main_loop()**. The handle to our window's frame is the element **window1** in the instance structure; each element takes its name from the objects we created using Devguide. Finally, we provide a defined exit value for the program.

The entire structure of handles for the window is defined in **dmesg_check_ui.h**, which is also automatically created by GXV; it looks like this:

```
          typedef struct {
              Xv_opaque window1;
              Xv_opaque textpane1;
              Xv_opaque controls1;
              Xv_opaque check_button;
          } dmesg_check_window1_objects;
```

CALLBACK STUBS

GXV creates a template for each callback function you specify. This is a big win, as the parameter lists and expected return types of each object's callback function can be hard to remember and painful to look up each time you need it. The callback stub for our check button, as generated by GXV, looks like this:

```
          /*
           * Notify callback function for `check_button'.
           */
          void
          check_button_notify ( item, event )
          Panel_item item;
          Event *event;
          {
              dmesg_check_window1_objects *ip =
                (dmesg_check_window1_objects *) xv_get ( item,
                  XV_KEY_DATA, INSTANCE );

              fputs ( "dmesg_check: check_button_notify\n", stderr );

              /* gxv_start_connections DO NOT EDIT THIS SECTION */

              /* gxv_end_connections */

          }
```

You can compile and run the program with this stub routine in place as you prototype your application, but it turns out, in our style of coding with Devguide, that you can safely eliminate the entire function body GXV provides as you develop your own application. With these lines removed, and our application code added in (plus some minor reformatting), our callback looks like this:

```
/*
 * Notify callback function for 'check_button'.
 */
void
check_button_notify ( item, event )
Panel_item item;
Event *event;
{
    FILE *pipe;
    char buf[150];

    textsw_reset ( main_ip->textpanel, 0, 0 );
    pipe = popen ( "/usr/etc/dmesg", "r" );
    while ( fgets ( buf, 150, pipe ) != NULL )
        textsw_insert ( main_ip->textpanel, buf, strlen ( buf ) );
    textsw_possibly_normalize ( main_ip->textpanel, 0 );
    pclose ( pipe );
}
```

MODIFYING THE APPLICATION

Because of the way GXV keeps the UI generation code and the application code in separate files, many aspects of the UI can often be modified without changing the application code, and vice versa. For example, in our example, the control pane is located below the text pane. If you run this application and try to resize it, you'll find that since the default action of GXV-generated code is to allow the lowest pane to resize dynamically, the control pane will be the one to increase and decrease in height, rather than the text pane.

Finally, Devguide doesn't automatically enforce Open Look GUI compliance. You'll have to do a little work to get that. To see what's required for Open Look compliance, check the OLFS and OLSG.

Frames

When users look at an application, they typically don't see the frame. They take it for granted and don't realize that programmers actually have to put some thought into the design of the frames.

There are three main frames that are used: base window frames (**FRAME_BASE**), help frames (**FRAME_HELP**), and popup window frames (**FRAME_CMD**). These three packages can provide a basis for other useful frame packages, such as a property frame (Sun reserves **FRAME_PROPS** for this), through subclassing.

FRAME ATTRIBUTES

Frames have the attributes shown in Figure 11.1. A popup window frame has, in addition, a *pushpin,* which is defined by the attributes shown in Figure 11.2.

STANDARD BASE WINDOW

The standard OL-compliant window has resize corners, a title, a close button, and no footer. It's created with a call like this:

```
Frame base;

base = xv_create ( XV_NULL, FRAME,
  XV_LABEL, argv[0],
  NULL );
```

You'll want to save the frame's handle for use as a parent item. It has **XV_NULL** as a parent because we're creating a base frame.[1] I like windows that identify themselves, so I usually set the **XV_LABEL** to the name of the program. If you're feeling creative, there are a number of other things you can do with this label—just look at the DeskSet for examples.

If you want to deviate from the standard, you can use the attributes that are mentioned in Figure 11.1.

---

[1] **XV_NULL** parents an object to the Root Window. Frames and other objects can also be parented to other objects (like other base windows).

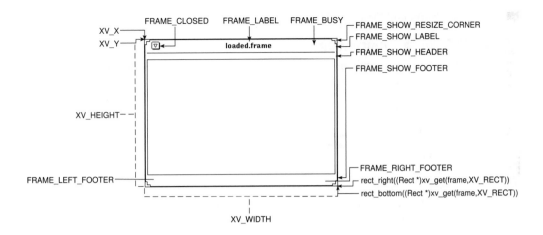

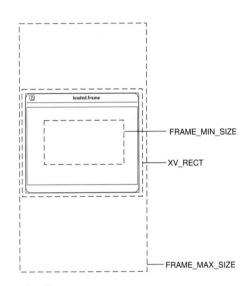

FIGURE 11.1 Frame Attributes

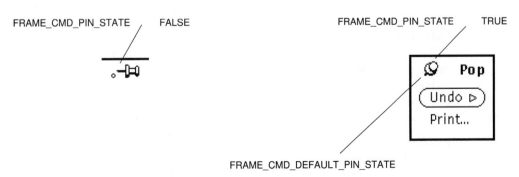

FIGURE 11.2 Pushpin Attributes

▮▮▮▮▮ **P**OPUP WINDOWS

Standard OL-compliant command frames have a title, a pushpin, no resize corners, and, usually, no footer.[2] They're created with a call like this:

```
Frame base, subframe;

subframe = xv_create ( base, FRAME_CMD,
  XV_LABEL, "Subwindow",
  NULL );
```

It looks a lot like the previous call to create a standard base window, but notice the package name: **FRAME_CMD** instead of **FRAME**. This simple change removes the resize corners and substitutes a pushpin for a close button.

Besides using another frame as a parent, you can also create a popup with the root window (workspace) as the parent by making the parent **XV_NULL**.

Another important difference is that **FRAME_CMD** windows come with a built-in panel. To get the panel's handle, use the following:

```
Frame subframe;    /* the subframe previously described */
Panel Psubframe;

Psubframe = (Panel) xv_get ( subframe, FRAME_CMD_PANEL );
```

With a normal window, you would have to use an xv_create() to create a panel, so this is an important difference.

Pushpin Control   When you create your command frame, you can set the initial state of the pushpin with the **FRAME_CMD_DEFAULT_PIN_STATE**. **FRAME_CMD_PIN_OUT** is the default; you can change it to **FRAME_CMD_PIN_IN**.

If you want to change the pin's state, use **FRAME_CMD_PIN_STATE** instead of **FRAME_CMD_DEFAULT_PIN_STATE**.

Blocking Popups   To create popup windows that block the application, use the **NOTICE** package.[3] More is included on the **NOTICE** package in Chapter 20.

Property Windows   Although there is a **FRAME_PROPS** defined in the frame header file, it is just an alias for the **FRAME_CMD** package (in other words, it doesn't do anything for you yet).

All property window–specific appearances and behavior must be taken care of by the programmer. An "Apply" button and a "Reset" button should be added (and centered) at the bottom of the **FRAME_PROPS**. You can also include the optional "Set Default" button in between the "Apply" and "Reset" buttons.

There are a few places where I wish XView was *more* fascist. This is one of them. It would be nice if the **FRAME_PROPS** package automatically did this sort of thing for you.

Property windows are also supposed to use change bars to show fields that have been changed from the defaults. Samples of how to implement this are shown in the section on Panel Messages.

---

[2]Footers are optional on popups. If you need to supply status or error messages from within the popup, then you should have a footer. See OLSG, p. 121, for more details.

[3]You can also block using `xv_window_loop()` and `xv_window_return()`, which are not discussed here.

MULTIPLE BASE FRAMES

To create a program that uses multiple base windows, create the multiple base windows like this:

```
Frame base, base2;

base = (Frame) xv_create ( XV_NULL, FRAME,
    XV_LABEL, argv[0],
    NULL );
base2 = (Frame) xv_create ( base, FRAME,
    XV_LABEL, "The other Base",
    NULL );
```

The **xv_main_loop()** call needs to be set to

```
xv_main_loop ( base );
```

Since both windows are base windows, they can both be iconified, and they can have different icons related to each window.

SETTING WINDOW SIZE

Some applications need control over the size of their windows. If your application uses resize buttons, you may want to define maximum (and minimum) dimensions for the windows.

Maximum Window Size   You have a panel with a lot of controls, which you've carefully designed. Should the user be able to change this window's size? If so, what happens when the user selects "Full Size" on the window menu?

Your application may elect to expand choice stacks into choice settings, change the spacing between panel items, expand the size of a canvas, and so on. Then again, you may wish to disable the ability to resize (by hiding the resize corners—see Figure 11.1 for the appropriate attributes) or by fixing a maximum size for the window.

You can set the maximum size of a window with the **FRAME_MAX_SIZE** attribute:

```
xv_set ( frame, FRAME_MAX_SIZE, max_width, max_height,
    NULL );
```

If you set the maxima to 0, you'll turn control of the maximum size over to the window manager (which may or may not impose its own limits).

To find out what the maximum window size is currently set to, do the following (where **max_width** and **max_height** are **int**s that are to contain the returned width and height):

```
int max_width, max_height;

xv_get ( frame, FRAME_MAX_SIZE, &max_width, &max_height );
```

Minimum Window Size   Besides setting a maximum size for your window, you may also want to set a minimum size. You may want to force the window to stay at a certain height or width to prevent panel items from being forced together or any other loss.

You can set the minimum size of a window with the **FRAME_MIN_SIZE** attribute:

```
int min_width, min_height;

xv_set ( frame, FRAME_MIN_SIZE, min_width, min_height,
  NULL );
```

If you set the minima to 0, you'll turn control of the minimum size over to the window manager (which may or may not impose its own limits).

To find out what the minimum window size is currently set to, do the following (where **min_width** and **min_height** are **int**s that are to contain the returned width and height):

```
int min_width, min_height;

xv_get ( frame, FRAME_MIN_SIZE, &min_width, &min_height );
```

Default Window Size   The default window size is usually the size of the window on startup. You can set the default window size with the **XV_WIDTH** and **XV_HEIGHT** attributes. If you wanted your program to have a default height of 300 and a default width of 200, you could set them with the following code:

```
Frame base;

xv_create ( base, FRAME,
  XV_WIDTH, 200,
  XV_HEIGHT, 300,
  NULL );
```

WINDOW_FIT

XView provides a number of "convenience" functions for prettifying your windows. The **window_fit_width()** function, for example, is used to compute a width for the window so that all of the defined subitems will fit horizontally in the window. The **window_fit_height()** function is used to compute a height for the window so all of the defined subitems will fit vertically in the window.

Finally, there is a **window_fit()** macro, which will compute a width and a height for the window so that all of the defined subitems will fit in the window.

A typical sequence of **window_fit()**s for a standard base frame with canvas and panel is the following:

```
Frame  base;
Canvas canvas;
Panel  panel;

window_fit_height ( panel );
canvas = xv_create ( base, CANVAS, NULL );
window_fit ( base );
```

The panel fits only the height, because we want it to fill the top section of the frame. The canvas is then created. When we do the **window_fit()** on the base window, it now has a fitted panel at the top and a canvas underneath. This will give you a window similar in look to a **shelltool** window.

Occasionally, things don't "look" right and you have to play with the order of the `window_fit()`s to get things to work.

SAMPLE PROGRAMS

The sample programs show examples of different window setups.

`frame.basic.c`	Basic frame
`frame.multiple.c`	Multiple base frames
`frame.w.menus.c`	Base frame with menus
`frame.size.c`	Frame with sizing controls

```
/* frame.basic.c -- Open Look basic frame
 * Author:  Kenneth Bibb
 * January 1992 -- Arastar Consulting
 *------------------------------------
 * Basic frame with panel and canvas
 */

#include <xview/xview.h>
#include <xview/panel.h>
#include <xview/canvas.h>

main ( argc, argv )
int argc;
char **argv;
{
  Frame                 frame;
  Canvas                canvas;
  Panel                 panel;

  xv_init ( XV_INIT_ARGC_PTR_ARGV, &argc, argv, NULL );

  /* create the base frame */
  frame = (Frame) xv_create ( NULL, FRAME,
              FRAME_LABEL,          argv[0],
              FRAME_SHOW_FOOTER,    TRUE,
              XV_X,                 300,
              XV_Y,                 175,
              NULL );

  /* create the panel */
  panel = (Panel) xv_create ( frame, PANEL, NULL );
  window_fit_height ( panel );

  /* create the canvas */
  canvas = (Canvas) xv_create ( frame, CANVAS,
              XV_X,                 0,
              XV_HEIGHT,            WIN_EXTEND_TO_EDGE,
              XV_WIDTH,             WIN_EXTEND_TO_EDGE,
              CANVAS_X_PAINT_WINDOW,  TRUE,
              NULL );

  /* fit the frame around the canvas and panel */
  window_fit ( frame );

  xv_main_loop ( frame );
}
```

```c
/* frame.multiple.c -- Multiple Base Windows
 * Author:   Kenneth Bibb
 * January 1992 -- Arastar Consulting
 *----------------------------------------
 */

#include <stdlib.h>
#include <sys/param.h>
#include <xview/xview.h>
#include <xview/panel.h>
#include <xview/canvas.h>
#include <xview/xv_xrect.h>
#include <xview/openmenu.h>

Attr_attribute BASE_FRAME_KEY;
Attr_attribute SITE_FRAME_KEY;

void
menu_stub ( menu, menu_item )
Menu menu;
Menu_item menu_item;
{
      char s[64];

      sprintf ( s,"Menu: [%s]\n", (char *) xv_get ( menu_item,
      MENU_STRING) );
xv_set ( xv_get ( menu,XV_KEY_DATA,BASE_FRAME_KEY ),FRAME_LEFT_FOOTER,s,
                        NULL);
}

void
sites ( menu,  menu_item )
Menu menu;
Menu_item menu_item;
{
      xv_set ( xv_get ( menu, XV_KEY_DATA, SITE_FRAME_KEY ),
            XV_SHOW, TRUE, NULL);
}

void push_me_proc ( button,event )
Panel_item button;
Event *event;
{
      char s[64];

      sprintf ( s,"Button: [%s]\n", (char *) xv_get ( button,
            PANEL_LABEL_STRING ) );
      xv_set ( xv_get ( button, XV_KEY_DATA, BASE_FRAME_KEY ),
            FRAME_LEFT_FOOTER, s, NULL );
}

int
main ( argc, argv )
int argc;
char **argv;
{
      Frame               frame;
      Frame               site_frame;
      Canvas              canvas;
```

```
        Panel                    panel;
        Panel                    Psite;
        Menu                     m, m_undo;


xv_init ( XV_INIT_ARGC_PTR_ARGV, &argc, argv, NULL );
        SITE_FRAME_KEY = xv_unique_key ();
        BASE_FRAME_KEY = xv_unique_key ();

        /* create the base frame
        */
        frame = (Frame) xv_create ( NULL, FRAME,
                     FRAME_LABEL,            argv[0],
                     FRAME_SHOW_FOOTER,      TRUE,
                     XV_X,                   300,
                     XV_Y,                   175,
                     NULL );

        /* create the other base frame
        */
        site_frame = (Frame) xv_create ( frame, FRAME,
                     FRAME_LABEL, "Sites",
                     XV_X,          350,
                     XV_Y,          300,
                     NULL );

        panel = (Panel) xv_create ( frame, PANEL, NULL );
        Psite = (Panel) xv_create ( site_frame, PANEL, NULL );

        m = (Menu) xv_create ( NULL, MENU,
                     MENU_ACTION_ITEM,        "New...", menu_stub,
                     MENU_ACTION_ITEM,        "Save...", menu_stub,
                     MENUITEM_SPACE,          NULL,
                     MENU_ACTION_ITEM,        "Print...",menu_stub,
                     MENU_ACTION_ITEM,        "Quit",exit,
                     XV_KEY_DATA, BASE_FRAME_KEY, frame,
                     NULL );

        (void) xv_create ( panel, PANEL_BUTTON,
                     PANEL_LABEL_STRING, "File",
                     PANEL_ITEM_MENU,        m,
                     NULL );

        m = (Menu) xv_create ( NULL, MENU,
                     MENU_ACTION_ITEM,              "Sites...", sites,
                     XV_KEY_DATA, SITE_FRAME_KEY,   site_frame,
                     NULL );

        (void) xv_create ( panel, PANEL_BUTTON,
                     PANEL_LABEL_STRING, "View",
                     PANEL_ITEM_MENU,        m,
                     NULL );

        m_undo = (Menu) xv_create ( NULL, MENU,
                     MENU_ACTION_ITEM,               "Undo Last Change",
                                                     menu_stub,

                     MENU_ACTION_ITEM,               "Undo All Changes",
                                                     menu_stub,
```

```
                             XV_KEY_DATA, BASE_FRAME_KEY,    frame,
                             NULL );

         m = (Menu) xv_create ( NULL, MENU,
                     MENU_ACTION_ITEM,                    "Again", menu_stub,
                     MENU_PULLRIGHT_ITEM,                 "Undo", m_undo,
                     MENUITEM_SPACE,                      NULL,
                     MENU_ACTION_ITEM,                    "Cut", menu_stub,
                     MENU_ACTION_ITEM,                    "Copy", menu_stub,
                     MENU_ACTION_ITEM,                    "Paste", menu_stub,
                     MENUITEM_SPACE,                      NULL,


MENU_ACTION_ITEM,                    "Select All", menu_stub,
MENU_ACTION_ITEM,                    "Clear", menu_stub,
XV_KEY_DATA, BASE_FRAME_KEY,   frame,
NULL );

         (void) xv_create ( panel, PANEL_BUTTON,
                     PANEL_LABEL_STRING, "Edit",
                     PANEL_ITEM_MENU,     m,
                     NULL );

         (void) xv_create ( Psite, PANEL_BUTTON,
                     PANEL_LABEL_STRING,              "Push Me",
                     PANEL_NOTIFY_PROC,               push_me_proc,
                     XV_KEY_DATA, BASE_FRAME_KEY,   frame,
                     NULL );

     window_fit ( Psite);
     window_fit ( site_frame);
     window_fit_height ( panel);

     canvas = (Canvas) xv_create ( frame, CANVAS,
                     XV_X,                       0,
                     XV_WIDTH,                   WIN_EXTEND_TO_EDGE,
                     XV_HEIGHT,                  WIN_EXTEND_TO_EDGE,
                     CANVAS_X_PAINT_WINDOW,  TRUE,
                     NULL );

     window_fit ( frame );

      * will follow
      */
     xv_main_loop ( frame );
     return ( 0 );
}
```

```
/* frame.w.menus.c -- Open Look basic frame with menus
 * Author:  Kenneth Bibb
 * February 1992 -- Arastar Consulting
 */

#include <xview/xview.h>
```

```
#include <xview/panel.h>
#include <xview/canvas.h>
#include <xview/xv_xrect.h>
#include <xview/openmenu.h>

Attr_attribute BASE_FRAME_KEY;

/* menu callback for testing
 */
void menu_stub(menu, menu_item)
Menu menu;
Menu_item menu_item;


{
 char s[64];

 sprintf(s,"Menu: [%s]\n", (char *)xv_get(menu_item, MENU_STRING));
 xv_set(xv_get(menu,XV_KEY_DATA,BASE_FRAME_KEY),FRAME_LEFT_FOOTER,
  s, NULL);
}

/* display the popup menu
 */
void show_it(window, event)
Xv_Window window;
Event *event;
{
 if((event_action(event) == ACTION_MENU) && (event_is_down(event)))
 {
  menu_show(xv_get(window, WIN_CLIENT_DATA),
    window, event, NULL);
 }
}

/* canvas repaint function
 */
void repaint(canvas, win, dpy, xwin, xrect)
Canvas canvas;
Xv_Window win;
Display *dpy;
Window xwin;
Xv_xrectlist *xrect;
{
       GC gc;
       int width, height;

       gc = DefaultGC(dpy, DefaultScreen(dpy));
       width = (int)xv_get(win, XV_WIDTH);
       height = (int)xv_get(win, XV_HEIGHT);
}

int main(argc, argv)
int argc;
char **argv;
{
       Frame           frame;
```

```
Canvas        canvas;
Icon          icon;
Server_image cimage;
Panel         panel;
Menu  m,      m_undo;

xv_init(XV_INIT_ARGC_PTR_ARGV, &argc, argv, NULL);
BASE_FRAME_KEY = xv_unique_key();

frame = (Frame)xv_create(XV_NULL, FRAME,
        FRAME_LABEL, argv[0],
        XV_X,           300,
        XV_Y,           175,
        NULL);


panel = (Panel)xv_create(frame, PANEL, NULL);



/* file menu--replace menu_stubs with names of
 *            real functions
 */
m = (Menu) xv_create ( XV_NULL, MENU,
        MENU_ITEM,
                MENU_STRING,        "New...",
                MENU_NOTIFY_PROC, menu_stub,
                NULL,
        MENU_ITEM,
                MENU_STRING,        "Save...",
                MENU_NOTIFY_PROC, menu_stub,
                NULL,
        MENUITEM_SPACE, NULL,
        MENU_ITEM,
                MENU_STRING,        "Print...",
                MENU_NOTIFY_PROC, menu_stub,
                NULL,
        XV_KEY_DATA, BASE_FRAME_KEY, frame,
        NULL);

(void)xv_create(panel, PANEL_BUTTON,
        PANEL_LABEL_STRING, "File",
        PANEL_ITEM_MENU, m,
        NULL);

/* create the view menu.  since this is application
 * specific, I put generic strings in
 */
m = (Menu)xv_create(XV_NULL, MENU,
        MENU_ITEM,
                MENU_STRING,        "Item 1",
                MENU_NOTIFY_PROC, menu_stub,
                NULL,
        MENU_ITEM,
                MENU_STRING,        "Item 2",
                MENU_NOTIFY_PROC, menu_stub,
                NULL,
        NULL);
```

```
(void)xv_create(panel, PANEL_BUTTON,
        PANEL_LABEL_STRING, "View",
        PANEL_ITEM_MENU, m,
        NULL);

/* undo sub menu
 */
m_undo = (Menu)xv_create(XV_NULL, MENU,
        MENU_ITEM,
                MENU_STRING,        "Undo Last Change",
                MENU_NOTIFY_PROC, menu_stub,
                NULL,
        MENU_ITEM,
                MENU_STRING,        "Undo All Changes",
                MENU_NOTIFY_PROC, menu_stub,
                NULL,
        NULL);




/* edit menu
 */
m = (Menu)xv_create(XV_NULL, MENU,
        MENU_ITEM,
                MENU_STRING,        "Again",
                MENU_NOTIFY_PROC, menu_stub,
                NULL,
        MENU_ITEM,
                MENU_STRING,     "Undo",
                MENU_PULLRIGHT, m_undo,
                NULL,
        MENUITEM_SPACE, NULL,
        MENU_ITEM,
                MENU_STRING,        "Cut",
                MENU_NOTIFY_PROC, menu_stub,
                NULL,
        MENU_ITEM,
                MENU_STRING,        "Copy",
                MENU_NOTIFY_PROC, menu_stub,
                NULL,
        MENU_ITEM,
                MENU_STRING,        "Paste",
                MENU_NOTIFY_PROC, menu_stub,
                NULL,
        MENUITEM_SPACE, NULL,
        MENU_ITEM,
                MENU_STRING,        "Select All",
                MENU_NOTIFY_PROC, menu_stub,
                NULL,
        MENU_ITEM,
                MENU_STRING,        "Clear",
                MENU_NOTIFY_PROC, menu_stub,
                NULL,
        NULL);

(void)xv_create ( panel, PANEL_BUTTON,
        PANEL_LABEL_STRING, "Edit",
```

```
                    PANEL_ITEM_MENU, m,
                    NULL);

        /* fit panel to created panel items
         */
        window_fit_height(panel);
        /* create the canvas
         */
        canvas = (Canvas)xv_create ( frame, CANVAS,
                XV_X,                    0,
                XV_WIDTH,                WIN_EXTEND_TO_EDGE,
                XV_HEIGHT,               WIN_EXTEND_TO_EDGE,
                CANVAS_REPAINT_PROC,     repaint,
                CANVAS_X_PAINT_WINDOW,   TRUE,
                NULL);

        /* fit frame around panel and canvas
         */
        window_fit(frame);

        /* create the popup menu
         */
        m = (Menu)xv_create ( XV_NULL, MENU,
                MENU_GEN_PIN_WINDOW, frame, "Popup Menu",
                MENU_PULLRIGHT_ITEM, "Undo", m_undo,
                MENU_ACTION_ITEM, "Print...", menu_stub,
                NULL);


        /* attach popup menu and event procedure to paint window
         */
        xv_set(canvas_paint_window(canvas),
                WIN_CONSUME_EVENTS, WIN_MOUSE_BUTTONS, NULL,
                WIN_EVENT_PROC,     show_it,
                WIN_CLIENT_DATA,    m,
                NULL);

        xv_main_loop(frame);
        return(0);
}
```

```
/* frame.size.c -- Default, minimum, maximum size
 * Author:   Kenneth Bibb
 * April 1992 -- Arastar Consulting
 *-------------------------------------
 * frame with size params
 * minimum, default, max sizes
 * also, footer and header
 */

#include <stdlib.h>
#include <sys/param.h>
#include <xview/xview.h>
```

```
#include <xview/panel.h>
#include <xview/canvas.h>
#include <xview/xv_xrect.h>
#include <xview/openmenu.h>
#include <xview/icon.h>
#include <xview/svrimage.h>

main(argc, argv)
int argc;
char **argv;
{
  Frame                 frame;
  Canvas                canvas;
  Panel                 panel;

  xv_init(XV_INIT_ARGC_PTR_ARGV, &argc, argv, NULL);
  frame = (Frame)xv_create ( NULL, FRAME,
                  FRAME_LABEL,          argv[0],
                  FRAME_SHOW_FOOTER,    TRUE,
                  FRAME_SHOW_HEADER,    TRUE,
                  XV_WIDTH,             200,
                  XV_HEIGHT,            300,
                  FRAME_MIN_SIZE,       20, 30,
                  FRAME_MAX_SIZE,       400, 600,
                  XV_X,                 300,
                  XV_Y,                 175,
                  NULL);
  panel = (Panel)xv_create ( frame, PANEL, NULL);



  window_fit_height ( panel);
  canvas = (Canvas)xv_create ( frame, CANVAS,
                  XV_X, 0,
                  XV_HEIGHT,                WIN_EXTEND_TO_EDGE,
                  XV_WIDTH,                 WIN_EXTEND_TO_EDGE,
                  CANVAS_X_PAINT_WINDOW, TRUE,
                  NULL);
  window_fit(frame);

  xv_main_loop(frame);
}
```

Gauges

The gauge is a simple object. It looks like a thermometer (especially when you set **PANEL_LAYOUT** to **PANEL_VERTICAL**) and even behaves like one. You can use gauges to visually express percentages, among other things. You can also think of them as read-only sliders. A gauge has the attributes shown in Figure 12.1.

SETTING THE GAUGE

The main thing you do with a gauge is *set* it to some value. The **dftool** program, listed at the end of this chapter, shows an example of this. It creates a gauge for each partition on your system and then sets the gauge to the value of that partition (blocks or percents).

PANEL_DIRECTION, PANEL_HORIZONTAL

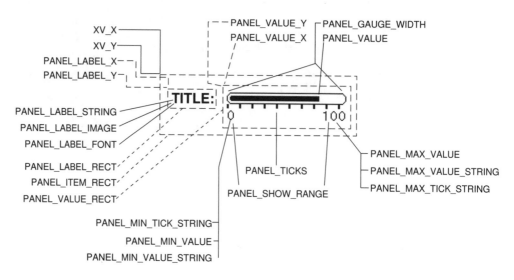

FIGURE 12.1 Gauge Attributes

To set **gauge** to a value of 50, you could

```
(void) xv_set ( gauge, PANEL_VALUE, 50, NULL );
```

Difficult, huh?

SAMPLE PROGRAM

The sample program shows off a number of the attributes used by the gauge package. It displays a dynamic picture of how full various partitions are. It will display the information in blocks or percentages; you can turn the tick marks on and off; and you can change the delay between times that the program checks the partitions.

```
/* dftool.c -- Open Look gauge
 * Author:  Kenneth Bibb
 * January 1992 -- Arastar Consulting
 *-------------------------------------
 * Sample of how to use gauge
 *
 * What should I demo?
 *
 */

#include <stdlib.h>
#include <stdio.h>   /* for getmntent() etc */
#include <mntent.h>  /* for getmntent() etc */
#include <math.h>    /* for nint()  */
#include <sys/param.h>
#include <sys/vfs.h>
#include <errno.h>

#include <xview/xview.h>
#include <xview/panel.h>
#include <xview/xv_xrect.h>
#include <xview/openmenu.h>
#include <xview/icon.h>
#include <xview/svrimage.h>

#define PTN_MAX  50  /* Max number of partitions */

int first_time = FALSE;
int max_partitions=0;
struct itimerval timer;
struct statfs  *fs[PTN_MAX];
struct mntent *me[PTN_MAX];

Frame                  frame;
Panel                  panel;
Attr_attribute FRAME_PROP_KEY;
Attr_attribute CHOICE_UNIT_KEY;
Attr_attribute CHOICE_TICK_KEY;
Attr_attribute TEXT_DELAY_KEY;
void                   check_disk ();

struct ption
{
```

```
        Panel_item              msg;
        Panel_item              gauge;
        Panel_item              val;
} ptn[PTN_MAX];

struct defaults
{
        Bool                    percent;
        Bool                    ticks;
        int                     delay;
} defs, udefs;


void
button_set ( Cunit, Ctick, Tdlay )
Panel_item Cunit;
Panel_item Ctick;
Panel_item Tdlay;
{
        (void) xv_set ( Cunit,
                PANEL_VALUE, defs.percent,
                NULL );
        (void) xv_set ( Ctick,
                PANEL_VALUE, defs.ticks,
                NULL );
        (void) xv_set ( Tdlay,
                PANEL_VALUE, defs.delay,
                NULL );
}

void
group_def ( button,event )
Panel_item  button;
Event *event;
{
        Panel_item Cunit = (Panel_item) xv_get ( button, XV_KEY_DATA,
                CHOICE_UNIT_KEY );
        Panel_item Ctick = (Panel_item) xv_get ( button, XV_KEY_DATA,
                CHOICE_TICK_KEY );
        Panel_item Tdlay = (Panel_item) xv_get ( button, XV_KEY_DATA,
                TEXT_DELAY_KEY );

        if ( strcmp ( xv_get ( button, PANEL_LABEL_STRING ), "Apply" ) == 0 )
        {
                defs.percent = (Bool) xv_get ( Cunit, PANEL_VALUE );
                defs.ticks   = (Bool) xv_get ( Ctick, PANEL_VALUE );
                defs.delay   = (int) xv_get ( Tdlay, PANEL_VALUE );
                check_disk ();
        } else {
                defs.percent = udefs.percent;
                defs.ticks   = udefs.ticks;
                defs.delay   = udefs.delay;
                button_set ();
                }
}

void
prop_display ( button, event )
Panel_item  button;
```

```
Event        *event;
{
        (void) xv_set ( xv_get ( button, XV_KEY_DATA, FRAME_PROP_KEY ),
                XV_SHOW, TRUE,
                NULL );
}


void
my_usage ( name )
char *name;
{
        printf ( "%s specific options\n", name );
        printf ( " -b use blocks instead of percentages\n" );
        printf ( " -d n change the delay to n seconds\n" );
        printf ( "   (range between 1 and 300 seconds\n" );
        printf ( " -t show tick marks on gauges\n\n" );
        xv_usage ( name );
        exit ( XV_OK );
}


set_defs ()
{
        /* set defaults
         */
        udefs.percent = defs.percent;
        udefs.ticks   = defs.ticks;
        udefs.delay   = defs.delay;
}

/* This reads disk information for setting the gauges.
 * This is pretty much equivalent to the df command.
 */
void check_disk ()
{
        FILE         *f;
        int          i;
        int          percentage;
        int          used;
        static int   hold_delay=-1;
        char         sbuf[8];
        char         *s=sbuf;

        if ( ( f = fopen ( "/etc/mtab", "r" ) ) == NULL ) {
                printf ( "unable to open mount table\n" );
                exit ( 1 );
        }
        for (i=0; ; i++) {
                me[i] = (struct mntent *) getmntent ( f );
                if ( me[i] == (struct mntent *) NULL )
                        break;
                if ( ! ( fs[i] = (struct statfs *) malloc
                ( sizeof ( struct statfs ) ) ) ) {
                        printf ( "unable to alloc\n" );
                        exit ( 2 );
                }
                statfs ( me[i]->mnt_dir, fs[i] );
                percentage = nint ( 100. - (float) ( (float) fs[i]->f_bavail
                lli *100.   / ( (float) fs[i]->f_blocks * .9 ) ) );
```

```
                    used = fs[i]->f_blocks - fs[i]->f_bfree;
                    if ( first_time ) {
                            ptn[i].msg = (Panel_item) xv_create ( panel,
                                    PANEL_MESSAGE,
                                    PANEL_NEXT_ROW,      -1,
                                    PANEL_LABEL_STRING, me[i]->mnt_dir,
                                    PANEL_LABEL_BOLD,    TRUE,
                                    NULL );
                            ptn[i].gauge = (Panel_item) xv_create ( panel,
                                    PANEL_GAUGE,
                                    PANEL_VALUE,        (defs.percent)?percentage:used,
                                    PANEL_TICKS,        (defs.ticks) ? 10 : 0,
                                    PANEL_MAX_VALUE, (defs.percent) ? 100 :
                                    fs[i]->f_blocks,
                                    NULL );
                            if ( defs.percent )
                                    sprintf ( s,"%10d%%",percentage );
                            else
                                    sprintf ( s,"%10d",used );
                            ptn[i].val  = (Panel_item) xv_create ( panel,
                                    PANEL_MESSAGE,
                                    PANEL_LABEL_STRING, s,
                                    PANEL_LABEL_BOLD,    TRUE,
                                    NULL );
                            timer.it_interval.tv_sec = defs.delay;
                            timer.it_interval.tv_usec = 0;
                            timer.it_value.tv_sec = defs.delay;
                            timer.it_value.tv_usec = 0;
                    } else {
                            (void) xv_set ( ptn[i].gauge,
                                    PANEL_VALUE,        (defs.percent) ?percentage : used,
                                    PANEL_TICKS,        (defs.ticks) ? 10 : 0,
                                    PANEL_MAX_VALUE, (defs.percent) ? 100 :
                                    fs[i]->f_blocks,
                                    NULL );
                            if ( defs.percent )
                                    sprintf ( s,"%10d%%",percentage );
                            else
                                    sprintf ( s,"%10d",used );
                            (void) xv_set ( ptn[i].val,
                                    PANEL_LABEL_STRING, s,
                                    NULL );
                            if ( defs.delay != hold_delay ) {
                                    hold_delay = defs.delay;
                                    timer.it_interval.tv_sec = defs.delay;
                                    timer.it_value.tv_sec = defs.delay;
                                    notify_set_itimer_func ( frame, check_disk,
                                    ITIMER_REAL, &timer,
                                    NULL );
                            }
                    }
            }
            (void) endmntent ( f ); /* closes file */
            max_partitions = i;
}

int
main ( argc, argv )
int argc;
```

```
char **argv;
{
        Frame   Fprop;
        Panel   Pprop;
        int     c;
        int     i=0;
        int     hold=-1;
        int     holdi=0;
        Bool    helpme=FALSE;
        Panel_item pi;
        Panel_item Cunit;
        Panel_item Ctick;
        Panel_item Tdlay;
        extern char *optarg;

        xv_init ( XV_INIT_ARGC_PTR_ARGV, &argc, argv,
                XV_USAGE_PROC, my_usage,
                NULL );
        FRAME_PROP_KEY  = xv_unique_key ();
        CHOICE_UNIT_KEY = xv_unique_key ();
        CHOICE_TICK_KEY = xv_unique_key ();
        TEXT_DELAY_KEY  = xv_unique_key ();
        /* set initial defaults
        */
        defs.percent = TRUE;
        defs.ticks = FALSE;
        defs.delay = 60;
         /* check to see if any defaults are overridden
        */
        while ( ( c = getopt ( argc, argv, "btd:" ) ) != -1 )
                switch(c) {
                case 'b':
                        defs.percent = FALSE;
                        break;
                case 't':
                        defs.ticks = TRUE;
                        break;
                case 'd':
                        defs.delay = atoi ( optarg );
                        break;
                case '?':
                case 'h':
                        helpme = TRUE;
                }
        if ( helpme ) {
                xv_usage ();
                exit ( 3 );
        }

        set_defs ();


        /* create base frame and panel
        */
        frame = (Frame) xv_create ( NULL, FRAME,
                FRAME_LABEL,                    argv[0],
                XV_X,                           300,
                XV_Y,                           175,
                FRAME_SHOW_RESIZE_CORNER, FALSE,
                NULL );
```

```
panel = (Panel) xv_create ( frame, PANEL, NULL );
pi = (Panel_item) xv_create ( panel, PANEL_BUTTON,
        PANEL_LABEL_STRING,  "Properties...",
        PANEL_NOTIFY_PROC,  prop_display,
        NULL );
Fprop = (Frame) xv_create ( frame, FRAME_CMD,
        FRAME_LABEL,  "Properties",
        XV_X,         350,
        XV_Y,         200,
        NULL );
(void) xv_set ( pi,
XV_KEY_DATA, FRAME_PROP_KEY, Fprop,
NULL );
Pprop = (Panel) xv_get ( Fprop, FRAME_CMD_PANEL, NULL);
Cunit = (Panel_item) xv_create ( Pprop, PANEL_CHOICE,
        PANEL_LABEL_STRING,  "Units:",
        PANEL_CHOICE_STRINGS, "Use Blocks",
                              "Use Percentages",
                              NULL,
        NULL );
Ctick= (Panel_item) xv_create ( Pprop, PANEL_CHOICE,
        PANEL_LABEL_STRING,  "Tickmarks:",
        PANEL_NEXT_ROW,      -1,
        PANEL_CHOICE_STRINGS, "Hide tickmarks",
                              "Show tickmarks",
                              NULL,
        NULL );
Tdlay = (Panel_item) xv_create ( Pprop, PANEL_NUMERIC_TEXT,
        PANEL_NEXT_ROW,      -1,
        PANEL_LABEL_STRING,  "Delay (in seconds):",
        PANEL_VALUE,         defs.delay,
        PANEL_MAX_VALUE,     300, /* 5 minute interval */
        PANEL_MIN_VALUE,     1, /* 1 second interval */
        NULL );
pi = (Panel_item) xv_create ( Pprop, PANEL_BUTTON,
        PANEL_NEXT_ROW,              -1,
        XV_X,                        xv_get ( Tdlay, XV_X )+80,
        PANEL_LABEL_STRING,          "Apply",
        PANEL_NOTIFY_PROC,           group_def,
        XV_KEY_DATA, CHOICE_UNIT_KEY, Cunit,
        XV_KEY_DATA, CHOICE_TICK_KEY, Ctick,
        XV_KEY_DATA, TEXT_DELAY_KEY,  Tdlay,
        NULL );
(void) xv_set ( Pprop,
        PANEL_DEFAULT_ITEM, pi,
        NULL );
(void) xv_create ( Pprop, PANEL_BUTTON,
        PANEL_LABEL_STRING, "Reset",
        PANEL_NOTIFY_PROC,  group_def,
        XV_X,   xv_get ( pi, XV_X )+100,
        XV_KEY_DATA, CHOICE_UNIT_KEY, Cunit,
        XV_KEY_DATA, CHOICE_TICK_KEY, Ctick,
        XV_KEY_DATA, TEXT_DELAY_KEY,  Tdlay,
        NULL );
button_set ( Cunit,Ctick,Tdlay );
window_fit ( Pprop );
window_fit ( Fprop );

first_time = TRUE;
```

```
      check_disk ();
      first_time = FALSE;

      ptn[max_partitions].msg = ptn[max_partitions].gauge = (Panel_item)
            NULL;
      for (i=0; i<max_partitions; i++) {
            if ( strlen ( xv_get ( ptn[i].msg,PANEL_LABEL_STRING ) ) >
                  hold ) {
                  hold = strlen ( xv_get ( ptn[i].msg,
                  PANEL_LABEL_STRING ));
                  holdi = i;
            }
      }
      for (i=0; i<max_partitions; i++) {
            (void) xv_set ( ptn[i].gauge,
                  XV_X, xv_get ( ptn[holdi].msg, XV_X ) +
                        xv_get ( ptn[holdi].msg, XV_WIDTH ) +
                        xv_get ( panel, PANEL_ITEM_X_GAP ),
                  NULL );

            (void) xv_set ( ptn[i].val,
                  XV_X, xv_get ( ptn[holdi].gauge, XV_X ) +
                        xv_get ( ptn[holdi].gauge, XV_WIDTH ) +
                        xv_get ( panel, PANEL_ITEM_X_GAP ),
                  NULL );
      }

      window_fit ( panel );
      window_fit ( frame );

      notify_set_itimer_func ( frame, check_disk, ITIMER_REAL, &timer,
            NULL );
      xv_main_loop ( frame );

      return ( 0 );
}
```

Figure 13.1 shows general features of XView which work with most of the packages.

FONTS

When working with fonts, you need to **xv_find()** the font first (so it will be available to your program). After you've found the font, you can use it to change the font of certain items. The attributes used to specify the fonts for items are listed in Table 13.1.

Warning: Changing the font on items will violate Open Look standards, along with standards of consistency in interfaces. Use font changes sparingly if you must change the font.

LOCATION

Table 13.2 lists calls that can be used to retrieve the dimensions of an XView object. These calls can be used with any XView object that is displayed. **XV_X**, as shown in Table 13.2 and Figure 13.1, is the attribute that controls the left edge, whereas **XV_Y** controls the top. By using **xv_create()** or **xv_set()** on these variables, you can explicitly control an object's position in the panel. For example, you can make panel button **b**'s left side line up with panel button **a**'s left side:

```
Panel_button_item a, b;

(void) xv_set ( b, XV_X, xv_get ( a, XV_X ), NULL );
```

When working with panel items, you also have label and value rectangles (**label_rect** and **value_rect**, respectively) to work with. The attributes that control the positions of these rectangles are listed in Table 13.3. It's usually not a good idea to move the label and value parts of a panel item around independently. Doing so can give your application a nonstandard interface.

The main method of manipulating the spaces around your panel items is by letting XView automatically handle them. This is called "relative" placement, as opposed to the "explicit" placement provided by **XV_X** and **XV_Y**. Occasionally, you'll find that you need to make changes to

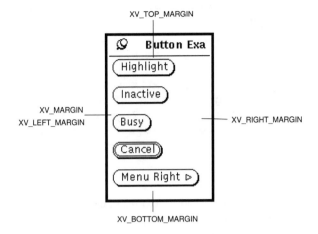

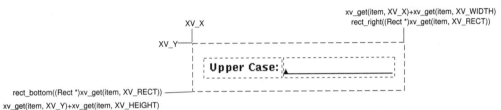

FIGURE 13.1 General Attributes

Attribute	Description
XV_FONT	The most general font attribute. It will work on most of the objects used in XView.
PANEL_LABEL_FONT	Lets you change the font of the label portion of some panel items.
PANEL_VALUE_FONT	Lets you change the font of the value portion of some panel items.
PANEL_LIST_FONT	Lets you change the font of a row in a panel list.

TABLE 13.1 Font Attributes

Edge	Call
Left	**xv_get (item, XV_X)**
Top	**xv_get (item, XV_Y)**
Right	**xv_get (item, XV_X) + xv_get (item, XV_WIDTH)**
Right	**rect_right ((Rect *) xv_get (item, XV_RECT))**
Bottom	**xv_get (item, XV_Y) + xv_get (item, XV_HEIGHT)**
Bottom	**rect_bottom ((Rect *) xv_get (item,XV_RECT))**

TABLE 13.2 Object Locations

this behavior. XView uses **PANEL_ITEM_X_GAP** and **PANEL_ITEM_Y_GAP** to control the spacing between columns and rows, respectively.

To force a panel item onto the next row or column, use **PANEL_NEXT_ROW** or **PANEL_NEXT_COL**, respectively, and set the value to the gap you want to use. A value of −1 uses the default values that were set by **PANEL_ITEM_X_GAP** and **PANEL_ITEM_Y_GAP**. So

```
xv_set ( item, PANEL_NEXT_ROW, -1, NULL );
```

is the same as

```
xv_set ( item, PANEL_NEXT_ROW, xv_get ( panel, PANEL_ITEM_X_GAP ), NULL );
```

If you wanted to change the gap between the last item and the current item to 50, you could use

```
xv_set ( item, PANEL_NEXT_ROW, 50, NULL );
```

■ MARGINS

The margin attributes that are available are listed in Table 13.4. These let you change the margins of text subwindows and the margins around panel items on panels.

Attribute	Description
PANEL_LABEL_X	Left side of the label rectangle
PANEL_LABEL_Y	Top side of the label rectangle
PANEL_VALUE_X	Left side of the value rectangle
PANEL_VALUE_Y	Top side of the value rectangle
PANEL_ITEM_LABEL_RECT	Used to manipulate the label rectangle
PANEL_ITEM_VALUE_RECT	Used to manipulate the value rectangle

TABLE 13.3 Panel Item Locations

Attribute	Description
XV_TOP_MARGIN	Top
XV_LEFT_MARGIN	Left
XV_BOTTOM_MARGIN	Bottom
XV_RIGHT_MARGIN	Right
XV_MARGIN	Border offset

TABLE 13.4 Object Margins

SAMPLE PROGRAM

The sample program **general.c** shows some of these features.

```
/* general.c -- XView general attributes
 * Author:   Kenneth Bibb
 * January 1992 -- Arastar Consulting
 *-------------------------------------
 * Basic frame with panel and canvas
 */

#include <xview/xview.h>
#include <xview/panel.h>
#include <xview/font.h>

main ( argc, argv )
int argc;
char **argv;
{
  Frame    frame;
  Font     fixed;
  Canvas   canvas;
  Panel    panel;

  xv_init ( XV_INIT_ARGC_PTR_ARGV, &argc, argv, NULL );

  /* get a fixed font */
  fixed = (Font) xv_find ( XV_NULL, FONT, FONT_NAME, "fixed", NULL);

  /* create the base frame */
  frame = (Frame) xv_create ( NULL, FRAME,
            FRAME_LABEL,         argv[0],
            FRAME_SHOW_FOOTER,   TRUE,
            XV_X,                300,
            XV_Y,                175,
            NULL );

  /* create the panel */
  panel = (Panel) xv_create ( frame, PANEL, PANEL_LAYOUT, PANEL_VERTICAL,
            NULL );
  ( void ) xv_create ( panel, PANEL_CHOICE,
    PANEL_LABEL_STRING,    "Rocks:",
    PANEL_CHOICE_STRINGS,  "Amethyst",
                           "Beryl",
```

```
                              "Chalcedony",
                              "Diamond",
                              "Emerald",
                              NULL,
          /*
          XV_X,           100,
          XV_Y,           100,
          PANEL_LABEL_X,  100,
          PANEL_LABEL_Y,  100,
          PANEL_VALUE_X,  200,
          PANEL_VALUE_Y,  200,
          */
          NULL );

    (void) xv_create ( panel, PANEL_BUTTON,
        PANEL_LABEL_FONT,   fixed,
        PANEL_LABEL_STRING, "Hobo",
        PANEL_NEXT_COL,     50,
        NULL );
    window_fit_height ( panel );
    window_fit ( frame );

    xv_main_loop ( frame );
}
```

Help

CHAPTER 14

Programmers don't like help. They want the user to learn the program inside out through osmosis or telepathy. Making up help messages is like teaching or writing—a horrible task for only the lowliest of creatures.

On the other hand, users love help. They'll ask for help on panel buttons, on the canvas, even on the Close button.

Writing help messages can be intimidating at first, but write them. The users will appreciate your program more if it has good help messages. Also, make your help messages useful. Explain why inactive items are inactive; explain how to reactivate them. Explain functionality when it isn't going to be obvious to the first-time user. Most important, make your help clear and concise.

When you release a program to your users, you should provide help for them (unfortunately, Bellevue is not usually an option). The most common help areas are listed below in this chapter with examples.

HELP MESSAGE FORMAT

A help message has two parts:

- Help tag
- Help text

You provide help by setting the **XV_HELP_DATA** attribute of an object. When the user presses the Help key while the mouse pointer is over that object, this data will be used. A typical **XV_HELP_DATA** would look like this:

```
XV_HELP_DATA, "myinfo:baseframe",
```

where "**myinfo**" refers to the file **myinfo.info**, which would be in one of the directories on the help path, and the help tag "**baseframe**" would refer to a help text message within the file **myinfo.info**. The help text would look like:

```
:baseframe
Base Frame
This is the help message associated
with the Base Frame. It is boring
and generic because I don't know
what application would
actually be using this.
#
```

Line length can't exceed 50 characters, so set your editor appropriately when creating the help file. Everything should be left-justified. The tags are also case-sensitive, so that **HelpMessage** is different from **Helpmessage**. The help message is terminated with a # or by the next tag.

GENERAL HELP MESSAGE (FOR FRAME BACKGROUND)

If an object does not have **XV_HELP_DATA** specified, but a help message has been specified for one of the object's ancestor objects, that message will serve for this object as well. Therefore, to provide a general help message, associate a tag with the main canvas, panel, or both, of your application.

```
Frame  frame;
Canvas canvas;
Panel  panel;

panel = (Panel) xv_create(frame, PANEL,
                          XV_HELP_DATA, "helpfile:general",
                          NULL );
canvas = (Canvas) xv_create ( frame, CANVAS,
                          XV_HELP_DATA, "helpfile:general",
                          NULL);
```

This will create a help message that will be shared between the two objects.

CONTROL HELP

When you create a control, you can associate a help tag with that control. There already are general messages that explain how to use many of the controls (look in **$OPENWINHOME/lib/help**'s files for examples), so what you should really be putting here is a description of the control's purpose.

```
Panel      panel;
Panel_item pi;

pi = (Panel_item) xv_create ( panel, PANEL_BUTTON,
                 PANEL_LABEL_STRING, "Xkill",
                 PANEL_NOTIFY_PROC,  xkill,
                 XV_HELP_DATA, "helpfile:xkill",
                 NULL );
```

When the user asks for help (by pressing the Help key with the mouse pointer over this button), the **xkill** tag's text will be displayed.

INACTIVE CONTROL HELP

When users ask for help on an inactive control, they usually want to know how to activate it. Provide information on why the control is inactive and on how to activate the control.

To attach help to an inactive control, associate the help tag when you inactivate the item:

```
Panel_item button;

(void) xv_set ( button,
         PANEL_INACTIVE,    TRUE,

         XV_HELP_DATA,      "helpfile:buttonInactive",
         NULL );
```

Remember to set the help message back to what it originally was when you reactivate the control.

PANE HELP

Attaching help to a pane is easiest when you are creating the pane:

```
Canvas canvas;
Frame    frame;

canvas = (Canvas) xv_create ( frame, CANVAS,
                         XV_HELP_DATA, "helpfile:panehelp",
                         NULL );
```

POPUP HELP

To attach help to a popup, associate the help tag with the popup at creation time (using **xv_create ( )**) or at run time (using **xv_set ( )**), as in the following example:

```
Panel subpanel;

(void) xv_set ( subpanel,
         XV_HELP_DATA, "helpfile:subpanel",
         NULL );
```

HELP TEXT

Creating Text Files   To create .**info** help files, use your favorite editor. If you want examples of existing help files, look at (or copy) the files in **$OPENWINHOME/lib/help**. A "good" choice would be **textedit.info**. Look at the help file from within **textedit**, try out each of the tokens, and see how each help token displays.

Text Attributes   Text attributes for bold and italicized text will (we hope) eventually be supported. At this time (XView 3.0), however, there is no support. There is also no support for embedded glyphs at this time.

Debugging Help   If you run into problems where your program isn't able to find the help text, your problem is in one of two places:

- The helpfile is not being found.
- The text is not being found within the file.

The first thing to do is check the **HELPPATH** environment variable. You can do this from the shell with:

```
host% printenv | grep HELPPATH
```

Or you can do it from a program by using the following:

```
printf ( "HELPPATH: [%s]\n",getenv ( "HELPPATH" ) );
```

You'll usually find that the problem is related to your help file not being found.

If you see the required directory in the path, and the file definitely exists in the directory, you should check the permissions on the file, to make sure that the people who are going to use this application (including you, during development) have read the permission.

If you still have a problem, you may not have your tag left-justified.

Sample Program   The **help.c** program demonstrates the attachment of help to a number of different controls. It is a copy of the **button.c** program presented in Chapter 6, but it now has help associated with many of the items.

```
/* help.c -- demonstration of different kinds of help
 * Author:  Kenneth Bibb
 * March 1992 -- Arastar Consulting
 *------------------------------------------------
 *
 * This is the button.c program with help attached to it.
 *
 */

#include <stdlib.h>
#include <xview/xview.h>
#include <xview/panel.h>
#include <xview/canvas.h>
#include <xview/xv_xrect.h>
#include <xview/openmenu.h>

/* set up key data variables
 */
Attr_attribute BASE_FRAME_KEY = NULL;
Attr_attribute POPUP_WINDOW_KEY = NULL;
Attr_attribute POPUP_PANEL_KEY = NULL;
Attr_attribute BUTTON_HI_KEY = NULL;
Attr_attribute BUTTON_IN_KEY = NULL;
Attr_attribute BUTTON_BU_KEY = NULL;
Attr_attribute BUTTON_CA_KEY = NULL;
Attr_attribute BUTTON_ME_KEY = NULL;


/* test menu stub
 */
void menu_stub ( menu, menu_item )
Menu menu;
Menu_item menu_item;
{
        char s[64];
        Frame frame = (Frame) xv_get ( menu, XV_KEY_DATA,
                                       BASE_FRAME_KEY, NULL );

        sprintf ( s,"Menu: [%s]\n", xv_get ( menu_item, MENU_STRING ) );
        (void) xv_set ( frame, FRAME_LEFT_FOOTER, s, NULL );
}
```

```
/* highlight a button
 */
void highlight ( button, event )
Panel_item button;
Event *event;
{
}

/* inactivate all buttons except the "inactivate" button
 */
void inactive ( button, event )
Panel_item button;
Event *event;
{
    Panel Pbutton = (Panel) xv_get ( button, XV_KEY_DATA,
                                                POPUP_PANEL_KEY );
    Panel_item ph = (Panel_item) xv_get ( button, XV_KEY_DATA,
                                                BUTTON_HI_KEY );
    Panel_item pi = (Panel_item) xv_get ( button, XV_KEY_DATA,
                                                BUTTON_IN_KEY );
    Panel_item pb = (Panel_item) xv_get ( button, XV_KEY_DATA,
                                                BUTTON_BU_KEY );
    Panel_item pc = (Panel_item) xv_get ( button, XV_KEY_DATA,
                                                BUTTON_CA_KEY );
    Panel_item pm = (Panel_item) xv_get ( button, XV_KEY_DATA,
                                                BUTTON_ME_KEY );

    Panel_item i  = NULL;

   /* if the highlight button is inactive
    *           activate all panel items (in this case, buttons)
    * else
    *           inactivate all panel items (in this case, buttons)
    *           activate the inactivate button
    */
    if ( xv_get ( ph, PANEL_INACTIVE ) == TRUE ) {
        xv_set ( ph,
                PANEL_INACTIVE, FALSE,
                XV_HELP_DATA, "help:Highlight",
                NULL );
        xv_set ( pb,
                PANEL_INACTIVE, FALSE,
                XV_HELP_DATA, "help:BusyButton",
                NULL );
        xv_set ( pc,
                PANEL_INACTIVE, FALSE,
                XV_HELP_DATA, "help:Cancel",
                NULL );
        xv_set ( pm,
                PANEL_INACTIVE, FALSE,
                XV_HELP_DATA, "help:MenuRight",
                NULL );
    } else {
        PANEL_EACH_ITEM(Pbutton, i)
                        xv_set ( i,
                            PANEL_INACTIVE, TRUE,
                            XV_HELP_DATA,
                            "help:InactiveButton",
                        NULL );
        PANEL_END_EACH
```

```
            xv_set ( button,
                    PANEL_INACTIVE, FALSE,
                    XV_HELP_DATA,  "help:inactivebutton",
                    NULL );
    }

}

/* busy all buttons except the "Busy" button
 */
void busy ( button, event )
Panel_item button;
Event *event;
{
    Panel Pbutton = (Panel) xv_get ( button, XV_KEY_DATA,
                                                    POPUP_PANEL_KEY );
    Panel_item ph = (Panel_item) xv_get ( button, XV_KEY_DATA,
                                                    BUTTON_HI_KEY );
    Panel_item pi = (Panel_item) xv_get ( button, XV_KEY_DATA,
                                                    BUTTON_IN_KEY );
    Panel_item pb = (Panel_item) xv_get ( button, XV_KEY_DATA,
                                                    BUTTON_BU_KEY );
    Panel_item pc = (Panel_item) xv_get ( button, XV_KEY_DATA,
                                                    BUTTON_CA_KEY );
    Panel_item pm = (Panel_item) xv_get ( button, XV_KEY_DATA,
                                                    BUTTON_ME_KEY );

    Panel_item i  = NULL;

    /* if the highlight button is busy
     * turn busy off on all panel items
     * else
     * turn busy on for all panel items
     * turn busy off on busy button
     */
    if ( xv_get ( ph, PANEL_BUSY ) == TRUE ) {
        xv_set ( ph,
                PANEL_BUSY, FALSE,
                XV_HELP_DATA, "help:Highlight",
                NULL );
        xv_set ( pi,
                PANEL_BUSY, FALSE,
                XV_HELP_DATA, "help:BusyButton",
                NULL );
        xv_set ( pc,
                PANEL_BUSY, FALSE,
                XV_HELP_DATA, "help:Cancel",
                NULL );
        xv_set ( pm,
                PANEL_BUSY, FALSE,
                XV_HELP_DATA, "help:MenuRight",
                NULL );
} else {
        PANEL_EACH_ITEM(Pbutton, i)
                xv_set ( i,
                        PANEL_BUSY, TRUE,
                        XV_HELP_DATA, "help:BusyButtons",
                        NULL );
        PANEL_END_EACH
        xv_set ( button, PANEL_BUSY, FALSE, NULL );
    }
```

```
}
/* "Button Window..." callback:  display button window
 */
void button_window ( button, event )
Panel_item button;
Event *event;
{
     xv_set ( xv_get ( button, XV_KEY_DATA, POPUP_WINDOW_KEY ),
                  XV_SHOW, TRUE, NULL);
}

/* "Cancel" button callback
 */
void cancel ( button, event )
Panel_item button;
Event *event;
{
  Frame frame = (Frame) xv_get ( button, XV_KEY_DATA, POPUP_WINDOWKEY );

  /* pull the pushpin and unmap the window
   */
  (void) xv_set ( frame,
                FRAME_CMD_PIN_STATE, FALSE,
                XV_SHOW,             FALSE,
                NULL );
}

/* display the popup window
 */
void show_it ( window, event )
Xv_Window window;
Event *event;
{
     if ( event_action ( event ) == ACTION_MENU && event_is_down
                                              ( event ) ) {
                 Menu m = (Menu) xv_get ( window, WIN_CLIENT_DATA );
                 menu_show ( m, window, event, NULL );
     }
     else if ( event_action ( event ) == ACTION_HELP )
                 xv_help_show ( window, "help:general", event );
}

/* repaint the canvas
 */
void repaint ( canvas, win, dpy, xwin, xrect )
Canvas canvas;
Xv_Window win;
Display *dpy;
Window xwin;
Xv_xrectlist *xrect;
{
     GC gc;
     int width, height;
     gc = DefaultGC ( dpy, DefaultScreen ( dpy ) );
     width = (int) xv_get ( win, XV_WIDTH );
     height = (int) xv_get ( win, XV_HEIGHT );
}

int main ( argc, argv )
```

```
int argc;
char **argv;
{
     Frame        frame;
     Frame        Fbutton;
     Panel        Pbutton;
     Panel_item   ph, pi, pb, pc, mb;
     Canvas       canvas;
     Panel        panel;
     Menu         m, m_undo;



     /* initialization
      */
     xv_init ( XV_INIT_ARGC_PTR_ARGV, &argc, argv, NULL );
     BASE_FRAME_KEY  = xv_unique_key ();
     POPUP_WINDOW_KEY = xv_unique_key ();
     POPUP_PANEL_KEY  = xv_unique_key ();
     BUTTON_HI_KEY  = xv_unique_key ();
     BUTTON_IN_KEY  = xv_unique_key ();
     BUTTON_BU_KEY  = xv_unique_key ();
     BUTTON_CA_KEY  = xv_unique_key ();
     BUTTON_ME_KEY  = xv_unique_key ();

     /* create base frame
      */
     frame = (Frame) xv_create ( XV_NULL, FRAME,
             FRAME_LABEL,       argv[0],
             FRAME_SHOW_FOOTER, TRUE,
             XV_X,              300,
             XV_Y,              175,
             NULL );

 /* create button subframe
  */
 Fbutton = (Frame) xv_create ( frame, FRAME_CMD,
             FRAME_LABEL, "Button Examples",
             XV_X,        400,
             XV_Y,        200,
             NULL );

 /* retrieve subframe's panel
  */
 Pbutton = (Panel) xv_get ( Fbutton, FRAME_CMD_PANEL );
 xv_set ( Pbutton,
             PANEL_LAYOUT, PANEL_VERTICAL,
             XV_HELP_DATA, "help:buttonpanel",
             NULL );
 panel = (Panel) xv_create ( frame, PANEL,
             XV_HELP_DATA, "help:general",
             NULL );
 /* create file menu
  */
 m = (Menu) xv_create ( XV_NULL, MENU,
             MENU_ITEM,
                                      MENU_STRING, "New...",
                                      NULL,
```

```
                MENU_ITEM,
                                                MENU_STRING,  "Save...",
                                                NULL,
                MENU_ITEM,
                                                MENU_STRING,  "Print...",
                                                NULL,
                MENU_NOTIFY_PROC,               menu_stub,
                XV_KEY_DATA, BASE_FRAME_KEY, frame,
                NULL );

    (void) xv_create ( panel, PANEL_BUTTON,
                PANEL_LABEL_STRING,  "File",
                PANEL_ITEM_MENU, m,
                NULL );

    /* command window button
     *          display "Button Window"
     */
    (void) xv_create ( panel, PANEL_BUTTON,
                PANEL_LABEL_STRING,              "Button Window...",
                PANEL_NOTIFY_PROC,               button_window,
                XV_KEY_DATA,   POPUP_WINDOW_KEY, Fbutton,
                NULL );
/*-------------B u t t o n    W i n d o w-------------------*/

    /* create the "Highlight button
     */
    ph = (Panel_item) xv_create ( Pbutton,  PANEL_BUTTON,
                        XV_HELP_DATA,         "help:Highlight",
                        PANEL_LABEL_STRING, "Highlight",
                        PANEL_NOTIFY_PROC,  highlight,
                        NULL );

    /* create the "Inactive" button
     */
    pi = (Panel_item) xv_create ( Pbutton,  PANEL_BUTTON,
                        XV_HELP_DATA,         "help:inactivebutton",
                        PANEL_LABEL_STRING, "Inactive",
                        PANEL_NOTIFY_PROC,  inactive,
                        NULL );

    /* create the Busy signal
     */
    pb = (Panel_item) xv_create ( Pbutton,  PANEL_BUTTON,
                        XV_HELP_DATA,          "help:BusyButton",
                        PANEL_LABEL_STRING, "Busy",
                        PANEL_NOTIFY_PROC,  busy,
                        NULL );
    /* create the "Cancel" button
     */
    pc = (Panel_item) xv_create ( Pbutton, PANEL_BUTTON,
                XV_HELP_DATA,         "help:Cancel",
                PANEL_LABEL_STRING, "Cancel",
                PANEL_NOTIFY_PROC,  cancel,
                NULL );

    /* create the "Menu Right" button
     */
    m = (Menu) xv_create ( XV_NULL, MENU,
```

```
                    MENU_ITEM,

                                        MENU_STRING, "Marillion",
                                        XV_HELP_DATA, "help:Marillion",
                                        NULL,
                    MENU_ITEM,

                                        MENU_STRING, "Genesis",
                                        XV_HELP_DATA, "help:Genesis",
                                        NULL,

                    MENU_ITEM,

                                        MENU_STRING, "IQ",
                                        XV_HELP_DATA, "help:IQ",
                                        NULL,
                    MENU_ITEM,

                                        MENU_STRING, "Twelfth Night",
                                        XV_HELP_DATA,
                                                "help:TwelfthNight",
                                        NULL,
                    MENU_NOTIFY_PROC,       menu_stub,
                XV_KEY_DATA, BASE_FRAME_KEY, frame,
                NULL );
    mb = (Panel_item) xv_create ( Pbutton, PANEL_BUTTON,
                XV_HELP_DATA,           "help:MenuRight",
                PANEL_LABEL_STRING,     "Menu Right",
                PANEL_ITEM_MENU,        m,
                NULL );
    /* set the key data on the buttons
     */
    (void) xv_set ( ph,
                XV_KEY_DATA,    BUTTON_HI_KEY,      ph,
                XV_KEY_DATA,    BUTTON_IN_KEY,      pi,
                XV_KEY_DATA,    BUTTON_BU_KEY,      pb,
                XV_KEY_DATA,    BUTTON_CA_KEY,      pc,
                XV_KEY_DATA,    BUTTON_ME_KEY,      mb,
                XV_KEY_DATA,    POPUP_WINDOW_KEY,   Fbutton,
                XV_KEY_DATA,    POPUP_PANEL_KEY,    Pbutton,
                NULL );
    (void) xv_set ( pi,
                XV_KEY_DATA,    BUTTON_HI_KEY,      ph,
                XV_KEY_DATA,    BUTTON_IN_KEY,      pi,
                XV_KEY_DATA,    BUTTON_BU_KEY,      pb,
                XV_KEY_DATA,    BUTTON_CA_KEY,      pc,
                XV_KEY_DATA,    BUTTON_ME_KEY,      mb,
                XV_KEY_DATA,    POPUP_WINDOW_KEY,   Fbutton,
                XV_KEY_DATA,    POPUP_PANEL_KEY,    Pbutton,
                NULL );
    (void) xv_set ( pb,
                XV_KEY_DATA,    BUTTON_HI_KEY,      ph,
                XV_KEY_DATA,    BUTTON_IN_KEY,      pi,
                XV_KEY_DATA,    BUTTON_BU_KEY,      pb,
                XV_KEY_DATA,    BUTTON_CA_KEY,      pc,
                XV_KEY_DATA,    BUTTON_ME_KEY,      mb,
                XV_KEY_DATA,    POPUP_WINDOW_KEY,   Fbutton,
                XV_KEY_DATA,    POPUP_PANEL_KEY,    Pbutton,
                NULL );
    (void) xv_set ( pc,
                XV_KEY_DATA,    BUTTON_HI_KEY,      ph,
                XV_KEY_DATA,    BUTTON_IN_KEY,      pi,
                XV_KEY_DATA,    BUTTON_BU_KEY,      pb,
                XV_KEY_DATA,    BUTTON_CA_KEY,      pc,
```

```
                           XV_KEY_DATA,    BUTTON_ME_KEY,     mb,
                           XV_KEY_DATA,    POPUP_WINDOW_KEY,  Fbutton,
                           XV_KEY_DATA,    POPUP_PANEL_KEY,   Pbutton,
                           NULL );
    (void) xv_set ( mb,
                           XV_KEY_DATA,    BUTTON_HI_KEY,     ph,
                           XV_KEY_DATA,    BUTTON_IN_KEY,     pi,
                           XV_KEY_DATA,    BUTTON_BU_KEY,     pb,
                           XV_KEY_DATA,    BUTTON_CA_KEY,     pc,
                           XV_KEY_DATA,    BUTTON_ME_KEY,     mb,
                           XV_KEY_DATA,    POPUP_WINDOW_KEY,  Fbutton,
                           XV_KEY_DATA,    POPUP_PANEL_KEY,   Pbutton,
                           NULL );
    /* make "Cancel" the default button
     */
    (void) xv_set ( Pbutton, PANEL_DEFAULT_ITEM, pc, NULL );

    /* make everything nice
     */
    window_fit_height ( Pbutton );
    window_fit ( Fbutton );
    window_fit_height ( panel );

    /* set up the canvas
     */
    canvas = (Canvas) xv_create ( frame, CANVAS,
                   XV_X,                      0,
                   XV_WIDTH,                  WIN_EXTEND_TO_EDGE,
                   XV_HEIGHT,                 WIN_EXTEND_TO_EDGE,
                   CANVAS_REPAINT_PROC,       repaint,
                   CANVAS_X_PAINT_WINDOW,     TRUE,
                   NULL );
    window_fit ( frame );

    /* create the popup */
    m = (Menu) xv_create ( XV_NULL, MENU,
                   XV_HELP_DATA,              "help:popup",
                   MENU_GEN_PIN_WINDOW, frame,    "Popup Menu",
                   MENU_ACTION_ITEM, "Quit",      exit,
                   NULL );
    xv_set ( canvas_paint_window ( canvas ),
                   WIN_CONSUME_EVENTS,    WIN_MOUSE_BUTTONS,
                                          ACTION_HELP,
                                          NULL,
                   WIN_EVENT_PROC,        show_it,
                   WIN_CLIENT_DATA,       m,
                   NULL );
    xv_main_loop ( frame );
    return ( 0 );
}


# help.info -- help file for help.c
#    your help file will usually need a more distinctive name than this;)
#

:notice
does this work?
```

```
:general
General

This program demonstrates the use of
XV_HELP_DATA to implement the various
Open Look GUI help screens.

:popup
Popup

This is an example of help for a
popup.  This popup lets you
Quit the application.

:InactiveButton
Inactive Buttons

These buttons are inactive because you have
pressed the "Inactive" button.  Press it again
to activate these buttons.

Note that the tag is case-sensitive.
(This is :InactiveButton)
:inactivebutton
Inactive

This button will make the other buttons in the
frame inactive.

Note that the tag is case-sensitive.
(This is :inactivebutton)

:buttonpanel
Button Window

This window has buttons that demonstrate various
Open Look GUI buttons.  Press a panel button
using the SELECT mouse button and see a
demonstration of that button type.  (For example,
the inactive button will make the other buttons
in the panel inactive.)

:ActiveButton

These buttons are active and will do the
action that is on their face.
:Highlight
Highlight

This button will turn highlighted when
you hold the SELECT mouse button down
over it.

:BusyButton
Busy

This button will turn the other buttons
```

on this panel to the busy pattern. To
restore the buttons, press Busy a second
time.

:BusyButtons
Busy Button pattern

This item is busy and cannot be used
until the busy pattern is removed. To
reset the button so that the busy pattern
goes away, press the Busy panel button
with the SELECT mouse button again.

:Cancel
Cancel

This button will pull the pushpin out of
the popup (if it is in) and then make
the popup vanish.

:MenuRight
Menu Right

The Menu Right panel button will pull up
a popup menu of Progressive Rock bands.
When you select one of the menu items,
the string associated with that item
will be displayed in the footing of the
base frame.

:Marillion
Marillion

A Progressive Rock group formed in the early
'80s, their best albums are "Script for a
Jester's Tear," "B'Sides Themselves," and
"Clutching at Straws." Fish (now solo) was
their original vocalist. He has now been
replaced with Steve Hogarth.

:Genesis
Genesis

A Progressive Rock group formed in the late
'60s, their best albums are "Selling England
by the Pound," "Trespass," "Foxtrot," and
"Nursery Cryme." Peter Gabriel (now solo)
was their original vocalist. He has now
been "replaced" by former drummer Phil
Collins.

:IQ
IQ

A Progressive Rock group formed in the late
'70s/early '80s. Their best albums are
"Are You Sitting Comfortably?", "The Wake,"
and "Tales From the Lush Attic." They
have also gone through a vocalist change.

```
:TwelfthNight
Twelfth Night

A Progressive Rock group formed in the late
'70s/early '80s.  Their best albums are
"XII," "Fact or Fiction," "Live and Let
Live," "Live at the Target," and "Collector's
Item."  Geoff Mann (now solo) was their
original vocalist.
```

I cons are yet another lowly part of the interface. Those with a Macintosh mentality love keeping everything iconized on the screen—unaware that because they are in Unix, those programs are still stealing cycles.

The attributes of an icon are shown in Figure 15.1. Icons can be beautiful, with a little work. See the animated sequence shown in the sample program. (Dogs like it too.) It's definitely worthwhile to learn one of the icon editors available, discussed in the next section.

CREATING ICON IMAGES

There are three main ways of creating icons. Even a programmer who likes handcoding everything will prefer to use **iconedit** or another one of the following editors for generating icons.

iconedit What we recommend using. It has a nice interface, it comes with OpenWindows, and it's probably the nicest icon editor available in OpenWindows. It is probably the most popular way of creating icons on Sun systems.

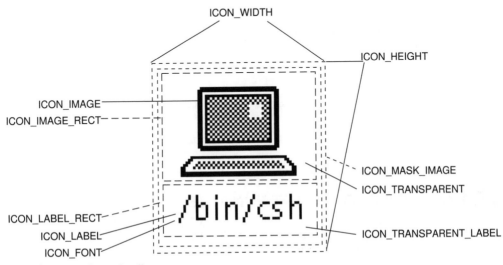

FIGURE 15.1 Icon Attributes

119

bitmap   An Xlib program rather than an XView program, so it doesn't have as nice an interface. It *is* usable, though; it is distributed with OpenWindows and is probably the second most popular way of creating icons on Sun systems.

olpixmap The icon editor that comes with AT&T's Open Look. It has many of the same features available in **iconedit**.

For more info on these packages, see the appropriate **man** pages.

▮IMPORTING THE ICON IMAGE

To bring an externally created icon in, you can use the following steps:

- #**include** the file created by **iconedit**, creating a bitmap.
- Create a server image from the bitmap.
- Tie the server image to the icon instance.

If you create a file like **state0.icon** (listed in Appendix B), you can bring it into your program with the following code:

```
short state0_image[] = {
#include "state0.icon"
};
```

You would then create a server image as follows:

```
Server_image s0_image;

s0image = (Server_image) xv_create ( XV_NULL, SERVER_IMAGE,
        XV_WIDTH,          64,
        XV_HEIGHT,         64,
        SERVER_IMAGE_BITS, state0_image,
        NULL );
```

The height and width of a typical icon is 64. The rest is straightforward. Finally, we tie the image to an icon:

```
Icon state;

state = (Icon) xv_create (XV_NULL, ICON,
                          ICON_IMAGE, s0image,
                          ICON_LABEL, "state",
                          NULL );
```

We also give the icon a label, making it easier to identify. This isn't always necessary.

▮LOADING AN ICON AT RUN TIME

Occasionally, you may want to load an icon image in at run time. You can do this with X11 bitmaps, but not with **pixrects,** so make sure you save your icons correctly.

To load the icon, create the server image like this:

```
char *filename;
```

```
SvrImage = (Server_image) xv_create (XV_NULL, SERVER_IMAGE,
                    SERVER_IMAGE_BITMAP_FILE, filename,
                    NULL) ;
```

A common error is to not include a path to the bitmap file, which can be used from any directory.

ANIMATED ICONS (TIED TO STATE)

Tying icon images to the state of the program is much easier than tying them to a timer. This technique (or a similar one) is used by programs like **mailtool** to change the icon image to reflect the state of the program.

To create the state animation used in the sample program, first include all the bitmaps, and then create server images as already shown in the section "Importing the Icon Image." Along with the **state0_image**, there must also be a **state1_image**, and so on for all the states that are to be displayed.

Here are the included bitmaps:

```
short state0_image[] = {
#include "state0.icon"
};

short state1_image[] = {
#include "state1.icon"
};
```

Here are the server images:

```
Server_image s0image;
Server_image s1image;

s0image = (Server_image) xv_create ( XV_NULL, SERVER_IMAGE,
        XV_WIDTH,           64,
        XV_HEIGHT,          64,
        SERVER_IMAGE_BITS,  state0_image,
        NULL );
s1image = (Server_image) xv_create ( XV_NULL, SERVER_IMAGE,
        XV_WIDTH,           64,
        XV_HEIGHT,          64,
        SERVER_IMAGE_BITS,  state1_image,
        NULL );
```

Here's the icon:

```
Icon   state0;

state0 = (Icon) xv_create ( XV_NULL, ICON,
                    ICON_IMAGE, s0image,
                    ICON_LABEL, "state",
                    NULL );
```

The state change is detected in some other routine. In this program's case, we're checking for a button press, so the state change is tied to the button's callback. The button was created like this:

```
Panel panel;

(void) xv_create ( panel, PANEL_BUTTON,
        PANEL_LABEL_STRING,        "Change State",
        PANEL_NOTIFY_PROC,         change_state_icon,
        XV_KEY_DATA, S0_ICON_KEY,  state0,
        NULL);
```

Note that the handle of the icon is passed to the callback through the use of key data.

The button's callback toggles the state of the icon by checking the value of a variable, setting the server image appropriately, then toggling the variable's value.

```
void
change_state_icon ( item, event )
Panel_item       item;
Event            *event;
{
        Icon state0 = (Icon) xv_get ( item, XV_KEY_DATA, S0_ICON_KEY );

        if ( current_state )  {
                        xv_set ( state0, ICON_IMAGE, s0image, NULL );
                        current_state = 0;
        } else {
                        xv_set ( state0, ICON_IMAGE, s1image, NULL );
                        current_state = 1;
        }
}
```

When the **current_state** is 1, the image and **current_state** are changed to 0. When the **current_state** is 0, the image and **current_state** are changed to 1. The **xv_set()** will make the icon refresh itself.

You could have the state represent the existence of a file, the value returned by a program, or any other information, instead of being tied to a button action. State-animated icons can be created for compilers (four images: idle, compiling, errors in compilation, and clean compilation), communication programs (three images: autodialing, failed to connect, connected), and many other applications.

▰ ANIMATED ICONS (TIED TO TIME)

Time-animated sequences can eat a lot of that idle CPU time you have lying around. They can be occasionally interesting, but they can easily be overused.

To create a time-animated sequence (like a blinking icon or the animated sequence included in the sample program), start by creating the images. This example will be of a three-frame animation. For a similar (but longer) animated sequence, see the sample program at the end of the chapter.

First, include the bitmaps:

```
short a0_image[] = {
#include "a0.icon"
};

short a1_image[] = {
#include "a1.icon"
};
```

```
short a2_image[] = {
#include "a2.icon"
};
```

Next the server images:

```
Server_image a0image;
Server_image a1image;
Server_image a2image;

a0image = (Server_image) xv_create ( XV_NULL, SERVER_IMAGE,
        XV_WIDTH,          64,
        XV_HEIGHT,         64,
        SERVER_IMAGE_BITS, a0_image,
        NULL ) ;

a1image = (Server_image) xv_create ( XV_NULL, SERVER_IMAGE,
        XV_WIDTH,          64,
        XV_HEIGHT,         64,
        SERVER_IMAGE_BITS, a1_image,
        NULL ) ;

a2image = (Server_image) xv_create ( XV_NULL, SERVER_IMAGE,
        XV_WIDTH,          64,
        XV_HEIGHT,         64,
        SERVER_IMAGE_BITS, a2_image,
        NULL ) ;
```

And we need an icon:

```
Icon icon;

icon = (Icon) xv_create ( XV_NULL, ICON,
                ICON_IMAGE, a0image,
                ICON_LABEL, "icon",
                NULL ) ;
```

All of this is familiar, and it should be fairly easy. When we create the timer routine, we enter unfamiliar territory:

```
Frame base;
struct itimerval t;

t.it_interval.tv_usec = t.it_value.tv_usec = 500000;
notify_set_itimer_func ( frame, animate, ITIMER_REAL, &t, NULL, NULL ) ;
```

This sets an arbitrary frame time delay of 500,000 microseconds. The sample program uses a slider for setting the delay. By playing with the slider you can find the speed you want in your program.

The **notify_set_itimer_func()** is used to call the **animate()** function at intervals specified by the **itimerval** structure **t**. The **animate()** function looks like this:

```
int animate_counter = -1;

void
```

```
animate ( item,event )
Panel_item item;
Event    *event;
{
        switch ( ++animate_counter ) {
        case 0:
                xv_set ( icon, ICON_IMAGE, a0image, NULL );
                break;
        case 1:
                xv_set ( icon, ICON_IMAGE, a1image, NULL );
                break;
        case 2:
                xv_set ( icon, ICON_IMAGE, a2image, NULL );
                animate_counter = -1;
                break;
        }
}
```

To speed up the animation, decrease the size of the **itimerval** delay stored in the **tv_used** and **tv_sec** fields. To slow it down, increase the size of the delay. Another thing you can do is to change the **animate()** function to something like this:

```
void
animate ( item,event )
Panel_item item;
Event *event;
{
        if ( ++animate_counter < 100 )
                        xv_set ( icon, ICON_IMAGE, a0image, NULL );
        else if ( animate_counter > 99 && animate_counter < 120 )
                        xv_set ( icon, ICON_IMAGE, a1image, NULL );
        else if ( animate_counter > 119 && animate_counter < 150 )
                        xv_set ( icon, ICON_IMAGE, a2image, NULL );
        else {
                        xv_set ( icon, ICON_IMAGE, a0image, NULL );
                        animate_counter = 0;
        }
}
```

In a setup like this, the **itimerval** delay will be used to determine how long the delay between each loop will be.

BLINKING

You can make an icon blink by doing time animation on it, alternating one image with another. You can change the rate of the blink by altering the frame delay. Here is an icon with two images: **a0image** and **a1image**. The **a1image** is the flash.

```
void
animate ( item,event )
Panel_item item;
Event *event;
{
        if(++animate_counter < 10000)
                        xv_set ( icon,
                                ICON_IMAGE,
                                (animate_counter % 10) ? a1image : a0image,
                                NULL );
```

```
          else  {
                              xv_set ( icon, ICON_IMAGE, a0image, NULL );
                              animate_counter = 0;
          }
}
```

COLOR ICONS

ICCCM.compliant icons are window-based instead of pixmap-based. Window-based icons suffer from poor performance when compared to pixmap-based icons, because the client is responsible for repainting instead of the window manager.

So, if you need ICCCM compliance, make sure your icons are window-based. If you like performance, make them pixmap-based. But use them (if you detect that the user's screen is color), because they're neat! And remember that **iconedit** can now do color.

SAMPLE PROGRAMS

The first sample program shows how to load an icon in at run time.

```
/* iconload.c -- Load an icon at run time
 * Author:  Kenneth Bibb
 * April 1992 -- Arastar Consulting
 *-------------------------------------------
 *
 * o Load an icon from a file
 *
 * o Only works with X11 bitmap format files
 */

#include <xview/xview.h>
#include <xview/panel.h>
#include <xview/svrimage.h>
#include <xview/icon.h>


usage ( s )
char *s;
{
      printf( "Usage: %s filename\n",s );
      exit ( 1 );
}

main ( argc, argv )
int argc;
char **argv;
{
      Frame                     base;
      Icon                      ldicon;
      Server_image              image0;
      Panel                     panel;

      xv_init ( XV_INIT_ARGC_PTR_ARGV, &argc, argv, NULL );

      if ( argc < 2 )
                  usage ( argv[0] );
```

```
        image0 = (Server_image) xv_create ( XV_NULL, SERVER_IMAGE,
                    SERVER_IMAGE_BITMAP_FILE, argv[1],
                    NULL );
        ldicon = (Icon) xv_create ( XV_NULL, ICON,
                                    ICON_IMAGE, image0,
                                    ICON_LABEL, "loaded",
                                    NULL );
        base = (Frame) xv_create ( NULL, FRAME,
                    FRAME_LABEL,   argv[0],
                    FRAME_CLOSED,  TRUE,
                    FRAME_ICON,    ldicon,
                    XV_X,          300,
                    XV_Y,          175,
                    NULL );
    panel = (Panel) xv_create ( base, PANEL, NULL );

    xv_main_loop ( base );
}
```

The sample program will iconize into the default icon (which is boring). The subwindows are also iconizable, and they are more interesting. Using the View menu, you can invoke a "State" animated icon or an "Animated" (time animation) icon. When the icon is visible, the "Change State" button will toggle the state icon between two states. The "Animate" button will start or pause the animated sequence on its icon.

The listings for the icons are in Appendix B.

```
/* icon.c -- Icon test program
 * Author:  Kenneth Bibb
 * April 1992 -- Arastar Consulting
 *-----------------------------------------
 *
 * o Icon State animation
 *    animation based on some state
 * o Icon Time animation
 *    animation based on a timer
 */

#include <stdlib.h>
#include <sys/param.h>
#include <xview/xview.h>
#include <xview/panel.h>
#include <xview/xv_xrect.h>
#include <xview/openmenu.h>
#include <xview/svrimage.h>
#include <xview/icon.h>
#include <xview/notify.h>

/* external bitmaps for the state animation
 * are state0_image and state1_image
 */
short state0_image[] = {
```

```
#include "state0.icon"
};
short state1_image[] = {
#include "state1.icon"
};

/* external bitmaps for the time animation
 * are anime[0-8]_image
 */
short anime0_image[] = {
#include "a0.icon"
};

short anime1_image[] = {
#include "a1.icon"
};

short anime2_image[] = {
#include "a2.icon"
};

short anime3_image[] = {
#include "a3.icon"
};

short anime4_image[] = {
#include "a4.icon"
};

short anime5_image[] = {
#include "a5.icon"
};

short anime6_image[] = {
#include "a6.icon"
};

short anime7_image[] = {
#include "a7.icon"
};

short anime8_image[] = {
#include "a8.icon"
};


Attr_attribute BASE_FRAME_KEY;      /* handle of base frame */
Attr_attribute STATE_FRAME_KEY;     /* handle of state frame */
Attr_attribute ANI_FRAME_KEY;       /* handle of animate frame */
Attr_attribute S0_ICON_KEY;         /* handle of state icon */

Server_image s0image;               /* server images for the bitmaps */
Server_image s1image;
Server_image a0image;
Server_image a1image;
Server_image a2image;
Server_image a3image;
Server_image a4image;
```

```
Server_image a5image;
Server_image a6image;
Server_image a7image;
Server_image a8image;
Icon animate0;               /* the icon for the time animation window */
int current_state = 0;       /* which state icon image is used         */
int animate_state = 0;       /* which part of the animation are we in   */
int anime_toggle = FALSE;    /* start/pause the animation               */
int slider_val = 60;         /* frame time delay slider controlled      */
struct itimerval t;          /* timer structure used by timing function */



/*======================================
 * State Animation callbacks
 *--------------------------------------------------------------------------
 */

/* the "State..." menu item's callback
 * this function displays the state animation frame
 */
void
state ( m, mi )
Menu m;
Menu_item mi;
{
        xv_set ( (Frame) xv_get ( mi, XV_KEY_DATA, STATE_FRAME_KEY ),
                        XV_SHOW, TRUE,
                        NULL );
}



/* the "Change State" button's callback
 * this is where the image is changed
 *
 *    current_state toggles between 0 and 1 displaying alternate
 *    images.
 */
void
change_state_icon ( item, event )
Panel_item item;
Event *event;
{
        Icon state0 = (Icon) xv_get ( item, XV_KEY_DATA, S0_ICON_KEY );

        if ( current_state ) {
                        xv_set ( state0, ICON_IMAGE, s0image, NULL );
                        current_state = 0;
        } else {
                        xv_set ( state0, ICON_IMAGE, s1image, NULL );
                        current_state = 1;
        }
}
```

```
/*===================================
 * Time Animation callbacks
 *----------------------------------------------------------------------
 */

/* The "Animate..." menu item callback
 * this function displays the animate animation frame
 *
 *     animate_state determines which frame to show.  0 sets this
 *                   to the beginning of the range (see animate_state_icon()
 *                   for more details)
 *     then we show the Fanime frame
 */
void
anime ( m, mi )
Menu m;
Menu_item mi;
{
        animate_state=0;
        xv_set ( (Frame) xv_get( mi, XV_KEY_DATA, ANI_FRAME_KEY),
                        XV_SHOW, TRUE,
                        NULL );
}

/* The workhorse routine.  This routine is responsible for deciding
 * which frame to display next.  While the counter animate_state is below
 * 300, it will display a0image, except for every 50th frame, where it will
 * show a8image.  This makes the cat flick its tail.
 *
 * Then we have a whirlwind of activity between 300 and 304, where
 * the ball comes flying and smacks the cat in the head.
 *
 * From 305 to 399 the corpse twitches in a comically gruesome manner.
 *
 * From 400 to 599 the corpse lies there dead.
 * At 600, the animate_state is reset to 0, resurrecting the little beastie
 */
void
animate_state_icon ( item,event )
Panel_item
item;
Event *event;
{
        if ( ++animate_state < 300 )
                        xv_set ( animate0, ICON_IMAGE, (animate_state %50)
                                ? a0image : a8image, NULL );
        else if ( animate_state == 300 )
                        xv_set ( animate0, ICON_IMAGE, a1image, NULL );
        else if ( animate_state == 301 )
                        xv_set ( animate0, ICON_IMAGE, a2image, NULL );
        else if ( animate_state == 302 )
                        xv_set ( animate0, ICON_IMAGE, a3image, NULL );
        else if ( animate_state == 303 )
                        xv_set ( animate0, ICON_IMAGE, a4image, NULL );
        else if ( animate_state == 304 )
                        xv_set ( animate0, ICON_IMAGE, a5image, NULL );
        else if ( animate_state > 304 && animate_state < 400 )
                        xv_set ( animate0, ICON_IMAGE, (animate_state % 10)
                                ? a6image : a7image, NULL );
```

```
            else if ( animate_state > 399 && animate_state < 600 )
                        xv_set ( animate0, ICON_IMAGE, a6image, NULL );
        else {
                        xv_set ( animate0, ICON_IMAGE, a6image, NULL );
                        animate_state = 0;
        }
}

/* the "Animate" button callback
 *
 *     anime_toggle reflects whether you should pause (FALSE) or
 *                  go (TRUE).
 *     t.it_interval.tv_usec and t.it_value.tv_usec are used to
 *                  determine the delay between frames.  Smaller numbers
 *                  mean faster animation.
 *     notify_set_itimer_func() actually does the animation
 *                  by calling animate_state_icon().
 */
void
toggle_animation ( item,event )
Panel_item item;
Event *event;
{
        Frame frame = (Frame) xv_get ( item, XV_KEY_DATA, BASE_FRAME_KEY );
        int value = slider_val;

        if (!anime_toggle) {
                        t.it_interval.tv_usec = t.it_value.tv_usec = (value+40)
                            * 1000;
                        notify_set_itimer_func ( frame, animate_state_icon,
                            ITIMER_REAL, &t, NULL);
                        anime_toggle = TRUE;
        } else {
                        notify_set_itimer_func ( frame, NOTIFY_FUNC_NULL,
                            ITIMER_REAL, NULL, NULL);
                        anime_toggle = FALSE;
        }
}

/* the slider's callback
 *
 *     slider_val is scaled, then used as the frame delay.
 *                  Small values make the animation faster,
 *                  While large values slow it down.
 */
void
movie ( item, value, event )
Panel_item item;
int value;
Event *event;
{
        slider_val = value;
}

/*---------------------------------------------------------------------*/

main ( argc, argv )
int argc;
char **argv;
```

```
{
        Frame                   frame;
        Frame                   Fstate;
        Frame                   Fanime;
        Icon                    state0;
        Panel                   panel;
        Panel                   Pstate;                          /* site panel */
        Panel                   Panime;                          /* site panel */
        Menu                    m;

        xv_init ( XV_INIT_ARGC_PTR_ARGV, &argc, argv, NULL );
        BASE_FRAME_KEY = xv_unique_key(); /* assign keys */
        STATE_FRAME_KEY = xv_unique_key();
        ANI_FRAME_KEY = xv_unique_key();
        S0_ICON_KEY = xv_unique_key();
        s0image = (Server_image) xv_create ( XV_NULL, SERVER_IMAGE,
                        XV_WIDTH,               64,
                        XV_HEIGHT,              64,
                        SERVER_IMAGE_BITS, state0_image,
                        NULL );
        s1image = (Server_image) xv_create ( XV_NULL, SERVER_IMAGE,
                        XV_WIDTH,               64,
                        XV_HEIGHT,              64,
                        SERVER_IMAGE_BITS, state1_image,
                        NULL );

        a0image = (Server_image) xv_create ( XV_NULL, SERVER_IMAGE,
                        XV_WIDTH,               64,
                        XV_HEIGHT,              64,
                        SERVER_IMAGE_BITS, anime0_image,
                        NULL );
        a1image = (Server_image) xv_create ( XV_NULL, SERVER_IMAGE,
                        XV_WIDTH,               64,
                        XV_HEIGHT,              64,
                        SERVER_IMAGE_BITS, anime1_image,
                        NULL );
        a2image = (Server_image) xv_create ( XV_NULL, SERVER_IMAGE,
                        XV_WIDTH,               64,
                        XV_HEIGHT,              64,
                        SERVER_IMAGE_BITS, anime2_image,
                        NULL );
        a3image = (Server_image) xv_create ( XV_NULL, SERVER_IMAGE,
                        XV_WIDTH,               64,
                        XV_HEIGHT,              64,
                        SERVER_IMAGE_BITS, anime3_image,
                        NULL );
        a4image = (Server_image) xv_create ( XV_NULL, SERVER_IMAGE,
                        XV_WIDTH,               64,
                        XV_HEIGHT,              64,
                        SERVER_IMAGE_BITS, anime4_image,
                        NULL );
        a5image = (Server_image) xv_create ( XV_NULL, SERVER_IMAGE,
                        XV_WIDTH,               64,
                        XV_HEIGHT,              64,
                        SERVER_IMAGE_BITS, anime5_image,
                        NULL );
        a6image = (Server_image) xv_create ( XV_NULL, SERVER_IMAGE,
                        XV_WIDTH,               64,
                        XV_HEIGHT,              64,
```

```
                              SERVER_IMAGE_BITS, anime6_image,
                              NULL );
        a7image = (Server_image) xv_create ( XV_NULL, SERVER_IMAGE,
                    XV_WIDTH,           64,
                    XV_HEIGHT,          64,
                    SERVER_IMAGE_BITS, anime7_image,
                    NULL );
        a8image = (Server_image) xv_create ( XV_NULL,SERVER_IMAGE,
                    XV_WIDTH,           64,
                    XV_HEIGHT,          64,
                    SERVER_IMAGE_BITS, anime8_image,
                    NULL );
        state0 = (Icon) xv_create ( XV_NULL, ICON,
                                    ICON_IMAGE, s0image,
                                    ICON_LABEL, "state",
                                    NULL );
        animate0 = (Icon) xv_create ( XV_NULL, ICON,
                                    ICON_IMAGE, a0image,
                                    ICON_LABEL, "time",
                                    NULL );
        frame = (Frame) xv_create ( NULL, FRAME,
                    FRAME_LABEL, argv[0],
                    XV_X,           300,
                    XV_Y,           175,
                    NULL );
        Fstate = (Frame) xv_create ( frame, FRAME,
                    FRAME_LABEL,  "State",
                    FRAME_ICON,    state0,
                    FRAME_CLOSED, TRUE,
                    XV_X,           350,
                    XV_Y,           300,
                    NULL );
        Fanime = (Frame) xv_create ( frame, FRAME,
                    FRAME_LABEL,  "Animate",
                    FRAME_ICON,    animate0,
                    FRAME_CLOSED, TRUE,
                    XV_X,           400,
                    XV_Y,           300,
                    NULL );
        panel = (Panel) xv_create ( frame, PANEL, NULL );
        Pstate= (Panel) xv_create ( Fstate, PANEL, NULL );
        Panime= (Panel) xv_create ( Fanime, PANEL, NULL );

        m = (Menu) xv_create ( NULL, MENU,
                    MENU_ITEM,
                                    MENU_STRING,                        "State...",
                                    MENU_NOTIFY_PROC,            state,
                                    XV_KEY_DATA, STATE_FRAME_KEY, Fstate,
                                    NULL,
                    MENU_ITEM,
                                    MENU_STRING,                "Animated...",
                                    MENU_NOTIFY_PROC,            anime,
                                    XV_KEY_DATA, ANI_FRAME_KEY,Fanime,
                                    NULL,
                    NULL );
        (void) xv_create ( panel, PANEL_BUTTON,
                    PANEL_LABEL_STRING, "View",
                    PANEL_ITEM_MENU,    m,
                    NULL );
```

```
        (void) xv_create ( panel, PANEL_BUTTON,
                    PANEL_LABEL_STRING,        "Change State",
                    PANEL_NOTIFY_PROC,         change_state_icon,
                    XV_KEY_DATA, S0_ICON_KEY, state0,
                    NULL );
        (void) xv_create ( panel, PANEL_BUTTON,
                    PANEL_LABEL_STRING,         "Animate",
                    PANEL_NOTIFY_PROC,          toggle_animation,
                    XV_KEY_DATA, BASE_FRAME_KEY, frame,
                    NULL );
        (void) xv_create ( panel, PANEL_SLIDER,
                    PANEL_NEXT_ROW,       -1,
                    PANEL_LABEL_STRING,   "Frame Delay:",
                    PANEL_VALUE,          10,
                    PANEL_MIN_VALUE,      0,
                    PANEL_MAX_VALUE,      100,
                    PANEL_NOTIFY_PROC,    movie,
                    NULL );
    window_fit_height ( panel );
    window_fit ( frame );

    xv_main_loop ( frame );
}
```

Keyboard Accelerators

There are two kinds of keyboard accelerator attributes that you can set for an object:

FRAME_ACCELERATOR Accepts a Meta-key combination
FRAME_X_ACCELERATOR Accepts an XKeySym

They have the following syntax:

```
FRAME_ACCELERATOR, char, routine, object
FRAME_X_ACCELERATOR, Xkeysym, routine, object
```

where **char** is a normal C **char**; **Xkeysym** is an XKeySym (as defined in **X11 /keysymdef.h**); **routine** is a callback routine of the following format:

```
void
accel_callback ( object, event )
Xv_opaque object;
Event *event;
{

}
```

and **object** is an object that we arbitrarily pass to the routine.

To create a key accelerator that will quit the application when the user presses Meta-**q**, we would do the following:

```
Frame frame;

(void) xv_set ( frame,
        FRAME_ACCELERATOR, 'q', quit, frame,
        NULL );
```

where **quit()** is

```
void
quit ( frame, event )
Frame frame;
```

```
Event *event;
{
        exit ();
}
```

SAMPLE PROGRAM

The sample program generates a basic frame and then waits for the following accelerators:

Meta-**m**   Change the frame to maximum size

Meta-**r**   Change the frame to default size

Meta-**q**   Quit the application

```
/* keybd.c -- Keyboard Accelerators
 * Author:  Kenneth Bibb
 * January 1992 -- Arastar Consulting
 *----------------------------------------
 * Basic frame with panel and canvas
 */

#include <stdlib.h>
#include <xview/xview.h>
#include <xview/panel.h>
#include <xview/canvas.h>
#define XK_LATIN1 1
#include <X11/keysymdef.h>

void
fullsize ( frame, event )
Frame frame;
Event *event;

{
        printf ( "fullsize \n" );
        (void) xv_set ( frame,
                        XV_WIDTH,  200,
                        XV_HEIGHT, 300,
                        XV_SHOW,   TRUE,
                        NULL );
}
void restore ( frame,event )
Frame frame;
Event *event;
{
        printf ( "restore\n" );
        (void) xv_set ( frame,
                        XV_WIDTH,  200,
                        XV_HEIGHT, 100,
                        XV_SHOW,   TRUE,
                        NULL );
}

void
quit ( frame, event )
```

```
Frame frame;
Event *event;
{
        printf ( "quit\n" );
        exit ();
}

main ( argc, argv )
int argc;
char **argv;
{
        Frame frame;
        Canvas canvas;
        Panel panel;

        xv_init ( XV_INIT_ARGC_PTR_ARGV, &argc, argv, NULL );


        /* create the base frame */
        frame = (Frame) xv_create ( NULL, FRAME,
                        FRAME_LABEL,              argv[0],
                        FRAME_SHOW_FOOTER, TRUE,
                        XV_X,                     300,
                        XV_Y,                     175,
                        XV_WIDTH,                 200,
                        XV_HEIGHT,                100,
                        NULL );
        (void) xv_set ( frame,
                        FRAME_X_ACCELERATOR, XK_m, fullsize, frame,
                        FRAME_ACCELERATOR,    'q', quit, frame,
                        FRAME_ACCELERATOR,    'r', restore, frame,
                        NULL );

/* create the panel */
panel = (Panel) xv_create ( frame, PANEL, NULL );
window_fit_height ( panel );

/* create the canvas */
canvas = (Canvas) xv_create ( frame, CANVAS,
                        XV_X,                     0,
                        XV_HEIGHT,                WIN_EXTEND_TO_EDGE,
                        XV_WIDTH,                 WIN_EXTEND_TO_EDGE,
                        CANVAS_X_PAINT_WINDOW, TRUE,
                        NULL );

/* fit the frame around the canvas and panel */
window_fit ( frame );

xv_main_loop ( frame );
}
```

Menus

When most users think of window-based applications, they think of the menus. (Lotus likes thinking about menus, too.) It's easy to make a program unusable by organizing your menus in a strange way.

Figure 17.1 shows the attributes for both pulldown and popup menus. A menu item has the attributes shown in Figure 17.2.

MENU CALLBACK

The menu callback is called as follows:

```
void
menu_notify_proc ( menu, menu_item )
Menu menu;
Menu_item menu_item;
{

}
```

GOOD MENU DESIGN

The Open Look GUI provides a number of guidelines concerning good menu design. When designing menus you should do the following:

- Group items using white space.
- Group using pullright menus.
- Use ellipsis (. . .) to indicate menu items that call command windows (dialog boxes).
- Order items in logical groups.
- Order item groups by use.
- Don't create menu items that have the same name as the menu button.
- Provide pushpins for menus that are used often.
- Avoid glyphs unless their meanings are clear.
- Do not mix glyphs and text within the same menu.

Look at the programs you use. Which ones are easy to use? If you notice the menu system while using it, there should be a better way of organizing it. Good organization will make the use of the application as transparent as possible.

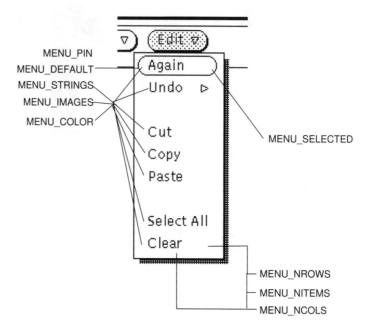

Popup Menu Attributes

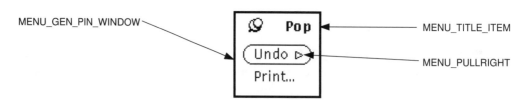

FIGURE 17.1 Menu Attributes

CREATE A STANDARD MENU

Creating the menu system comes after the base windows have been designed. In the following examples, we'll work with a base window setup using a single base window and a single panel. The frame will be called **Fmain** and the panel will be **Pmain**.

When creating a menu system, it is usually helpful to use the following steps:

- Copy the standard menus in.
- Comment out features that will not be used in the current application.
- Design and implement pulldown menus.

MENU_ITEM

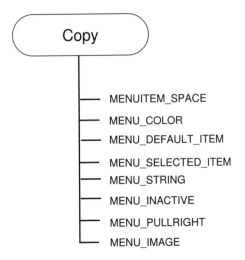

FIGURE 17.2 Menu Item Attributes

- Design and implement pullright menus.
- Design and implement popup menu.
- Test menu prototype.
- Get user feedback.
- Iterate until acceptable.

Delete a Menu   You can delete a menu with **xv_destroy_safe()**. If your menu is called **menu_1**, you could delete it with

```
xv_destroy_safe ( menu_1 );
```

MENU TYPES
The Open Look GUI supports pulldown, pullright, and popup menus. You can make menus with nonexclusive choices (you can choose multiple items from the same menu simultaneously); push-pins; keyboard accelerators; multicolumns; and graphics. You can also dynamically generate menus.

Pulldown Menus   Most of your menus will be pulldown menus. This is the kind of menu that you see in most window applications regardless of interface. You'll actually need to create two items to create one of these: the menu button and the menu itself. As an example of a pulldown menu, we'll create the standard Edit menu.

First, variables need to be defined:

```
Menu m;            /* the menu handle for the menu button */
Panel Pmain;       /* Panel for main window */
```

The panel should already be created when you created the base window. It will be needed for the menu button.

Next, you should set up your menu notify procedures. In most cases, there will be a lot of work involved in creating the actual routines. Prototyping these routines makes it easy to see if the menu system will work as planned. A stub routine you can use is the following:

```
void
menu_stub ( Menu m, Menu_item mi )
{
#ifdef DEBUG
        printf ( "Menu: [%s]\n", xv_get ( mi,MENU_STRING ) );
#endif
}
```

This function is plugged into your notify procedure. It's easy to replace with real code, and since it's only a single line that is shared among all the menu notify procedures, it's easy to add to your code. Using the first menu notify procedure from the Edit menu ("Again") as an example, we have

```
void
again ( Menu m, Menu_item mi )
{
        menu_stub ( m,mi );
}
```

Now it's time to make the actual menu. Notice that the parent of the menu is **XV_NULL**—you'll associate the menu with an item later. Because you are doing the association at a later time, you need to save the menu handle in a variable. If the menu's button is created immediately after the menu is created, you only need to allocate the one variable for all your menus.

```
m = (Menu) xv_create ( XV_NULL, MENU,
        MENU_ITEM,
                        MENU_STRING,        "Again",
                        MENU_NOTIFY_PROC,   new,
                        NULL,
        MENU_ITEM,
                        MENU_STRING,        "Undo",
                        MENU_NOTIFY_PROC,   load,
                        NULL,
        MENU_ITEM_SPACE, NULL,
        MENU_ITEM,
                        MENU_STRING,        "Cut",
                        MENU_NOTIFY_PROC,   save,
                        NULL,
        MENU_ITEM,
                        MENU_STRING,        "Copy",
                        MENU_NOTIFY_PROC,   import,
                        NULL,
        MENU_ITEM,
                        MENU_STRING,        "Paste",
                        MENU_NOTIFY_PROC,   export,
                        NULL,
        MENU_ITEM_SPACE, NULL,
```

```
     MENU_ITEM,
                     MENU_STRING,         "Select All",
                     MENU_NOTIFY_PROC,    browse,
                     NULL,
     MENU_ITEM,
                     MENU_STRING,         "Delete",
                     MENU_NOTIFY_PROC,    print,
                     NULL,
     MENU_ITEM,
                     MENU_STRING,         "Clear",
                     MENU_NOTIFY_PROC,    exit,
                     NULL,
     NULL );
```

These attributes are used to create menu entries with associated notify procedures.

When doing initial testing, you can also assign a **MENU_NOTIFY_PROC** attribute to the menu, instead of to each menu item.

```
menu = (Menu) xv_create ( XV_NULL, MENU,
     MENU_NOTIFY_PROC, menu_stub,
     MENU_STRINGS, "Cut", "Copy", "Paste", NULL,
     NULL );
```

The **MENU_ITEM** is more useful if you're going to need to assign things separately to each menu item. The latter example is useful when you're initially creating the menu, or if you have a menu that doesn't need anything sent for an individual menu item.

We could also have used a shorthand form for declaring each menu item:

```
MENU_ACTION_ITEM, "Again", new,
```

which is equivalent to

```
MENU_ITEM, MENU_STRING,         "Again",
           MENU_NOTIFY_PROC,    new,
           NULL,
```

The Open Look GUI uses spaces instead of lines to separate groups of menu items. Here is a macro that can be used to put a space in a menu:

```
#define MENU_ITEM_SPACE   MENU_ITEM, \
                               MENU_STRING, "", \
                               MENU_FEEDBACK, FALSE,
```

There is a similar macro defined in **xview/openmenu.h** for the **MENU_ITEM** package, upon which this is based.

Finally, we need to create a menu button to hang the menu on:

```
(void) xv_create ( Pmain, PANEL_BUTTON,
     PANEL_LABEL_STRING, "Edit",
     PANEL_ITEM_MENU, m,
     NULL );
```

The return value of **xv_create()** is not needed here, so it is cast to **void**. The parent item is **Pmain** (the main window's panel), and we're creating a button, so we use the **PANEL_BUTTON** package. The **PANEL_LABEL_STRING** attribute sets the text that will go into the button. The **PANEL_ITEM_MENU** attribute associates the menu (in this case **m**) with the button being defined. You also do not need to assign a **PANEL_NOTIFY_PROC** to the button—the default action is to display the menu when the button is pressed.

Pulldown Menu with Pullright Submenu   Submenus in the Open Look GUI are pullright menus. They are used to organize the menu commands into a hierarchical, logical structure. In the standard Edit menu, the Undo item is often defined as a pullright. (This is done to allow the user not only to undo the last change, but also to undo all changes that have been made to the file.) To create the Edit menu with a pullright, you first need to define the variables:

```
Menu m;            /* Generic menu handle for menu buttons */
Menu Mundo;        /* menu handle for the undo submenu */
Panel Pmain;       /* Panel for main window */
```

Define the menu notify procedures in the same way as for a normal pulldown menu. The menu button is also created in exactly the same way. With a pullright menu, you need to define the submenu first and then the main menu, as follows:

```
m_undo = (Menu) xv_create(XV_NULL, MENU,
        MENU_ITEM,
                    MENU_STRING, "Undo Last Change",
                    MENU_NOTIFY_PROC, undo_last,
                    NULL,
        MENU_ITEM,
                    MENU_STRING, "Undo All Changes",
                    MENU_NOTIFY_PROC, undo_all,
                    NULL,
        NULL );

m = (Menu) xv_create ( XV_NULL, MENU,
        MENU_ITEM,
                    MENU_STRING, "Again",
                    MENU_NOTIFY_PROC, new,
                    NULL,
        MENU_ITEM,
                    MENU_STRING, "Undo",
                    MENU_PULLRIGHT, m_undo,
                    NULL,
        MENU_ITEM_SPACE, NULL,
        MENU_ITEM,
                    MENU_STRING, "Cut",
                    MENU_NOTIFY_PROC, save,
                    NULL,
        MENU_ITEM,
                    MENU_STRING, "Copy",
                    MENU_NOTIFY_PROC, import,
                    NULL,
        MENU_ITEM,
                    MENU_STRING, "Paste",
                    MENU_NOTIFY_PROC, export,
```

```
                    NULL,
   MENU_ITEM_SPACE, NULL,
   MENU_ITEM,
                    MENU_STRING, "Select All",
                    MENU_NOTIFY_PROC, browse,
                    NULL,
   MENU_ITEM,
                    MENU_STRING, "Delete",
                    MENU_NOTIFY_PROC, print,
                    NULL,
   MENU_ITEM,
                    MENU_STRING, "Clear",
                    MENU_NOTIFY_PROC, exit,
                    NULL,
       NULL );
```

When we create the Undo submenu, we have to save its handle for the Edit menu. When defining Undo on the Edit menu, **MENU_NOTIFY_PROC** is not used. Instead, **MENU_PULLRIGHT** is used. This attribute associates a submenu with a menu item, to which it appends a pullright triangle. Instead of **MENU_ACTION_ITEM**, the shorthand form of this item would be

```
   MENU_PULLRIGHT_ITEM, "Undo", m_undo,
```

Popup Menu   The most frequently used commands should be added to the popup menu. According to the OLSG, you shouldn't duplicate the menu buttons that are in your base window. (For an example of what *not* to do, take a look at **textedit**'s popup.)

The prototype of the **uusetup** program's popup will be used as an example. I wanted a simple popup that looked like the one shown in Figure 17.3.

Since I make a lot of mistakes, I wanted the Undo functions as part of the popup (I was, conveniently, already storing the handle of the submenu). The users at my office like to waste a lot of paper by making a lot of printouts, so the Print command should also go here to aid them in destroying the rain forests.

As usual, we start with the variables:

```
Menu;           /* Generic menu handle for menu buttons */
Menu Mundo;     /* menu handle for the undo submenu */
Canvas Cmain;   /* Canvas for main window */
```

FIGURE   17.3
Simple Popup
Menu

The only new variable is **Cmain**, the Canvas variable. I wanted the base window to look like a **shelltool** window, so the canvas was a necessary evil.

The **Mundo** menu is straightforward. However, the **m** menu has a few tricks thrown in:

```
M = (Menu) xv_create ( NULL, MENU,
          MENU_GEN_PIN_WINDOW, frame, "Popup",
          MENU_ITEM,
               MENU_STRING, "Undo",
               MENU_PULLRIGHT, Mundo,
               NULL,
          MENU_ITEM,
               MENU_STRING, "Print...",
               MENU_NOTIFY_PROC, print,
               NULL,
          NULL);
```

Since Print is going to invoke a command window, we append an ellipsis (...) to it. Appending ellipsis to commands that invoke command windows (dialog boxes) is standard in most GUIs.

The main difference is the **MENU_GEN_PIN_WINDOW** attribute, which creates a popup menu with a pushpin. **MENU_GEN_PIN_WINDOW** needs a parent frame and a title provided. The title is truncated if it's longer than the menu items. If your title is chopped, you will need to extend the length of one of your menu items, shorten the title, or both.

Finally, you need to set up the event handling for the window. There are two steps involved: You need to tell the canvas to activate a window event procedure, and you need to create the window event procedure. A typical canvas event procedure looks like

```
Attr_attribute POPUP_MENU_KEY;

(void) xv_set ( canvas_paint_window ( canvas ),
        WIN_CONSUME_EVENTS,           WIN_MOUSE_BUTTONS, NULL,
        WIN_EVENT_PROC,               show_popup,
        XV_KEY_DATA,POPUP_MENU_KEY,   menu,
        NULL );
```

The event handler, **show_popup()**, looks like

```
void
show_popup ( xwin, event )
Xv_window window;
Event *event;
{
        if ( event_is_down ( event ) && event_action (event)==
                        ACTION_MENU  ) {
                        menu_show(
                                  xv_get(xwin,XV_KEY_DATA, POPUP_MENU_KEY),
                                  xwin, event, NULL );
        }
}
```

MENU ACCELERATORS

To assign a menu accelerator key to a menu item, you need to use the **FRAME_X_ACCELERATOR** or **FRAME_ACCELERATOR** attribute. The use of these attributes applies to the entire frame, so make sure you're not overlaying a key that you want to use as an accelerator elsewhere.

Instructions on how to use **FRAME_X_ACCELERATOR** and **FRAME_ACCELERATOR** are provided in Chapter 16.

OPEN LOOK STANDARD MENUS

There are three standard Open Look menus:

- File
- View
- Edit

They are shown in Figure 17.4.

SAMPLE PROGRAM

The following sample program includes examples of the Open Look GUI menus.

```
/* menus.c -- Open Look basic frame with menus
 * Author:  Kenneth Bibb
 * February 1992 -- Arastar Consulting
 */

#include <stdlib.h>
#include <xview/xview.h>
#include <xview/panel.h>
#include <xview/canvas.h>
#include <xview/xv_xrect.h>
#include <xview/openmenu.h>

Attr_attribute BASE_FRAME_KEY;
Attr_attribute  POPUP_KEY;
/* menu callback for testing
 */
void
menu_stub ( menu, menu_item )
Menu menu;
Menu_item menu_item;
{
     char s[64];

     sprintf ( s,"Menu: [%s]\n", (char *) xv_get ( menu_item,
                                          MENU_STRING ) );
     xv_set ( xv_get ( menu, XV_KEY_DATA, BASE_FRAME_KEY ),
     FRAME_LEFT_FOOTER, s, NULL );
}

/* display the popup menu
 */
void
show_popup ( xwin, event )
Xv_Window xwin;
Event *event;
{
     if ( ( event_action ( event ) ==ACTION_MENU ) && ( event_is_down
                                          ( event ) ) ) {
                    menu_show ( xv_get ( xwin, XV_KEY_DATA, POPUP_KEY ),
                                          xwin, event, NULL );

     }
}
```

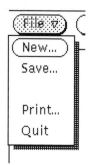

Standard File Menu

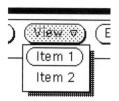

View Menu

The contents of the view menu are not standard, but can contain items like "Zoom In", "Actual Size", "Refresh Screen", "Show Grid", etc.

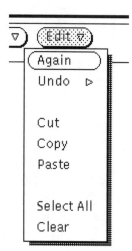

Standard Edit Menu

The Undo submenu contains an "Undo Last" and an "Undo All" item.

FIGURE 17.4 Standard Open Look Menus

```
/* canvas repaint function
 */
void
repaint ( canvas, win, dpy, xwin, xrect )
Canvas canvas;
Xv_Window win;
Display *dpy;
Window xwin;
Xv_xrectlist *xrect;
{
```

```
        GC gc;
        int width, height;

        gc = DefaultGC ( dpy, DefaultScreen ( dpy ) );
        width = (int) xv_get ( win, XV_WIDTH );
        height = (int) xv_get ( win, XV_HEIGHT );
}

int
main ( argc, argv )
int argc;
char **argv;
{
        Frame                       frame;
        Canvas                      canvas;
        Icon                        icon;
        Server_image                cimage;
        Panel                       panel;
        Menu                        m, m_undo;

        xv_init ( XV_INIT_ARGC_PTR_ARGV, &argc, argv, NULL );
        BASE_FRAME_KEY = xv_unique_key ();

        frame = (Frame) xv_create ( XV_NULL, FRAME,
                    FRAME_LABEL,        argv[0],
                    FRAME_ACCELERATOR,  "q", exit, frame,
                    XV_X,               300,
                    XV_Y,               175,
                    NULL );

        panel = (Panel) xv_create ( frame, PANEL, NULL );

        /* file menu--replace menu_stubs with names of
         *            real functions--use short cuts
         */
        m = (Menu) xv_create ( XV_NULL, MENU,
                    MENU_NOTIFY_PROC, menu_stub,
                    MENU_ITEM,
                                MENU_STRING, "New...",
                                NULL,
                    MENU_ITEM,
                                MENU_STRING, "Save...",
                                MENU_NOTIFY_PROC, menu_stub,
                                NULL,
                    MENUITEM_SPACE, NULL,
                    MENU_ITEM,
                                MENU_STRING, "Print...",
                                MENU_NOTIFY_PROC, menu_stub,
                                NULL,
                    MENU_ITEM,
                                MENU_STRING, "Quit",
                                MENU_NOTIFY_PROC, exit,
                                NULL,
                    XV_KEY_DATA, BASE_FRAME_KEY, frame,
                    NULL );

        (void) xv_create ( panel, PANEL_BUTTON,
                    PANEL_LABEL_STRING, "File",
                    PANEL_ITEM_MENU,    m,
                    NULL );
```

```
/* Create the view menu.  Since this is application -
 * specific, I put generic strings in.
 */
m = (Menu) xv_create ( XV_NULL, MENU,
                MENU_ITEM,
                                MENU_STRING, "Item 1",
                                MENU_NOTIFY_PROC, menu_stub,
                                NULL,

                MENU_ITEM,
                                MENU_STRING, "Item 2",
                                MENU_NOTIFY_PROC, menu_stub,
                                NULL,
                NULL );

(void) xv_create ( panel, PANEL_BUTTON,
                PANEL_LABEL_STRING, "View",
                PANEL_ITEM_MENU,    m,
                NULL );

/* Undo submenu
 */
m_undo = (Menu) xv_create ( XV_NULL, MENU,
                MENU_STRINGS, "Undo Last Change", "Undo All Changes",
                                                NULL,
                MENU_NOTIFY_PROC, menu_stub,
                NULL );

/* edit menu
 */
m = (Menu) xv_create ( XV_NULL, MENU,
                MENU_ITEM,
                                MENU_STRING, "Again",
                                MENU_NOTIFY_PROC, menu_stub,
                                NULL,
                MENU_ITEM,
                                MENU_STRING, "Undo",
                                MENU_PULLRIGHT, m_undo,
                                NULL,
                MENUITEM_SPACE, NULL,
                MENU_ITEM,
                                MENU_STRING, "Cut",
                                MENU_NOTIFY_PROC, menu_stub,
                                NULL,
                MENU_ITEM,
                                MENU_STRING, "Copy",
                                MENU_NOTIFY_PROC, menu_stub,
                                NULL,
                MENU_ITEM,
                                MENU_STRING, "Paste",
                                MENU_NOTIFY_PROC, menu_stub,
                                NULL,
                MENUITEM_SPACE, NULL,
                MENU_ITEM,
                                MENU_STRING, "Select All",
                                MENU_NOTIFY_PROC, menu_stub,
                                NULL,
                MENU_ITEM,
                                MENU_STRING, "Clear",
                                MENU_NOTIFY_PROC, menu_stub,
                                NULL,
```

```
                    NULL );
(void) xv_create ( panel, PANEL_BUTTON,
            PANEL_LABEL_STRING, "Edit",
            PANEL_ITEM_MENU,      m,
            NULL );

/* fit panel to created panel items
 */
window_fit_height ( panel );

/* create the canvas
 */
 canvas = (Canvas) xv_create ( frame, CANVAS,
            XV_X,                  0,
            XV_WIDTH,              WIN_EXTEND_TO_EDGE,

            XV_HEIGHT,             WIN_EXTEND_TO_EDGE,

            CANVAS_REPAINT_PROC,   repaint,
            CANVAS_X_PAINT_WINDOW, TRUE,
            NULL );

/* fit frame around panel and canvas
 */
window_fit ( frame );

/* create the popup menu
 */
m = (Menu) xv_create ( XV_NULL, MENU,
            MENU_GEN_PIN_WINDOW, frame, "Popup Menu",
            MENU_PULLRIGHT_ITEM, "Undo", m_undo,
            MENU_ACTION_ITEM, "Print...", menu_stub,
            NULL );

/* attach popup menu and event procedure to paint window

 */
xv_set ( canvas_paint_window ( canvas ),
            WIN_CONSUME_EVENTS,             WIN_MOUSE_BUTTONS, NULL,
            WIN_EVENT_PROC,              show_popup,
            XV_KEY_DATA,         POPUP_KEY, m,
            NULL );

xv_main_loop ( frame );
return ( 0 );
}
```

Miscellaneous

18

CHAPTER

The following topics didn't really seem to fit into any definite categories, so I've lumped them together here.

WINDOW START STATE

To start a program as an icon, set the base frame's **FRAME_CLOSED** attribute to **TRUE**.

```
Frame base;

(void) xv_set ( base, FRAME_CLOSED, TRUE, NULL );
```

If users will normally keep your program as an icon until needed, it's best to set the default to **FRAME_CLOSED**. The user can still control whether or not the program comes up as an icon, by using the **−Wi** (icon) and **+Wi** (open) command line switches.

```
host% misc +Wi
```

This can be useful if the icon uses animation tied to conditions. When a certain condition that requires user intervention is encountered (like the arrival of mail or connection to a remote site), you can change the icon to alert the user that the condition has arrived.

CHECKING FOR MONO/COLOR

The easiest way to see whether the monitor is monochrome or color is to check the depth of the window. In XView 3.0, you can use

```
xv_get ( base_frame, XV_DEPTH )
```

to check. If **xv_get()** returns 1, the screen is monochrome. Otherwise, it's color. XView 2.0 did not support **XV_DEPTH**, so you should use **WIN_DEPTH** instead.

150

CHECKING XVIEW VERSION

Starting with version 3.0 of XView, there are ways of testing which version of XView is being used. One way is to use the variable **xv_version**, which contains a string that describes which version of XView you're using.

From what I've seen, the usual question is, "Is this XView 2.0 or XView 3.0?" I use the **XV_VERSION_NUMBER** **#define** for this. If it's defined, then I have XView 3.0 or better. Otherwise, I probably have XView 2.0. For example, I could do the following to determine which attribute to use to find out whether the monitor has color:

```
printf ( "This system is %s\n", ( xv_get ( frame,
#ifdef XV_VERSION_NUMBER
                XV_DEPTH,
#else
                WIN_DEPTH,
#endif
                         ) == 1 )
                            ? "monochrome" : "color" );
```

If **XV_VERSION_NUMBER** is defined, then **XV_DEPTH** will be used instead of **WIN_DEPTH**.

A better way of checking would be to explicitly test what version is being used:

```
#if XV_VERSION_NUMBER == 3000
```

This determines whether you're using version 3.0. Since there will continually be updates, it's best to check for the version that you're using as a target version.

USAGE HELP MESSAGE FUNCTION

If your program uses any custom command line switches, you should define a custom *usage message* function, which can be invoked to tell the user what switches are available. XView automatically defines its own usage message, **xv_usage()**, which it attaches as the main usage function. To add your own command line options, create your usage function:

```
int my_usage ( name )
char *name;
{
    printf( "This is a defined message\n\n" );
    xv_usage ( name );
    exit ( XV_OK );
}
```

This will print the message "This is a defined message" before printing the XView-defined command line args with **xv_usage()**.

You tell your program about this usage function with the **XV_USAGE_PROC** attribute in the **xv_init()** call.

```
xv_init ( XV_INIT_ARGC_PTR_ARGV, &argc, argv,
        XV_USAGE_PROC, my_usage,
        NULL);
```

The following example will use a function, **my_usage()**, as the usage procedure.

SAMPLE PROGRAM

The sample program demonstrates how these features work. It will display the version number (if one exists) and state whether it is running on a monochrome or a color system. It also has a usage function, which can be invoked by running the program with the **−help** option.

```c
/* misc.c -- Open Look miscellaneous features
 * Author:   Kenneth Bibb
 * Jan 1992 -- Arastar Consulting
 *------------------------------------------
 */

#include <stdlib.h>
#include <sys/param.h>
#include <xview/xview.h>
#include <xview/panel.h>
#include <xview/canvas.h>
#include <xview/xv_xrect.h>
#include <xview/openmenu.h>
#include <xview/icon.h>
#include <xview/svrimage.h>

int my_usage ( name )
char *name;
{
        printf ( "This is a programmer defined\n" );
        printf ( "Usage message\n\n" );
        xv_usage ( name );
        exit ( XV_OK );
}

int main ( argc, argv )
int argc;
char **argv;
{
        Frame               frame;
        Canvas              canvas;
        Panel               panel;

        /* initialization
         */
        xv_init ( XV_INIT_ARGC_PTR_ARGV, &argc, argv,
                    XV_USAGE_PROC, my_usage,
                    NULL);
        /* Create something for the DEPTH attribute to work on
         */
        frame = (Frame) xv_create (NULL, FRAME,
                    FRAME_LABEL,  argv[0],
                    FRAME_CLOSED, TRUE,
                    XV_X,         300,
                    XV_Y,         175,
                    NULL );

/* version check */
#ifdef XV_VERSION_NUMBER
        printf( "XV_version: [%s]\n",xv_version );
#else
```

```
            printf( "There is no version number\n" );
#endif




/* color check */
#ifdef XV_VERSION_NUMBER
        printf ( "This system is %s\n", ( xv_get ( frame, XV_DEPTH ) == 1 )
                        ? "monochrome" : "color" );
#else
        printf( "This system is %s\n", ( xv_get ( frame, WIN_DEPTH ) == 1 )
                        ? "monochrome" : "color" );
#endif

        xv_main_loop ( frame );
        return( 0 );
}
```

Multiline Text Fields

19

C H A P T E R

Multiline text fields let you display a larger amount of text than is possible with a normal text field. Although they appear to be multiline, they are really just a single large text field. Because of this, you can't embed linefeeds or returns in the field. There are still places where these things are useful. A multiline text field has the attributes shown in Figure 19.1.

MULTILINE TEXT FIELD CALLBACK

Multiline text fields have a callback like the following:

```
Panel_setting text_notify_proc ( Panel_item multitext, Event *event )
{

}
```

This function is the same as the one used for normal panel text items. For more information on them, see Chapter 27.

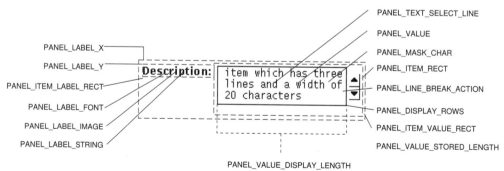

FIGURE 19.1 Multiline Text Field Attributes

PUTTING TEXT INTO A MULTILINE FIELD

Assigning text to a multiline text field is the same as assigning text to a normal text field—you use the **PANEL_VALUE** attribute:

```
Panel_item multiline;

(void) xv_set ( multiline,
        PANEL_VALUE,                 "This is a string which will"
                                     "be put into a multiline text"
                                     "field.",

        NULL );
```

RETRIEVING TEXT FROM A MULTILINE FIELD

Retrieving text from a multiline text field is the same as retrieving text from a normal text field. You use the **PANEL_VALUE** attribute:

```
Panel_item multiline;
char      *s;

s = (char *) xv_get ( multiline, PANEL_VALUE );
```

SAMPLE PROGRAM

The sample program displays a multiline object with three rows and 20 columns.

```
/* multi.c -- demonstration of a multiline text field
 * Author:  Kenneth Bibb
 */

#include <xview/xview.h>
#include <xview/panel.h>
#include <xview/canvas.h>

main ( argc, argv )
int argc;
char **argv;
{
      Frame frame;
      Panel panel;

      xv_init ( XV_INIT_ARGC_PTR_ARGV, &argc, argv, NULL );

      /* create the base frame */
      frame = (Frame) xv_create ( NULL, FRAME,
                  FRAME_LABEL,        argv[0],
                  FRAME_SHOW_FOOTER,  TRUE,
                  XV_X,               300,
                  XV_Y,               175,
                  NULL );

      /* create the panel */
      panel = (Panel) xv_create ( frame, PANEL, NULL );
      (void) xv_create ( panel, PANEL_MULTILINE_TEXT,
                  PANEL_LABEL_STRING,        "Description:",
                  PANEL_DISPLAY_ROWS,        3,
```

```
                  PANEL_VALUE_DISPLAY_LENGTH, 20,
                  PANEL_VALUE,                 "This is an example of \
a multiline text item that has three lines and a width of 20 characters ",
                  NULL );
      window_fit ( panel );
      window_fit ( frame );

      xv_main_loop ( frame );
}
```

Notices

Although notices aren't as sexy as frames, they are an important part of a GUI. Used sparingly, they can enhance a program. Make the most commonly used option the default, try to be clear in what you say, and your notices will make you proud.

But first, you can't do fully compliant notices with XView 3.0. When you enable **NOTICE_LOCK_SCREEN**, it *looks* as if you have an Open Look GUI–compliant notice, but it locks the whole screen, which is not compliant. (Blocking the application is compliant, but you shouldn't be blocking the entire screen.)

On the other hand, you can create a notice with **NOTICE_LOCK_SCREEN** set to **FALSE**. It won't *look* like the Open Look–compliant notice, but it at least won't block events to other windows. This is more compliant than the previous example, since the OLFS says that the shadow is optional for implementations that don't support nonrectangular windows. Sun will, we hope, create a fully compliant notify package as part of the next XView release.

The attributes of a notice are shown in Figure 20.1.

NOTICE CALLBACK

The callback for a notice has the following prototype:

```
void
notice_proc ( XV_Notice notice, int value, Event *event );
```

XVIEW 2.0 NOTICES VS. XVIEW 3.0 NOTICES

XView 2.0 did not have a **NOTICE** package—it used the SunView1–compatible **notice_prompt()** function for generating notices. Since a lot of programs were written using the old method, **notice_prompt()** is still provided for backward compatibility. Since it isn't consistent with XView packages, you should avoid **notice_prompt()** for any new programming projects that you're working on.

The new **NOTICE** package is used like any other XView package, using **xv_create()**, **xv_set()**, and **xv_get()**. Notices do not use **xv_find()**.

GOOD NOTICE DESIGN

Some of the recommended design is done by XView. It will handle things like the shadow (yeah, right) and beeps (it looks at how the resources are set). But other things have to be done by you.

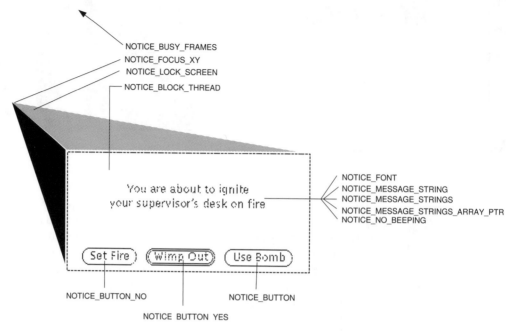

FIGURE 20.1 Notice Attributes

You should always provide a way of canceling the action. Providing situations with no means of backing out are good only if you're writing user-hostile software. A user who feels comfortable exploring your program will become more effective in using it.

Don't have the buttons set to strings like "Yes," "No," "Maybe," or "OK." The user may be in a hurry and may not realize what the notice is really saying. Also, try to word the action in a positive way: "Apply" instead of "Don't Abandon," for instance. If there are multiple actions available, provide them all on the notice.

Avoid locking the entire screen! Window systems are meant for multitasking—the user probably has something running in another window while using your system. If you do a full screen block, the user may not be able to take care of time-sensitive events in other windows in time. It's recommended that you lock the current event, but don't lock the entire screen. Be a good screen neighbor.

Make all of the current application's frames show the busy pattern. It's fairly easy to implement, and it helps associate the notice to a program. It also has the added advantage of showing you where you *can't* type until the notice is dismissed.

If you are displaying a notice for informational purposes, have a confirm button (XView will automatically create this for you if you don't include any strings) and turn off beeps, with **NOTICE_NO_BEEPING** set to **TRUE**.

Make the default action the most commonly used action. Notices that try to make the system foolproof are useful only to fools.

Finally, the OLFS recommends that you flush the input buffer when you first bring up the notice. This prevents mouse-ahead (or type-ahead) commands from activating unexpectedly.

In summary:

- Let the user cancel actions.
- Clearly label your buttons.
- Avoid locking the full screen.
- The current application's frames should go "Busy."
- Information notices should have a "Confirm" button.
- Information notices should not beep.
- The most-used action should be the default.
- Flush the input buffer.

AN OPEN LOOK–COMPLIANT SKELETON NOTICE_EVENT_PROC

It's easy to say things like "flush when you're done," but how do you actually implement these things? This is left as an exercise for the reader to figure out. (Not really—it just seemed like an appropriate thing to say.)

These attributes are spread over the notice definition and the notify callback. The following is an example of a minimal notice definition that meets all of these Open Look compliance criteria.

```
#include <xview/xview.h>
#include <xview/notice.h>
#include <xview/panel.h>

Frame frame, Fnotice;
Panel panel;

(void) xv_create ( panel, NOTICE,
      NOTICE_MESSAGE_STRINGS, "Before you show those pictures",
            "to your friends at work,",
            "remember that your wife",
            "will kill you when she finds out",
            NULL,
      NOTICE_BUTTON,          "Show them anyway", 200,
      NOTICE_BUTTON,          "Wimp Out", 201,
      NOTICE_BUSY_FRAMES,     frame, Fnotice, NULL,
      NULL );
```

The default button is determined by the notice package as one of the following:

- **NOTICE_BUTTON_YES**
- First **NOTICE_BUTTON**
- A (Confirm) button, which **NOTICE** creates

In the foregoing example, the "Show them anyway" button will be the default because of the second rule. Alternatively, we could have written

```
NOTICE_BUTTON_YES, "Show them anyway",
NOTICE_BUTTON_NO, "Wimp Out",
```

This may not be as clear as the **NOTICE_BUTTON** attribute, so I tend to use the **NOTICE_BUTTON** attribute instead. You can also mix **NOTICE_BUTTON_YES** in with the **NOTICE_BUTTON**s (useful if you don't want the first button to be the default). Generally, however, it would be better to keep them separated (it's also best to have the leftmost option as the default).

This notice blocks only the current application (the default). If we wanted to defy Open Look standards, we would have to add an additional attribute to the **xv_create()**.

Finally, the **NOTICE_BUSY_FRAMES** sets the frames of the named windows to the busy pattern. It accepts a list of frames, terminated with a **NULL**.

BLOCKING NOTICES

Notices that block all applications on the screen are not functionally Open Look–compliant. We will not go into them here. Use nonblocking (default) notices whenever possible. It's true that they don't look Open Look–compliant, but at least they provide the correct Open Look feel.

FLUSHING INPUT BUFFER

To flush the input buffer, you can do the following:

```
(void) xv_set ( server, SERVER_SYNC_AND_PROCESS_EVENTS, NULL);
```

If you do not have the server, you can get it with the following routine:

```
Xv_Server server;

server = (Server) xv_get ( screen, SCREEN_SERVER );
```

If you don't have the screen, you can get it with

```
Xv_Screen screen;

screen = xv_get ( base, XV_SCREEN );
```

MAKING WINDOWS GO BUSY

According to the Open Look GUI standards, when a notice is displayed, all associated windows should have their headers change to the busy pattern. The **NOTICE_BUSY_FRAMES** attribute is used for this. You need to provide a **NULL**-terminated list of frames as an argument to this attribute. For example, if your application has two frames, **frame** and **Fnotice**, you could say

```
xv_set ( notice, NOTICE, NOTICE_BUSY_FRAMES, frame, Fnotice,
NULL);
```

Alternatively, you could use the following routine, which will recursively walk through a frame tree, making all of the subframes busy. This routine is invoked with a function call like

```
subtree_walk ( base, FRAME_BUSY, TRUE );
```

where **base** is the application's base frame, **FRAME_BUSY** is the attribute that you want to set, and **TRUE** is the value that you want **FRAME_BUSY** to assume. The **subtree_walk()** function looks like the following:

```
int
stw ( base, attrib, val, i)
Frame base;
Attr_attribute attrib;
int val;
int i;
{
      Frame sub = (Frame) xv_get ( base, FRAME_NTH_SUBFRAME, i );

      if(sub)  {
         subtree_walk ( sub, attrib, val );
         stw ( base, attrib, val, i+1);
      } else
      return;
}

void subtree_walk ( base, attrib, val )
Frame base;
Attr_attribute attrib;
int val;
{
      xv_set ( base, attrib, val, NULL );
      stw ( base, attrib, val, 1);
}
```

SAMPLE PROGRAM

The following sample program demonstrates a couple of different notices.

```
/* notice.c -- Open Look basic notice types
 * Author:  Kenneth Bibb
 * March 1992 -- Arastar Consulting
 *------------
 */

#include <stdlib.h>
#include <sys/param.h>
#include <xview/xview.h>
#include <xview/panel.h>
#include <xview/openmenu.h>
#include <xview/xv_xrect.h>
#include <xview/notice.h>
#include <xview/server.h>

Attr_attribute FRAME_BASE_KEY;
Attr_attribute PANEL_BASE_KEY;
Attr_attribute SERVER_KEY;

/* This routine shows an Open Look--compliant notice,
 * complete with input queue flushing and default buttons,
 * and it doesn't block all input to the window.
 * It does NOT have the shadow showing where it
 * came from, however.  A future attribute?
 */
void
show_notice ( item, event )
Panel_item item;
```

```
Event *event;
{
        Xv_Server server = xv_get ( item, XV_KEY_DATA, SERVER_KEY);
        Frame frame  = xv_get ( item, XV_KEY_DATA, FRAME_BASE_KEY);
        Panel panel  = xv_get ( item, XV_KEY_DATA, PANEL_BASE_KEY);

        /* flush input buffer */
        xv_set ( server,
                        SERVER_SYNC_AND_PROCESS_EVENTS,
                        NULL);

        /* create notify popup
         *------------------------
         * The weird use of buttons lets us define
         * a default button that is not the first button.
         * We are also able to find out which button was pressed
         * this way.
         */
        (void) xv_create ( panel, NOTICE,
                        XV_HELP_DATA,            "help:notice",
                        NOTICE_BLOCK_THREAD,     TRUE,
                        NOTICE_LOCK_SCREEN,      FALSE,
                        NOTICE_MESSAGE_STRINGS,  "You are about to ignite",
                                                 "your supervisor's
                                                 "desk on fire",

                        NULL,
                        NOTICE_BUTTON_NO,        "Set Fire",
                        NOTICE_BUTTON_YES,       "Wimp Out",
                        NOTICE_BUTTON,           "Use Bomb", 202,

                        NOTICE_BUSY_FRAMES,      frame, NULL,
                        XV_SHOW,                 TRUE,
                        NULL );
}

/* This is a standard Xview notice.
 * It is missing some of the things suggested by the OLSG,
 * but it gets the job done.
 */
void
show_xview ( item, event )
Panel_item item;
Event *event;
{
        Panel panel = xv_get ( item, XV_KEY_DATA, PANEL_BASE_KEY
        );

        (void) xv_create ( panel, NOTICE,
                        NOTICE_MESSAGE_STRINGS, "Standard XView Notice",

                                                NULL,
                                XV_SHOW,        TRUE,
                                NULL );
}

/* This is not a useful notice.
 * Just thought you might like to see what the defaults are.
```

```
*/
void
show_dxv ( item, event )
Panel_item item;
Event *event;
{
        Panel panel = xv_get ( item, XV_KEY_DATA, PANEL_BASE_KEY );

        (void) xv_create ( panel, NOTICE,
                        XV_SHOW,                    TRUE,
                        NULL);
}

/* This is a blocking notice.
 * It is not Open Look--compliant, but it looks nice.
 */
void
show_block ( item, event )
Panel_item item;
Event *event;
{
        Panel panel = xv_get ( item, XV_KEY_DATA, PANEL_BASE_KEY );

        (void) xv_create ( panel, NOTICE,
                        NOTICE_MESSAGE_STRINGS, "This is not compliant",
                                                "Full screen blocking is bad",
                                                NULL,
                        NOTICE_LOCK_SCREEN,     TRUE,
                        XV_SHOW,                TRUE,
                        NULL );
}




int
main ( argc, argv )
int argc;
char **argv;
{
      Frame               frame;
      Panel               panel;
      Panel_item          ph, pi, pj;

      xv_init ( XV_INIT_ARGC_PTR_ARGV, &argc, argv, NULL );

      FRAME_BASE_KEY = xv_unique_key ();
      PANEL_BASE_KEY = xv_unique_key ();
      SERVER_KEY = xv_unique_key ();

      frame = (Frame) xv_create ( NULL, FRAME,
                      FRAME_LABEL, argv[0],
                      XV_X,          300,
                      XV_Y,          175,
                      NULL );
      panel = (Panel) xv_create ( frame, PANEL,
                      NULL );
```

```
        ph = (Panel_item) xv_create ( panel, PANEL_BUTTON,
                PANEL_LABEL_STRING,             "OL Std Notice",
                PANEL_NOTIFY_PROC,              show_notice,
                XV_KEY_DATA, FRAME_BASE_KEY, frame,

                XV_KEY_DATA, PANEL_BASE_KEY, panel,

                XV_KEY_DATA, SERVER_KEY,

                                       xv_get ( xv_get(
                                              frame,XV_SCREEN ),
                                          SCREEN_SERVER ),

                NULL );
    xv_set ( panel, PANEL_DEFAULT_ITEM, ph );
        ph = (Panel_item) xv_create ( panel, PANEL_BUTTON,
                PANEL_LABEL_STRING,             "Std XView Notice",

                PANEL_NOTIFY_PROC,              show_xview,

                XV_KEY_DATA, PANEL_BASE_KEY,  panel,
                NULL );
        ph = (Panel_item) xv_create ( panel, PANEL_BUTTON,
                PANEL_LABEL_STRING,             "Default Std XView Notice",
                PANEL_NOTIFY_PROC,              show_dxv,
                XV_KEY_DATA, PANEL_BASE_KEY,  panel,
                NULL );
        ph = (Panel_item) xv_create ( panel, PANEL_BUTTON,
                PANEL_LABEL_STRING,             "Blocking Notice",
                PANEL_NOTIFY_PROC,              show_block,

                XV_KEY_DATA, PANEL_BASE_KEY,  panel,
                NULL );

    window_fit ( panel );
    window_fit ( frame );

    xv_main_loop ( frame );
}
```

The Notifier

All input to an XView program is handled through the Notifier. The Notifier acts as the central switching station for keystrokes, mouse movements, button clicks, and UNIX signals. All such actions are translated to *events* and are delivered to XView objects that have registered an interest in them.

A great deal of a program's interaction with the Notifier is handled automatically by the various XView packages. For example, keystrokes on a text item are handled by the panel package and converted into the **PANEL_VALUE** of that item without the Notifier's actions ever being directly exposed to the programmer.

A closer level of interaction with the Notifier takes places when you register a *notify procedure* for a particular item. One place where you're almost sure to do this is with a button, since it's not very useful without such a procedure. This is still a quite heavily filtered interaction; the panel package handles most of the events the button receives, such as the Select mouse button is pressed over it, delivering a "button down" event, and the button provides its previewing feedback. Your notify procedure is only called when the Select button is released and the "button up" event is delivered.

Your closest contact with the Notifier is done via *event procedures,* which may be associated with XView objects, such as panel items, or events external to your program, such as UNIX signals.

Because the Notifier sits between your program and the rest of the outside world, it is unsafe to use certain UNIX system calls or procedures that use these system calls. The XVPM lists these; and they are recapped briefly in Table 21.1.

◼ REPLACEMENT FOR SYSTEM()

For many of the UNIX functions and system calls that should not be used in an XView program, the Notifier has a direct replacement. One that isn't directly replaced is **system**(3).

One reason for this is that **system**(3) is *mainline-based* (to use the terminology described in the XVPM): When you make the call to **system**(3), your program blocks until the program you're executing returns.

The other reason that **system**(3) isn't directly replaced is perhaps that since it is a fairly simple routine, made up of a little bit of signal handling, a **fork()**, an **exec∗()** of some kind, and a **wait()**, its implementation is left as an exercise to the programmer. Arguably, this isn't the perfect attitude for a toolkit library to take, so we'll try to fill the void with something we'll cleverly call **xv_system()**, listed at the end of this chapter.

165

Function	Use This
sigvec(2)	notify_set_signal_func() or notify_set_destroy_func()
signal(3)	notify_set_signal_fun() or notify_set_destroy_func()
setitimer(2)	notify_set_itimer_func()
getitimer(2)	notify_set_itimer_func()
alarm(3)	notify_set_itimer_func()
wait(2)	notify_set_wait3_func()
wait3(2)	notify_set_wait3_func()
ioctl(FIONBIO, ...)	notify_set_input_func() and notify_set_output_func()
ioctl(FIOASYNC, ...)	notify_set_input_func() and notify_set_output_func()
system(3)	xv_system()

TABLE 21.1 Bad Functions and Their Replacements

As we mentioned, the original **system**(3) is a blocking function: Internally, it calls **wait()** and thus does not return until **wait()** returns. This isn't how **wait()**'s Notifier-based replacement, **notify_set_wait3_func()**, works; in typical event-driven fashion, you use it to register a procedure that is called when the child process dies or is stopped.

Because of this, **xv_system()** differs from **system()** in a couple of important ways. First, it returns immediately, rather than waiting for the child process to exit. This is fine in many instances, as many programs that call **system()** never check its return value anyway. The other differences relate to the first. **xv_system()** cannot return the return value of the child, since the child may not have exited yet. Instead, it returns the process ID of the child. The final difference is that **xv_system()** takes a second argument, which may be either **NULL** or the name of a function you provide. If you pass a function, that function will be called when the child process invoked by **xv_system()** exits. The differences in operation between the two calls are shown in Figure 21.1.

The **commander** program, listed at the end of this chapter, is a simple XView program that uses the **xv_system()** call; **wait_return()** is the function that we pass to get the return value.

█████ █N INTERPOSITION EXAMPLE

The **interpose.c** program, listed at the end of this chapter, shows how interposition can be used to create a panel item to support floating-point integers without modifying the XView library itself. This sort of extensibility can be used to change the behavior of XView by intercepting an event before it arrives at its destination and then making modifications to the event data before passing it along. The interpositions this program performs are illustrated in Figure 21.2.

█████ █NTERPOSING ON A TEXT SUBWINDOW

Although most of the XView Notifier functionality is identical to what was available under Sunview, some of the additional features of XView require minor changes. One example came up recently in porting a user's code. They had been interposing on a text window as follows:

```
Textsw textsw;

textsw = (Textsw) xv_create ( frame, TEXTSW, NULL );

(void) notify_interpose_event_func ( textsw, mynotifier, NOTIFY_SAFE );
```

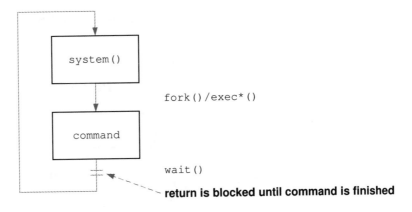

return is blocked until command is finished

system()

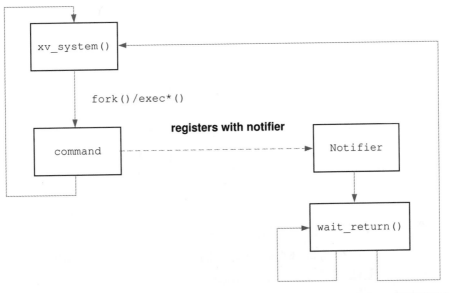

xv_system()   **loop until done**   **return if WIFEXITED**

FIGURE 21.1 `xv_system()` and Processes

normal process

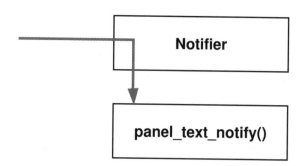

upper case

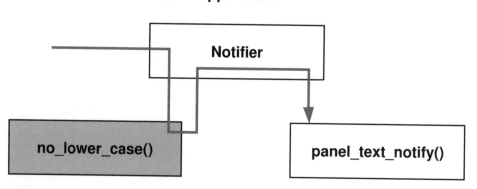

FIGURE 21.2a How `interpose.c` Works

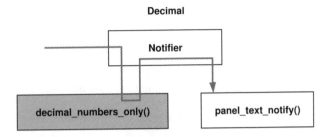

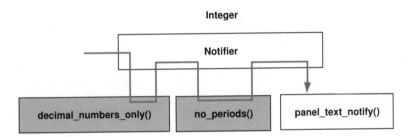

FIGURE 21.2b How `interpose.c` Works

This worked under SunView, but under XView there's a new wrinkle. Text windows, like other objects subclassed from the **OPENWIN** class, may have their windows split into subwindows. These subwindows are each known as *views;* events for each view are handled by the **OPENWIN** associated with it.

The last line in the foregoing fragment can be changed to get events from the "zeroth" view, which is currently the view associated with the first window created, and it will work:

```
(void) notify_interpose_event_func (
        xv_get ( textsw, OPENWIN_NTH_VIEW, 0 ),
        mynotifier,
        NOTIFY_SAFE );
```

To capture events on every view, you may need to change the code still further, using the **OPENWIN_EACH_VIEW** and **OPENWIN_END_EACH** macros, which will loop you through every existing view:

```
Xv_Window view;
OPENWIN_EACH_VIEW(textsw, view)
        notify_interpose_event_func ( view, mynotifier, NOTIFY_SAFE );
OPENWIN_END_EACH
```

SAMPLE PROGRAMS

Makefile	A Makefile for creating the **commander** example
commander.c	Front-end test for **xv_system()**
xv_system.c	The **xv_system()** replacement function call
interpose.c	Panel text item interposition demonstration

```
#
# Makefile for commander demonstration
#

CC = cc
CFLAGS += -g
CPPFLAGS += -I$(OPENWINHOME)/include
LDFLAGS += -L$(OPENWINHOME)/lib
LDLIBS += -lxview -lolgx -lX11

commander: commander.o xv_system.o
    $(CC) $(LDFLAGS) -o commander commander.o xv_system.o $(LDLIBS)
```

```
/* commander.c - Test of xv_system() call.
 * Author: Larry Wake
 */

#include <stdio.h>
#include <xview/xview.h>
#include <xview/panel.h>
#include <xview/notify.h>


/*
 * Global object definitions.
 */
Frame base_frame;

/*
 *  Function to receive the return value of the child process invoked by
 *  xv_system().
 */
Notify_value
wait_return ( client, pid, status, rusage )
Notify_client client;
int pid;
union wait *status;
struct rusage *rusage;
{
    if ( WIFEXITED ( *status ) ) {
        char msg[50];
```

```
           sprintf ( msg, "Process %d returned with status %d.", pid,
               status->w_retcode );
           xv_set ( base_frame, FRAME_LEFT_FOOTER, msg, NULL );


           return NOTIFY_DONE;
        } else
           return NOTIFY_IGNORED;
}


/*
 * Notify callback function for `cmd_item'.
 */
Panel_setting
cmd_notify ( item, event )
Panel_item item;
Event *event;
{
    char msg[50];
    int pid;

    pid = xv_system ( (char *) xv_get ( item, PANEL_VALUE ), wait_return );
    sprintf ( msg, "Process %d launched.", pid );
    xv_set ( base_frame, FRAME_LEFT_FOOTER, msg, NULL );
    return panel_text_notify ( item, event );
}

main ( argc, argv )
int     argc;
char    **argv;
{
    Panel panel;

    xv_init ( XV_INIT_ARGC_PTR_ARGV, &argc, argv, NULL );

    base_frame = xv_create ( NULL, FRAME,
        XV_LABEL,           "Command Executor",
        FRAME_SHOW_FOOTER, TRUE,
        NULL );

    panel = xv_create ( base_frame, PANEL,
        WIN_BORDER, TRUE,
        NULL );

    (void) xv_create ( panel, PANEL_TEXT,
        XV_X,                         16,
        XV_Y,                         16,
        PANEL_VALUE_DISPLAY_LENGTH,   40,
        PANEL_VALUE_STORED_LENGTH,    80,
        PANEL_LABEL_STRING,           "Command:",
        PANEL_NOTIFY_PROC,            cmd_notify,
        NULL );

    window_fit ( panel );
    window_fit ( base_frame );

    xv_main_loop ( base_frame );
    exit ( 0 );
}
```

```
/* xv_system.c -- an XView replacement for system().
 * Author:  Larry Wake
 *------------------------
 * xv_system() -- an XView replacement for system().  First argument is
 * that of a string to be passed to /bin/sh executed as a child process,
 * second argument is the function to be called when the child process
 * returns.  If func is NULL, the default proc will be called.

 *
 * return is pid if we forked successfully, -1 if we didn't.

 */

#include <xview/notify.h>

int xv_system ( s, func )
char *s;
Notify_func func;
{
    static Notify_client xv_sys_client = 42;    /* Life, the Universe,...  */
    pid_t pid;
    pid = fork ();
    if ( pid == -1 )              /* error */
                return -1;
    else
        if ( pid == 0 ) { /* child */
                    execl ( "/usr/bin/sh","sh","-c", s, (char *) NULL );
                    _exit ( 127 );
        }

    if ( func == NULL )
                notify_set_wait3_func ( xv_sys_client, notify_default_wait3,
                                        pid );
    else
                notify_set_wait3_func ( xv_sys_client, func, pid );

    return pid;
}
```

```
/*
 * item_interpose.c -- demonstration of interposition on Panel_items.
 * Richard M. Goldstein, Window Developer Environment
 * SunSoft, Inc.
 * April 1992
 */


/*
 * Example of a generic method of interposing on Panel_item's
 * without modifying the XView library to support this directly.
 */
```

```
#include <stdio.h>
#include <xview/xview.h>
#include <xview/panel.h>
#include <xview/notify.h>


static Notify_value   base_item_event_handler ();
static Notify_value   decimal_numbers_only ();
static Notify_value   no_periods ();
static Notify_value   no_lower_case ();
static void           post_panel_item_events ();
static void           register_panel_items ();


static Attr_attribute EVENT_PROC_KEY;


#define isdot(chr) ( (chr) == '.' )


/***********************************************************************/


void
main ( argc,argv )
int argc;
char **argv;
{
    Frame frame;
    Panel panel;
    Panel_text_item upper_text;
    Panel_text_item number_text;
    Panel_text_item decimal_text;

    (void) xv_init ( XV_INIT_ARGC_PTR_ARGV, &argc, argv, NULL );
    EVENT_PROC_KEY = xv_unique_key ();

    frame = xv_create ( XV_NULL, FRAME,
                            XV_LABEL, "Modified Textfields",
                            NULL );

    panel = xv_create ( frame, PANEL,
                            PANEL_LAYOUT, PANEL_VERTICAL,
                            NULL );

    upper_text = xv_create ( panel, PANEL_TEXT,
                                    PANEL_LABEL_STRING,           "Upper Case:",
                                    PANEL_VALUE_DISPLAY_LENGTH, 16,
                                    NULL );

    decimal_text = xv_create ( panel, PANEL_TEXT,
                                    PANEL_LABEL_STRING,           "Decimal:",
                                    PANEL_VALUE_DISPLAY_LENGTH, 12,
                                    NULL );

    number_text = xv_create ( panel, PANEL_TEXT,
                                    PANEL_LABEL_STRING, "Integer:",
                                    PANEL_VALUE_DISPLAY_LENGTH, 12,
                                    NULL );
```

```
    /* register panel items with the notifier */
    register_panel_items ( panel );

    /* application-specific handlers */
    notify_interpose_event_func ( upper_text, no_lower_case, NOTIFY_SAFE );
    notify_interpose_event_func ( decimal_text, decimal_numbers_only,
                                  NOTIFY_SAFE );

    /*
     * Implement integer by using existing decimal handler and weeding
     * out the periods.  Note:  Interposers are stacked, so order is
     * important.
     */
    notify_interpose_event_func ( number_text, decimal_numbers_only,
                                  NOTIFY_SAFE );
    notify_interpose_event_func ( number_text, no_periods, NOTIFY_SAFE );

    window_fit ( panel );
    window_fit ( frame );
    xv_main_loop ( frame );
    exit ( 0 );
}


/*************************************************************************/
/* These routines are generic to the panel items.   */
/*************************************************************************/


/*
 * Traverse each item in the given Panel and register our base event handler
 * for it with the Notifier.  Also, replace the default event handler with
 * one that posts events via the Notifier and attach the old one onto the
 * item with key-data.  Note:  Once this is done, our Panel_item's are
 * functionally no different than when we started, except that they can
 * now be interposed on.
 */
static void
register_panel_items ( panel )
Panel panel;
{
    Panel_item item;
    void (* items_event_proc)();

    PANEL_EACH_ITEM(panel, item)
        items_event_proc = (void (*)()) xv_get ( item, PANEL_EVENT_PROC );
        xv_set ( item,
                    PANEL_EVENT_PROC,                post_panel_item_events,
                    XV_KEY_DATA,  EVENT_PROC_KEY, items_event_proc,
                    NULL );
        notify_set_event_func ( item, base_item_event_handler, NOTIFY_SAFE);
    PANEL_END_EACH

}


/*
```

```
 * This routine is "generic" in that it will work
 * with any panel item, presuming you set the equally
 * generic "base_item_event_handler" on each panel item
 * you use this with.
 */
static void
post_panel_item_events ( item, event )
Panel_item item;
Event *event;
{
    /*
     * Rather than let the brain-damaged Panel delegate
     * the event directly, post it to the panel item so
     * that an interposition stream can deal with it.
     */
    notify_post_event ( (Notify_client) item, (Notify _event)
                        event, NOTIFY_SAFE );
}




/*
 * The generic base handler for panel items.  This makes
 * a direct call to the items default event handler, just
 * as the Panel would normally do.  Note: A base handler
 * is always the LAST handler to see the event.
 */
static Notify_value
base_item_event_handler ( client, event, arg, type )
Notify_client client;
Notify_event event;
Notify_arg arg;
Notify_event_type type;
{
    void (* items_event_proc)() = (void (*)()) xv_get ( (Panel_item) client,
            XV_KEY_DATA, EVENT_PROC_KEY );

    if ( items_event_proc )
        (* items_event_proc) ( (Panel_item) client, (Event *)event );

    /*
     * Assume the panel item handled the event, as the Panel
     * doesn't return any useful status information.
     */
    return NOTIFY_DONE;
}




/**********************************************************************/
/* These routines are for item/application specific purposes. */
/* For the sake of example, they don't attempt to handle all  */
/* possible events--they are intended to be simple and        */
/* understandable.                                            */
/**********************************************************************/


/*
 * An interposer that can weed out all printable characters
```

```
 * that don't comprise decimal values for a Textfield.
 */
static Notify_value
decimal_numbers_only ( client, event, arg, type )
Notify_client client;
Notify_event event;
Notify_arg arg;
Notify_event_type type;
{
    int id = event_action ( (Event *) event );
    int found_decimal = FALSE;
    char *value;
    char *ptr;

    /*
     * Don't bother to muck with editing events, just
     * make sure they get through.
     */
    if ( !isprint ( id ) )
        return notify_next_event_func ( client, event, arg, type );

    /*
     * For good measure, make sure there is not
     * already a decimal point in the item.
     */
    value = (char *) xv_get ( (Panel_item) client, PANEL_VALUE);
    for ( ptr=value; *ptr; ptr++ )
        if ( isdot (*ptr) ) {
            found_decimal = TRUE;
            break;
        }

    if ( isdigit (id) || (isdot (id) && !found_decimal) )
        return notify_next_event_func ( client, event, arg, type );

    /* Invalid Character! */
    if ( event_is_down ( (Event *) event ) )
        window_bell( (Panel) xv_get ( (Panel_item) client, XV_OWNER) );
        return NOTIFY_DONE;
}



/*
 * An interposer that can filter out the '.' characters
 */
static Notify_value
no_periods ( client, event, arg, type )
Notify_client client;
Notify_event event;
Notify_arg arg;
Notify_event_type type;
{
    int id = event_action ( (Event *) event );

    if ( !isdot (id) )
        return notify_next_event_func ( client, event, arg, type );
    /* No '.' allowed! */
```

```
        if ( event_is_down ( (Event *) event) )
            window_bell ( (Panel) xv_get ( (Panel_item) client, XV_OWNER) );
            return NOTIFY_DONE;
}



/*
 * Force all characters to be upper case
 */
static Notify_value
no_lower_case ( client, event, arg, type )
Notify_client client;
Notify_event event;
Notify_arg arg;
Notify_event_type type;
{
    int id = event_action ( (Event *) event );

    /*
     * It is perfectly legal to modify an event from
     * an interposer.
     */
    if ( !(isalpha (id) && isupper (id) ) )
        event_set_action ( (Event *) event, to upper (id) );

    return notify_next_event_func ( client, event, arg, type );
}
```

The Panel

Panels are where a lot of the design action happens. Your buttons, sliders, menus, and choice settings go here, to name just a few. So the panel itself is usually not noticed by the user, though the things on the panel are.

The attributes of a panel are shown in Figure 22.1.

PANELS AND FRAMES

To attach a panel to a standard frame, do the following:

```
Frame base;
Panel panel;
base = (Frame) xv_create ( XV_NULL, FRAME, NULL ); /* base frame */
panel = (Panel) xv_create ( base, PANEL, NULL );
```

First the standard frame, **base**, is created (I use default settings here to simplify the example). Then we create a **PANEL** object that uses **base** as the parent item. When we reach the program's main loop, the window we create will have a panel.

FRAME_CMDs are different. This subclass already has a panel created; you need to retrieve its handle:

```
Frame base, sub;
Panel Psub;
sub = (Frame) xv_create ( base, FRAME_CMD, NULL );
Psub = (Panel) xv_get ( sub, PANEL, NULL );
```

Here we create a subframe, **sub**. Instead of using an **xv_create()** to create a panel, we use **xv_get()** to retrieve the **FRAME_CMD**'s panel.

MULTIPLE CONTROL PANELS IN A FRAME

To create multiple panels in a single frame, you could use the following code:

```
Frame base;
Panel p1, p2;
base = (Frame) xv_create ( XV_NULL, FRAME,
        FRAME_LABEL, argv[0], NULL );

p1 = (Panel) xv_create ( base, PANEL, NULL);
p2 = (Panel) xv_create ( base, PANEL, NULL);
```

You may need to play with height and width or use the **window_fit()** macros to get things to fit correctly. See the sample program **multipanel.c** at the end of this chapter for an example.

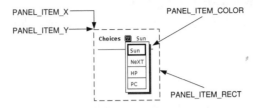

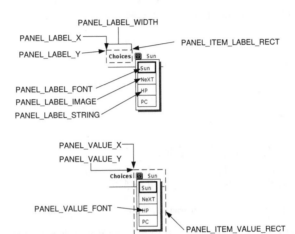

FIGURE 22.1 Panel Attributes

REFRESHING A PANEL

The **panel_paint ()** function can be used to refresh objects that have been hidden by showing other objects in front of them.

```
Panel panel;

panel_paint ( panel, PANEL_CLEAR )
```

This command will clear the panel first before refreshing the panel items.

```
Panel panel;

panel_paint ( panel, PANEL_NO_CLEAR )
```

This call will not clear the panel first, but it will repaint all of the panel's items.

If you need to refresh only certain items, you can refresh them by using a **panel_item** instead of a panel:

```
panel_paint ( panel_item, PANEL_CLEAR )
```

Once again, you can use **PANEL_CLEAR** or **PANEL_NO_CLEAR**.

▮MULTILINE PANEL LABELS

When you define labels on panel items, you can create multiline labels like the following:

```
Product
 Guide:
```

with this attribute:

```
PANEL_LABEL_STRING, "Product \nGuide:",
```

The embedded '\n' will split the string. Each line is right-justified (remember to include trailing spaces on lines that don't end with a colon, if you want the colon to hang). This example would create

```
Product
 Guide:
```

If we left that space out we'd get

```
Product
Guide:
```

▮ALIGNING PANEL ITEMS

The `align_items()` function, which is provided in the sample program `panelalign.c`, lets you align panel items. It is called as follows:

```
align_items ( align_command, item1, ..., NULL );
```

The `align_items()` function accepts a variable number of Panel items. The supported align commands are listed in Table 22.1. To align three buttons (**bi, bj, bk**) by their centers, you could use the following call:

```
align_items ( ALIGN_CENTER, bi, bj, bk, NULL );
```

▮DISTRIBUTING PANEL ITEMS

The `distribute_items()` function, which is provided in the sample program `panelalign.c`, lets you distribute panel items. It uses the items at the extremes as anchors

Command	Action
ALIGN_LEFT	Align left sides by moving horizontally
ALIGN_CENTER	Align centers by moving horizontally
ALIGN_RIGHT	Align right sides by moving horizontally
ALIGN_TOP	Align top sides by moving vertically
ALIGN_MIDDLE	Align middles by moving vertically
ALIGN_BOTTOM	Aign bottom sides by moving vertically

TABLE 22.1 Align Commands

Command	Action
`PANEL_HORIZONTAL`	Distribute horizontally
`PANEL_VERTICAL`	Distribute vertically

TABLE 22.2 Distribute Directions

and makes the centers of the other objects equidistant. The **distribute_items()** function accepts a variable number of panel items:

```
distribute_items ( direction, item1, ..., NULL );
```

The supported directions are listed in Table 22.2. To distribute three buttons (bi, bj, bk) horizontally, you could use the following code:

```
distribute_items ( PANEL_HORIZONTAL, bi, bj, bk, NULL);
```

Note: This routine distributes *and sorts* the items into the sequence given in the **distribute_items()** argument list. I consider this to be a feature...

PANEL ITEM LAYOUT

The **PANEL_LAYOUT** attribute is used for figuring out how the items are going to be laid out during creation. There are two supported layouts:

PANEL_HORIZONTAL Create things horizontally

PANEL_VERTICAL Create things vertically

If **PANEL_LAYOUT** was **PANEL_HORIZONTAL** and you created five buttons, they'd be laid out as shown in Figure 22.2. If **PANEL_LAYOUT** was **PANEL_VERTICAL**, the buttons would be laid out as shown in Figure 22.3.

SAMPLE PROGRAMS

There are two sample programs:

multipanel.c Demonstration of two panels in a frame

panel(align).c Demonstration of align/distribute

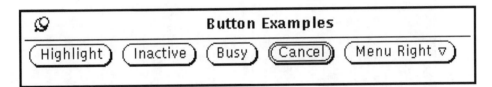

FIGURE 22.2 Horizontal Buttons

FIGURE   22.3
Vertical Buttons

The **multipanel.c** program doesn't do anything. It quietly creates a frame with two sub-panels, using **window_fit()**, and sits there.

```
/* multipanel.c -- Open Look panels
 * Author:  Kenneth Bibb
 * January 1992 -- Arastar Consulting
 *-------------------------------------
 * Is there supposed to be white space around the panels?
 */

#include <stdlib.h>
#include <sys/param.h>
#include <xview/xview.h>
#include <xview/panel.h>
#include <xview/canvas.h>
#include <xview/xv_xrect.h>
#include <xview/openmenu.h>
#include <xview/icon.h>
#include <xview/svrimage.h>

main ( argc, argv )
int argc;
char **argv;
{
        Frame frame;
        Canvas canvas;
        Panel panel;
        Panel p2;

        xv_init ( XV_INIT_ARGC_PTR_ARGV, &argc, argv, NULL );
        frame = (Frame) xv_create ( NULL, FRAME,
                    FRAME_LABEL, argv[0],
                    XV_X,          300,
                    XV_Y,          175,
                    NULL );
```

```
        panel = (Panel) xv_create ( frame, PANEL, NULL );
        (void) xv_create ( panel, PANEL_BUTTON,
                                   PANEL_LABEL_STRING, "Nada",
                                   NULL );
        window_fit_height ( panel );

        p2 = (Panel) xv_create ( frame, PANEL,
                                   XV_X,     0,
                                   XV_Y,     41,
                                   XV_WIDTH, 100,
                                   NULL );
        (void) xv_create ( p2, PANEL_BUTTON,
                                   PANEL_LABEL_STRING, "Nothing",
                                   NULL );

        canvas = (Canvas) xv_create ( frame, CANVAS,
                    XV_HEIGHT,            WIN_EXTEND_TO_EDGE,
                    XV_WIDTH,             WIN_EXTEND_TO_EDGE,
                    CANVAS_X_PAINT_WINDOW, TRUE,
                    NULL );
        window_fit ( frame );

        xv_main_loop ( frame );
}
```

The **panel.c** program shows a number of buttons spread across the bottom of the screen. The buttons at the top of the screen control the placement of the buttons. Since you can obliterate buttons by overlaying them, I've provided a reset button and also do panel refreshes with **panel_paint()** after every manipulation. (Note: The buttons used in controlling the button placement were aligned using the **align_items()** function.)

```
/* panelalign.c -- Alignment and Distribution Functions
 * Author:  Kenneth Bibb
 * January 1992 -- Arastar Consulting
 * Copyright (c) 1992  Ken Bibb
 *
 *-------------------------------------
 * usage:
 * align_items ( int,Panel_items ... ) ALIGN_LEFT, ALIGN_CENTER, ALIGN_RIGHT
 *                                                  ALIGN_TOP, ALIGN_BOTTOM,
 *
 * usage:
 * distribute_items ( int,Panel_items ... ) PANEL_HORIZONTAL, PANEL_VERTICAL
 */

#include <xview/xview.h>
#include <xview/panel.h>
#include <xview/canvas.h>
#include <xview/xv_xrect.h>
#include <xview/openmenu.h>
#include <xview/icon.h>
#include <xview/svrimage.h>
#include "align.h"

Attr_attribute PIX;
Attr_attribute PJX;
```

```
Attr_attribute PKX;
Attr_attribute PLX;
Attr_attribute PMX;
Attr_attribute PANEL_KEY;

int
distribute_items ( alignment,  va_alist )
va_dcl
{
     va_list      panel_items;
     Rect *r;
     Panel_item pitem;
     int  margin_a, margin_b;
     int n = 0; /* number of items */
     int span = 0; /* distance between centers */
     int i;
     int width=0;

     margin_a = 100000;    /* left/top margin */
     margin_b = 0;         /* right/bottom margin */
     va_start(panel_items);

     if ( alignment == PANEL_HORIZONTAL )  {
             while ( pitem = va_arg ( panel_items, Panel_item)) {
                         ++n;
                         r = (Rect *) xv_get ( pitem, XV_RECT );
                         if ( xv_get ( pitem, XV_X ) < margin_a )
                             margin_a = xv_get ( pitem, XV_X )
                                 + ( xv_get ( pitem,XV_WIDTH )  /2 );
                         if ( rect_right ( r ) > margin_b )
                             margin_b = rect_right ( r ) -
                             ( xv_get ( pitem, XV_WIDTH )/2 )+1;
             }
     } else {
             while ( pitem = va_arg(panel_items, Panel_item)) {
                         ++n;
                         r = (Rect *) xv_get ( pitem, XV_RECT );
                         if ( xv_get ( pitem, XV_Y ) < margin_a )
                                 margin_a = xv_get ( pitem, XV_Y ) +
                                 ( xv_get ( pitem, XV_HEIGHT )/2 );
                         if ( rect_bottom ( r ) > margin_b )
                                 margin_b = rect_bottom ( r ) -
                                 ( xv_get ( pitem, XV_HEIGHT )/2 );
             }
     }
     va_end(panel_items);

     va_start(panel_items);
     if ( alignment == PANEL_HORIZONTAL ) {
             /* do first item */
             if ( pitem = va_arg(panel_items, Panel_item)) {
                         span = ( margin_b - margin_a ) / (n - 1 );
                         width = xv_get ( pitem, XV_WIDTH ) / 2;
                         (void) xv_set ( pitem,
                                         XV_X, ( margin_a - width ),
                                         NULL );
             } else
                         return ( XV_ERROR );
             for (i=1; i<(n-1); i++) {
                         pitem = va_arg ( panel_items, Panel_item);
```

```
                                      width = xv_get ( pitem, XV_WIDTH ) / 2;
                                      (void) xv_set ( pitem,
                                              XV_X, margin_a + (span * i )
                                                      - width, NULL );
                  }
      } else {
                  /* do first item */
                  if ( pitem = va_arg ( panel_items, Panel_item )) {
                              span = ( margin_b - margin_a ) / ( n - 1 );
                              width = xv_get ( pitem, XV_HEIGHT ) / 2;
                              (void) xv_set ( pitem,
                                      XV_Y, ( margin_a - width ),
                                      NULL );
                  } else
                              return ( XV_ERROR );
                  for(i=1; i<(n-1); i++) {
                              pitem = va_arg(panel_items, Panel_item);
                              width = xv_get ( pitem, XV_HEIGHT ) / 2;
                              (void) xv_set ( pitem,
                                      XV_Y, margin_a + ( span * i )
                                                      - width,
                                      NULL );
                  }
      }
      va_end(panel_items);
      return ( XV_OK );
}

int
align_items ( alignment,  va_alist )
va_dcl
int alignment;
{
      va_list panel_items;
      Rect *r;
      Panel_item pitem;
      int old_margin, x;
      va_start(panel_items);
      if ( alignment != ALIGN_CENTER && alignment != ALIGN_MIDDLE ) {
                  if ( alignment == ALIGN_LEFT || alignment == ALIGN_TOP )
                              old_margin = 100000;
                  else
                              old_margin = 0;
                  while ( pitem = va_arg(panel_items,Panel_item)) {
                              r = (Rect *)xv_get(pitem,XV_RECT);
                              switch(alignment) {
                              case ALIGN_LEFT:    /* align left edge of rects */
                                          if ( xv_get ( pitem, XV_X )
                                                  < old_margin )
                                              old_margin = xv_get ( pitem,
                                                      XV_X );
                                          break;
                              case ALIGN_CENTER: /* align (left+right)/2 */
                                          /* center on first object */
                                          break;
                              case ALIGN_RIGHT:/* align right edge of rects */
                                          if ( rect_right ( r ) > old_margin )
                                              old_margin = rect_right ( r );
                                          break;
                              case ALIGN_TOP:    /* align top edge of rects */
                                          if ( xv_get ( pitem, XV_Y )
```

```
                                                    < old_margin)
                                    old_margin = xv_get ( pitem,
                                            XV_Y );
                                break;
                    case ALIGN_MIDDLE: /* align (top+bottom)/2 */
                                    /* center on first object */
                                    break;
                    case ALIGN_BOTTOM:/* align bottom of rects */
                                    if ( rect_bottom ( r )
                                        > old_margin )
                                        old_margin = rect_bottom ( r );
                                    break;
                    default: /* bad alignment--set XV_ERROR */
                    return ( XV_ERROR );
                    }
        }
    } else {
            pitem = va_arg(panel_items, Panel_item);
            if ( alignment == ALIGN_CENTER ) {
                    old_margin = xv_get ( pitem, XV_X ) + (int)
                            ( xv_get ( pitem, XV_WIDTH ) / 2 );
            } else
                    old_margin = xv_get ( pitem, XV_Y ) + (int) ( xv_get
                                    ( pitem, XV_HEIGHT ) / 2 );
    }
    va_end(panel_items);

    va_start(panel_items);
    while ( pitem = va_arg(panel_items, Panel_item) ) {
            switch ( alignment ) {
            case ALIGN_LEFT:    /* align left edge of rects */
                    (void) xv_set ( pitem, XV_X, old_margin, NULL );
                    break;
            case ALIGN_CENTER: /* align (left+right)/2 */
                    x = (int) xv_get ( pitem, XV_X );
                    (void) xv_set ( pitem,
                    XV_X, (old_margin    ( (int) xv_get
                        ( pitem, XV_WIDTH ) / 2 ) ),
                    NULL );
                    break;
            case ALIGN_RIGHT:   /* align right edge of rects */
                    (void) xv_set ( pitem,
                            XV_X, ( old_margin - xv_get
    ( pitem, XV_WIDTH
) ),
                            NULL );
                    break;
            case ALIGN_TOP:     /* align top edge of rects */
                    (void) xv_set ( pitem, XV_Y, old_margin, NULL );
                    break;
            case ALIGN_MIDDLE: /* align (top+bottom)/2 */
                    (void) xv_set ( pitem,
                            XV_Y, ( old_margin - ( (int) xv_get
                            ( pitem, XV_HEIGHT / 2 ) ) ),
                    NULL );
                    break;
            case ALIGN_BOTTOM: /* align bottom edge of rects */
                    (void) xv_set ( pitem, XV_Y, old_margin, NULL );
            default: /* bad alignment--set XV_ERROR */
                    return ( XV_ERROR );
        }
```

```
        }
        va_end(panel_items);
        return(XV_OK);
}

#ifdef TEST

/* the following code creates a panel with buttons that can be used
 * to try out the various routines
 */

void
left_proc ( button, event )
Panel_item  button;
Event *event;
{
        Panel       panel = (Panel)   xv_get ( button, XV_KEY_DATA, PANEL_KEY );
        Panel_item pi = (Panel_item) xv_get ( button, XV_KEY_DATA, PIX );
        Panel_item pj = (Panel_item) xv_get ( button, XV_KEY_DATA, PJX );
        Panel_item pk = (Panel_item) xv_get ( button, XV_KEY_DATA, PKX );
        Panel_item pl = (Panel_item) xv_get ( button, XV_KEY_DATA, PLX );
        Panel_item pm = (Panel_item) xv_get ( button, XV_KEY_DATA, PMX );

        align_items ( ALIGN_LEFT, pi, pj, pk, pl, pm, NULL );
        panel_paint ( panel, PANEL_CLEAR );
}

void
center_proc ( button, event )
Panel_item button;
Event *event;
{
        Panel       panel = (Panel)   xv_get ( button, XV_KEY_DATA, PANEL_KEY );
        Panel_item pi = (Panel_item) xv_get ( button, XV_KEY_DATA, PIX );
        Panel_item pj = (Panel_item) xv_get ( button, XV_KEY_DATA, PJX );
        Panel_item pk = (Panel_item) xv_get ( button, XV_KEY_DATA, PKX );
        Panel_item pl = (Panel_item) xv_get ( button, XV_KEY_DATA, PLX );
        Panel_item pm = (Panel_item) xv_get ( button, XV_KEY_DATA, PMX );

        align_items ( ALIGN_CENTER, pi, pj, pk, pl, pm, NULL );
        panel_paint ( panel, PANEL_CLEAR );
}

void
right_proc ( button, event )
Panel_item button;
Event *event;
{
        Panel       panel = (Panel)   xv_get ( button, XV_KEY_DATA, PANEL_KEY );
        Panel_item pi = (Panel_item) xv_get ( button, XV_KEY_DATA, PIX );
        Panel_item pj = (Panel_item) xv_get ( button, XV_KEY_DATA, PJX );
        Panel_item pk = (Panel_item) xv_get ( button, XV_KEY_DATA, PKX );
        Panel_item pl = (Panel_item) xv_get ( button, XV_KEY_DATA, PLX );
        Panel_item pm = (Panel_item) xv_get ( button, XV_KEY_DATA, PMX );

        align_items ( ALIGN_RIGHT, pi, pj, pk, pl, pm, NULL );
        panel_paint ( panel, PANEL_CLEAR );
}

void
top_proc(button, event)
```

```
Panel_item button;
Event *event;
{
     Panel       panel = (Panel)   xv_get ( button, XV_KEY_DATA, PANEL_KEY );
     Panel_item pi = (Panel_item) xv_get ( button, XV_KEY_DATA, PIX );
     Panel_item pj = (Panel_item) xv_get ( button, XV_KEY_DATA, PJX );
     Panel_item pk = (Panel_item) xv_get ( button, XV_KEY_DATA, PKX );
     Panel_item pl = (Panel_item) xv_get ( button, XV_KEY_DATA, PLX );
     Panel_item pm = (Panel_item) xv_get ( button, XV_KEY_DATA, PMX );

     align_items ( ALIGN_TOP, pi, pj, pk, pl, pm, NULL );
     panel_paint ( panel, PANEL_CLEAR );
}

void
middle_proc ( button, event )
Panel_item button;
Event *event;
{
     Panel       panel = (Panel)   xv_get ( button, XV_KEY_DATA, PANEL_KEY );
     Panel_item pi = (Panel_item) xv_get ( button, XV_KEY_DATA, PIX );
     Panel_item pj = (Panel_item) xv_get ( button, XV_KEY_DATA, PJX );
     Panel_item pk = (Panel_item) xv_get ( button, XV_KEY_DATA, PKX );
     Panel_item pl = (Panel_item) xv_get ( button, XV_KEY_DATA, PLX );
     Panel_item pm = (Panel_item) xv_get ( button, XV_KEY_DATA, PMX );

     align_items ( ALIGN_MIDDLE, pi, pj, pk, pl, pm, NULL );
     panel_paint ( panel, PANEL_CLEAR );
}

void
bottom_proc ( button, event )
Panel_item button;
Event *event;
{
     Panel       panel = (Panel)   xv_get ( button, XV_KEY_DATA, PANEL_KEY );
     Panel_item pi = (Panel_item) xv_get ( button, XV_KEY_DATA, PIX );
     Panel_item pj = (Panel_item) xv_get ( button, XV_KEY_DATA, PJX );
     Panel_item pk = (Panel_item) xv_get ( button, XV_KEY_DATA, PKX );
     Panel_item pl = (Panel_item) xv_get ( button, XV_KEY_DATA, PLX );
     Panel_item pm = (Panel_item) xv_get ( button, XV_KEY_DATA, PMX );

     align_items ( ALIGN_BOTTOM, pi, pj, pk, pl, pm, NULL );
     panel_paint ( panel, PANEL_CLEAR );
}

void
horiz_proc ( button, event )
Panel_item button;
Event *event;
{
     Panel       panel = (Panel)   xv_get ( button, XV_KEY_DATA, PANEL_KEY );
     Panel_item pi = (Panel_item) xv_get ( button, XV_KEY_DATA, PIX );
     Panel_item pj = (Panel_item) xv_get ( button, XV_KEY_DATA, PJX );
     Panel_item pk = (Panel_item) xv_get ( button, XV_KEY_DATA, PKX );
     Panel_item pl = (Panel_item) xv_get ( button, XV_KEY_DATA, PLX );
     Panel_item pm = (Panel_item) xv_get ( button, XV_KEY_DATA, PMX );

     if ( distribute_items ( PANEL_HORIZONTAL, pi, pj, pk, pl, pm, NULL )
                       == XV_ERROR )
                          printf ( "horiz error!\n" );
     panel_paint ( panel, PANEL_CLEAR );
```

```
}

void
vert_proc ( button, event )
Panel_item button;
Event *event;
{
    Panel      panel = (Panel)   xv_get ( button, XV_KEY_DATA, PANEL_KEY );
    Panel_item pi = (Panel_item) xv_get ( button, XV_KEY_DATA, PIX );
    Panel_item pj = (Panel_item) xv_get ( button, XV_KEY_DATA, PJX );
    Panel_item pk = (Panel_item) xv_get ( button, XV_KEY_DATA, PKX );
    Panel_item pl = (Panel_item) xv_get ( button, XV_KEY_DATA, PLX );
    Panel_item pm = (Panel_item) xv_get ( button, XV_KEY_DATA, PMX );

    if ( distribute_items ( PANEL_VERTICAL, pi, pj, pk, pl, pm, NULL )
                            == XV_ERROR )
            printf ( "vert error!\n" );
    panel_paint ( panel, PANEL_CLEAR );
}


void
display_proc ( button, event )
Panel_item button;
Event *event;
{
    Panel_item pi = (Panel_item) xv_get ( button, XV_KEY_DATA, PIX );
    Panel_item pj = (Panel_item) xv_get ( button, XV_KEY_DATA, PJX );
    Panel_item pk = (Panel_item) xv_get ( button, XV_KEY_DATA, PKX );
    Panel_item pl = (Panel_item) xv_get ( button, XV_KEY_DATA, PLX );
    Panel_item pm = (Panel_item) xv_get ( button, XV_KEY_DATA, PMX );
    int direction;

    printf( "-------------------------------\n" );
    printf( "pi (%d,%d)\t%d\t[%s]\n",
                xv_get ( pi, XV_X ), xv_get ( pi, XV_Y ),
                xv_get ( pi, XV_X ) + xv_get ( pi, XV_WIDTH ) / 2,
                xv_get ( pi, PANEL_LABEL_STRING )
                );
    printf( "pj (%d,%d)\t%d\t[%s]\n",
                xv_get ( pj, XV_X ), xv_get ( pj, XV_Y ),
                xv_get ( pj, XV_X ) + xv_get ( pj, XV_WIDTH ) / 2,
                xv_get ( pj, PANEL_LABEL_STRING )
                );
    printf( "pk (%d,%d)\t%d\t[%s]\n",
                xv_get ( pk, XV_X ), xv_get ( pk, XV_Y),
                xv_get ( pk, XV_X ) + xv_get ( pk, XV_WIDTH ) / 2,
                xv_get ( pk, PANEL_LABEL_STRING )
                );
    printf( "pl (%d,%d)\t%d\t[%s]\n",
                xv_get ( pl, XV_X ), xv_get ( pl, XV_Y),
                xv_get ( pl, XV_X ) + xv_get ( pl , XV_WIDTH ) / 2,
                xv_get ( pl, PANEL_LABEL_STRING)
                );
    printf( "pm (%d,%d)\t%d\t[%s]\n",
                xv_get ( pm, XV_X ), xv_get ( pm, XV_Y ),
                xv_get ( pm, XV_X ) + xv_get ( pm, XV_WIDTH ) / 2,
                xv_get ( pm, PANEL_LABEL_STRING )
                );
}
```

```
void
reset_proc ( button, event )
Panel_item button;
Event *event;
{
      Panel        panel = (Panel)    xv_get ( button, XV_KEY_DATA, PANEL_KEY );
      Panel_item pi = (Panel_item) xv_get ( button, XV_KEY_DATA, PIX );
      Panel_item pj = (Panel_item) xv_get ( button, XV_KEY_DATA, PJX );
      Panel_item pk = (Panel_item) xv_get ( button, XV_KEY_DATA, PKX );
      Panel_item pl = (Panel_item) xv_get ( button, XV_KEY_DATA, PLX );
      Panel_item pm = (Panel_item) xv_get ( button, XV_KEY_DATA, PMX );

      (void) xv_set ( pi, XV_X,  50, XV_Y, 200, NULL );
      (void) xv_set ( pj, XV_X, 150, XV_Y, 250, NULL );
      (void) xv_set ( pk, XV_X, 250, XV_Y, 300, NULL );
      (void) xv_set ( pl, XV_X, 350, XV_Y, 220, NULL );
      (void) xv_set ( pm, XV_X, 450, XV_Y, 350, NULL );
      panel_paint ( panel, PANEL_CLEAR );
}

int
main ( argc, argv )
int argc;
char **argv;
{
      Frame frame;
      Canvas canvas;
      Panel panel;
      Panel p2;
      Panel_item ml, mt, md;
      Panel_item pi, pj, pk, pl, pm;
      Panel_item bi, bj, bk, bl, bm, bn, bo, bp, bq, br;

      xv_init ( XV_INIT_ARGC_PTR_ARGV, &argc, argv, NULL );
      PIX = xv_unique_key ();
      PJX = xv_unique_key ();
      PKX = xv_unique_key ();
      PLX = xv_unique_key ();
      PMX = xv_unique_key ();
      PANEL_KEY = xv_unique_key ();
      frame = (Frame) xv_create ( NULL, FRAME,
                    FRAME_LABEL, argv[0],
                    XV_X,           200,
                    XV_Y,           175,
                    XV_WIDTH,       600,
                    NULL );
      panel = (Panel) xv_create ( frame, PANEL,
                                    PANEL_LAYOUT, PANEL_HORIZONTAL,
                                    NULL );
      ml = (Panel_item) xv_create ( panel, PANEL_MESSAGE,
                                    PANEL_LABEL_STRING, "L/R Alignment",
                                    PANEL_LABEL_BOLD,     TRUE,
                                    NULL );
      mt = (Panel_item) xv_create ( panel, PANEL_MESSAGE,
                                    PANEL_LABEL_STRING, "T/B Alignment",
                                    PANEL_LABEL_BOLD,     TRUE,
                                    NULL );
      md = (Panel_item) xv_create ( panel, PANEL_MESSAGE,
                                    PANEL_LABEL_STRING, "Distribute",
                                    PANEL_LABEL_BOLD, TRUE,
                                    NULL );
```

```
        bi = (Panel_item) xv_create ( panel, PANEL_BUTTON,
                                PANEL_NEXT_ROW,      -1,
                                PANEL_LABEL_STRING,  "Top",
                                PANEL_NOTIFY_PROC,   top_proc,
                                NULL );
        bp = (Panel_item) xv_create ( panel, PANEL_BUTTON,
                                PANEL_LABEL_STRING,  "Horizontal",
                                PANEL_NOTIFY_PROC,   horiz_proc,
                                NULL );
        bj = (Panel_item) xv_create ( panel, PANEL_BUTTON,
                                PANEL_NEXT_ROW,      -1,
                                PANEL_LABEL_STRING,  "Left",
                                PANEL_NOTIFY_PROC,   left_proc,
                                NULL );
        bk = (Panel_item) xv_create ( panel, PANEL_BUTTON,
                                PANEL_LABEL_STRING,  "Center",
                                PANEL_NOTIFY_PROC,   center_proc,
                                NULL );
        bl = (Panel_item) xv_create ( panel, PANEL_BUTTON,
                                PANEL_LABEL_STRING,  "Right",
                                PANEL_NOTIFY_PROC,   right_proc,
                                NULL );
        bm = (Panel_item) xv_create ( panel, PANEL_BUTTON,
                                XV_X, xv_get ( panel, PANEL_ITEM_X )+
                                xv_get ( bl, XV_WIDTH ) + 100,
                                PANEL_LABEL_STRING,  "Middle",
                                PANEL_NOTIFY_PROC,   middle_proc,
                                NULL );
        bq = (Panel_item) xv_create ( panel, PANEL_BUTTON,
                                XV_X, xv_get ( panel, PANEL_ITEM_X )
                                + xv_get ( bm, XV_WIDTH ) + 200,
                                PANEL_LABEL_STRING,  "Vertical",
                                PANEL_NOTIFY_PROC,   vert_proc,
                                NULL );
        (void) xv_set ( ml, XV_X, xv_get ( bj, XV_X ), NULL );
        (void) xv_set ( mt, XV_X, xv_get ( bm, XV_X ), NULL );
        (void) xv_set ( md, XV_X, xv_get ( bq, XV_X ), NULL );
        (void) xv_set ( bi, XV_X, xv_get ( bm, XV_X ), NULL );
        (void) xv_set ( bp, XV_X, xv_get ( bq, XV_X ), NULL );
        bn = (Panel_item) xv_create ( panel, PANEL_BUTTON,
                                PANEL_NEXT_ROW,      -1,
                                XV_X,                xv_get ( bm, XV_X ),
                                PANEL_LABEL_STRING,  "Bottom",
                                PANEL_NOTIFY_PROC,   bottom_proc,
                                NULL );

    align_items ( ALIGN_CENTER, mt, bi, bm, bn, NULL );
/*  align_items ( ALIGN_CENTER, md, bp, bq, NULL );*/
    align_items ( ALIGN_RIGHT, ml, bl, NULL );
    align_items ( ALIGN_CENTER, ml, bk, NULL );
    distribute_items ( PANEL_HORIZONTAL, bj, bk, bl, NULL );


    bo = (Panel_item) xv_create ( panel, PANEL_BUTTON,
                                PANEL_NEXT_ROW,      -1,
                                PANEL_LABEL_STRING,  "Reset",
                                PANEL_NOTIFY_PROC,   reset_proc,
                                NULL );
    br = (Panel_item) xv_create ( panel, PANEL_BUTTON,
                                PANEL_LABEL_STRING,  "Display",
```

```
                              PANEL_NOTIFY_PROC,  display_proc,
                              NULL );
      (void) xv_create ( panel, PANEL_MESSAGE,
                              PANEL_NEXT_ROW, -1,
                              PANEL_LABEL_STRING,
"------------------------------------------------------------- ---",
                              NULL );
      pi = (Panel_item) xv_create ( panel, PANEL_BUTTON,
                              PANEL_LABEL_STRING, "T r i t o n",
                              XV_X,             50,
                              XV_Y,             200,
                              NULL );
      pj = (Panel_item) xv_create ( panel, PANEL_BUTTON,
                              PANEL_LABEL_STRING, "Merman",
                              XV_X,             150,
                              XV_Y,             250,
                              NULL );
      pk = (Panel_item) xv_create ( panel, PANEL_BUTTON,
                              PANEL_LABEL_STRING, "Naiad",
                              XV_X,             250,
                              XV_Y,             300,
                              NULL );
      pl = (Panel_item) xv_create ( panel, PANEL_BUTTON,
                              PANEL_LABEL_STRING, "Fishman",
                              XV_X,             350,
                              XV_Y,             220,
                              NULL );
      pm = (Panel_item) xv_create ( panel, PANEL_BUTTON,
                              PANEL_LABEL_STRING, "li",
                              XV_X,             450,
                              XV_Y,             350,
                              NULL );
      (void) xv_set ( bi,
                 XV_KEY_DATA, PIX,        pi,
                 XV_KEY_DATA, PJX,        pj,
                 XV_KEY_DATA, PKX,        pk,
                 XV_KEY_DATA, PLX,        pl,
                 XV_KEY_DATA, PMX,        pm,
                 XV_KEY_DATA, PANEL_KEY, panel,
                 NULL );
      (void) xv_set ( bj,
                 XV_KEY_DATA, PIX,        pi,
                 XV_KEY_DATA, PJX,        pj,
                 XV_KEY_DATA, PKX,        pk,
                 XV_KEY_DATA, PLX,        pl,
                 XV_KEY_DATA, PMX,        pm,
                 XV_KEY_DATA, PANEL_KEY, panel,
                 NULL );
      (void) xv_set ( bk,
                 XV_KEY_DATA, PIX,        pi,
                 XV_KEY_DATA, PJX,        pj,
                 XV_KEY_DATA, PKX,        pk,
                 XV_KEY_DATA, PLX,        pl,
                 XV_KEY_DATA, PMX,        pm,
                 XV_KEY_DATA, PANEL_KEY, panel,
                 NULL );
      (void) xv_set ( bl,
                 XV_KEY_DATA, PIX,        pi,
                 XV_KEY_DATA, PJX,        pj,
                 XV_KEY_DATA, PKX,        pk,
```

```
                      XV_KEY_DATA, PLX,        pl,
                      XV_KEY_DATA, PMX,        pm,
                      XV_KEY_DATA, PANEL_KEY, panel,
                      NULL );
         (void) xv_set ( bm,
                      XV_KEY_DATA, PIX,        pi,
                      XV_KEY_DATA, PJX,        pj,
                      XV_KEY_DATA, PKX,        pk,
                      XV_KEY_DATA, PLX,        pl,
                      XV_KEY_DATA, PMX,        pm,
                      XV_KEY_DATA, PANEL_KEY, panel,
                      NULL );
         (void) xv_set ( bn,
                      XV_KEY_DATA, PIX,        pi,
                      XV_KEY_DATA, PJX,        pj,
                      XV_KEY_DATA, PKX,        pk,
                      XV_KEY_DATA, PLX,        pl,
                      XV_KEY_DATA, PMX,        pm,
                      XV_KEY_DATA, PANEL_KEY, panel,
                      NULL );
         (void) xv_set ( bo,
                      XV_KEY_DATA, PIX,        pi,
                      XV_KEY_DATA, PJX,        pj,
                      XV_KEY_DATA, PKX,        pk,
                      XV_KEY_DATA, PLX,        pl,
                      XV_KEY_DATA, PMX,        pm,
                      XV_KEY_DATA, PANEL_KEY, panel,
                      NULL );
         (void) xv_set ( bp,
                      XV_KEY_DATA, PIX,        pi,
                      XV_KEY_DATA, PJX,        pj,
                      XV_KEY_DATA, PKX,        pk,
                      XV_KEY_DATA, PLX,        pl,
                      XV_KEY_DATA, PMX,        pm,          )
                      XV_KEY_DATA, PANEL_KEY, panel,
                      NULL );
         (void) xv_set ( bq,
                      XV_KEY_DATA, PIX,        pi,
                      XV_KEY_DATA, PJX,        pj,
                      XV_KEY_DATA, PKX,        pk,
                      XV_KEY_DATA, PLX,        pl,
                      XV_KEY_DATA, PMX,        pm,
                      XV_KEY_DATA, PANEL_KEY, panel,
                      NULL );
         (void) xv_set ( br,
                      XV_KEY_DATA, PIX,        pi,
                      XV_KEY_DATA, PJX,        pj,
                      XV_KEY_DATA, PKX,        pk,
                      XV_KEY_DATA, PLX,        pl,
                      XV_KEY_DATA, PMX,        pm,
                      XV_KEY_DATA, PANEL_KEY, panel,
                      NULL );
      window_fit ( frame );

         xv_main_loop ( frame );

}
#endif
```

Panel Lists

23

Panel lists are one of the most often mentioned panel items in **alt.toolkits.xview**. Once you use them a few times, they aren't bad, but learning them can be rough.

A **PANEL_LIST** object has the attributes shown in Figure 23.1.

PANEL LIST CALLBACK

The panel list callback format is one of the more complicated ones:

```
void
list_proc ( item, string, client_data, op, event, row )
Panel_item item;
char *string;
caddr_t client_data;
Panel_list_op op;
Event *event;
int row;
{
}
```

where **item** is the handle of the panel list; **string** is the string on the selected row; **client_data** is user-definable data attached to the selected row; **op** is one of the values listed in Table 23.1; **event** is the event that occurred; and **row** (only in XView 3.0 and later) is the selected row number.

A STATIC PANEL LIST

Occasionally there is a need for a static panel list. They are pretty easy to create and are a good place to start if you're just learning how to use panel lists. The following is a typical panel list:

```
Panel panel;
Panel_item pl;

pl = (Panel_item) xv_create ( panel, PANEL_LIST,
        PANEL_LABEL_STRING, "Device Types",
        PANEL_LIST_STRINGS,
                    "Hayes", "V.32", "Microcom",
                    "Trailblazer", "ATI", "Unisys", "US Robotics", NULL,
        NULL );
```

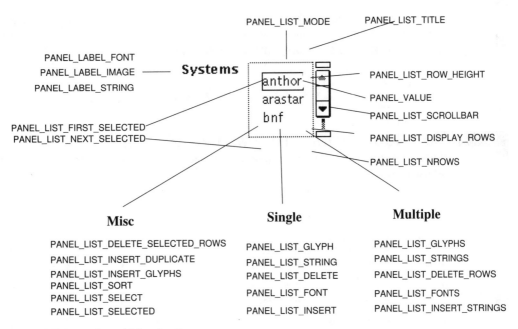

FIGURE 23.1 Panel List Attributes

This creates a panel list on **panel** having a list of rows that were created at compile time.

ADDING AN ITEM DYNAMICALLY

A more complicated task involves adding an item to the list while the program is running. The **PANEL_LIST_INSERT** attribute is used to do this as follows (the following examples all manipulate the panel list created in the previous example):

```
int    i;
char *s;

(void) xv_set ( pl,
     PANEL_LIST_INSERT, i,
     PANEL_LIST_STRING, i, s,
     NULL );
```

Op	In English
PANEL_LIST_OP_SELECT	Row selection
PANEL_LIST_OP_DESELECT	Row deselection
PANEL_LIST_OP_VALIDATE	Row insertion
PANEL_LIST_OP_DELETE	Row deletion

TABLE 23.1 Panel List Ops

where **i** is the row number that you want to add and **s** is the string that you're adding. If you want to protect against having duplicate items added to the panel list, you can use the XView 3.0 attribute **PANEL_LIST_INSERT_DUPLICATE** to prevent it:

```
(void) xv_set ( pl,
        PANEL_LIST_INSERT_DUPLICATE, FALSE,
        NULL );
```

ADDING A GROUP OF ITEMS DYNAMICALLY

If you're going to add a large group of items to the panel list, you'll probably want to do it in the following way:

```
(void) xv_set ( pl,
        XV_SHOW, FALSE,
        NULL );
(void) xv_set ( pl,
        PANEL_LIST_INSERT, 1,
        PANEL_LIST_STRING, 1, "row",
        NULL );

/* any other inserts go here */

(void) xv_set ( pl,
        XV_SHOW, TRUE,
        NULL );
```

The **XV_SHOW** attribute controls the display of the object. While **XV_SHOW** is set to **FALSE**, changes to that item will not appear on the user's screen. When **XV_SHOW** is set back to **TRUE**, the item will be displayed with the whole set of changes having taken place.

DELETING AN ITEM DYNAMICALLY

To delete an item from the panel list while the program is running, you use the **PANEL_LIST_DELETE** attribute. To delete the item on row **i**, you would use

```
(void) xv_set ( pl,
        PANEL_LIST_DELETE, i,
        NULL );
```

DELETING A GROUP OF ITEMS DYNAMICALLY

Deleting a group is similar to adding a group. Turn **XV_SHOW** off before doing the group of deletions and then turn it back on when you're finished.

```
(void) xv_set ( pl,
        XV_SHOW, FALSE,
        NULL );
(void) xv_set ( pl,
        PANEL_LIST_DELETE, 1,
        NULL );

/* any other deletes go here */

(void) xv_set ( pl,
        XV_SHOW, TRUE,
        NULL );
```

GETTING THE INDEX NUMBER OF AN ITEM

There are three ways of retrieving an index of an item:

- client_data
- **PANEL_LIST_FIRST_SELECTED**
- **for** loop

client_data Method In XView 3.0, the argument list for the panel list notify procedure includes the row as one of the values passed. In the following example, **client_data** is the row number and **string** is the string associated with that row.

```
void
list_proc ( item, string, client_data, op, event )
Panel_item item;
char *string;
caddr_t client_data;
Panel_list_op op;
Event *event;
{
        if ( op ==PANEL_LIST_OP_SELECT ) {
                        printf ( "selected: [%d][%s]\n", client_data, string );
                        xv_set ( system, PANEL_VALUE, string, NULL );
        }
}
```

PANEL_LIST_FIRST_SELECTED Method If you're trying to access the selected row from a function that is not the panel list notify procedure, the **PANEL_LIST_FIRST_SELECTED** (and, for panel toggle lists, **PANEL_LIST_NEXT_SELECTED**) attribute can be used.

```
Panel_item list;
int i;

i = (int) xv_get ( list, PANEL_LIST_FIRST_SELECTED );
```

Here we retrieve the row number of the first chosen row and store it in the **i** variable.

for Method Finally, you could use a **for** loop to list the selected items. The following code finds the first selected row in the panel list.

```
for (i=0; i<xv_get ( list, PANEL_LIST_NROWS ); i++)
        if ( xv_get ( list, PANEL_LIST_SELECTED, i ) )
                        break;
```

This can easily be modified to handle multiple selections by replacing **break** with the code you want used against any selected row.

CHANGING THE FONT ON A PANEL LIST ITEM

To set an individual row to the previously **xv_find()** ed font **fixed**, you would use the following code:

```
Panel_item list;
Xv_Font fixed;

(void) xv_set ( list,
        PANEL_LIST_FONT, i, fixed,
        NULL );
```

To change the fonts of a group of rows, use the **PANEL_LIST_FONTS** attribute:

```
Panel_item list;
Xv_Font fixed, f1, f2, f3;


(void) xv_set ( list,
        PANEL_LIST_FONTS, f1, fixed, f2, f3, f1, NULL,
        NULL );
```

This example would take fonts **fixed**, **f1**, **f2**, and **f3** (which had been successfully created or found using **xv_find()**), and assign them to the rows. The first panel list row would be shown in **f1**, the second in **fixed**, and so on until a terminating **NULL** is encountered.

HIERARCHICAL

Hierarchical panel lists are very useful in a large number of situations. Unfortunately, they aren't supported by XView yet. If you want to use them, you'll have to create something on your own. (The **xv** program has something close that you might want to use as a source.) Maybe we'll get hierarchical panel lists in XView 3.1.

SAMPLE PROGRAM

The sample program displays a panel list and lets the user dynamically add and delete names as entered in the text item; a predefined group of names can also be added and deleted; and finally, the font of a row can be toggled between the default font and the "fixed" font.

```
/* pl.c -- Panel List test program
 * Author:  Kenneth Bibb
 *-------------------------------------------
 */

#include <stdio.h>                          /* for file i/o             */
/* #include <stdlib.h> */
#include <sys/param.h>                      /* for MAXHOSTNAMELEN       */
#include <xview/xview.h>
#include <xview/panel.h>
#include <xview/notice.h>
#include <xview/font.h>
#include <xview/cms.h>

#define LINELENGTH 1024                     /* length of a site name    */
#define MATRIXLEN   64                      /* max num sites in list    */

int numsites;                               /* curr num sites in list   */
```

```
Attr_attribute FRAME_BASE_KEY;              /* base frame */
Attr_attribute PANEL_BASE_KEY;              /* base frame's panel      */
Attr_attribute PL_KEY;                      /* main panel list         */
Attr_attribute TXT_SYS_KEY;                 /* system name text item   */
Attr_attribute FONT_FIXED_KEY;              /* "fixed" font */
Attr_attribute FONT_DEFLT_KEY;              /* "lucida" font */

#define FIXED_NUM 5                         /* num items in fixed group */
int fixed_group_in_list = FALSE;            /* fg in panel list?        */
int first_group = -1;                       /* row of first fg item     */
char *fg[FIXED_NUM] = { "Propaganda",       /* fixed strings for insert */
                        "Proponent",
                        "Query",
                        "Quagmire",
                        "Renaissance"
};

/* Add a single system name to the panel list.
 *      The system name is taken from the panel text item,
 *      which is shown on the same panel.
 */
void
add_system ( item,event )
Panel_item item;
Event *event;
{
        Panel_item system = xv_get ( item, XV_KEY_DATA, TXT_SYS_KEY );
        Panel_item list   = xv_get ( item, XV_KEY_DATA, PL_KEY );
        Panel      panel  = xv_get ( item, XV_KEY_DATA, PANEL_BASE_KEY );

        char  sbuf[LINELENGTH];
        char *s = sbuf;
        int i;

        xv_set ( xv_get ( item, XV_KEY_DATA, FRAME_BASE_KEY ),
                    FRAME_LEFT_FOOTER, " ",
                    NULL );
        if(numsites < MATRIXLEN) {
                    ++numsites;
                    strcpy ( s, xv_get ( system, PANEL_VALUE) );
                    for ( i=0; i<xv_get ( list, PANEL_LIST_NROWS ) ; i++)
                        if ( xv_get ( list, PANEL_LIST_SELECTED, i ) )
                                            break;
                    xv_set ( list,
                        PANEL_LIST_INSERT,  i,
                        PANEL_LIST_STRING,  i, s,
                        NULL );
        } else
#ifdef XV_VERSION_NUMBER
                    (void) notice_prompt ( panel, NULL,
#else
                    (void) xv_create ( item, NOTICE,
#endif
                        NOTICE_FOCUS_XY, event_x ( event ), event_y(event),
                        NOTICE_MESSAGE_STRINGS,
                        "You Can't Add Any More Systems!", NULL,
                        NOTICE_BUTTON_YES, "Darn It",
                        NULL );
}
```

```
void
add_group ( item, event )
Panel_item item;
Event *event;
{
        Panel panel         = xv_get ( item, XV_KEY_DATA, PANEL_BASE_KEY );
        Panel_item system = xv_get ( item, XV_KEY_DATA, TXT_SYS_KEY );
        Panel_item list   = xv_get ( item, XV_KEY_DATA, PL_KEY );

        char  sbuf[LINELENGTH];
        char *s=sbuf;
        int i,j;

        xv_set ( xv_get ( item, XV_KEY_DATA, FRAME_BASE_KEY ),
              FRAME_LEFT_FOOTER, " ",
              NULL );
        if ( numsites + FIXED_NUM < MATRIXLEN ) {
                if ( fixed_group_in_list )
                        (void) xv_set ( xv_get ( item, XV_KEY_DATA,
                                                    FRAME_BASE_KEY ),
                                     FRAME_LEFT_FOOTER,
                          "The fixed group was already added",
                                     NULL );
                else {
                        (void) xv_set ( list,
                                     XV_SHOW, FALSE,
                                     NULL );
                        numsites += FIXED_NUM;
                        for (i=0; i<xv_get ( list, PANEL_LIST_NROWS ); i++)
                            if ( xv_get ( list, PANEL_LIST_SELECTED, i ) )
                                                break;
                        first_group = i;
                        for (j=0; j<FIXED_NUM; j++) {
                                     xv_set ( list,
                                     PANEL_LIST_INSERT, i + j,
                                     PANEL_LIST_STRING, i + j, fg[j],
#ifdef XV_VERSION_NUMBER
                                     PANEL_LIST_INSERT_DUPLICATE, FALSE,
#endif
                                     NULL );
                        }
                        (void) xv_set ( list,
                                     XV_SHOW, TRUE,
                                     NULL );
                        fixed_group_in_list = TRUE;
                }
        } else
#ifndef XV_VERSION_NUMBER
        (void) notice_prompt ( panel, NULL,
#else
        (void) xv_create ( item, NOTICE,
#endif
                NOTICE_FOCUS_XY, event_x ( event), event_y ( event),
                NOTICE_MESSAGE_STRINGS,
                    "You Can't Add Any More Systems!", NULL,
                NOTICE_BUTTON_YES, "Darn It",
                NULL );
}
```

```
void
del_system ( item, event )
Panel_item item;
Event *event;
{
        Panel_item system = xv_get ( item, XV_KEY_DATA, TXT_SYS_KEY );
        Panel_item list   = xv_get ( item, XV_KEY_DATA, PL_KEY );

        int    result;
        char   sbuf[LINELENGTH];
        char *s = sbuf;
        int    i, j;

        xv_set ( xv_get ( item, XV_KEY_DATA, FRAME_BASE_KEY ),
                        FRAME_LEFT_FOOTER, " ",
                        NULL );
        sprintf ( s, "Do you want to delete the %s system?",
                        (char *) xv_get ( system, PANEL_VALUE ) );
#ifdef XV_VERSION_NUMBER                              /*    XV 2.0 */
        result = notice_prompt ( xv_get ( item, XV_KEY_DATA,
                                                PANEL_BASE_KEY ), NULL,
#else                                                /* > XV 2.0 */
        (void) xv_create ( xv_get ( item, XV_KEY_DATA, PANEL_BASE_KEY),
    NOTICE,
                NOTICE_STATUS,              &result,
#endif
                NOTICE_FOCUS_XY,            event_x ( event), event_y ( event ),
                NOTICE_MESSAGE_STRINGS, s, NULL,
                NOTICE_BUTTON_YES,      "Delete It",
                NOTICE_BUTTON_NO,       " Cancel",
                NULL );
        if ( result ==NOTICE_YES ) {
                for (i=0; i<xv_get ( list, PANEL_LIST_NROWS ); i++)
                        if ( xv_get ( list, PANEL_LIST_SELECTED, i ) )
                                break;
                xv_set ( list, PANEL_LIST_DELETE, i, NULL); /* delete it */
                --numsites;
                for (i=0; i<xv_get ( list, PANEL_LIST_NROWS ); i++)
                        if ( xv_get ( list, PANEL_LIST_SELECTED, i ) )
                                break;
                xv_set ( system,
                        PANEL_VALUE, xv_get ( list, PANEL_LIST_STRING, i ),
                        NULL );
        }
}

void
del_group ( item, event )
Panel_item item;
Event *event;
{
        Panel_item list  = xv_get ( item, XV_KEY_DATA, PL_KEY );
        int    result;
        char   sbuf[LINELENGTH];
        char *s = sbuf;
        int    i, j;

        xv_set ( xv_get ( item, XV_KEY_DATA, FRAME_BASE_KEY ),
                        FRAME_LEFT_FOOTER, " ",
                        NULL );
```

```
        if ( fixed_group_in_list ) {
            for ( i=FIXED_NUM; i; i--)
                        xv_set ( list,
                                    PANEL_LIST_DELETE, first_group + i-1,
                                    NULL );
            numsites -= FIXED_NUM;
            for (i=0; i<xv_get ( list, PANEL_LIST_NROWS ); i++)
                    if ( xv_get ( list, PANEL_LIST_SELECTED, i ) )
                                        break;
            fixed_group_in_list = FALSE;
    } else
            (void) xv_set (xv_get ( item, XV_KEY_DATA, FRAME_BASE_KEY ),
                    FRAME_LEFT_FOOTER, "The fixed group does not exist",
                    NULL );
}

void
list_proc ( item, string, client_data, op, event, row )
Panel_item item;
char *string;
caddr_t client_data;
Panel_list_op op;
Event *event;
int row;
{
   char sbuf[LINELENGTH];
   char *s = sbuf;

   if ( op == PANEL_LIST_OP_SELECT ) {
                sprintf ( s,"selected: [%d][%s]\n", row, string );
                xv_set ( xv_get ( item, XV_KEY_DATA, FRAME_BASE_KEY ),
                                FRAME_LEFT_FOOTER, s,
                                NULL );
                xv_set ( xv_get ( item, XV_KEY_DATA, TXT_SYS_KEY),
                                PANEL_VALUE, string,
                                NULL );
    }
}

void
toggle_font ( button, event )
Panel_item button;
Event *event;
{
   Panel_item list    = xv_get ( button, XV_KEY_DATA, PL_KEY );
   Xv_Font fixed   = (Xv_Font) xv_get ( button, XV_KEY_DATA, FONT_FIXED_KEY);
   Xv_Font def     = (Xv_Font) xv_get ( button, XV_KEY_DATA, FONT_DEFLT_KEY);
   int i, j;

   i = (int) xv_get ( list, PANEL_LIST_FIRST_SELECTED );
   if ( ( j = xv_get ( list, PANEL_LIST_FONT, i ) ) == fixed) {
                    (void) xv_set ( list,
                                PANEL_LIST_FONT, i, def,
                                NULL );
    } else {
                    (void) xv_set ( list,
                                PANEL_LIST_FONT, i, fixed,
                                NULL );
```

```
        }
#ifdef NOT_NEEDED
        (void) xv_set ( list,
                        XV_SHOW, TRUE,
                        NULL );
#endif
}

void
toggle_all ( button, event )
Panel_item button;
Event *event;
{
   Panel_item list    = xv_get ( button, XV_KEY_DATA, PL_KEY );
   Xv_Font fixed   = (Xv_Font) xv_get ( button, XV_KEY_DATA, FONT_FIXED_KEY);
   Xv_Font def     = (Xv_Font) xv_get ( button, XV_KEY_DATA, FONT_DEFLT_KEY);
   int i, j;

   if ( ( j = xv_get ( list, PANEL_LIST_FONT, 0 ) ) == fixed ) {
                        printf ( "fixed: %d %d\n", fixed, def );
                        (void) xv_set ( list,
                                        XV_FONT, def,
                                        NULL );
   } else {
                        printf ( "deflt: %d %d\n", fixed, def );
                        (void) xv_set ( list,
                                        XV_FONT, fixed,
                                        NULL );
   }
   (void) xv_set ( list,
                        XV_SHOW, TRUE,
                        NULL );
}


int
scmp ( i,j )                                    /* string compare for qsort */
char **i, **j;
{
        return ( strcmp ( *i, *j ) );
}



int
main ( argc, argv )
int argc;
char **argv;
{
        FILE *sysfile;
        Frame frame;
        Panel panel;
        Panel_item list;
        Panel_item system;
        Panel_item pb;
        Xv_Font fixed;
        Xv_Font def_font;
```

```
        int i, j;
        int button_diff;
        int maxsite;
        char  sbuf[LINELENGTH];
        char *s = sbuf;
        char  site[LINELENGTH];
        char *sitelist[64];

        if ( ( sysfile = fopen ( "/etc/uucp/Systems", "r" ) ) == NULL ) {
                printf ( "%s: Unable to open Systems file\n", argv[0] );
                exit ( 1 );
        }
        s = fgets ( s, LINELENGTH, sysfile );
        for ( j=0; j<MATRIXLEN && !feof(sysfile); ) {
                if ( s[0] != '#' && !isspace ( s[0] ) ) {
                    if ( ( sitelist[j] = ( char *) malloc
                        ( LINELENGTH * sizeof ( char ) ) ) == NULL ) {
                        printf ( "%s: out of mem (%d)\n", argv[0], j );
                                exit ( 2 );
                        }
                        strtok ( s, "   ,.()" );
                        strcpy ( sitelist[j++], s );
                }
                s = fgets ( s, LINELENGTH, sysfile );
        }
        sitelist[j] = NULL;
        numsites = j;
        fclose ( sysfile );

        qsort ( sitelist, numsites, sizeof ( sitelist[0] ), scmp );

        xv_init ( XV_INIT_ARGC_PTR_ARGV, &argc, argv, NULL );
        FRAME_BASE_KEY = xv_unique_key ();
        PANEL_BASE_KEY = xv_unique_key ();
        PL_KEY         = xv_unique_key ();
        TXT_SYS_KEY    = xv_unique_key ();
        FONT_FIXED_KEY = xv_unique_key ();
        FONT_DEFLT_KEY = xv_unique_key ();

        frame = (Frame) xv_create ( NULL,FRAME,
                    FRAME_LABEL,         argv[0],
                    FRAME_SHOW_FOOTER, TRUE,
                    NULL );
        panel = (Panel) xv_create ( frame, PANEL, NULL );
        list = xv_create ( panel, PANEL_LIST,
                    PANEL_LABEL_STRING, "Systems",
#ifdef XVIEW3
                    PANEL_LIST_INSERT_DUPLICATE, FALSE,
#endif
                    PANEL_LIST_DISPLAY_ROWS, 3,
                    PANEL_NOTIFY_PROC, list_proc,
                    XV_KEY_DATA, FRAME_BASE_KEY, frame,
                    NULL );
        for (i=0; i<numsites; i++) {
                xv_set ( list,
                            PANEL_LIST_INSERT,       i,
                            PANEL_LIST_STRING,       i, sitelist[i],
```

```
                              PANEL_LIST_CLIENT_DATA, i, i,
                              NULL );
}
system = xv_create ( panel, PANEL_TEXT,
          PANEL_LABEL_STRING,          "System",
          PANEL_VALUE,                 sitelist[0],
          PANEL_VALUE_DISPLAY_LENGTH,  11,
          PANEL_VALUE_STORED_LENGTH,   MAXHOSTNAMELEN,
          NULL );
(void) xv_set ( system,
          XV_X, xv_get ( system, XV_X ) + 100,
          NULL );
(void) xv_set ( list,
          XV_KEY_DATA, TXT_SYS_KEY, system,
          NULL );
pb = (Panel_item) xv_create ( panel, PANEL_BUTTON,
          XV_X,                        xv_get ( system, XV_X ),
          XV_Y,                        xv_get ( system, XV_Y )+
                                       xv_get ( system, XV_HEIGHT )+
                                       xv_get ( panel,
                                                PANEL_ITEM_X_GAP ),
          PANEL_LABEL_STRING,          "Add",
          PANEL_NOTIFY_PROC,           add_system,
          XV_KEY_DATA, FRAME_BASE_KEY, frame,
          XV_KEY_DATA, PANEL_BASE_KEY, panel,
          XV_KEY_DATA, PL_KEY,         list,
          XV_KEY_DATA, TXT_SYS_KEY,    system,
          NULL );
button_diff = (int) xv_get ( pb, XV_Y ) - (int) xv_get ( system, XV_Y );
(void) xv_create ( panel, PANEL_BUTTON,
          XV_X,                        xv_get ( pb, XV_X ),
          XV_Y,                        xv_get ( pb, XV_Y ) + button_diff,
          PANEL_LABEL_STRING,          "Add Fixed Group",
          PANEL_NOTIFY_PROC,           add_group,
          XV_KEY_DATA, FRAME_BASE_KEY, frame,
          XV_KEY_DATA, PANEL_BASE_KEY, panel,
          XV_KEY_DATA, PL_KEY,         list,
          NULL );
(void) xv_create ( panel, PANEL_BUTTON,
          XV_X,                        xv_get ( pb, XV_X ),
          XV_Y,                        xv_get ( pb, XV_Y ) + (
                                                button_diff * 2 ),
          PANEL_LABEL_STRING,          "Delete",
          PANEL_NOTIFY_PROC,           del_system,
          XV_KEY_DATA, FRAME_BASE_KEY, frame,
          XV_KEY_DATA, PANEL_BASE_KEY, panel,
          XV_KEY_DATA, PL_KEY,         list,
          XV_KEY_DATA, TXT_SYS_KEY,    system,
          NULL );
(void) xv_create ( panel, PANEL_BUTTON,
          XV_X,                        xv_get ( pb, XV_X ),
          XV_Y,                        xv_get ( pb, XV_Y ) + (
                                                button_diff * 3 ),
          PANEL_LABEL_STRING,          "Delete Fixed Group",
          PANEL_NOTIFY_PROC,           del_group,
          XV_KEY_DATA, FRAME_BASE_KEY, frame,
          XV_KEY_DATA, PANEL_BASE_KEY, panel,
          XV_KEY_DATA, PL_KEY,         list,
          NULL );
```

```
        def_font = (Xv_Font) xv_get ( frame, XV_FONT );
        fixed    = (Xv_Font) xv_find ( frame, FONT,
                        FONT_NAME, "fixed",
                        NULL );
        if ( !fixed )
                printf ( "no fixed?!?\n" );
        (void) xv_create ( panel, PANEL_BUTTON,
                XV_X,                       xv_get ( pb, XV_X ),
                XV_Y,                       xv_get ( pb, XV_Y ) +
                                               ( button_diff * 4 ),
                PANEL_LABEL_STRING,         "Toggle Font",
                PANEL_NOTIFY_PROC,          toggle_font,
                XV_KEY_DATA, PL_KEY,        list,
                XV_KEY_DATA, FONT_FIXED_KEY, fixed,
                XV_KEY_DATA, FONT_DEFLT_KEY, def_font,
                NULL );
        (void) xv_create ( panel, PANEL_BUTTON,
                XV_X,                       xv_get ( pb, XV_X ),
                XV_Y,                       xv_get ( pb, XV_Y) +
                                               ( button_diff * 5 ),
                PANEL_LABEL_STRING,         "Toggle All",
                PANEL_NOTIFY_PROC,          toggle_all,

                XV_KEY_DATA, PL_KEY,        list,
                XV_KEY_DATA, FONT_FIXED_KEY, fixed,
                XV_KEY_DATA, FONT_DEFLT_KEY, def_font,
                NULL );
window_fit ( panel );
window_fit ( frame );
xv_main_loop ( frame );
return ( 1 );
}
```

Panel Messages

24

P anel messages, sometimes called read-only messages by the retentive, can be used for displaying things to the user. The user can't directly mangle these messages, because they are display-only. This occasionally leads to frustration and to graffiti on the screen. Panel messages have the attributes shown in Figure 24.1.

PANEL MESSAGE CALLBACK

The callback to a **PANEL_MESSAGE** object looks like

```
void
message_proc ( item, event )
Panel_item item;
Event *event;
{

}
```

where **item** is the handle of the panel message and **event** should be a Select button up event.

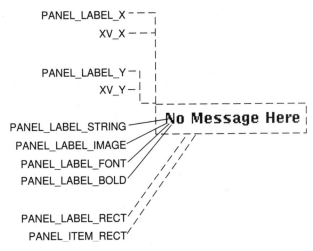

FIGURE 24.1 Panel Message Attributes

IMPLEMENTING CHANGE BARS USING PANEL MESSAGES

Although XView doesn't explicitly handle change bars on property windows, you can implement them by using panel messages.

Let's put a change bar in front of a choice item. Since the change bar needs to appear to the left of the choice item, it's easiest to create it first, rather than explicitly placing these items.

```
Panel_item chm;                          /* choice message */
Panel panel;

chm = xv_create ( panel, PANEL_MESSAGE, NULL );
(void) xv_create ( panel, PANEL_CHOICE,
        PANEL_CHOICE_STRINGS,    "Choice A",
                                 "Choice B",
                                 "Choice C",
                                 NULL,
        PANEL_NOTIFY_PROC,       choice_proc,
        XV_KEY_DATA, CH_ITEM_KEY, chm,
        NULL );
```

Using key data, we pass the panel message's handle into the callback. The callback looks like this:

```
void
choice_proc ( item, value, event )
Panel_item item;
int value;
Event *event;
{
        Panel_item cbar = xv_get ( item, XV_KEY_DATA, CH_ITEM_KEY );
        static int def_choice = 0;

        xv_set ( cbar
                PANEL_LABEL_STRING, ( ( value != def_choice ) ? "|" : " " ),
                NULL );
}
```

The **chm** item is retrieved as **cbar**. Next I have a hardcoded (Eeewww! Bad Programmer! Bad!!) value as the property window's default value for this choice setting. By comparing the current value against the default, I can see if the choice was changed. When it is changed, a " | " is displayed. If it is not changed, a " " is displayed.

THE SAMPLE PROGRAM

The sample program **message.c** shows a few common instances of panel messages. There are three things that are demonstrated by this program:

- A button that toggles a panel message
- A text item that displays a change bar if you type something into the field and press Tab or Return.
- A choice item that displays a change bar if you choose an item that is not the default.

```
/* message.c -- panel message demo
 * Author:  Kenneth Bibb
 * April 1992 -- Arastar Consulting
 *----------------------------------------
 *
 * o Toggle a message.
 *     TGL_ITEM_KEY will hold the handle of the PANEL_MESSAGE
 *     button_toggle_proc() is where the action is
 *     pb is the handle of the button in main()            h)
 *     tglm is the handle of the panel message in main()
 *
 * o Text item Change Bar
 *     TXT_ITEM_KEY will hold the handle of the PANEL_TEXT
 *     text_proc() is where the action is
 *     txtm is the handle of the panel message in main()
 *
 * o Choice Change Bar
 *     CH_ITEM_KEY will hold the handle of the PANEL_CHOICE
 *     choice_proc() is where the action is
 *     chm is the handle of the panel message in main()
 *
 * o Panel message callback
 *     detects SELECT up events
 *----------------------------------------
 * BUGS:  default value should not be hardcoded in production programs
 *     Text item's change bar should clear
 */

#include <stdio.h>
#include <xview/xview.h>
#include <xview/panel.h>



Attr_attribute TGL_ITEM_KEY;    /* toggled message handle    */
Attr_attribute TXT_ITEM_KEY;    /* panel_text cbar handle    */
Attr_attribute CH_ITEM_KEY;     /* choice cbar handle        */
char *blanks = "              ";  /* used with the toggled msg */



/* callback for the "Toggle Message" button
 */
void
button_toggle_proc ( item, event )
Panel_item item;
Event *event;
{
    /* retrieve the handle of the panel_message which we're going
     * to manipulate in the following xv_set()
     */
    Panel_item tm = (Panel_item) xv_get ( item, XV_KEY_DATA, TGL_ITEM_KEY);
    /* change the PANEL_LABEL_STRING on retrived panel_message.
     * if the string is not blank, replace PANEL_LABEL_STRING with blanks
     * if the string is blank,     replace PANEL_LABEL_STRING with message
     */
    xv_set ( tm, PANEL_LABEL_STRING,
                ( ( strcmp ( (char *) xv_get ( tm, PANEL_LABEL_STRING),
                                              blanks ) != 0 )
```

```
                              ? blanks : "No Message Here" ),
        NULL );
}

/* callback for the "What?" text item
 */
void
text_proc ( item, event )
Panel_item item;
Event *event;
{
        Panel_item tcb = xv_get ( item, XV_KEY_DATA, TXT_ITEM_KEY );

        /* change the PANEL_LABEL_STRING on retrieved panel_message.
         * if the PANEL_VALUE is not NULL, display "|"
         * if entering value use dimmed |
         */
        xv_set ( tcb, PANEL_LABEL_STRING, ( xv_get ( item, PANEL_VALUE) )
                                                        ? "|" : " ",
                    PANEL_INACTIVE, TRUE,
                    NULL );
}

/* callback for the "Who ate the cookies?" choice
 */
void
choice_proc ( item, value, event )
Panel_item item;
int value;
Event *event;
{
        /* hardcoded default value which should be replaced
         * with something more elegant
         */
        static int def_choice=0;
        Panel_item tcb = xv_get ( item, XV_KEY_DATA, CH_ITEM_KEY);

        xv_set ( tcb,
                    PANEL_LABEL_STRING, ( ( value != def_choice) ? "|" : " " ),
                    NULL);
}

/* callback for the "No Message Here" panel_message
 */
void
message_proc ( item, event )
Panel_item item;
Event *event;
{
        /* beep at any user stupid enough to click here ;) 
         */
        printf ( "\07" );
        fflush ( stdout );
}

main ( argc, argv )
int argc;
char **argv;
{
```

```
Frame         frame;                          /* base frame          */
Panel         panel;                          /* base panel          */
Panel_item    pb;                             /* toggle button handle */
Panel_item    tglm;                           /* toggle message handle */
Panel_item    txtm;                           /* text message handle  */
Panel_item    chm;                            /* choice message handle */
char          mbuf[20];
char          *message=mbuf;                  /* field for panel_text */

xv_init ( XV_INIT_ARGC_PTR_ARGV, &argc, argv, NULL );
TXT_ITEM_KEY = xv_unique_key ();         /* set the keys      */
TGL_ITEM_KEY = xv_unique_key ();
CH_ITEM_KEY  = xv_unique_key ();

frame = (Frame) xv_create ( XV_NULL, FRAME,
              FRAME_LABEL,                    argv[0],
              XV_X,                           300,
              XV_Y,                           175,
              FRAME_SHOW_RESIZE_CORNER, FALSE,
              NULL );
panel = (Panel) xv_create ( frame, PANEL, NULL );


/* set up toggle button
 */
pb =    (Panel_item) xv_create ( panel, PANEL_BUTTON,
              PANEL_LABEL_STRING, "Toggle Message",
              PANEL_NOTIFY_PROC,  button_toggle_proc,
              NULL );
tglm = (Panel_item) xv_create ( panel, PANEL_MESSAGE,
              PANEL_LABEL_STRING, blanks,
              PANEL_NOTIFY_PROC,  message_proc,
              NULL );
(void) xv_set ( pb, XV_KEY_DATA, TGL_ITEM_KEY, tglm, NULL);


/* set up text field
 */
txtm = (Panel_item) xv_create ( panel, PANEL_MESSAGE,
              PANEL_NEXT_ROW, -1,
              NULL );          h)
(void) xv_create ( panel, PANEL_TEXT,
              PANEL_LABEL_STRING,          "What?",
              PANEL_VALUE_DISPLAY_LENGTH, 10,
              PANEL_VALUE_STORED_LENGTH,  20,
              PANEL_VALUE,                message,
              XV_KEY_DATA, TXT_ITEM_KEY,  txtm,
              PANEL_NOTIFY_LEVEL,         PANEL_ALL,
              PANEL_NOTIFY_PROC,          text_proc,
              NULL );

/* set up choice
 */
chm = (Panel_item) xv_create ( panel, PANEL_MESSAGE,
              PANEL_NEXT_ROW,             -1,
              PANEL_LABEL_BOLD,           TRUE,
              NULL );

(void) xv_create ( panel, PANEL_CHOICE,
              PANEL_LABEL_STRING,         "Who ate the cookies?",
```

```
                    PANEL_CHOICE_STRINGS,        "April",
                                                 "Alene",
                                                 "Allison",
                                                 "Amber",
                                                 "Amy",
                                                 NULL,
                    PANEL_NOTIFY_PROC,           choice_proc,
                    XV_KEY_DATA, CH_ITEM_KEY,    chm,
                    NULL );
        window_fit ( panel );
        window_fit ( frame );

        xv_main_loop ( frame );
}
```

Panel Text Items

25

T ext items are, in a way, the missing link in the evolutionary chain that leads from the command line-oriented interface of **csh** and the full GUI context of the scroll list.

Setting these items up and getting values back out are easy. But manipulating the notify procedure can be confusing, and data validation can seem (at least slightly) off-the-wall. A **PANEL_TEXT** object has the attributes shown in Figure 25.1.

CALLBACK PROCEDURE

The callback function for a panel text item can be prototyped as follows:

```
Panel_setting panel_text_notify ( Panel_item item, Event *event)
```

Where **item** is the panel text item's handle, **event** is a pointer to the Event structure, and **Panel_setting** is one of the values listed in Table 25.1. You'll also need to set **PANEL_NOTIFY_LEVEL** appropriately, or you'll never get this far. The values are listed in Table 25.2. The specified level uses the chars in **PANEL_NOTIFY_STRING** to determine whether the notify procedure should be called. The default notify string is ″\n\t\r″, but you can use other chars depending on your needs.

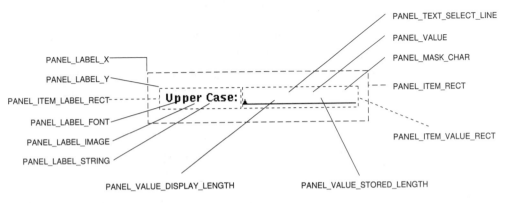

FIGURE 25.1 Panel Text Item Attributes

Setting	Moves Caret	Focus Point
PANEL_NONE	no	no
PANEL_NEXT	next	begin
PANEL_PREVIOUS	previous	begin
PANEL_INSERT	no	here

TABLE 25.1 PANEL Setting List

PUTTING TEXT INTO A PANEL TEXT ITEM

To put text into the value part of a panel text item, use

```
xv_set ( item, PANEL_VALUE, string, NULL );
```

where **item** is the panel text item that you want to modify, and **string** is the string that you want to display.

RETRIEVING TEXT FROM A PANEL TEXT ITEM

Retrieving text is very similar. To retrieve the text off of a panel text item, use

```
string = (char *) xv_get ( item, PANEL_VALUE );
```

where **string** is the retrieved text and **item** is the panel text item.

DATA VALIDATION ON A PANEL TEXT ITEM

As previously mentioned, there are four settings—**PANEL_NONE**, **PANEL_NON_PRINTABLE**, **PANEL_SPECIFIED**, and **PANEL_ALL**—that can be used for setting the notify level. If you want to do data validation, this gives you the chance to do validation at one of these levels.

You can wait until the user has finished entering the entire field before you do your validation. To do this you should use **PANEL_NON_PRINTABLE** or **PANEL_SPECIFIED**. Alternatively, you can capture everything that the user types and do validation on the fly. To do that, you'd use **PANEL_ALL**.

You can also tie an interposition routine to the text item and create a "new" text item that will "automatically" do the proper validation.

Validation by Field   Sometimes it's best to do validation on the whole field. Ensuring that a field contains a valid state abbreviation, for example, would be such a use.

Notify Level	Description
PANEL_NONE	Don't call the notify procedure.
PANEL_NON_PRINTABLE	Call notify procedure on nonprint chars.
PANEL_SPECIFIED	Call notify procedure on specified char.
PANEL_ALL	Call notify procedure on all chars.

TABLE 25.2 PANEL_NOTIFY_LEVEL Values

AB	Alberta
BC	British Columbia
MB	Manitoba
NB	New Brunswick
NF	Newfoundland
NS	Nova Scotia
NT	Northwest Territories
ON	Ontario
PE	Prince Edward Island
PQ	Quebec
SK	Saskatchewan
UT	Yukon Territory

TABLE 25.3 Canada Postal Code Directory Province Abbreviations

To do field validation, check the field using a notify level of **PANEL_NON_PRINTABLE** or **PANEL_SPECIFIED**.

Validation by Character You can also do verification on a character-by-character basis. If you wanted to ensure that a field contains a valid Canadian province code, for example, you could either check by field or by character. A more normal use is to restrict a field to numbers or to create a floating point entry.

Use a notify level of **PANEL_ALL** for this. You should pass nonprintable characters to **panel_text_notify()** (the default notify procedure for panel text items). Printable characters should return **PANEL_INSERT** so that they'll be inserted into the field (and so that they'll be displayed).

SAMPLE PROGRAM

The sample program **text.c** has three fields: a state field, which accepts a U.S. state abbreviation; a province field, which accepts a Canadian province abbreviation; and an integer field, which demonstrates **PANEL_NONE** validation.

The state field uses interposition to force characters into upper case. It then checks a table of state names, which it gets from the following header file:

```
/* states.h -- list of state abbreviations
 */
"AK", "AL", "AR", "AZ", "CA", "CO", "CT", "DE", "FL", "GA", "HI", "IA", "ID",
"IL", "IN", "KS", "KY", "LA", "MA", "MD", "ME", "MI", "MN", "MO", "MS", "MT",
"NC", "ND", "NE", "NH", "NJ", "NM", "NV", "NY", "OH", "OK", "OR", "PA", "RI",
"SC", "SD", "TN", "TX", "UT", "VA", "VT", "WA", "WI", "WV", "WY"
```

Provinces, listed in Table 25.3, are hardcoded in and should prevent invalid keystrokes from being entered.

Finally, here is the source:

```
/* text.c -- demonstration of text panel items
 * Author: Kenneth Bibb
 *-------------------------------------------------
 * demonstrate PANEL_NONE, PANEL_NONPRINTABLE, PANEL_ALL, PANEL_SPECIFIED
 * for separate items.
 *
 * by field check: state abbs
 * by char  check: province abbs
 * using PANEL_NONE (only checked with "validate"): integer
 */

#include <stdio.h>
#include <xview/xview.h>
#include <xview/panel.h>
#include <xview/notify.h>

char *valid_states[] = {
#include "states.h"
};

/* valid province codes according to the Canada Postal Code Directory:
 *      AB              Alberta
 *      BC              British Columbia
 *      MB              Manitoba
 *      NB              New Brunswick
 *      NF              Newfoundland
 *      NS              Nova Scotia
 *      NT              Northwest Territories
 *      ON              Ontario
 *      PE              Prince Edward Island
 *      PQ              Quebec
 *      SK              Saskatchewan
 *      YT              Yukon Territory
 */

static Notify_value   base_item_event_handler ();
static Notify_value   decimal_numbers_only ();
static Notify_value   no_periods ();
static Notify_value   no_lower_case ();
static void           post_panel_item_events ();
static void           register_panel_items ();


Attr_attribute FRAME_BASE_KEY;
Attr_attribute TEXT_STATE_KEY;
Attr_attribute TEXT_PROVINCE_KEY;
Attr_attribute TEXT_INTGR_KEY;
Attr_attribute EVENT_PROC_KEY;


#define NUM_STATES 50              /* shouldn't change any time soon */

#define isdot(chr) ( ( chr ) =='.' )


Panel_setting
state_check ( text,event )
Panel_item text;
Event *event;
```

```
{
        Frame base = (Frame) xv_get ( text, XV_KEY_DATA, FRAME_BASE_KEY);
        char *value = (char *) xv_get ( text, PANEL_VALUE );
        int   i, found = FALSE;
        for (i=0; i<NUM_STATES; i++) {
                if ( strcmp ( value,valid_states[i] ) ==0 ) {
                                found = TRUE;
                                break;
                }
        } if ( found ) {
                (void) xv_set ( base,
                                FRAME_LEFT_FOOTER, " ",
                                NULL );
                return ( PANEL_NEXT );
        } else {
                (void) xv_set ( base,
                                FRAME_LEFT_FOOTER, "Not a valid state",
                                NULL );
                window_bell ( (Panel) xv_get ( (Panel_item) text, XV_OWNER ) );
                return ( PANEL_NONE );
        }
}

Panel_setting
province_check ( c,text )
int    c;
Panel_item text;
{
        char *string = (char *) xv_get ( text, PANEL_VALUE );

        if ( string[0] == NULL ) {
                switch ( c ) {
                case 'A':
                case 'B':
                case 'M':
                case 'N':
                case 'O':
                case 'P':
                case 'S':
                case 'Y':
                                return(PANEL_INSERT);
                default:
                                window_bell ( (Panel) xv_get (
                                                (Panel_item) text, XV_OWNER ) );
                                return ( PANEL_NONE );
                }
        } else if ( string[1] == NULL ) {
                switch ( string[0] ) {
                case 'A':
                                if ( c == 'B' )
                                                return ( PANEL_INSERT );
                                break;
                case 'B':
                                if (c == 'C')
                                                return ( PANEL_INSERT );
                                break;
                case 'M':
                                if ( c == 'B' )
                                                return ( PANEL_INSERT );
                                break;
```

```
                    case 'N' :
                                  switch(c) {
                                  case 'B' :
                                  case 'F' :
                                  case 'S' :
                                  case 'T' :
                                                       return ( PANEL_INSERT );
                                  default:
                                                       break;
                                  }
                    case 'O' :
                                  if ( c == 'N' )
                                                       return ( PANEL_INSERT );
                                  break;
                    case 'P' :
                                  if ( c == 'E' || c == 'Q' )
                                                       return ( PANEL_INSERT );
                                  break;
                    case 'S' :
                                  if ( c == 'K' )
                                                       return ( PANEL_INSERT );
                                  break;
                    case 'Y' :
                                  if ( c == 'T' )
                                                       return ( PANEL_INSERT );
                                  break;
                    }
              window_bell ( (Panel) xv_get ( (Panel_item) text, XV_OWNER ) );
              return( PANEL_NONE );
        }
        return ( PANEL_INSERT );
}
Panel_setting
province_notify ( text,event )
Panel_item text;
Event *event;
{
        char *string = (char *) xv_get ( text, PANEL_VALUE );
        int   c = event_action ( (Event *) event );
        extern Panel_setting panel_text_notify ();

        if ( string[0] == NULL )
              return ( province_check ( c, text ) );
        else if ( !isprint ( c ) ) {
              switch ( c ) {
              case '\n':
              case '\t':
              case '\r':
                                  return ( PANEL_NEXT );
              default:
                                  return ( panel_text_notify ( text, event) );
              }
        } else {
              if ( string[1] == NULL )
                                  return ( province_check ( c,text ) );
              else {
              window_bell ( (Panel) xv_get ( (Panel_item) text, XV_OWNER ) );
```

```
                                return ( PANEL_NONE );
                }
        }
}

Panel_setting
integer_check ( text, event )
Panel_item text;
Event *event;
{
    Frame base = (Frame) xv_get ( text, XV_KEY_DATA, FRAME_BASE_KEY);
    char *string = (char *) xv_get ( text, PANEL_VALUE );
    int   len = strlen ( string );
    int   i, found = FALSE;

    for ( i=0; i<len; i++)
        if ( !isdigit ( string[i] ) )
                                found = TRUE;
    if ( found ) {
        (void) xv_set ( base,
            FRAME_LEFT_FOOTER, "Only decimal digits are allowed",
            NULL );
        window_bell ( (Panel) xv_get ( (Panel_item) text, XV_OWNER ) );
            return ( PANEL_NONE );
    } else {
        (void) xv_set ( base,
            FRAME_LEFT_FOOTER, " ",
            NULL );
        return ( PANEL_NEXT );
    }
}

void
bval ( button, event )
Panel_item button;
Event *event;
{
    Frame          base = xv_get ( button, XV_KEY_DATA, FRAME_BASE_KEY );
    Panel_item     state = xv_get ( button, XV_KEY_DATA, TEXT_STATE_KEY );
    Panel_item province = xv_get ( button, XV_KEY_DATA, TEXT_PROVINCE_KEY );
    Panel_item     intgr = xv_get ( button, XV_KEY_DATA, TEXT_INTGR_KEY );
    char *province_string = (char *) xv_get ( province, PANEL_VALUE );
    char  sbuf[80];
    char *s = sbuf;

    if ( (state_check ( state, event ) ==PANEL_NONE ) ||
       ( province_notify ( province, event ) ==NULL ) ||
       ( integer_check ( intgr, event ) ==PANEL_NONE ) )
                return;

    sprintf ( s, "State: %s Province: %s",
        (char *) xv_get ( state, PANEL_VALUE ),
        province_string );
    (void) xv_set ( base,
        FRAME_LEFT_FOOTER, s,
        NULL );
}
```

```
int
main ( argc, argv )
int argc;
char **argv;
{
        Frame base;
        Panel panel;
        Panel_text_item state;
        Panel_text_item province;
        Panel_text_item decint;


        (void) xv_init ( XV_INIT_ARGC_PTR_ARGV, &argc, argv, NULL );
        EVENT_PROC_KEY = xv_unique_key ();
        FRAME_BASE_KEY = xv_unique_key ();
        TEXT_STATE_KEY = xv_unique_key ();
        TEXT_PROVINCE_KEY = xv_unique_key ();
        TEXT_INTGR_KEY = xv_unique_key ();

        base = (Frame) xv_create ( XV_NULL, FRAME,
                    XV_LABEL,                argv[0],
                    FRAME_SHOW_FOOTER, TRUE,
                    NULL );

        panel = (Panel_item) xv_create ( base, PANEL,
                    PANEL_LAYOUT, PANEL_VERTICAL,
                    NULL );

        state = (Panel_item) xv_create ( panel, PANEL_TEXT,
                    PANEL_LABEL_STRING,          "U.S. State:",
                    PANEL_VALUE_DISPLAY_LENGTH,  2,
                    PANEL_VALUE_STORED_LENGTH,   2,
                    PANEL_NOTIFY_PROC,           state_check,
                    XV_KEY_DATA, FRAME_BASE_KEY, base,
                    NULL );

        province = (Panel_item) xv_create ( panel, PANEL_TEXT,
                    PANEL_LABEL_STRING,          "Canadian Province:",
                    PANEL_VALUE_DISPLAY_LENGTH,  2,
                    PANEL_VALUE_STORED_LENGTH,   2,
                    PANEL_NOTIFY_LEVEL,          PANEL_ALL,
                    WIN_IGNORE_EVENTS,           WIN_UP_EVENTS, NULL,
                    PANEL_NOTIFY_PROC,           province_notify,
                    XV_KEY_DATA, FRAME_BASE_KEY, base,
                    NULL );

        decint = (Panel_item) xv_create ( panel, PANEL_TEXT,
                    PANEL_LABEL_STRING,          "Decimal Integer:",
                    PANEL_VALUE_DISPLAY_LENGTH,  8,
                    PANEL_VALUE_STORED_LENGTH,   8,
                    XV_KEY_DATA, FRAME_BASE_KEY, base,
                    PANEL_NOTIFY_LEVEL,          PANEL_NONE,
                    PANEL_NOTIFY_PROC,           integer_check,
                    NULL );

        (void) xv_create ( panel, PANEL_BUTTON,
                    PANEL_LABEL_STRING,              "Validate",
                    PANEL_NOTIFY_PROC,               bval,
```

```
                          XV_KEY_DATA, FRAME_BASE_KEY,    base,
                          XV_KEY_DATA, TEXT_STATE_KEY,    state,
                          XV_KEY_DATA, TEXT_PROVINCE_KEY, province,
                          XV_KEY_DATA, TEXT_INTGR_KEY,    decint,
                          NULL );
        register_panel_items ( panel );
        notify_interpose_event_func ( state, no_lower_case, NOTIFY_SAFE);
        notify_interpose_event_func ( province, no_lower_case, NOTIFY_SAFE );

        window_fit ( panel );
        window_fit ( base );
        xv_main_loop ( base );
        return ( 0 );
}


/*******************************************************************/
/* These routines are generic to the panel items.  */
/*******************************************************************/


/*
 * Traverse each item in the given Panel and register our base event handler
 * for it with the Notifier.  Also, replace the default event handler with
 * one that posts events via the Notifier, and attach the old one onto the
 * item with key-data.  Note:  Once this is done, our Panel_item's are
 * functionally no different than when we started, except that they can
 * now be interposed on.
 */
static void
register_panel_items ( panel )
Panel panel;
{
        Panel_item item;
        void (*items_event_proc) ();

        PANEL_EACH_ITEM(panel, item)
        items_event_proc = (void(*) ()) xv_get ( item, PANEL_EVENT_PROC );
        xv_set ( item,
                    PANEL_EVENT_PROC,             post_panel_item_events,
                    XV_KEY_DATA, EVENT_PROC_KEY, items_event_proc,
                    NULL );
        notify_set_event_func ( item, base_item_event_handler, NOTIFY_SAFE );
        PANEL_END_EACH
}

static void
post_panel_item_events ( item, event )
Panel_item item;
Event *event;
{
        notify_post_event ( (Notify_client)item,
                            (Notify_event)event,NOTIFY_SAFE );
}


/*
 * The generic base handler for panel items.  This makes
 * a direct call to the items' default event handler, just
```

```
 * as the Panel would normally do.  Note:  A base handler
 * is always the LAST handler to see the event.
 */
static Notify_value
base_item_event_handler ( client, event, arg, type )
Notify_client client;
Notify_event event;
Notify_arg arg;
Notify_event_type type;
{
        void (*items_event_proc)() = (void (*)()) xv_get ( (Panel_item)
                    client, XV_KEY_DATA, EVENT_PROC_KEY );

        if ( items_event_proc )
             (*items_event_proc) ( (Panel_item) client, (Event *) event );
        return NOTIFY_DONE;
}


/*
 * Force all characters to be upper case
 */
static Notify_value
no_lower_case ( client, event, arg, type )
Notify_client client;
Notify_event event;
Notify_arg arg;
Notify_event_type type;
{
        int id = event_action ( (Event *) event);

        if ( !( isalpha ( id ) && isupper ( id ) ) )
                    event_set_action ( (Event *) event, toupper ( id ) );
        return ( notify_next_event_func ( client, event, arg, type ) );
}
```

The Selection Package

26

The selection package is a generalized method of interprocess communication. In its most abstract conception, it gives programs a virtually unlimited number of "rendezvous" locations through which they can pass data to each other.

The most well-known example of such a rendezvous is the concept of the "clipboard" —one program can be thought of as posting its data up on the wall for any other to copy.

If you look at that description carefully, you may find it to be slightly different from many people's concept of the clipboard. The clipboard is usually thought of as "common" area of memory, disk, or what-have-you, into which a program duplicates its data, so that another program can then come along, grab this chunk of memory, and drag it back home with it.

That view is misleading, at least when dealing with X. In X, a program that wishes to make its data available via the selection package only announces its intention to do so; it does this by *acquiring the clipboard selection*. No data is transferred at this time to another location; the program is merely announcing that another program can rendezvous with it by asking the selection service who holds the clipboard selection at this time.

When the program that wants the data on the clipboard makes its request, only then does the offering program transfer data, and it does so directly to the client; the data is never really held in an intermediate location (other than the transient buffers necessary to copy the data from one process to another). In fact, it's entirely possible that the program holding the clipboard selection has only *decided what to offer* on the clipboard until the time a potential recipient asks for it.

The clipboard is not the only rendezvous point for data. There are three such rendezvous points defined by the ICCCM, but in fact, programs are free to define their own. Of course, these are useless unless other programs know that they exist and are being used. The other ICCCM-defined selection ranks are **PRIMARY** and **SECONDARY**, but because these two ranks are almost always handled internally by the XView packages, our examples will focus on how to implement the **CLIPBOARD** selection.

Here's a typical sequence of events involved in transferring data via the clipboard, from the point of view of the program offering the data:

1. The user of the program makes an action to be interpreted as "copying something to the clipboard."

2. The program informs the X server that it now wants to be the "owner" of the clipboard selection; this request is granted. The program should provide some kind of feedback to the user indicating that the copy has taken place.

3. At this point, the program is likely to do something to identify the data that will be given to a program that asks for the contents of the clipboard; this could be a good time to copy this data to a separate area of memory or disk, in case the data in question is modified by future actions before the clipboard selection that's just been acquired is to be relinquished.

4. The user of another program (or the same program!) makes an action to be interpreted as a copy from the clipboard.

5. The requesting program asks the X server for the clipboard's data; the X server in turn checks to see who it has given the clipboard selection to and asks it for the data, which it then passes to the requestor.

There is one more element to this transaction that we haven't mentioned yet: The selection holder and the selection requestor will negotiate what *kind* of data is to be transferred. For example, if the selection is a file, the selection requestor may want only the *name* of the file. Another selection holder may want the *contents* of the file. The type of data being transferred can be tested at a higher level, as well; a graphics program requesting the contents of the clipboard may reject it on being informed that the data is an audio file.

XVIEW AND THE SELECTION PACKAGE

The XView programmer interacts with X's selection service through the *selection package*. A program wishing to hold a selection uses a **SELECTION_OWNER** object; a program asking for the contents of a selection uses a **SELECTION_REQUESTOR** object. A program can actually hold several selections at once by using multiple **SELECTION_OWNER** objects.

Note that many XView objects automatically handle selections, through internal use of such objects. A text subwindow, for example, will hold three selections if you double click on any word in its window (it now holds the **PRIMARY** selection), press the Copy key (it now holds the **CLIPBOARD** selection), then hold down the Paste key and double click on any other word (it now holds the **SECONDARY** selection).

OWNING A SELECTION

Here's a simple example of a program that will copy the current time as a text string to the clipboard whenever a "Copy to Clipboard" button is pressed. Remember, there is no location outside of this program that can be considered the clipboard. It's not in the X server, it's not in some background process — it's all up to whatever program has announced that it wants to be the holder of the clipboard selection. In our example, the program itself allocates an area of memory where it stores the time that the button was pressed.

The action starts in the button's notify routine. The current time of day is stored in the global string `clip_buf`, and its length is stored the global int `clip_len`. Then the function `own_clipboard()` is called.

```
void
own_clipboard ()
{
static Selection_owner sel_owner = NULL;

if (sel_owner ==NULL)
    sel_owner = xv_create ( base_frame, SELECTION_OWNER,
        SEL_CONVERT_PROC, clip_conv_proc,
        SEL_LOSE_PROC,    sel_lose_proc,
        NULL );
```

```
    xv_set ( sel_owner,
            SEL_OWN,        TRUE,
            SEL_RANK_NAME,  "CLIPBOARD",
            NULL );

    xv_set ( base_frame,
            FRAME_LEFT_FOOTER, "Acquired clipboard.",
            NULL);
    }
```

In this code **sel_owner** is an object of type **Selection_owner**. The first time **own_clipboard()** is called, this object is created, and two procedures are associated with it: **clip_conv_proc()** is the *selection conversion procedure* that will be called whenever a program asks for the contents of the clipboard, and **sel_lose_proc()** is the procedure that will be called whenever our program loses the selection.

Now we make the call that actually acquires the clipboard selection. By setting the attributes **SEL_OWN** to **TRUE** and **SEL_RANK_NAME** to **"CLIPBOARD"**, we become the owner of the clipboard selection. From now until the time we lose the selection, any procedure that asks to copy from the clipboard will trigger our function **clip_conv_proc()**.

The **clip_conv_proc()** function must be written to answer requests appropriate to this application. It will be passed a "target," which is an *X atom* designating what kind of data the requesting application wants. One target we must always be prepared to answer is the **TARGETS** target—we should pass a list of all the targets we know how to deal with in response to this request.

Digression: An X atom is merely an opaque handle with a string associated with it. The X server guarantees that there is only one atom associated with any string, so a convenient shorthand is established. Rather than two programs passing a string such as **"PHASE_OF_THE_MOON"**, they may register an atom by that name with the X server and pass the much shorter atom whenever that particular piece of data needs to be exchanged. A short list of atoms is predefined; the values of the predefined atoms are associated with symbolic constants beginning with **XA_**, such as **XA_PRIMARY**. Other atoms, such as **"TARGETS"**, are created on the fly the first time they are needed and do not have a predefined numeric value; their value must be requested from the server via the Xlib **XInternAtom()** call or by using the XView function

```
    targ_atom = (Atom) xv_get ( server_object, SERVER_ATOM, "TARGETS" );
```

(For more information on the server object, see XVPM Section 15.3.)

In our example, we convert (or handle, if you prefer) requests for the **"TARGETS"**, **"LENGTH"**, and **XA_STRING** atoms, which is the minimum set of atoms required to interoperate with XView programs that request strings from the clipboard.

For any **clip_conv_proc()** call, we need to place values in four locations that have been passed to us: **format**, **length**, **type**, and **data**. The **format** is the length of each element of the data, **length** is the number of items of that size we're returning, **type** is an atom describing the type of data being returned, and the **data** is the actual data being returned.

Handling the **TARGETS** request is as simple as creating an array of the atoms we handle. We do this the first time **clip_conv_proc()** is called. Atoms are four bytes long, so we pass 32 as the **format**. We're returning three atoms, so we set **length** to 3. The **type** is **XA_ATOM**, and **data** is the array of atoms we can deal with.

The **LENGTH** request is handled similarly. We return an integer, so we pass 32, 1, **XA_INTEGER**, and the length of our clipboard data. For the **XA_STRING** request, we pass 8, the length of the buffer, **XA_STRING** and the buffer itself.

Our function **sel_lose_proc()** will be called when another program decides to acquire the **CLIPBOARD** selection. In our example, all we do is put a message on the frame footer, but if we had dynamically allocated space to hold the clipboard data, this would be the place to free it up.

⬛ REQUESTING A SELECTION'S DATA

Our next example program will copy the contents of any of the **PRIMARY**, **SECONDARY**, or **CLIPBOARD** selections to a text subwindow.

The menu associated with the "Rank" button has three choices, corresponding with the three types of selections we wish to request. At the time we create the menu, we set each menu item's **MENU_CLIENT_DATA** to the selection's atom, so it's a simple matter, during the menu's notification routine, to use that atom to make the request.

The **button_notify()** function is where we make the actual request. The first time this routine is called, we create the **SELECTION_REQUESTOR** object we use for this and subsequent requests. Notice that the defaults for the **SELECTION_REQUESTOR** item are sufficient for our program: specifically, the default for **SEL_TYPE** is **XA_STRING**.

For each call, we set the requestor object's **SEL_RANK** attribute to the atom, which was attached to the menu item as just described. We then use **xv_get()** to make the actual request for the data. If the request is successful, we're returned a pointer to a **malloc()**ed buffer of the data, and the length and format of the data are returned in the two variables whose addresses we passed. If the request failed, **SEL_ERROR** is returned in the length variable.

This example shows a blocking request—that is, the request is executed and completes sequentially. This is probably the most natural way to retrieve a selection for those used to a procedural model of programming. The disadvantage to making the call in this way is that if the program holding the selection is slow to reply to the request, or if there is a large amount of data to transfer, your program will hang until the request completes.

It is also possible to make a nonblocking request. You do this by "posting" the request, specifying a reply procedure to be called when the data transfer is complete. The call to post the request, **sel_post_req()**, returns immediately.

There are only a few changes we'd need to make to our example program to change it from a blocking to a nonblocking request. First, we'd need to create a reply procedure; we can do this by taking the appropriate code from **button_notify()** and putting it in a wrapper:

```
void
reply_proc ( req, target, type, data, length, format )
Selection_requestor req;
Atom target, type;
Xv_opaque data;
unsigned long length;
int format;
{
        char msg[30];
        textsw_reset ( textsw, 0, 0 );
        textsw_insert ( textsw, data, strlen ( data ) );
        textsw_possibly_normalize ( textsw, 0 );
        free ( data );
```

```
        sprintf ( msg, "Selection length: %d", length );
        xv_set ( base_frame, FRAME_LEFT_FOOTER, msg, NULL );
}
```

Now we change **button_notify()** so that instead of using **xv_get()** against the selection requestor object, we call **sel_post_req()**. We also specify a selection reply procedure when we create the selection requestor object.

```
void
button_notify ( menu, result )
Menu menu;
Menu_item result;
{
        static Selection_requestor sel_requestor = NULL;
        if ( sel_requestor ==NULL )
            sel_requestor = xv_create ( base_frame, SELECTION_REQUESTOR,

                    SEL_REPLY_PROC, reply_proc,
                    NULL );

        xv_set ( sel_requestor,
            SEL_RANK, (Atom) xv_get ( result, MENU_CLIENT_DATA ),
            NULL );

        (void) sel_post_req ( sel_requestor );
}
```

SAMPLE PROGRAMS

There are four files here:

Makefile   A Makefile for creating these programs

sor.c   A blocking requestor example

sor_nb.c   A nonblocking requestor example

stopwatch.c   An example of taking over the clipboard

```
#
# Makefile for the selection chapter
#
CFLAGS += -g
CPPFLAGS += -I$(OPENWINHOME)/include
LDFLAGS += -L$(OPENWINHOME)/lib
LDLIBS += -lxview -lolgx -lX11

all: stopwatch sor sor_nb
stopwatch: stopwatch.o
        $(LINK.c) -o $@ $(@).o $(LDLIBS)

sor: sor.o
        $(LINK.c) -o $@ $(@).o $(LDLIBS)

sor_nb: sor_nb.o
        $(LINK.c) -o $@ $(@).o $(LDLIBS)

clean:
        $(RM) *.o *.BAK *% core
```

```
/*
 * sor.c - An example of a blocking selection requestor.
 */

#include <stdio.h>
#include <X11/Xlib.h>
#include <xview/xview.h>
#include <xview/panel.h>
#include <xview/textsw.h>
#include <xview/sel_pkg.h>

/*
 * Global object definitions.
 */
Frame               base_frame;
Textsw              textsw;

void
button_notify ( menu, result )
Menu menu;
Menu_item result;
{
    static Selection_requestor sel_requestor = NULL;
    char *data;
    int length, format;

    if ( sel_requestor == NULL )
        sel_requestor = xv_create ( base_frame, SELECTION_REQUESTOR, NULL );

    xv_set ( sel_requestor,
        SEL_RANK, (Atom) xv_get ( result, MENU_CLIENT_DATA ),
        NULL );

    data = (char *) xv_get ( sel_requestor, SEL_DATA, &length, &format );

        if ( length == SEL_ERROR )
            xv_set ( base_frame, FRAME_LEFT_FOOTER,
                                            "Could not get selection.", NULL );
    else {
        char msg[30];

        textsw_reset ( textsw, 0, 0 );
        textsw_insert ( textsw, data, strlen ( data ) );
        textsw_possibly_normalize ( textsw, 0 );
        free ( data );
        sprintf ( msg, "Selection length: %d", length );
        xv_set ( base_frame, FRAME_LEFT_FOOTER, msg, NULL );

    }

}

/*
 * Create menu for rank button.
 */
Menu
sor_menu_create ( owner )
Frame owner;
{
    Menu menu;
```

```
    Display *dpy;

    dpy = (Display *) xv_get ( owner, XV_DISPLAY );

    menu = xv_create(XV_NULL, MENU_COMMAND_MENU,
        MENU_TITLE_ITEM, "Selection Rank",
        MENU_ITEM,
                        MENU_STRING,  "PRIMARY",
                        MENU_CLIENT_DATA, XA_PRIMARY,
                        NULL,
        MENU_ITEM,
                        MENU_STRING,  "SECONDARY",
                        MENU_CLIENT_DATA, XA_SECONDARY,
                        NULL,
        MENU_ITEM,
                        MENU_STRING,  "CLIPBOARD",
                        MENU_CLIENT_DATA, XInternAtom ( dpy,
                                            "CLIPBOARD", False ),
                        NULL,
        MENU_GEN_PIN_WINDOW, owner, "Sel. Rank",
        MENU_NOTIFY_PROC, button_notify,
        NULL );
    return menu;
}

void
setup_window ()
{
    Panel panel;

    base_frame = xv_create ( NULL, FRAME,
        XV_LABEL, "Select-O-Rama",
        FRAME_SHOW_FOOTER, TRUE,
        NULL );

    panel = xv_create ( base_frame, PANEL,
        XV_WIDTH, 414,
        NULL );

    (void) xv_create ( panel, PANEL_BUTTON,
        XV_X,               16,
        XV_Y,               16,
        PANEL_LABEL_STRING, "Rank",
        PANEL_ITEM_MENU,    sor_menu_create ( base_frame ),
        NULL );

    window_fit_height ( panel );

    textsw = xv_create ( base_frame, TEXTSW,
        XV_X,                   0,
        XV_Y,                   (int) xv_get ( panel, XV_HEIGHT ),
        XV_WIDTH,               414,
        XV_HEIGHT,              121,
        TEXTSW_BROWSING,        TRUE,
        TEXTSW_DISABLE_LOAD,    TRUE,
        TEXTSW_IGNORE_LIMIT,    TEXTSW_INFINITY,
        NULL);

    window_fit ( base_frame );

}
```

```
main ( argc, argv )
int     argc;
char    **argv;
{
    xv_init ( XV_INIT_ARGC_PTR_ARGV, &argc, argv, NULL );

    setup_window ();

    xv_main_loop ( base_frame );
    exit ( 0 );
}
```

```
/*
 *  sor_nb.c - An example of a non-blocking selection requestor.
 */

#include <stdio.h>
#include <X11/Xlib.h>
#include <xview/xview.h>
#include <xview/panel.h>
#include <xview/textsw.h>
#include <xview/sel_pkg.h>

/*
 * Global object definitions.
 */
Frame               base_frame;
Textsw              textsw;
void
reply_proc ( req, target, type, data, length, format )
Selection_requestor req;
Atom target, type;
Xv_opaque data;
unsigned long length;
int format;
{
    char msg[30];

    textsw_reset ( textsw, 0, 0 );
    textsw_insert ( textsw, data, strlen ( data ) );
    textsw_possibly_normalize ( textsw, 0 );
    free ( data );

    sprintf ( msg, "Selection length: %d", length );
    xv_set ( base_frame, FRAME_LEFT_FOOTER, msg, NULL );
}
void
button_notify ( menu, result )
Menu menu;
Menu_item result;
{
    static Selection_requestor sel_requestor ==NULL;
```

```
    if ( sel_requestor == NULL )
      sel_requestor = xv_create ( base_frame, SELECTION_REQUESTOR,
          SEL_REPLY_PROC, reply_proc,
          NULL );

    xv_set ( sel_requestor,
          SEL_RANK, (Atom) xv_get ( result, MENU_CLIENT_DATA),
          NULL );

    (void) sel_post_req ( sel_requestor );
}

/*
 * Create menu for rank button.
 */
Menu
sor_menu_create ( owner )
Frame owner;
{
    Menu menu;
    Display *dpy;

    dpy = (Display *) xv_get ( owner, XV_DISPLAY );

    menu = xv_create ( XV_NULL, MENU_COMMAND_MENU,
        MENU_TITLE_ITEM, "Selection Rank",
        MENU_ITEM,
            MENU_STRING, "PRIMARY",
            MENU_CLIENT_DATA, XA_PRIMARY,
            NULL,
        MENU_ITEM,
            MENU_STRING, "SECONDARY",
            MENU_CLIENT_DATA, XA_SECONDARY,
            NULL,
        MENUITEM,
            MENU_STRING, "CLIPBOARD",
            MENU_CLIENT_DATA, XInternAtom ( dpy, "CLIPBOARD", False ),
            NULL,
        MENU_GEN_PIN_WINDOW, owner, "Sel. Rank",
        MENU_NOTIFY_PROC, button_notify,
        NULL);
    return menu;

}

void
setup_window ()
{
    Panel panel;

    base_frame = xv_create (XV_NULL, FRAME,
        XV_LABEL,           "Select-O-Rama",
        FRAME_SHOW_FOOTER, TRUE,
        NULL );

    panel = (Panel) xv_create ( base_frame, PANEL,
        XV_WIDTH, 414,
        NULL );
```

```
    (void) xv_create ( panel, PANEL_BUTTON,
        XV_X,                 16,
        XV_Y,                 16,
        PANEL_LABEL_STRING,   "Rank",
        PANEL_ITEM_MENU,      sor_menu_create ( base_frame ),
        NULL );

    window_fit_height ( panel );

    textsw = (Textsw) xv_create ( base_frame, TEXTSW,
        XV_X,                 0,
        XV_Y,                 (int) xv_get ( panel, XV_HEIGHT ),
        XV_WIDTH,             414,
        XV_HEIGHT,            121,
        TEXTSW_BROWSING,      TRUE,
        TEXTSW_DISABLE_LOAD,  TRUE,
        TEXTSW_IGNORE_LIMIT,  TEXTSW_INFINITY,
        NULL );

    window_fit ( base_frame );
}

main ( argc, argv )
int     argc;
char    **argv;
{
    xv_init ( XV_INIT_ARGC_PTR_ARGV, &argc, argv, NULL );

    setup_window ();

    xv_main_loop ( base_frame );
    exit ( 0 );
}
```

```
/*
 * stopwatch.c - Example of a program that takes ownership of the clipboard
 *                    selection.
 */

#include <stdio.h>
#include <time.h>
#include <X11/Xlib.h>
#include <xview/xview.h>
#include <xview/panel.h>
#include <xview/sel_pkg.h>

/*
 * Global object definitions.
 */
Frame base_frame;
Display *dpy;
```

```
char clip_buf[26];
int clip_len;

/*
 *  Respond to a request for the contents of the CLIPBOARD selection
 */
static int
clip_conv_proc ( owner, type, buf, length, format )
Selection_owner owner;
Atom *type;
Xv_opaque *buf;
unsigned long *length;
int *format;
{
    Atom TARGETS, LENGTH;
    static Atom targs[3] = { NULL, NULL, NULL };

    /*
     *  Initialize list of atoms we will respond to
     */
    if (targs[0] == NULL ) {
        TARGETS = XInternAtom ( dpy, "TARGETS", False );
        LENGTH = XInternAtom ( dpy, "LENGTH", False );

        targs[0] = TARGETS;
        targs[1] = LENGTH;
        targs[2] = XA_STRING;
    }

    if ( *type == TARGETS ) {
        *format = 32;
        *length = 3;
        *type = XA_ATOM;
        *buf = (Xv_opaque) targs;
        return TRUE;
    } else if ( *type == LENGTH ) {
        *format = 32;
        *length = 1;
        *type = XA_INTEGER;
        *buf = (Xv_opaque) &clip_len;
        return TRUE;
    } else if ( *type == XA_STRING ) {
        *format = 8;
        *length = clip_len;
        *buf = (Xv_opaque) clip_buf;
        return TRUE;
    } else
        return FALSE;
}

/*
 *  Handle loss of the selection

 */
void
sel_lose_proc ( sel )
Selection_owner sel;
{
    xv_set ( base_frame, FRAME_LEFT_FOOTER, "Clipboard relinquished.", NULL);
```

```
    /*
     *  If you dynamically allocated an area to hold clipboard contents,
     *  this is where you'd free it.
     */
}

/*
 *  Become the owner of the CLIPBOARD selection
 */
void
own_clipboard ()
{
    static Selection_owner sel_owner = NULL;

    if ( sel_owner == NULL )
        sel_owner = (Selection_owner) xv_create ( base_frame, SELECTION_OWNER,
            SEL_CONVERT_PROC, clip_conv_proc,
            SEL_LOSE_PROC,    sel_lose_proc,
            NULL );

    xv_set ( sel_owner,
        SEL_OWN,        TRUE,
        SEL_RANK_NAME, "CLIPBOARD",
        NULL );

    xv_set ( base_frame, FRAME_LEFT_FOOTER, "Acquired clipboard.", NULL );
}

/*
 * Notify callback function for `button_item'.
 */
void
button_notify ( item, event )
Panel_item item;
Event *event;
{
    struct timeval t;

    (void) gettimeofday ( &t, NULL );
    strcpy ( clip_buf, ctime ( &t.tv_sec ) );

    clip_len = strlen ( clip_buf );

    own_clipboard ();
}

void
setup_window ()
{
    Panel panel;

    base_frame = (Frame) xv_create ( XV_NULL, FRAME,
        XV_LABEL,         "Stopwatch",
        FRAME_SHOW_FOOTER, TRUE,
        NULL );

    panel = (Panel) xv_create ( base_frame, PANEL,
        WIN_BORDER, TRUE,
        NULL );
```

```
    (void) xv_create ( panel, PANEL_BUTTON,
        XV_X,               16,
        XV_Y,               16,
        PANEL_LABEL_STRING, "Copy Time to Clipboard",
        PANEL_NOTIFY_PROC,  button_notify,
        NULL );

    window_fit ( panel );
    window_fit ( base_frame );
}

main ( argc, argv )
int     argc;
char    **argv;
{
    xv_init ( XV_INIT_ARGC_PTR_ARGV, &argc, argv, NULL );

    setup_window ();

    dpy = (Display *) xv_get ( base_frame, XV_DISPLAY );

    xv_main_loop ( base_frame );
    exit ( 0 );
}
```

Sliders

Sliders are useful when you need to set a value within what can be easily thought of as a range. A slider has the attributes shown in Figure 27.1.

SLIDER CALLBACK

The callback for a slider looks like

```
void
slider_proc ( item, val, event )
Panel_item item;
int val;
Event *event;
{
}
```

where **item** is the handle of the slider, **val** is the current value (position of the slider), and **event** is the event that triggered the callback.

SLIDER LABELS

The purposes of some of the various slider attributes can be arcane.

PANEL_SLIDER_END_BOXES is responsible for toggling the display of the end boxes of the slider. If you want to let your users go quickly to the endpoints of the slider's range, set this to **TRUE**.

PANEL_MIN_VALUE sets the lower limit of the slider. This can be an unsigned integer.

PANEL_MAX_VALUE sets the upper limit of the slider. This can be an unsigned integer.

PANEL_SHOW_RANGE set to **TRUE** shows the min value at the minimum end of the slider and the max value at the maximum end of the slider. These values can be overridden by setting the **PANEL_MIN_VALUE_STRING** and **PANEL_MAX_VALUE_STRING** attributes, respectively. You can also turn off the display of the values by setting this to **FALSE**.

PANEL_MIN_VALUE_STRING controls an optional string that can be placed at the minimum end of the slider. If end boxes are displayed, this string is placed on the other side of the end box from the slider.

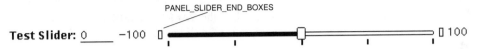

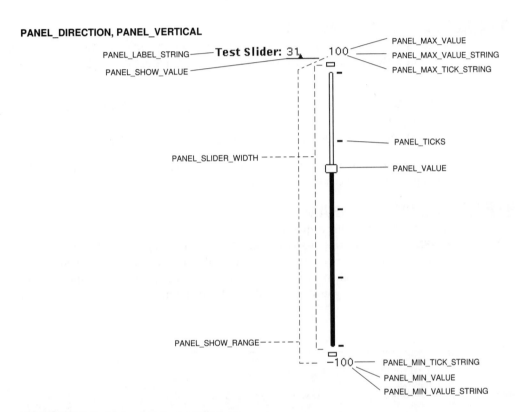

FIGURE 27.1 Slider Attribute Diagram

PANEL_MAX_VALUE_STRING controls an optional string that can be placed at the maximum end of the slider. If end boxes are displayed, this string is placed on the other side of the end box from the slider.

PANEL_MIN_TICK_STRING controls an optional string that can be placed next to the tick mark on the minimum end of the range. This can be used with the **PANEL_MIN_VALUE_STRING**, since they appear in different locations.

PANEL_MAX_TICK_STRING controls an optional string that can be placed next to the tick mark on the maximum end of the range. This can be used with the **PANEL_MAX_VALUE_STRING**, since they appear in different locations.

PANEL_SLIDER_WIDTH controls the length (in pixels) of the slider. This can be used to set the slider to a fixed length.

PANEL_TICKS sets the number of ticks along the slider, between the minimum and maximum tick marks.

SETTING THE SLIDER

Although the slider can be intimidating because of the many attributes that are available, it is easy to set the slider to a fixed value. Use the **PANEL_VALUE** attribute to set the slider to whatever value is required. For example, to set the slider **sl** to a value of 15:

```
(void) xv_set ( sl, PANEL_VALUE, 15, NULL );
```

READING THE SLIDER

To read the slider, you need to have a **PANEL_NOTIFY_PROC** set up for the slider. You also need to set the **PANEL_NOTIFY_LEVEL** to tell the notifier what kinds of events you're interested in.

- **PANEL_DONE** tells the notifier that you're only interested in Select button up events within the panel.
- **PANEL_ALL** tells the notifier that you're interested in all changes made to the slider.

The notify procedure receives the value as the second argument of the argument list. Within the notify procedure you can access this value.

SAMPLE PROGRAM

The following program displays a slider. You can change the orientation of the slider from **PANEL_HORIZONTAL** to **PANEL_VERTICAL** by clicking on the "Flip Direction" button.

The slider has a number of attributes set. Look at its **xv_create()** in the **main()** function and you'll see some others, which have been commented out. By commenting and uncommenting the various attributes, you should be able to figure out how the different attributes relate to each other.

```
/* slider.c -- slider demo
 * Author:   Kenneth Bibb
 * January 1992 -- Arastar Consulting
 *------------------------------------------
 * o Change the slider's layout by pressing the "Flip Direction" button
 * o Toggle attributes by (un)commenting them and compiling
 *
 */

#include <xview/xview.h>
#include <xview/panel.h>


Attr_attribute SLIDER_ITEM_KEY;   /* slider handle */
Attr_attribute FRAME_KEY;                      /* base frame handle */


/* callback for the "Flip Direction" button
 */
void
button_flip_proc ( item, event )
Panel_item item;
```

```
Event *event;
{
        /* retrieve the handle of the slider which we're going
         * to manipulate in the following xv_set ()
         */
        Panel_item sl = (Panel_item) xv_get ( item, XV_KEY_DATA,
                                                    SLIDER_ITEM_KEY );

        /* retrieve the current PANEL_DIRECTION with the xv_get ()
         * then toggle it
         */
        xv_set ( sl,
                    PANEL_DIRECTION, ( ( xv_get ( sl, PANEL_DIRECTION ) ==
                                                        PANEL_VERTICAL )
                                    ? PANEL_HORIZONTAL
                                    : PANEL_VERTICAL ),
                NULL);
}

/* callback for the slider -- written by Rick Goldstein
 */
void
slider_proc ( item, val, event )
Panel_item item;
int val;
Event *event;

{
        char buf[32];
        Frame frame = (Frame) xv_get ( item, XV_KEY_DATA, FRAME_KEY, NULL );

        sprintf ( buf, "You stopped on %d", val );
        (void) xv_set ( frame, FRAME_LEFT_FOOTER, buf, NULL );
}

main ( argc, argv )
int argc;
char **argv;
{
        Frame       frame;                          /* base frame */
        Panel       panel;                          /* base panel */
        Panel_item  sl;                             /* slider handle */


        xv_init ( XV_INIT_ARGC_PTR_ARGV, &argc, argv, NULL );
        SLIDER_ITEM_KEY = xv_unique_key ();
        FRAME_KEY = xv_unique_key ();


        frame = (Frame) xv_create ( NULL, FRAME,
                    FRAME_LABEL,                argv[0],
                    FRAME_SHOW_RESIZE_CORNER,FALSE,
                    FRAME_SHOW_FOOTER,          TRUE,
                    XV_X,                       300,
                    XV_Y,                       175,
                    NULL );
        panel = (Panel) xv_create ( frame, PANEL, NULL );
```

```
    /* create the slider
     * many of these attributes use defaults
     */
    sl = xv_create ( panel, PANEL_SLIDER,
                PANEL_LABEL_STRING,    "Test Slider:",
                PANEL_DIRECTION,       PANEL_HORIZONTAL,
                PANEL_VALUE,           0,      /* default value */
                PANEL_MIN_VALUE,       -100,   /* low end of range */
#ifdef XV_VERSION_NUMBER
                PANEL_MIN_TICK_STRING,  "-100", /* XView 3.0 */
                PANEL_MIN_VALUE_STRING, "min",  /* XView 3.0 */
#endif
                PANEL_MAX_VALUE,        100, /* high end of range */
#ifdef XV_VERSION_NUMBER
/*              PANEL_MAX_VALUE_STRING, "max", /* XView 3.0 */
                PANEL_MAX_TICK_STRING,  "100", /* XView 3.0 */
#endif
                PANEL_SLIDER_END_BOXES, TRUE,   /* show boxes        */
                PANEL_SLIDER_WIDTH,     300,    /* width in pixels   */
                PANEL_TICKS,            5,      /* number of ticks   */
                PANEL_SHOW_VALUE,       TRUE,   /* text field        */
                PANEL_SHOW_RANGE,       TRUE,   /* show endpoint vals */
                PANEL_NOTIFY_PROC,      slider_proc,
                PANEL_NOTIFY_LEVEL,     PANEL_DONE, /* only on stops */
                XV_KEY_DATA, FRAME_KEY, frame,
    NULL );

    /* create the button
     * the XV_Y is used to force the button onto the same row
     * as the slider
     */
    (void) xv_create ( panel, PANEL_BUTTON,
                XV_Y,                     xv_get(sl,XV_Y),
                PANEL_LABEL_STRING,       "Flip Direction",
                XV_KEY_DATA, SLIDER_ITEM_KEY, sl,
                PANEL_NOTIFY_PROC,        button_flip_proc,
                NULL );

    xv_main_loop ( frame );
}
```

Textsw

When you need a text subwindow, the **TEXTSW** package provides a quick and dirty way of doing things. For more control (multiple fonts, sizes, and so on), you'll need to use a canvas. But for most applications a textsw will be good enough.

A **TEXTSW** object has the attributes shown in Figure 28.1.

GENERAL COMMENTS ON TEXTSWS

Textsws are pretty straightforward—if you want to do something, you can typically do it with an attribute or a function. Message logs can be confusing, so I'm giving them a separate section, but everything else is pretty straightforward.

MESSAGE LOG WINDOWS

Message Logs[1] can be quite useful for debugging, general status info, and other purposes. They're even (relatively) easy to implement.

Here's some code for creating a pinnable message log window:

```
Frame   Flog;
Textsw  textsw;
char    sbuf[80];
char    *s = sbuf;

sprintf ( s, "%s: Message Log", argv[0] );
Flog = (Frame) xv_create ( frame, FRAME_CMD,
        FRAME_LABEL,  s,
        XV_X,         305,
        XV_Y,         220,
        NULL );
textsw = (Textsw) xv_create ( Flog, TEXTSW,
        XV_X,                       0,
        XV_Y,                       0,
        XV_WIDTH,                   WIN_EXTEND_TO_EDGE,
        XV_HEIGHT,                  WIN_EXTEND_TO_EDGE,
        TEXTSW_AGAIN_RECORDING,     FALSE,
        TEXTSW_CHECKPOINT_FREQUENCY, 0,
        TEXTSW_DISABLE_CD,          TRUE,
        TEXTSW_DISABLE_LOAD,        TRUE,
```

---

[1]For more information on Message Logs, see the OLSG, p. 302.

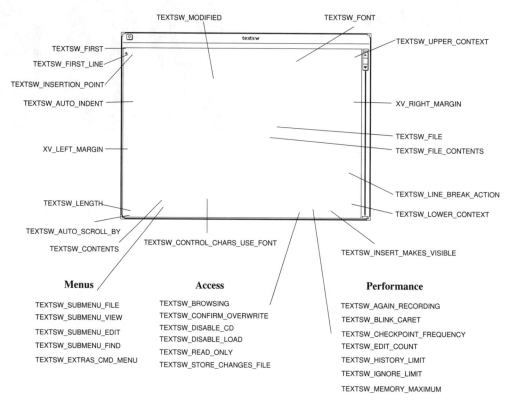

FIGURE 28.1 Textsw Attributes

```
        TEXTSW_HISTORY_LIMIT,        0,
        TEXTSW_IGNORE_LIMIT,         TEXTSW_INFINITY,
        TEXTSW_READ_ONLY,            TRUE,
        NULL );
window_fit ( Flog );
```

We start by formatting a window label like the one described in the OLGS. We then create the window and the textsw, which is going to fill the frame. We set the origin, height, and width of the textsw; then we turn off a number of features that won't be required (since we're not allowing the user to edit the log). The **TEXTSW_IGNORE_LIMIT** and **TEXTSW_READ_ONLY** combination disables the notice that comes up when you destroy the window, and it makes the window read-only (respectively).

We can now write to the message log by using

```
Textsw  textsw;
char    *string;
int     len;

textsw_insert ( textsw, string, len );
```

where **textsw** is the textsw that we want to write to, **string** is the message which we want to add to the message log, and len is the length of the string that we're adding.

SAMPLE PROGRAMS

There are two sample programs: **msglog.c**, which implements a simple message log window with buttons that write one of two strings into the message log, and **textsw.c**, which lets you edit a file.

msglog.c   The sample program is fairly straightforward, especially when compared against the previous section on message log windows. Following are some notes I'd like to make.

I include the time and date on each line—this is useful when tracking errors on a message log and is highly recommended. I use some standard UNIX time functions to format this part of the message. Since **strlen()** returns an incorrect size on strings created by **strftime()**, I use the length returned by **strftime()** and add the length of the strings that I'm going to add to it to generate a length usable by **textsw_insert()**.

```c
/* msglog.c -- Open Look message log
 * Author:  Kenneth Bibb
 * February 1992 -- Arastar Consulting
 */

#include <time.h>
#include <xview/xview.h>
#include <xview/panel.h>
#include <xview/canvas.h>
#include <xview/xv_xrect.h>
#include <xview/openmenu.h>
#include <xview/textsw.h>
#include <xview/notice.h>

Attr_attribute  LOGWIN_KEY;
Attr_attribute TEXTSW_KEY;

void
view_log ( menu, menu_item )
Menu menu;
Menu_item menu_item;
{
        Frame frame = xv_get ( menu, XV_KEY_DATA, LOGWIN_KEY );

        if ( xv_get ( frame, XV_SHOW ) ==FALSE )
                        xv_set ( frame,
                                        XV_SHOW, TRUE,
                                        NULL );

}


void
err_buttons ( item, event )
Panel_item item;
Event *event;
{
```

```
        Textsw te = xv_get ( item, XV_KEY_DATA, TEXTSW_KEY );
        char sbuf[80], s2buf[80];
        char *s = sbuf, *s2 = s2buf;
        time_t tt;
        struct tm *tm;
        int len;

        time ( &tt );
        tm=localtime ( &tt );
        len = strftime ( s2, 80, "%a %m/%d/%y %H:%M:%S", tm );
        if ( strcmp ( xv_get ( item, PANEL_LABEL_STRING ), "Error 1" )== 0)
        {
                    sprintf ( s, "%s\tQuietly decapitating
                            kittens\n", s 2 );
                    len += 30;
                    textsw_insert ( te, s,len );
        } else {
                    sprintf ( s, "%s\tLoudly punting a tomcat \n", s2);
                    len += 25;
                    textsw_insert ( te, s, len );
        }
}


int
main ( argc, argv )
int argc;
char **argv;
{
        Frame                       frame;
        Frame                       Flog;
        Textsw                      textsw;
        Panel                       panel;
        Menu                        menu;
        char                        sbuf[48];
        char                        *s = sbuf;


        xv_init ( XV_INIT_ARGC_PTR_ARGV, &argc, argv, NULL );
        TEXTSW_KEY = xv_unique_key ();
        LOGWIN_KEY = xv_unique_key ();

        /* create the base frame
         */
        frame = (Frame) xv_create ( XV_NULL, FRAME,
                    FRAME_LABEL,                argv[0],
                    XV_X,                       300,
                    XV_Y,                       175,
                    NULL );

        /* create the message log frame and associated stuff
         */
        sprintf ( s, "%s: Message Log", argv[0] );
        Flog =  (Frame) xv_create ( frame, FRAME_CMD,
                    FRAME_LABEL,                s,
                    XV_X,                       305,
                    XV_Y,                       220,
                    NULL );
```

```
        textsw = (Textsw) xv_create ( Flog, TEXTSW,
                    XV_X,       0,
                    XV_Y,       0,
                    XV_WIDTH,                       WIN_EXTEND_TO_EDGE,
                    XV_HEIGHT,                      WIN_EXTEND_TO_EDGE,
                    TEXTSW_AGAIN_RECORDING,         FALSE,
                    TEXTSW_CHECKPOINT_FREQUENCY,    0,
                    TEXTSW_DISABLE_CD,              TRUE,
                    TEXTSW_DISABLE_LOAD,            TRUE,
                    TEXTSW_HISTORY_LIMIT,           0,
                    TEXTSW_IGNORE_LIMIT,            TEXTSW_INFINITY,
                    TEXTSW_READ_ONLY,               TRUE,
                    NULL );
    window_fit ( Flog );

    /* back to our regularly scheduled program
     */
    menu  = (Menu) xv_create ( XV_NULL, MENU,
                    MENU_ITEM,
                            MENU_STRING, "Message Log",
                            NULL,
                    MENU_NOTIFY_PROC, view_log,
                    XV_KEY_DATA, LOGWIN_KEY, Flog,
                    NULL ),


    panel = (Panel) xv_create ( frame, PANEL,
                    NULL );

    (void) xv_create ( panel, PANEL_BUTTON,
                    PANEL_LABEL_STRING, "View",
                    PANEL_ITEM_MENU,    menu,
                    NULL );

    (void) xv_create ( panel, PANEL_BUTTON,
                    PANEL_LABEL_STRING,     "Error 1",
                    XV_KEY_DATA, TEXTSW_KEY, textsw,
                    PANEL_NOTIFY_PROC,      err_buttons,
                    NULL );

    (void) xv_create ( panel, PANEL_BUTTON,
                    PANEL_LABEL_STRING,     "Error 2",
                    PANEL_NOTIFY_PROC,      err_buttons,
                    XV_KEY_DATA, TEXTSW_KEY, textsw,
                    NULL );

    window_fit ( panel );
    window_fit ( frame );

    xv_main_loop ( frame );
    return ( 0 );
}
```

textsw.c This is a working editor implemented in less than 20 lines of code. You could use it to write code, but I prefer the logical, powerful, and omnipresent **vi** to any of these upstart editors (including **emacs**) (and no, there is no smiley on this line).

This was done in response to those nagging NeXT ads that show NeXT in a poor light by misrepresenting the Sun side of things. One of them (or it might have been a magazine article) mentioned that a fully working editor could be created on a NeXT in less than 15 minutes. I suspect that this editor has fewer lines of code in it than the NeXT version; plus, it took me probably no more than two minutes to crank out.

This is a good "demo" program, which you can use to experiment with the different attributes and commands that are used with the textsw package.

```
/* textsw.c -- basic editor
 * Author:  Kenneth Bibb -- May 1992 -- Arastar Consulting
 */

#include <xview/xview.h>
#include <xview/textsw.h>

void main ( int argc, char **argv )
{
        Frame frame;

        xv_init ( XV_INIT_ARGC_PTR_ARGV, &argc, argv, NULL );
        frame = (Frame) xv_create ( XV_NULL, FRAME,
                        FRAME_LABEL, argv[0],
                        NULL );
        (void) xv_create ( frame, TEXTSW, NULL );
        xv_main_loop ( frame );
}
```

TTY Subwindow

T he **TTY** subwindow package creates a subwindow that acts like a terminal. It understands the curses package and can be used in creating interactive windows like **shelltool** (although **shelltool** actually uses something else).

The biggest drawback to the **TTY** subwindow is that you're allowed only one per process. If you can live with that restriction, **TTY** will do a lot for you.

A **TTY** subwindow has the attributes shown in Figure 29.1.

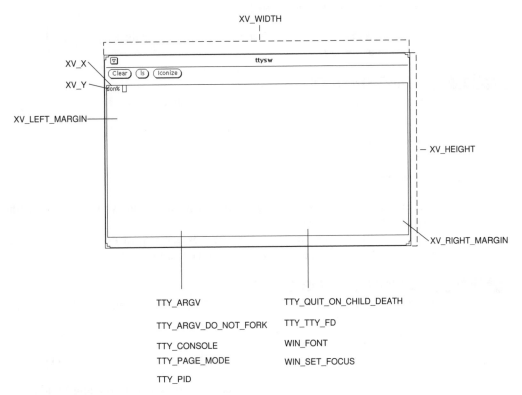

FIGURE 29.1 TTY Subwindow Attributes

▌SENDING DATA IN

There are times when you'll want to control what happens in the **TTY** subwindow. You can invoke the window with a command line so that it will execute just the requested command. You can also set things up so that your program can send certain lines into the **TTY** subwindow. For example, you can add macro buttons to a program and have each macro button generate a key sequence that you would normally have to type.

To include a command line, you can do the following:

```
for (i=1; i<argc; i++)
        argv[i - 1] = argv[i];
argv[i-1] = NULL;

tty = (Tty) xv_create ( frame, TTY,
        WIN_ROWS,     24,
        WIN_COLUMNS, 80,
        TTY_ARGV,     argv,
        NULL );
```

If you want to write to the input of the **tty**, you can use

```
Tty    tty;
char *string;
int    len;

tty_input ( tty, string, len );
```

This will send **string** to the **tty**'s *input*. This means that the **tty** will handle **string** as if it were typed in by the user.

▌GETTING DATA OUT

If you want to write to the output of the **tty**, you can use

```
Tty    tty;
char *string;
int    len;

tty_output ( tty, string, len );
```

Remember: This is going to the **tty**'s *output*. This means that you're doing something similar to a **printf()** to the screen.

You can use this to execute one of the **TTY** escape sequences. Table 29.1 lists **TTY** escape sequences; it is taken from the **xview/tty.h** header file.

▌CHECKING ON JOB STATUS

The following routine will monitor the status of a job that is running within a **TTY** subwindow:

```
Tty tty;

notify_set_wait3_func ( tty, wait_func, (int) xv_get ( tty, TTY_PID ));
```

The **TTY_PID** is the process id of the child process that is running within the **tty**. The **wait_func** is a function that is called as follows:

Escape Sequence	Action
\E[1t	Open
\E[2t	Close (become iconic)
\E[3t	Move, with interactive feedback
\E[3;top;leftt	Move to *top*, *left* in pixels
\E[4t	Change size, with interactive feedback
\E[5t	Top (expose)
\E[6t	Bottom (hide)
\E[7t	Refresh
\E[8;rows;colst	Change size to rows × cols in characters
\E[11t	Report open or iconic; sends back \E[1t or \E[2t
\E[13t	Report position; sends back \E[3;top \E;left \Et
\E[14t	Report size in pixels; sends back \E[8;rows\E;cols\Et
\E[18t	Report size in chars; sends back \E[4;rows \E;cols \Et
\E[20t	Report icon label; sends back \E]Llabel \E\
\E[21t	Report tool label; sends \E]llabel \E\
\E]1text \E\	Set tool label to text
\E]1text \E\	Set icon file to file
\E]Llabel \E\	Set icon file to label

TABLE 29.1 Escape Sequences [The \E is an ESC character (^[or 0x1b).]

```
Notify_value
wait_func ( tty, pid, wait, rusage )
Tty tty;
int pid;
union wait *wait;
struct rusage *rusage;
{

}
```

■ SAMPLE PROGRAM

The first sample program invokes a window that can be used as a terminal window (similar to **shelltool**). Three buttons are provided. "Clear" will execute the **clear** command, clearing the text from the window; "ls" will execute the **ls** command, displaying the files in the current directory; and "Iconize" will iconize the window by using one of the **TTY** escape sequences shown in Table 29.1. The first two commands use **tty_input()**, and the last uses **tty_output()**.

```
/* ttysw.c -- Open Look TTY subwindow
 * Author:   Kenneth Bibb
 * April 1992 -- Arastar Consulting
 *-----------------------------------
 * Basic frame with panel and ttysw
 */
```

```
#include <xview/xview.h>
#include <xview/panel.h>
#include <xview/tty.h>

Attr_attribute TTY_KEY = NULL;

void
ls ( button, event )
Panel_item button;
Event *event;
{
     char *lsmsg = "ls\n";

     ttysw_input ( xv_get ( button, XV_KEY_DATA, TTY_KEY ),
                  lsmsg, strlen ( lsmsg ) );
}

void
clear ( button, event )
Panel_item button;
Event *event;
{
     char *clmsg = "clear\n";

     ttysw_input ( xv_get ( button, XV_KEY_DATA, TTY_KEY ),
                  clmsg, strlen ( clmsg ) );
}

void
iconize ( button, event )
Panel_item button;
Event *event;
{
     char *icmsg = "^[[2t";

     ttysw_output ( xv_get ( button, XV_KEY_DATA, TTY_KEY ), icmsg,
                   strlen ( icmsg ) );
}

int
main ( argc, argv )
int argc;
char **argv;

{    Frame base;
     Tty tty;
     Panel panel;
     Panel_item pc, pl, pi;

     xv_init ( XV_INIT_ARGC_PTR_ARGV, &argc, argv, NULL );
     TTY_KEY = xv_unique_key ();

     /* create the base frame */
     base = (Frame) xv_create ( NULL, FRAME,
                  FRAME_LABEL,         argv[0],
                  FRAME_SHOW_FOOTER,   TRUE,
                  XV_X,                300,
                  XV_Y,                175,
                  NULL );
```

```
    /* create the panel */
    panel = (Panel) xv_create ( base, PANEL, NULL );

    /* create some buttons */
    pc = (Panel_item) xv_create ( panel, PANEL_BUTTON,
                    PANEL_LABEL_STRING, "Clear",
                    PANEL_NOTIFY_PROC,  clear,
                    NULL );
    pl = (Panel_item) xv_create ( panel, PANEL_BUTTON,
                    PANEL_LABEL_STRING, "ls",
                    PANEL_NOTIFY_PROC,  ls,
                    NULL );
    pi = (Panel_item) xv_create ( panel, PANEL_BUTTON,
                    PANEL_LABEL_STRING, "Iconize",
                    PANEL_NOTIFY_PROC, iconize,
                    NULL );
    window_fit_height ( panel );

    /* create the ttysw */
    tty = (Tty) xv_create ( base, TTY,
                    WIN_ROWS,                   24,
                    WIN_COLUMNS,                80,
                    TTY_QUIT_ON_CHILD_DEATH,    TRUE,
                    NULL );
    (void) xv_set ( pc, XV_KEY_DATA, TTY_KEY, tty, NULL );
    (void) xv_set ( pl, XV_KEY_DATA, TTY_KEY, tty, NULL );
    (void) xv_set ( pi, XV_KEY_DATA, TTY_KEY, tty, NULL );

    /* fit the frame around the ttysw and panel */
    window_fit ( base );

    xv_main_loop ( base );
    return ( 0 );
}
```

The second program takes the command line and uses that to run a program within a **TTY** subwindow. When the program inside the **TTY** subwindow either stops or completes, a message is displayed at the bottom of the frame.

A good command to use as an argument is **man df**. Try a ^**Z** and a **q** at the **more** prompt.

```
/* shtty.c -- Execute a command from the command line
 * Author:   Kenneth Bibb


 * April 1992 -- Arastar Consulting
 *------------------------------------
 * Basic frame with panel and ttysw
 */

#include <xview/xview.h>
#include <xview/panel.h>
#include <xview/tty.h>
#include <sys/wait.h>

Attr_attribute FRAME_BASE_KEY;
```

```
Notify_value
wait_func ( tty, pid, wait, rusage )
Tty tty;
int pid;
union wait *wait;
struct rusage *rusage;
{
        if ( !WIFSTOPPED(*wait) )
        {
                    xv_set ( xv_get ( tty, XV_KEY_DATA, FRAME_BASE_KEY),
                              FRAME_LEFT_FOOTER,
                    "Your job has completed: Please quit from window menu",
                              NULL );
        } else {
                    xv_set ( xv_get ( tty, XV_KEY_DATA, FRAME_BASE_KEY
),
                              FRAME_LEFT_FOOTER,
                    "Your job has stopped: Please quit from window menu",
                              NULL );
        }
        return ( NOTIFY_DONE );
}

int
main ( argc, argv )
int argc;
char **argv;
{
        Frame frame;
        Tty tty;
        Panel panel;
        Panel_item pc, pl, pi;
        int i;

        xv_init ( XV_INIT_ARGC_PTR_ARGV, &argc, argv, NULL );
        FRAME_BASE_KEY = xv_unique_key ();

        for (i=1; i<argc; i++)
                    argv[i - 1] = argv[i];
        argv[i - 1] = NULL;
        /* create the base frame */
        frame = (Frame) xv_create ( NULL, FRAME,
                    FRAME_LABEL,         argv[0],
                    FRAME_SHOW_FOOTER,   TRUE,
                    XV_X,                300,
                    XV_Y,                175,
                    NULL );

        /* create the panel */
        panel = (Panel) xv_create ( frame, PANEL, NULL );
        window_fit_height ( panel );

        /* create the ttysw */
        tty = (Tty) xv_create ( frame, TTY,
                    WIN_ROWS,                              24,
                    WIN_COLUMNS,                           80,
                    TTY_ARGV,                              argv,
                    XV_KEY_DATA, FRAME_BASE_KEY,        frame,
                    NULL );
```

```
        /* monitor the child process */
        notify_set_wait3_func ( tty, wait_func, (int) xv_get ( tty,TTY_PID ));
        /* fit the frame around the ttysw and panel */
        window_fit ( frame );

        xv_main_loop ( frame );
        return ( 0 );
}
```

PART

RELATED PACKAGES

Using CC with XView

30

WHAT IT IS

The **cc** is the standard C compiler, which comes with Suns. It is not an ANSI C compiler—it is a standard C compiler, so you'll need to avoid the various ANSI-isms when using it.

HOW TO USE IT WITH XVIEW

When I compile files using **cc**, I use the following line:

```
cc -O file.c -o file -L$OPENWINHOME/lib -lxview -lolgx -lX11
```

If you are not using **make** to compile your programs, I recommend setting up a shell script like the following:

```
#!/bin/csh
cc -O $1.c -o $1 -L$OPENWINHOME/lib -lxview -lolgx -lX11
```

If you named the shell script **xcc**, this will let you say

```
host% xcc textsw
```

This will compile the **textsw.c** program down to an executable called **textsw**.

During debugging, you will want to use the **-g** option instead of the **-O** option.

The **-lxview**, **-lolgx**, and **-lX11** libraries are required to enable all of the XView things that you do in your program.

DBX and DBXTOOL

31

CHAPTER

f you're a typical programmer, you'll spend a lot of time debugging. If you're a seasoned programmer, you'll never admit it.

WHERE DID I GO WRONG?

If your program dumps core, you can see where the problem is by doing the following:

```
host% dbx program core
dbx> where
```

The **where** command of **dbx** will produce a stack dump like the following:

```
anthor% dbx msglog core
Reading symbolic information...
Read 900 symbols
warning: core file read error: address not in data space
program terminated by signal SEGV (no mapping at the fault address)
(dbx) where
warning: core file read error: address not in data space
localsub() at 0xf755a14c
localtime() at 0xf755a2a4
err_buttons(item = 165648, event = 0xf7fff6ec), line 40 in "msglog.c"
panel_btn_accepted() at 0xf76a4d28
eY__btn_accept_preview() at 0xf76a46c8
panel_accept_preview() at 0xf76a9d8c
panel_default_event() at 0xf76aa91c
panel_notify_event() at 0xf76a9054
cx__ndet_p_event() at 0xf7657734
notify_post_event_and_arg() at 0xf76579c8
hr__win_send() at 0xf7658a40
xv_input_pending() at 0xf765acdc
dI__notify_fd() at 0xf7657bac
dG__ndis_send_ascending_fd() at 0xf7657afc
ndis_default_prioritizer() at 0xf7651d84
notify_client() at 0xf7652890
ndis_default_scheduler() at 0xf7652924
gh__scheduler() at 0xf7653578
```

```
ndis_dispatch() at 0xf7652024
notify_start() at 0xf76f5284
xv_main_loop() at 0xf773525c
main(argc = 1, argv = 0xf7fffd0c), line 125 in "msglog.c"
(dbx) quit
```

You can usually see where your program's problem is using this technique. Occasionally, it will only give you a clue, but usually it is quite useful. (In this example, it was line 126 that had the bug).

SOME COMMON XVIEW ERRORS

The following are some of the more common errors that people make when using XView.

Terminating Null in Variable Lists

Symptom: "Random" core dump.

Comment: It's easy to leave one of these off, especially if you have a nested group of variable lists.

Object Reference Before Creation

Symptom: "Null passed to **xv_set**"

Comment: If you're going to reference an object (like a menu with a **PANEL_ITEM_MENU**) the object must already be created.

Help File Not in Helppath

Symptom: "Unable to find" error when you invoke help.

Comment: If you're having problems with help, take a look at your helppath and verify that your help file is in the path. You may need to redefine your **HELPPATH** in your **.login** so that it includes the correct directories.

Using a Forbidden System Call

Symptom: "Random" core dump.

Comment: If you use one of the system calls that circumvents the Notifier, it will occasionally work in very small programs. When you do it in a larger program, you're almost guaranteeing disaster. Use the recommended substitutes.

Using the Wrong Reference

Symptom: "It used to work, but it stopped when I upgraded."

Comment: There have been some significant changes to the behavior of drag-n-drop, selection service (now package), and notices (now a package). A lot of minor changes have been made to other packages, too. So get the reference that matches the version of the toolkit you're interested in.

Using GCC with XView **32**

WHAT IT IS

The **gcc** program is the FSF's ANSI C compiler. It has features making it backward compatible with "standard" C, and it can be used with XView.

One of the major advantages of **gcc** is that you can use ANSI-style prototypes and function declarations to enable some data type checking. Not only does this catch many errors, but I feel that ANSI code is more readable than standard C code.

HOW TO USE IT WITH XVIEW

The line I use to compile my files is

```
gcc -O file.c -o file -traditional -L$OPENWINHOME/lib -lxview -lolgx -lX11
```

If you are not using **make** to compile your programs (if your programs are relatively small, being made of a single source file, for example), you might want to create a small shell script like the following **csh** script:

```
#!/bin/csh
gcc -O $1.c -o $1 -traditional -L$OPENWINHOME/lib -lxview -lolgx -lX11
```

If you call the shell script **xcc**, you could compile a program like the **textsw.c** program with the following command line:

```
host% xcc textsw
```

Your resulting executable will be called **textsw**.

AN EXPLANATION OF THE SWITCHES USED

The **-traditional** option of **gcc** supports a number of features that are typically used by common C compilers.

The **-L** option tells the linker that **$OPENWINHOME/lib** should be used as part of the library search path.

The **-lxview**, **-lolgx**, and **-lX11** options link the **xview**, **olgx**, and **X11** libraries into your application. These libraries are what give XView to your program.

The **-O** option turns optimization on (you'll want to replace this with **-g** when debugging).

SOME PROBLEMS WITH XVIEW

There have been different problems with different versions of **gcc**. If you encounter a problem while using it with XView, make sure to report it to the **bugs** alias.

One problem I encountered was with the **-g** switch when used with one of the older version (1.39). There have also been problems when structures are passed in certain situations. My understanding is that these bugs are now fixed (they are now on version 2.1). The latest copy of **gcc** is kept on **prep.ai.mit.edu** and is available via anonymous FTP. You should probably check with **archie** for a closer, less heavily used site to anonymous FTP the source.

LIMITED ARGUMENT CHECKING PACKAGE

The following is a description of a patch that is available through the Internet.

```
From: abraham@hugin.dk
Newsgroups: gnu.gcc.help,alt.toolkits.xview,comp.windows.open-look

Subject: ANNOUNCE: XView argument checking with gcc 2.0.
Message-ID: <ABRAHAM.92Feb28090113@thor.iesd.auc.dk>
Date: 28 Feb 92 09:01:13 GMT
Article-I.D.: thor.ABRAHAM.92Feb28090113
Sender: root@iesd.auc.dk (Operator)
Organization: HUGIN Expert A/S
Lines: 82

A patch to gcc 2.0 providing limited argument checking for
xv_set and xv_create (like gcc 2.0 already does for *printf
and *scanf), is available by anonymous ftp. See the README file,
which is included below.

Warning: I began working on the patch yesterday...

******************************************************************

XView support for gcc:
----------------------

HISTORY:

Inspired by the way gcc now checks the arguments to printf
and scanf family of varargs functions, I decided to try to
implement similar support for the xv_set and xv_create
functions used by the XView graphical toolkit.

* Version 0.0 alpha for gcc-2.0

It now finds the single (harmless) error in Ftptool 4.1, and
does not crash in the process, so I will let it go. Use on your
own risk.

Version 0.0 alpha should work with XView 3.0 or older. Future
versions of XView will most likely cause "-Wxview" and
"-Wxview-type" to generate more spurious warnings.

DESCRIPTION:

Add two new warnings to gcc.  They are both disabled by defaults.
```

"-Wxview": Generate warnings if xv_set or xv_create are called
with the wrong number of arguments, if a XView attribute is not
an integer constant, or if any argument is more than 32 bits
wide.

"-Wxview-type": Generate warnings if an argument to an XView
attribute is not of the expected type. Distinguishes between
three types: integer, pointer, and opaque, where opaque can
match any type. May generate spurious warnings, since the
XView include files contain incorrect type information for
many attributes. Does not work without "-Wxview".

PROBLEMS:

- Does not support xv_get or xv_find.
- Does not check if attribute is defined for the receiving object.
- "-Wxview" does not complain about structure arguments.
- "-Wxview-type" should distinguish between more types.
- "-Wxview" complains about attribute variables.
- XView extensions may cause more spurious warnings.

INSTALLATION:

Get gcc-2.0 from your favorite source of free software.

Get /pub/gcc-2.0-xview-0.0.tar.Z by anonymous ftp
from hugin.dk (129.142.51.10).

Replace the "c-decl.c" and "c-typeck.c" files in gcc source
directory, and place the xview directory also in the gcc
source directory.

Compile and install the new version of gcc using the normal
procedure.

Hint:
    If you want to keep both the official and the XView
    versions of gcc, then create a $gnulib/gcc/$ARCH/xview,
    and keep the official version in $gnulib/gcc/$ARCH/2.0.

    Make symbolic links from everything in $gnulib/gcc/$ARCH/2.0
    to $gnulib/gcc/$ARCH/xview, except cc1. cc1 is the only
    program affected by the changes.

    You will now be able to invoke the official version with
    "gcc" and the XView version with "gcc -V xview".

LEGAL NOTICE:

Everything in the XView directory is owned by SMI, the
changes to the "c-decl.c" are owned by me, and the
changes to "c-typeck.c" are owned by me and possibly by SMI.

Read the file xview/LEGAL_NOTICE for SMI's position. I
would be happy to transfer ownership to the FSF.

Written by Per Abrahamsen (abraham@hugin.dk).

PART

IV

SAMPLE PROGRAMS

SlingShot

SlingShot is a package of extensions to XView that lets you draw various objects and lets you create things like multicolumn scrolling lists, spreadsheets, and movable objects, which could be used for creating a File Manager-like interface. It is not an official part of XView, but it is included here because these functions are often requested.

The SlingShot package is currently at version 1.0 with two patches. A version 2.0 will probably be available by the time this book is in print. Information on how to obtain it is provided further in this chapter.

SLINGSHOT PACKAGES

The following classes are supported by SlingShot and are organized into the hierarchy shown in Figure 33.1.

ARRAY_TILE This package is used to create an array, which can be filled with objects from the other packages. When used with **DRAWTEXT**, it can be used to implement multicolumn scroll lists or spreadsheets.

CANVAS_SHELL Required for the other packages—they draw onto a canvas shell.

DRAWAREA A package that creates an object used as a place to draw. It takes care of many of your low-level worries automatically.

DRAWICON A package used to create a File Manager-like icon that can be manipulated within a canvas shell. This can be used to write File Manager-like interfaces.

DRAWIMAGE This package creates an object that contains a server image, which can be manipulated. This can be used to create "buttons" and other objects that can be manipulated on the canvas.

DRAWLINE A package used to draw a line. A few style-related attributes can be manipulated.

DRAWRECT A package used to draw a rectangle. You can change a few style-related attributes.

DRAWTEXT A package used to create an object that contains a string, which can be manipulated. This can be used in creating spreadsheets, multicolumn scrollpanels, objects comprised exclusively of text, and so forth.

265

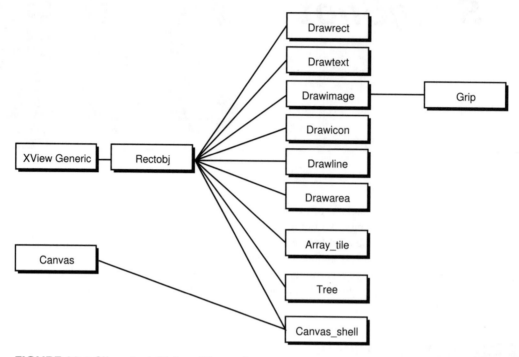

FIGURE 33.1 Slingshot Object Hierarchy

GRIP	A package that creates an object that can be dragged within a window. It can be used to manipulate an object.
RECT_OBJ	The base class of the package. All the other classes are subclasses of this class.
TREE	An object that positions its children in a hierarchy connected with lines.

HOW TO GET IT

You can get SlingShot by emailing a message to **archive-server@gazoo.eng.sun** with a **Subject:** line of

```
help
```

To have **gazoo** send you a file, email **archive-server@gazoo.eng.sun** with a message body of

```
send sspkg1.0
```

(This will send you version 1.0—you should first check to see if version 2.0 is out.)

If you do not have Internet access, ordering information is provided at the front of the book.

SAMPLE PROGRAMS

The Slingshot package comes with a number of sample programs, which demonstrate most of the features of the package. The new version of the toolkit will also come with extended documentation (possibly the nicest looking documentation I've seen with a freely copyable package like this).

ADDU— Add User Interface

34

This program was written by Larry, who used Devguide to generate it. Those readers who aren't using Devguide won't be able to compile these files. There is still some coding that may be of interest to you in the .c files, though.

addu.G

The following is the .G file for the **addu** interface.

```
;GIL-3
(
(
        :type                   :menu
        :name                   shell_menu
        :help                   ""
        :columns                1
        :menu-type              :exclusive
        :menu-handler           shell_menu_notify
        :menu-title             "Shells"
        :menu-item-labels       ("/bin/csh" "/bin/sh" )
        :menu-item-label-types  (:string :string )
        :menu-item-states       (:active :active )
        :menu-item-defaults     (nil nil )
        :initial-selections     (nil nil )
        :menu-item-handlers     (nil nil )
        :menu-item-menus        (nil nil )
        :menu-item-colors       ("" "" )
        :pinnable               t
        :user-data              ()
        :actions                (
                        (
                        :from           (shell_menu)
                        :when           (Notify )
                        :to             (shell_menu)
                        :function_type  CallFunction
                        :arg_type       ()
                        :action         (shell_menu_notify)
                        )
                )
        )
)
```

```
(
        :type                   :menu
        :name                   logid_rule_menu
        :help                   ""
        :columns                1
        :menu-type              :command
        :menu-handler           nil
        :menu-title             "Login ID Rules"
        :menu-item-labels       ("Jane Doe -> jdoe" "Jane Doe -> jane"
                                 "Jane Doe -> janed" "Jane Doe -> doej"
                                 "Jane Doe -> doe" )
        :menu-item-label-types  (:string :string :string :string :string )
        :menu-item-states       (:active :active :active :active :active )
        :menu-item-defaults     (nil nil nil nil nil )
        :initial-selections     (nil nil nil nil nil )
        :menu-item-handlers     (nil nil nil nil nil )
        :menu-item-menus        (nil nil nil nil nil )
        :menu-item-colors       ("" "" "" "" "" )
        :pinnable               t
        :user-data              ()
        :actions                ()
)
(
        :type                   :base-window
        :name                   window1
        :owner                  nil
        :width                  371
        :height                 274
        :background-color       ""
        :foreground-color       ""
        :label                  "Add User"
        :label-type             :string
        :initial-state          :open
        :show-footer            t
        :resizable              t
        :icon-file              ""
        :icon-label             ""
        :icon-mask-file         ""
        :event-handler          nil
        :user-data              ()
        :actions                ()
)
(
        :type                   :control-area
        :name                   main_upper_pane
        :owner                  window1
        :help                   "This is \"addu\", the GUI-based add user
program. Press help over any item to see how to use it."
        :x                      0
        :y                      0
        :width                  371
        :height                 45
        :background-color       ""
        :foreground-color       ""
        :initial-state          :visible
        :show-border            nil
        :menu                   nil
        :event-handler          nil
        :user-data              ()
        :actions                ()
)
```

```
(
      :type                     :button
      :name                     props_item
      :owner                    main_upper_pane
      :help                     "Press this button to make configuration
changes for the program, using its property sheet."
      :x                        16
      :y                        16
      :width                    89
      :height                   19
      :constant-width           nil
      :button-type              :normal
      :foreground-color         ""
      :label                    "Properties..."
      :label-type               :string
      :initial-state            :active
      :menu                     nil
      :notify-handler           nil
      :event-handler            nil
      :user-data                ()
      :actions                  (
                    (
                    :from                 (window1 props_item)
                    :when                 (Notify )
                    :to                   (props_win)
                    :function_type        :user_defined
                    :arg_type             ()
                    :action               (Show)
                    )
      )
)
(
      :type                     :control-area
      :name                     main_lower_pane
      :owner                    window1
      :help                     "This is \"addu\", the GUI-based add user
program. Press help over any item to see how to use it."
      :x                        0
      :y                        45
      :width                    371
      :height                   229
      :background-color         ""
      :foreground-color         ""
      :initial-state            :visible
      :show-border              t
      :menu                     nil
      :event-handler            nil
      :user-data                ()
      :actions                  ()
)
(
      :type                     :text-field
      :name                     fname_item
      :owner                    main_lower_pane
      :help                     "Enter the full name of the user
you wish to add, in the format \"Firstname Lastname\" -- when you press
Return, this will be used to construct a default login ID for this person,
based on the rule you've specified on the properties
sheet."
```

```
            :x                      69
            :y                      16
            :width                  240
            :height                 15
            :value-x                149
            :value-y                16
            :value-length           20
            :stored-length          20
            :rows                   3
            :foreground-color       ""
            :text-type              :alphanumeric
            :label                  "Full Name:"
            :label-type             :string
            :layout-type            :horizontal
            :value-underlined       t
            :initial-value          ""
            :initial-state          :active
            :read-only              nil
            :notify-handler         fname_notify
            :event-handler          nil
            :user-data              ()
            :actions                (
                    (
                    :from                   (window1 fname_item)
                    :when                   (Notify )
                    :to                     (window1 fname_item)
                    :function_type          CallFunction
                    :arg_type               ()
                    :action                 (fname_notify)
                    )
            )
    )
    (
            :type                   :text-field
            :name                   logid_item
            :owner                  main_lower_pane
            :help                   "Enter the login ID for this user here.  When
you press Return on the Full Name blank, a default login ID is automatically
placed here for you."
            :x                      43
            :y                      41
            :width                  170
            :height                 15
            :value-x                149
            :value-y                41
            :value-length           8
            :stored-length          8
            :rows                   3
            :foreground-color       ""
            :text-type              :alphanumeric
            :label                  "UNIX Login ID:"
            :label-type             :string
            :layout-type            :horizontal
            :value-underlined       t
            :initial-value          ""
            :initial-state          :active
            :read-only              nil
            :notify-handler         logid_notify
            :event-handler          nil
            :user-data              ()
            :actions                (
```

```
(
                    :from                          (window1 logid_item)
                    :when                          (Notify )
                    :to                            (window1 logid_item)
                    :function_type                 CallFunction
                    :arg_type                      ()
                    :action                        (logid_notify)
                    )
       )
)
(
        :type                  :text-field
        :name                  uid_field_item
        :owner                 main_lower_pane
        :help                  "Enter the user ID for this user.  The program
automatically selects the lowest free UID in the range specified on the
properties sheet, but you may override it if you wish."
        :x                     87
        :y                     66
        :width                 102
        :height                15
        :value-x               149
        :value-y               66
        :value-length          5
        :stored-length         5
        :rows                  3
        :foreground-color      ""
        :text-type             :alphanumeric
        :label                 "User ID:"
        :label-type            :string
        :layout-type           :horizontal
        :value-underlined      t
        :initial-value         ""
        :initial-state         :active
        :read-only             nil
        :notify-handler        nil
        :event-handler         nil
        :user-data             ()
        :actions               ()
)
(
        :type                  :button
        :name                  gid_item
        :owner                 main_lower_pane
        :help                  "Pressing this button brings up a window with
a list of the groups defined on this system."
        :x                     64
        :y                     88
        :width                 81
        :height                19
        :constant-width        nil
        :button-type           :normal
        :foreground-color      ""
        :label                 "Group ID..."
        :label-type            :string
        :initial-state         :active
        :menu                  nil
        :notify-handler        nil
        :event-handler         nil
        :user-data             ()
        :actions               (
```

```
(
                    :from                 (window1 gid_item)
                    :when                 (Notify )
                    :to                   (gid_win)
                    :function_type        :user_defined
                    :arg_type             ()
                    :action               (Show)
                    )

        )
)
(
        :type                 :text-field
        :name                 gid_field_item
        :owner                main_lower_pane
        :help                 "Enter the number of the group you would like
this user to belong to.  Press the Group ID... button to choose from the
existing list of groups."
        :x                    149
        :y                    91
        :width                40
        :height               15
        :value-x              149
        :value-y              91
        :value-length         5
        :stored-length        32
        :rows                 3
        :foreground-color     ""
        :text-type            :alphanumeric
        :label                ""
        :label-type           :string
        :layout-type          :horizontal
        :value-underlined     t
        :initial-value        ""
        :initial-state        :active
        :read-only            nil
        :notify-handler       nil
        :event-handler        nil
        :user-data            ()
        :actions              ()
)
(
        :type                 :text-field
        :name                 home_dir_item
        :owner                main_lower_pane
        :help                 "Enter the home directory for this user.  When
you press Return on the UNIX Login ID blank, a default home directory is
automatically constructed, based on the home directory location you
specified on the properties sheet."
        :x                    32
        :y                    116
        :width                277
        :height               15
        :value-x              149
        :value-y              116
        :value-length         20
        :stored-length        80
        :rows                 3
        :foreground-color     ""
        :text-type            :alphanumeric
        :label                "Home Directory:"
        :label-type           :string
        :layout-type          :horizontal
```

```
         :value-underlined          t
         :initial-value             ""
         :initial-state             :active
         :read-only                 nil
         :notify-handler            nil
         :event-handler             nil
         :user-data                 ()
         :actions                   ()
)
(

         :type                      :button
         :name                      shell_menu_button
         :owner                     main_lower_pane
         :help                      "Enter the login shell you wish this user to
have.  You may select possible shells from the abbreviated menu button,
which lists the shells found in /etc/shells, if that file exists."
         :x                         61
         :y                         144
         :width                     108
         :height                    15
         :constant-width            nil
         :button-type               :abbreviated
         :foreground-color          ""
         :label                     "Login Shell:"
         :label-type                :string
         :initial-state             :active
         :menu                      shell_menu
         :notify-handler            nil
         :event-handler             nil
         :user-data                 ()
         :actions                   ()
)
(

         :type                      :text-field
         :name                      shell_field_item
         :owner                     main_lower_pane
         :help                      "Enter the login shell you wish this user to
have.  You may select possible shells from the abbreviated menu button,
which lists the shells found in /etc/shells, if that file exists."
         :x                         181
         :y                         144
         :width                     64
         :height                    15
         :value-x                   181
         :value-y                   144
         :value-length              8
         :stored-length             80
         :rows                      3
         :foreground-color          ""
         :text-type                 :alphanumeric
         :label                     ""
         :label-type                :string
         :layout-type               :horizontal
         :value-underlined          t
         :initial-value             "/bin/csh"
         :initial-state             :active
         :read-only                 nil
         :notify-handler            nil
         :event-handler             nil
         :user-data                 ()
         :actions                   ()
)
```

```
(
        :type                   :button
        :name                   apply_item
        :owner                  main_lower_pane
        :help                   "Press the Apply button to create the user
whose attributes you have filled in above."
        :x                      133
        :y                      184
        :width                  53
        :height                 19
        :constant-width         nil
        :button-type            :normal
        :foreground-color       ""
        :label                  "Apply"
        :label-type             :string
        :initial-state          :active
        :menu                   nil
        :notify-handler         apply_notify
        :event-handler          nil
        :user-data              ()
        :actions                (
                        (
                        :from                   (window1 apply_item)
                        :when                   (Notify )
                        :to                     (window1 apply_item)
                        :function_type          CallFunction
                        :arg_type               ()
                        :action                 (apply_notify)
                        )
        )
)
(
        :type                   :button
        :name                   reset_item
        :owner                  main_lower_pane
        :help                   "Press this button to return the values on
this window to their original state."
        :x                      221
        :y                      184
        :width                  51
        :height                 19
        :constant-width         nil
        :button-type            :normal
        :foreground-color       ""
        :label                  "Reset"
        :label-type             :string
        :initial-state          :active
        :menu                   nil
        :notify-handler         reset_notify
        :event-handler          nil
        :user-data              ()
        :actions                (
                        (
                        :from                   (window1 reset_item)
                        :when                   (Notify )
                        :to                     (window1 reset_item)
                        :function_type          CallFunction
                        :arg_type               ()
                        :action                 (reset_notify)
                        )
        )
)
```

```
(
        :type                   :popup-window
        :name                   gid_win
        :owner                  window1
        :width                  249
        :height                 206
        :background-color       ""
        :foreground-color       ""
        :label                  "Group ID Chooser"
        :label-type             :string
        :initial-state          :invisible
        :show-footer            t
        :resizable              t
        :pinned                 t
        :done-handler           nil
        :event-handler          nil
        :user-data              ()
        :actions                ()
)
(
        :type                   :control-area
        :name                   gid_pane
        :owner                  gid_win
        :help                   "This is the Group ID Chooser window.
                                Selecting a group name from the list places
                                its number in the Group blank on
the main window."
        :x                      0
        :y                      0
        :width                  249
        :height                 206
        :background-color       ""
        :foreground-color       ""
        :initial-state          :visible
        :show-border            nil
        :menu                   nil
        :event-handler          nil
        :user-data              ()
        :actions                ()
)
(
        :type                   :scrolling-list
        :name                   gid_list
        :owner                  gid_pane
        :help                   ""
        :x                      24
        :y                      16
        :width                  200
        :height                 164
        :value-x                24
        :value-y                16
        :rows                   8
        :foreground-color       ""
        :label                  ""
        :title                  ""
        :label-type             :string
        :layout-type            :horizontal
        :read-only              nil
        :multiple-selections    nil
        :selection-required     nil
        :initial-state          :active
        :droppable              nil
```

```
        :default-drop-site      nil
        :menu                   nil
        :notify-handler         gid_list_notify
        :event-handler          nil
        :initial-list-values    ()
        :initial-list-glyphs    ()
        :initial-selections     ()
        :user-data              ()
        :actions                (
                    (
                    :from                   (gid_win gid_list)
                    :when                   (Notify )
                    :to                     (gid_win gid_list)
                    :function_type          CallFunction
                    :arg_type               ()
                    :action                 (gid_list_notify)
                    )
            )
    )
    (
        :type                   :popup-window
        :name                   props_win
        :owner                  window1
        :width                  393
        :height                 189
        :background-color       ""
        :foreground-color       ""
        :label                  "Add User: Properties"
        :label-type             :string
        :initial-state          :invisible
        :show-footer            t
        :resizable              t
        :pinned                 nil
        :done-handler           nil
        :event-handler          nil
        :user-data              ()
        :actions                ()
    )
    (
        :type                   :control-area
        :name                   props_pane
        :owner                  props_win
        :help                   "This is the property sheet for addu.  Make
configuration changes for the program by changing the appropriate items,
then pressing \"Apply.\""

        :x                      0
        :y                      0
        :width                  393
        :height                 189
        :background-color       ""
        :foreground-color       ""
        :initial-state          :visible
        :show-border            nil
        :menu                   nil
        :event-handler          nil
        :user-data              ()
        :actions                ()
    )
    (
        :type                   :setting
        :name                   logid_rule_item
```

```
        :owner                  props_pane
        :help                   "Select the rule to use to construct a login
ID based on the full name you enter."
        :x                      58
        :y                      16
        :width                  289
        :height                 23
        :value-x                198
        :value-y                16
        :rows                   1
        :columns                0
        :layout-type            :horizontal
        :foreground-color       ""
        :setting-type           :stack
        :selection-required     t
        :label                  "Default Login ID Is:"
        :label-type             :string
        :notify-handler         nil
        :event-handler          nil
        :choices                ("Jane Doe -> jdoe" "Jane Doe -> jane"
                                "Jane Doe -> janed" "Jane Doe -> doej"
                                "Jane Doe -> doe" "Jane Q. Doe -> jqd" )
        :choice-label-types     (:string :string :string :string :string
                                                            :string )
        :choice-colors          ("" "" "" "" "" "" )
        :choice-defaults        (nil nil nil nil nil nil )
        :initial-selections     (nil nil nil nil nil nil )
        :initial-state          :active
        :user-data              ()
        :actions                ()
)
(
        :type                   :text-field
        :name                   range_from_item
        :owner                  props_pane
        :help                   "Enter the lowest possible UID that you wish
this program to create."
        :x                      38
        :y                      47
        :width                  235
        :height                 15
        :value-x                198
        :value-y                47
        :value-length           5
        :stored-length          5
        :rows                   3
        :foreground-color       ""
        :text-type              :numeric
        :label                  "Lowest Allowable UID:"
        :label-type             :string
        :layout-type            :horizontal
        :value-underlined       t
        :min-value              0
        :initial-value          0
        :initial-state          :active
        :read-only              nil
        :notify-handler         nil
        :event-handler          nil
        :user-data              ()
        :actions                ()
)
```

```
(
        :type                   :text-field
        :name                   range_to_item
        :owner                  props_pane
        :help                   "Enter the highest possible UID that you wish
this program to create."
        :x                      33
        :y                      70
        :width                  240
        :height                 15
        :value-x                198
        :value-y                70
        :value-length           5
        :stored-length          5
        :rows                   3
        :foreground-color       ""
        :text-type              :numeric
        :label                  "Highest Allowable UID:"
        :label-type             :string
        :layout-type            :horizontal
        :value-underlined       t
        :max-value              65533
        :min-value              0
        :initial-value          0
        :initial-state          :active
        :read-only              nil
        :notify-handler         nil
        :event-handler          nil
        :user-data              ()
        :actions                ()
)
(
        :type                   :text-field
        :name                   props_home_item
        :owner                  props_pane
        :help                   "Enter the name of the directory that home
directories should be placed in.  For example, if you wish user fred to have
his home directory in /home/bedrock/fred, enter \"/home/bedrock\" here."
        :x                      24
        :y                      93
        :width                  334
        :height                 15
        :value-x                198
        :value-y                93
        :value-length           20
        :stored-length          80
        :rows                   3
        :foreground-color       ""
        :text-type              :alphanumeric
        :label                  "Put Home Directories In:"
        :label-type             :string
        :layout-type            :horizontal
        :value-underlined       t
        :initial-value          ""
        :initial-state          :active
        :read-only              nil
        :notify-handler         nil
        :event-handler          nil
        :user-data              ()
        :actions                ()
)
(
        :type                   :text-field
```

```
        :name                   default_gid_item
        :owner                  props_pane
        :help                   "Fill in the number of the group you would
like most users at your site to belong to.  It will be presented as the
default group for each new user you create."
        :x                      72
        :y                      116
        :width                  190
        :height                 15
        :value-x                198
        :value-y                116
        :value-length           8
        :stored-length          80
        :rows                   3
        :foreground-color       ""
        :text-type              :alphanumeric
        :label                  "Default Group ID:"
        :label-type             :string
        :layout-type            :horizontal
        :value-underlined       t
        :initial-value          ""
        :initial-state          :active
        :read-only              nil
        :notify-handler         nil
        :event-handler          nil
        :user-data              ()
        :actions                ()
)
(
        :type                   :button
        :name                   props_apply_item
        :owner                  props_pane
        :help                   "Press the Apply button to save the
configuration choices that you have made on this window."
        :x                      120
        :y                      160
        :width                  53
        :height                 19
        :constant-width         nil
        :button-type            :normal
        :foreground-color       ""
        :label                  "Apply"
        :label-type             :string
        :initial-state          :active
        :menu                   nil
        :notify-handler         props_apply_notify
        :event-handler          nil
        :user-data              ()
        :actions                (
                        (
                        :from                   (props_win props_apply_item)
                        :when                   (Notify )
                        :to                     (props_win props_apply_item)
                        :function_type          CallFunction
                        :arg_type               ()
                        :action                 (props_apply_notify)
                        )
        )
)
(
        :type                   :button
        :name                   props_reset_item
```

```
       :owner                  props_pane
       :help                   "Press this button to return the values on the
property sheet to what they were the last time you applied them."
       :x                      192
       :y                      160
       :width                  51
       :height                 19
       :constant-width         nil
       :button-type            :normal
       :foreground-color       ""
       :label                  "Reset"
       :label-type             :string
       :initial-state          :active
       :menu                   nil
       :notify-handler         props_reset_notify
       :event-handler          nil
       :user-data              ()
       :actions                (
                       (
               :from                   (props_win props_reset_item)
               :when                   (Notify )
               :to                     (props_win props_reset_item)
               :function_type          CallFunction
               :arg_type               ()
               :action                 (props_reset_notify)
                       )
       )
)
)
```

a ddu_ui.h

```
#ifndef addu_HEADER
#define addu_HEADER

/*
 * addu_ui.h - User interface object and function declarations.
 * This file was generated by 'gxv' from 'addu.G'.
 * DO NOT EDIT BY HAND.
 */

extern Attr_attribute INSTANCE;

extern Xv_opaque addu_shell_menu_create();
extern Xv_opaque addu_logid_rule_menu_create();

typedef struct {
        Xv_opaque       window1;
        Xv_opaque       main_upper_pane;
        Xv_opaque       props_item;
        Xv_opaque       main_lower_pane;
        Xv_opaque       fname_item;
        Xv_opaque       logid_item;
        Xv_opaque       uid_field_item;
        Xv_opaque       gid_item;
        Xv_opaque       gid_field_item;
        Xv_opaque       home_dir_item;
```

```
        Xv_opaque       shell_menu_button;
        Xv_opaque       shell_field_item;
        Xv_opaque       apply_item;
        Xv_opaque       reset_item;
} addu_window1_objects;

extern addu_window1_objects *addu_window1_objects_initialize();

extern Xv_opaque addu_window1_window1_create();
extern Xv_opaque addu_window1_main_upper_pane_create();
extern Xv_opaque addu_window1_props_item_create();
extern Xv_opaque addu_window1_main_lower_pane_create();
extern Xv_opaque addu_window1_fname_item_create();
extern Xv_opaque addu_window1_logid_item_create();
extern Xv_opaque addu_window1_uid_field_item_create();
extern Xv_opaque addu_window1_gid_item_create();
extern Xv_opaque addu_window1_gid_field_item_create();
extern Xv_opaque addu_window1_home_dir_item_create();
extern Xv_opaque addu_window1_shell_menu_button_create();
extern Xv_opaque addu_window1_shell_field_item_create();
extern Xv_opaque addu_window1_apply_item_create();
extern Xv_opaque addu_window1_reset_item_create();

typedef struct {
        Xv_opaque       gid_win;
        Xv_opaque       gid_pane;
        Xv_opaque       gid_list;
} addu_gid_win_objects;

extern addu_gid_win_objects *addu_gid_win_objects_initialize();

extern Xv_opaque addu_gid_win_gid_win_create();
extern Xv_opaque addu_gid_win_gid_pane_create();
extern Xv_opaque addu_gid_win_gid_list_create();

typedef struct {
        Xv_opaque       props_win;
        Xv_opaque       props_pane;
        Xv_opaque       logid_rule_item;
        Xv_opaque       range_from_item;
        Xv_opaque       range_to_item;
        Xv_opaque       props_home_item;
        Xv_opaque       default_gid_item;
        Xv_opaque       props_apply_item;
        Xv_opaque       props_reset_item;
  } addu_props_win_objects;

extern addu_props_win_objects *addu_props_win_objects_initialize();

extern Xv_opaque addu_props_win_props_win_create();
extern Xv_opaque addu_props_win_props_pane_create();
extern Xv_opaque addu_props_win_logid_rule_item_create();
extern Xv_opaque addu_props_win_range_from_item_create();
extern Xv_opaque addu_props_win_range_to_item_create();
extern Xv_opaque addu_props_win_props_home_item_create();
extern Xv_opaque addu_props_win_default_gid_item_create();
extern Xv_opaque addu_props_win_props_apply_item_create();
extern Xv_opaque addu_props_win_props_reset_item_create();
#endif
```

█████ `addu_ui.c`

```c
/*
 * addu_ui.c - User interface object initialization functions.
 * This file was generated by 'gxv' from 'addu.G'.
 * DO NOT EDIT BY HAND.
 */

#include <stdio.h>
#include <sys/param.h>
#include <sys/types.h>
#include <xview/xview.h>
#include <xview/canvas.h>
#include <xview/panel.h>
#include <xview/scrollbar.h>
#include <xview/svrimage.h>
#include <xview/termsw.h>
#include <xview/text.h>
#include <xview/tty.h>
#include <xview/xv_xrect.h>
#include "addu_ui.h"


/*
 * Create object 'shell_menu' in the specified instance.
 */
Xv_opaque
addu_shell_menu_create(ip, owner)
        caddr_t      ip;
        Xv_opaque    owner;
{
        extern Menu   shell_menu_notify();
        Xv_opaque     obj;

        obj = xv_create(XV_NULL, MENU_CHOICE_MENU,
                        XV_KEY_DATA, INSTANCE, ip,
                        MENU_GEN_PROC, shell_menu_notify,
                        MENU_TITLE_ITEM, "Shells",
                        MENU_ITEM,
                                    XV_KEY_DATA, INSTANCE, ip,
                                    MENU_STRING, "/bin/csh",
                                    NULL,
                        MENU_ITEM,
                                    XV_KEY_DATA, INSTANCE, ip,
                                    MENU_STRING, "/bin/sh",
                                    NULL,
                        MENU_GEN_PIN_WINDOW, owner, "Shells",
                        NULL);
        return obj;
}

/*
 * Create object 'logid_rule_menu' in the specified instance.
 */
Xv_opaque
addu_logid_rule_menu_create(ip, owner)
        caddr_t      ip;
        Xv_opaque    owner;
{
        Xv_opaque     obj;
```

```
        obj = xv_create(XV_NULL, MENU_COMMAND_MENU,
                XV_KEY_DATA, INSTANCE, ip,
                MENU_TITLE_ITEM, "Login ID Rules",
                MENU_ITEM,
                        XV_KEY_DATA, INSTANCE, ip,
                        MENU_STRING, "Jane Doe -> jdoe",
                        NULL,
                MENU_ITEM,
                        XV_KEY_DATA, INSTANCE, ip,
                        MENU_STRING, "Jane Doe -> jane",
                        NULL,
                MENU_ITEM,
                        XV_KEY_DATA, INSTANCE, ip,
                        MENU_STRING, "Jane Doe -> janed",
                        NULL,
                MENU_ITEM,
                        XV_KEY_DATA, INSTANCE, ip,
                        MENU_STRING, "Jane Doe -> doej",
                        NULL,
                MENU_ITEM,
                        XV_KEY_DATA, INSTANCE, ip,
                        MENU_STRING, "Jane Doe -> doe",
                        NULL,
                MENU_GEN_PIN_WINDOW, owner, "Login ID Rules",
                NULL);
        return obj;
}

/*
 * Initialize an instance of object `window1'.
 */
addu_window1_objects *
addu_window1_objects_initialize(ip, owner)
        addu_window1_objects *ip;
        Xv_opaque           owner;
{
        if (!ip && !(ip = (addu_window1_objects *) calloc(1,
        sizeof (addu_window1_objects))))
                return (addu_window1_objects *) NULL;
        if (!ip->window1)
                ip->window1 = addu_window1_window1_create(ip, owner);
        if (!ip->main_upper_pane)
                ip->main_upper_pane =
                    addu_window1_main_upper_pane_create (ip, ip->window1)
        if (!ip->props_item)
                ip->props_item = addu_window1_props_item_create(ip,
                    ip->main_upper_pane);
        if (!ip->main_lower_pane)
                ip->main_lower_pane =
                    addu_window1_main_lower_pane_create (ip, ip->window1)
        if (!ip->fname_item)
                ip->fname_item = addu_window1_fname_item_create(ip,
                    ip->main_lower_pane);
        if (!ip->logid_item)
                ip->logid_item = addu_window1_logid_item_create(ip,
                    ip->main_lower_pane);
        if (!ip->uid_field_item)
                ip->uid_field_item = addu_window1_uid_field_item_create
                    (ip, ip->main_lower_pane);
        if (!ip->gid_item)
```

```
                        ip->gid_item = addu_window1_gid_item_create(ip,
                                ip->main_lower_pane);
        if (!ip->gid_field_item)
                ip->gid_field_item = addu_window1_gid_field_item_create (ip,
                        ip->main_lower_pane);
        if (!ip->home_dir_item)
                ip->home_dir_item = addu_window1_home_dir_item_create(ip,
                        ip->main_lower_pane);
        if (!ip->shell_menu_button)
                ip->shell_menu_button =
                        addu_window1_shell_menu_button_create (ip,
                                                ip->main_lower_pane);
        if (!ip->shell_field_item)
                ip->shell_field_item =
                        addu_window1_shell_field_item_create (ip,
                                                ip->main_lower_pane);
        if (!ip->apply_item)
                ip->apply_item = addu_window1_apply_item_create(ip,
                        ip->main_lower_pane);
        if (!ip->reset_item)
                ip->reset_item = addu_window1_reset_item_create(ip,
                        ip->main_lower_pane);
        return ip;
}


/*
 * Create object 'window1' in the specified instance.
 */
Xv_opaque
addu_window1_window1_create(ip, owner)
        addu_window1_objects * ip;
        Xv_opaque       owner;
{
        Xv_opaque       obj;

        obj = xv_create(owner, FRAME,
                        XV_KEY_DATA, INSTANCE, ip,
                        XV_WIDTH, 371,
                        XV_HEIGHT, 274,
                        XV_LABEL, "Add User",
                        FRAME_SHOW_FOOTER, TRUE,
                        FRAME_SHOW_RESIZE_CORNER, TRUE,
                        NULL);
        return obj;
}


/*
 * Create object 'main_upper_pane' in the specified instance.
 */
Xv_opaque
addu_window1_main_upper_pane_create(ip, owner)
        addu_window1_objects * ip;
        Xv_opaque       owner;
{
        Xv_opaque       obj;

        obj = xv_create(owner, PANEL,
                        XV_KEY_DATA, INSTANCE, ip,
                        XV_HELP_DATA, "addu:main_upper_pane",
                        XV_X, 0,
                        XV_Y, 0,
```

```
                                XV_WIDTH, WIN_EXTEND_TO_EDGE,
                                XV_HEIGHT, 45,
                                WIN_BORDER, FALSE,
                                NULL);
                return obj;
        }


        /*
         * Create object `props_item' in the specified instance.
         */
        Xv_opaque
        addu_window1_props_item_create(ip, owner)
                addu_window1_objects *ip;
                Xv_opaque    owner;
        {
                extern void  addu_window1_props_item_notify_callback();
                Xv_opaque    obj;

                obj = xv_create(owner, PANEL_BUTTON,
                                XV_KEY_DATA, INSTANCE, ip,
                                XV_HELP_DATA, "addu:props_item",
                                XV_X, 16,
                                XV_Y, 16,
                                PANEL_LABEL_STRING, "Properties...",
                                PANEL_NOTIFY_PROC,
                                        addu_window1_props_item_notify_callback,
                                NULL);
                return obj;
        }


        /*
         * Create object `main_lower_pane' in the specified instance.
         */
        Xv_opaque
        addu_window1_main_lower_pane_create(ip, owner)
                addu_window1_objects *ip;
                Xv_opaque    owner;
        {
                Xv_opaque    obj;

                obj = xv_create(owner, PANEL,
                                XV_KEY_DATA, INSTANCE, ip,
                                XV_HELP_DATA, "addu:main_lower_pane",
                                XV_X, 0,
                                XV_Y, (int)xv_get(ip->main_upper_pane, XV_Y)
                                    + (int)xv_get(ip->main_upper_pane, XV_HEIGHT),
                                XV_WIDTH, WIN_EXTEND_TO_EDGE,
                                XV_HEIGHT, WIN_EXTEND_TO_EDGE,
                                WIN_BORDER, TRUE,
                                NULL);
                return obj;
        }


        /*
         * Create object `fname_item' in the specified instance.
         */
        Xv_opaque
        addu_window1_fname_item_create(ip, owner)
                addu_window1_objects *ip;
                Xv_opaque    owner;
```

```
{
        extern Panel_setting fname_notify();
        Xv_opaque    obj;
        obj = xv_create(owner, PANEL_TEXT,
                        XV_KEY_DATA, INSTANCE, ip,
                        XV_HELP_DATA, "addu:fname_item",
                        XV_X, 69,
                        XV_Y, 16,
                        PANEL_VALUE_DISPLAY_LENGTH, 20,
                        PANEL_VALUE_STORED_LENGTH, 20,
                        PANEL_LABEL_STRING, "Full Name:",
                        PANEL_LAYOUT, PANEL_HORIZONTAL,
                        PANEL_READ_ONLY, FALSE,
                        PANEL_NOTIFY_PROC, fname_notify,
                        NULL);
        return obj;
}

/*
 * Create object 'logid_item' in the specified instance.
 */
Xv_opaque
addu_window1_logid_item_create(ip, owner)
        addu_window1_objects *ip;
        Xv_opaque owner;
{
        extern Panel_setting logid_notify();
        Xv_opaque obj;

        obj = xv_create(owner, PANEL_TEXT,
                        XV_KEY_DATA, INSTANCE, ip,
                        XV_HELP_DATA, "addu:logid_item",
                        XV_X, 43,
                        XV_Y, 41,
                        PANEL_VALUE_DISPLAY_LENGTH, 8,
                        PANEL_VALUE_STORED_LENGTH, 8,
                        PANEL_LABEL_STRING, "UNIX Login ID:",
                        PANEL_LAYOUT, PANEL_HORIZONTAL,
                        PANEL_READ_ONLY, FALSE,
                        PANEL_NOTIFY_PROC, logid_notify,
                        NULL);
        return obj;
}

/*
 * Create object 'uid_field_item' in the specified instance.
 */
Xv_opaque
addu_window1_uid_field_item_create(ip, owner)
        addu_window1_objects *ip;
        Xv_opaque    owner;
{
        Xv_opaque    obj;

        obj = xv_create(owner, PANEL_TEXT,
                        XV_KEY_DATA, INSTANCE, ip,
                        XV_HELP_DATA, "addu:uid_field_item",
                        XV_X, 87,
                        XV_Y, 66,
                        PANEL_VALUE_DISPLAY_LENGTH, 5,
                        PANEL_VALUE_STORED_LENGTH, 5,
```

```
                            PANEL_LABEL_STRING, "User ID:",
                            PANEL_LAYOUT, PANEL_HORIZONTAL,
}

                            PANEL_READ_ONLY, FALSE,
                            NULL);
        return obj;
/*
 * Create object 'gid_item' in the specified instance.
 */
Xv_opaque
addu_window1_gid_item_create(ip, owner)
        addu_window1_objects *ip;
        Xv_opaque       owner;
{
        extern void   addu_window1_gid_item_notify_callback();
        Xv_opaque       obj;

        obj = xv_create(owner, PANEL_BUTTON,
                        XV_KEY_DATA, INSTANCE, ip,
                        XV_HELP_DATA, "addu:gid_item",
                        XV_X, 64,
                        XV_Y, 88,
                        PANEL_LABEL_STRING, "Group ID...",
                        PANEL_NOTIFY_PROC, addu_window1_gid_item_notify_callback,
                        NULL);
        return obj;
}

/*
 * Create object 'gid_field_item' in the specified instance.
 */
Xv_opaque
addu_window1_gid_field_item_create(ip, owner)
        addu_window1_objects *ip;
        Xv_opaque       owner;
{

        Xv_opaque       obj;

        obj = xv_create(owner, PANEL_TEXT,
                        XV_KEY_DATA, INSTANCE, ip,
                        XV_HELP_DATA, "addu:gid_field_item",
                        XV_X, 149,
                        XV_Y, 91,
                        PANEL_VALUE_DISPLAY_LENGTH, 5,
                        PANEL_VALUE_STORED_LENGTH, 32,
                        PANEL_LAYOUT, PANEL_HORIZONTAL,
                        PANEL_READ_ONLY, FALSE,
                        NULL);
        return obj;
}

/*
 * Create object 'home_dir_item' in the specified instance.
 */
Xv_opaque
addu_window1_home_dir_item_create(ip, owner)
        addu_window1_objects *ip;
        Xv_opaque       owner;
{
        Xv_opaque       obj;
```

```
        obj = xv_create(owner, PANEL_TEXT,
                    XV_KEY_DATA, INSTANCE, ip,
                    XV_HELP_DATA, "addu:home_dir_item",
                    XV_X, 32,
                    XV_Y, 116,
                    PANEL_VALUE_DISPLAY_LENGTH, 20,
                    PANEL_VALUE_STORED_LENGTH, 80,
                    PANEL_LABEL_STRING, "Home Directory:",
                    PANEL_LAYOUT, PANEL_HORIZONTAL,
                    PANEL_READ_ONLY, FALSE,
                    NULL);
        return obj;
}


/*
 * Create object 'shell_menu_button' in the specified instance.
 */
Xv_opaque
addu_window1_shell_menu_button_create(ip, owner)
        addu_window1_objects *ip;
        Xv_opaque     owner;
{

        Xv_opaque     obj;

        obj = xv_create(owner, PANEL_ABBREV_MENU_BUTTON,
                    XV_KEY_DATA, INSTANCE, ip,
                    XV_HELP_DATA, "addu:shell_menu_button",
                    XV_X, 61,
                    XV_Y, 144,
                    PANEL_LABEL_STRING, "Login Shell:",
                    PANEL_ITEM_MENU, addu_shell_menu_create((caddr_t) ip,
                    ip->window1),
                    NULL);
        return obj;
}


/*
 * Create object 'shell_field_item' in the specified instance.
 */
Xv_opaque
addu_window1_shell_field_item_create(ip, owner)
        addu_window1_objects *ip;
        Xv_opaque     owner;
{

        Xv_opaque     obj;

        obj = xv_create(owner, PANEL_TEXT,
                    XV_KEY_DATA, INSTANCE, ip,
                    XV_HELP_DATA, "addu:shell_field_item",
                    XV_X, 181,
                    XV_Y, 144,
                    PANEL_VALUE_DISPLAY_LENGTH, 8,
                    PANEL_VALUE_STORED_LENGTH, 80,
                    PANEL_LAYOUT, PANEL_HORIZONTAL,
                    PANEL_VALUE, "/bin/csh",
                    PANEL_READ_ONLY, FALSE,
                    NULL);
        return obj;
}
```

```
/*
 * Create object 'apply_item' in the specified instance.
 */
Xv_opaque
addu_window1_apply_item_create(ip, owner)
        addu_window1_objects *ip;
        Xv_opaque owner;
{
        extern void   apply_notify();
        Xv_opaque     obj;

        obj = xv_create(owner, PANEL_BUTTON,
                        XV_KEY_DATA, INSTANCE, ip,
                        XV_HELP_DATA, "addu:apply_item",
                        XV_X, 133,
                        XV_Y, 184,
                        PANEL_LABEL_STRING, "Apply",
                        PANEL_NOTIFY_PROC, apply_notify,
                        NULL);
        return obj;
}
```

MSGBOARD

The **msgboard** system is an office In/Out/message board and pager. Although the current version is pretty well tied to various bits of Sun-ness, the eventual plan is to support any system running ONC and XView.

Its purpose is to be the "Swiss Army knife" of personnel tracking and messaging, with three basic functions:

- A distributed In/Out board, making it easier to find out where people are
- A system for sending and reading phone messages (an electronic equivalent to the "While You Were Out" slip)
- A centralized system for sending (and eventually logging) messages to pagers

THE IN/OUT BOARD

The In/Out board is the heart of the system. It has a line for each user, showing their name and whether they're in or out; if they're out, it shows where they are and when they'll be back.

Each person may change the info on his or her line; people designated as "administrators" may change anyone's line. The latter is the key to the success of this board in a typical office, as there will be users who will resist using the board or will just forget to keep it up to date. **Msgboard**'s solution is to give one or more people (usually the office's receptionist) "admin" capabilities so that they can keep the board in sync with reality as lapses occur.

Users can use the following programs to change the board:

msgboard	The main program. Provides a full-screen interface on OpenWindows (or other X11) displays. The receptionist and other key personnel will always use this; other people can use this as they wish.
msglock	A program that marks the user as Out, runs their favorite screen lock program, then marks them as back In when they unlock their screen.
imin	A quick and easy command line program that allows a user to say they're "in" in five keystrokes.
imout	The flip side of "imin"; it also prompts for a return time and comment.
mbtty	Provides a text dump of the current board; use it if you're logged in on a nonbitmapped display.

PHONE MESSAGES

In **msgboard**, anyone can click on any person's status line—which selects that person—then press the "Send Pmsg..." button. A popup window prompts for the usual info, such as name, company, and phone number; when "Send" is chosen, an email message is sent to the selected user.

Phone messages are also kept within the **msgboard** system itself, so that the receptionist can scan for new, pending, or complete phone messages. This makes it easy for someone out of the office to call the receptionist and check his or her messages. For convenience, tempered by privacy concerns, this mechanism can be used by any user to check his or her own messages, but not anyone else's. (There is a compile-time option that will configure **msgboard** to allow anyone to read anyone else's "new" phone messages. See the installation notes.)

PAGERS

The program maintains a database of each person's pager type and number. Any user can press click on the "Page" button to send a page to any user with a pager. In a later release, pages will be logged, so that admin users can handle "who paged me?" questions.

The interface between **msgboard** and numeric pagers needs work. The preferred method would be to have a dedicated program that had exclusive access to a suitable modem; if anyone knows of such a program or wants to volunteer to write it, I'm more than willing to share the load and the glory.

DOCUMENTATION

The documentation consists of this file, the manual page (**msgboard.man**), and the file **instant**, which is intended as a one-pager for admin-mode users. The **instant** file is not available here, but it will be available, along with an **INSTALL** file, through the **boarders** mailing list—that email address is listed further in the chapter.

Spot help is also available for all features of **msgboard** and **msglock**. (If I missed one, let me know!)

BUGS

msgboard will occasionally crash. This problem will be fixed in an upcoming version of the program. Contact the **boarders** list for more info.

CODE

The code follows this introductory stuff. It is in the following order:

- Header files
- .c files

Each section will start with a listing of the files that are in that section.

The following files are also available. See "Further Sources" at the beginning of the book for information on how to obtain code.

- **man** page, **msgboard.man**
- .g files
- .awk files

- Miscellaneous files
- Icons

COMMENTS?

Please send any comments, bug reports, critiques of programming style, and other relevent or irrelevent prose to **larry.wake@west.sun.com**. You can even use the program itself to do this; see "About Message Board..." under the View button.

There's a mailing list, too: write to **boarders-request@runcible.west.sun.com** to get on it.

ABOUT MSGBOARD

It was written using Sun's Devguide interface builder and the XView Open Look toolkit. Original development work began in August 1989 in SunView and then was shelved for a while; more serious work using Devguide and XView began in January 1991.

If you have comments, criticism, suggestions, and/or bug reports, please let me know! The easiest way to do this is to press the "Send Mail" button on the "About Msgboard" popup and drop me an email message. This program has changed significantly (for the better, I hope) as I received feedback during the test process; I hope to make many more improvements as the program's distribution widens.

The **msgboard** is in the public domain, but the copyright on the source code is retained by myself and Sun Microsystems, my employer. This means that you can give the source code to anyone, but you cannot sell any part of the source code, nor can you incorporate any part of the source code into a product that is subsequently sold.

For more information on how the program works, you can use the Help key on any object; you should also be able to type **man msgboard** to see an online manual page.

CREDITS

- The pager routines are taken from **beeptool**, written by Gail Matthews.
- The look and feel of this "About" window, and the Send Mail feature, are based on similar features found in Chuck Musciano's **contool** program.
- The routine for sending an OWV2-style drag'n'drop event was written by Scott Oaks.

HEADER FILES

The following header files are used by this system:

db.h	Database header
hack/gdd.h	Bug workaround
mb_client.h	Message board client header
msgboard.h	Main header (site-specific info)
msgboard_xv.h	**msgboard_xv** includes
outs_menu.h	**outs_menu** includes
pagelog_ui.h	Object and function declarations
pmsg_client.h	Phone message includes
version.h	Version number

db.h

```
#define DBNAME "msgdata"
#define DB_COOKIE "msgdata"
#define DB_VERSION 2
```

hack/gdd.h

```
/*
 *  This file exists only to compensate for a minor bug in Devguide.
 */
```

mb_client.h

```
/*
 *  mb_client.h
 */

extern unsigned int last_seq_no;

extern char *msgd_err[];

enum msgd_types {
    MSGD_VOID,
    MSGD_GREC,
    MSGD_DREC,
    MSGD_UREC
};
```

msgboard.h

```
/*
 *  Site-definable constants.
 */

/*
 *  Default interval between each database check.
 */
#define CK_INT 30

/*
 *  Default name of the machine running the rpc.msgd server  User
 *  can override this with MB_SERVER envariable.
 */
/* #define MB_SERVER "msghost" */
#define MB_SERVER "baaa"

/*
 *  Where the server should look for the data file, error log, and pmsg
 *  directory.
 */
#define MB_TOPDIR "/var/spool/msgboard"
```

```
/*
 *  Uncomment this if you want everyone to be able to see everyone else's
 *  phone messages.  Used by the server; clients check the appropriate
 *  flag in the global record passed to them by the server.
 */
/* #define TRUSTED_OFFICE */


/*
 *  Minimum and maximum UID to consider as "real" users in passwd list
 */
#define MIN_UID      1001
#define MAX_UID      65533


/*
 *  Aging information, used by "nightly": how many days should a message
 *  stick around before being moved to the next lower category, and how
 *  long until it's deleted from trash?  Note that as delivered, things
 *  will never just disappear.  You might want to modify this by setting
 *  TO_COMPLETE_DAYS and TO_TRASH_DAYS to fairly high values.
 */
#define TO_PENDING_DAYS 14
#define TO_COMPLETE_DAYS 0 /* Never auto-move from pending */
#define TO_TRASH_DAYS 0    /* Never auto-move from complete */
#define DEL_DAYS     21


/*
 *  Beeper defines, used by rpc.msgd.
 */
#define  DIALHOST "suntan" /* hostname of machine with */
                           /* dialer program */
#define CU          "/usr/local/bin/cu"
#define  PAUSE      ",,,,,"
#define  SKYPAGE_PHONE "1-800-555-1212"
#define  MESSAGE    "555*1212"


/*
 *  Comment this out if you want to disable programmatic control of panel
 *  item positioning, defaulting to the DevGuide-defined coordinates; doing
 *  this is probably only useful for layout debugging.  I haven't checked
 *  to make sure this works, but code enabled by SCALABLE may also be
 *  obsoleted by DevGuide 3.0.
 */
#define SCALABLE


/*
 *  System mail delivery program.  The code expects a Berkeley-type
 *  mail program that groks tilde escapes, so you probably don't want
 *  to change this.
 */
#define MAILER      "/usr/ucb/Mail"


/*
 *  Authorization levels required for the different RPC services
 *  provided by rpc. msgd.  Server currently supports AUTH_NONE,
 *  AUTH_UNIX and AUTH_DES.  Clients do not use these constants directly;
 *  authorization levels are placed in struct srvinfo by connect_to_server().
 */

/*
 *  Authentication for GET_REC, GET_MOD_REC
 */
#define MB_GET_AUTH AUTH_NONE
```

```
/*
 *   Authentication for PUT_REC
 */
#define MB_PUT_AUTH AUTH_DES

/*
 *   Authentication for SEND_PAGE
 */
#define MB_PAGE_AUTH AUTH_DES

/*
 *   Authentication for SEND-PMSG
 */
#define MB_SNDPMSG_AUTH AUTH_DES

/*
 *   Authentication for SCAN-PMSG and friends
 */
#define MB_GETPMSG_AUTH AUTH_DES

/*
 *   Default parameter storage file
 */
#define PARAMFILE ".mb2rc"

/*
 * Nothing below here should need to be changed unless you're mucking
 * with the code.
 ************************************************************************
 */

#define CLASS_NAME "MsgBoard"

/*
 *   Choices for sendmsg window
 */
#define SM_CHOICE_DEFAULT 1 /* Default choice for sendmsg (2^0) */
#define SM_CHOICE_LV_MSG 16 /* Choice that opens text subwin (2^4) */
#define SM_MAX_CHOICE    4      /* Highest choice available (0-based) */

/*
 *   Choices for scan message window
 */

#define SCM_CHOICE_DEFAULT 0
#define SCM_CHOICE_NEW 0
#define SCM_CHOICE_PEN 1
#define SCM_CHOICE_COM 2
#define SCM_CHOICE_TRA 3
#define SCM_MAX_CHOICE 3

/*
 *   String lengths for various database fields
 */
#define LOGID_LEN 8
#define FNAME_LEN 20
#define UNTIL_LEN 15
#define COMMENT_LEN 40
#define MOTD_LEN 64
#define SITE_LEN 40
#define CAT_LEN 10
#define SORTBY_LEN FNAME_LEN
```

```
#define EXT_LEN *
#define PAGERNUM_LEN 13

/*
 *   String lengths for pmsg fields
 */
#define TO_LEN 64
#define TIME_LEN 16
#define CALLER_LEN 50
#define ORG_LEN 50
#define PHNUM_LEN 50

/*
 *   Printing stuff
 */
#define PRINTCMD "/usr/ucb/lpr"
#define PRINTERNAME_LEN 20
#define TO_PRINTER 0
#define TO_FILE 1
#define POSTSCRIPT 0
#define ASCII 1

/*
 *   Add/Modify window mode.
 */
#define IDLE 0
#define ADDING 1
#define MODIFYING 3

/*
 *   Display modes for the main window
 */
#define DISP-TEXT 0
#define DISP-DATES 1

/*
 *   Value representing bogosity
 */
#define BOGUS -1

/*
 *   The three modes for an entry
 */
#define MB-OUT 0
#define MB_IN 1
#define MB_UNK 2

/*
 *   Value representing "All" -- used for categories and status
 */
#define MB_ALL -1

/*
 *   Beeper types
 */
#define BEEP_ALPHA 0
#define BEEP_NUM 1
#define BEEP_SKY 2
#define BEEP_UNK 3

/*
 *   Masks for Mem_Rec.flags:
 *      MB_CHG_PLAN: Should msgboard automagically update .plan for you?
```

```
 *      MB_ADMIN:     Can you use msgboard's administrative functions?
 *                    (only settable by users with this flag already set)
 *      MB_PRESERVE:  Should the comment field NOT be zeroed when moving
 *                    from Out to In?
 *      MB_VIA_MAIL:  Should pmsgs be sent to you via email?
 *      MB_VIA_MB:    Should pmsgs be saved/accessible within msgboard?
 *      MB_NEWMSGS:   Do you have unread messages? (read-only)
 */
#define MB_CHG_PLAN 0x01
#define MB_ADMIN 0x02
#define MB_PRESERVE 0x04
#define MB_VIA_MAIL 0x08
#define MB_VIA_MB 0x10
#define MB_NEWMSGS 0x20


/*
 *  Masks for global flags:
 *      MB_G_CHG_PLAN: Default for MB_CHG_PLAN field; see above
 *      MB_G_VIA_MAIL: Default for MB_VIA_MAIL
 *      MB_G_PRESERVE: Default for MB_PRESERVE
 *      MB_G_VIA_MB:   Default for MB_VIA_MB
 *      MB_G_LASTNM1ST: Format for full names: if TRUE, last name first;
 *                      if FALSE, first name first.
 *      MB_G_TRUSTED: If TRUE, server is running in TRUSTED_OFFICE mode.
 *                    Note that this is a READ-ONLY variable as far as
 *                    clients are concerned.
 */
#define MB_G_CHG_PLAN 0x01
#define MB_G_PRESERVE 0x04
#define MB_G_VIA_MAIL 0x08
#define MB_G_VIA_MB 0x10
#define MB_G_LASTNM1ST 0x40
#define MB_G_TRUSTED 0x80


/*
 *  Status flags returned by the server.
 */
#define MSGD_OK 0
#define MSGD_DISCONNECTED 1      /* Not connected to server */
#define MSGD_RPC_FAIL 2          /* Pretty vauge, eh? */
#define MSGD_VALID_FAIL 3        /* Security validation error */
#define MSGD_NOT_FOUND 4         /* Record not found */
#define MSGD_ALREADY_EXISTS 5 /* Record already exists */
#define MSGD_ERROR 6             /* General failure */


/*
 *  Width of the In/Out/??? glyph
 */
#define INOUT_WIDTH 64

#ifndef TRUE
#define TRUE (1)
#define FALSE (0)
#endif

#define CNULL ((char *) 0)
#define FNULL ((FILE *) NULL)
#define ITIMER_NULL ((struct itimerval *) 0)


/*
 *  Structure for user records
 */
```

```
typedef struct mem_rec {
    char logid[LOGID_LEN+1],              /* UNIX login name */
         fname[FNAME_LEN+1],              /* Full name              */
         until[UNTIL_LEN+1],             /* "Out until" field */
         comment[COMMENT_LEN+1],         /* Message field */
         cat[CAT_LEN+1],                 /* Category  */
         sortby[SORTBY_LEN+1],           /* Sort key  */
         ext[EXT_LEN+1],                 /* Phone extension */
         pagernum[PAGERNUM_LEN+1];       /* Pager phone number */
    int
         row,                            /* on-screen row # */
         status,                         /* In, Out, or ??? */
         flags,                          /* In, Boolean flags:
                                                MG_CHG_PLAN
                                                MB_ADMIN
                                                MB_PRESERVE
                                                MB_VIA_MAIL
                                                MB_VIA_MB */
         pagertype;                      /* Pager type */
    time_t timestamp;                    /* Record mod time */

} Mem_Rec;

int comp_by_logid (), comp_by_sortby (), comp_strings ();

char *getenv (), *get_fname ();

Mem_Rec *find_urec ();

typedef struct global_rec {

    char  name [SITE_LEN + 1],           /* Name of the server's site */
          motd[MOTD_LEN + 1];            /* Message of the day */
    int   flags                          /* Global flags */
          pagertype;                     /* Default pager type */
} Global_Rec;

extern char **cats, mylogid[], mb_server[];
extern int users, admin, delay, numcats, cur_cat, cur_status, admin_enable;
extern Mem-Rec *ulist, *myentry;
extern Global_Rec globrec;
```

msgboard_xv.h

```
struct winparams {
        int             state;
        Rect            rect;
};

extern int prt_type, prt_dest, cur_sel, pop_mod, windowsys_up, fmt_msgs,
        timer_stopped, watchnum, dragstyle;

extern int wgrid;

extern char prt_name[], prt_dir[], prt_file[], **watchlist;

extern Frame base_frame;
```

```
extern struct winparams
                        send_params, scan_params, main_params, page_params,
                        outmod_params;

#ifdef _XLIB_H_
extern Display *dpy;
#endif
```

outs_menu.h

```
struct outent {
    char  *label,
                *until,
                *message;
    int pop;
};

extern struct outent *outlist;
extern int num_outs;
```

pagelog_ui.h

```
#ifndef pagelog_HEADER
#define pagelog_HEADER

/*
 * pagelog_ui.h - User interface object and function declarations.
 * This file was generated by `gxv' from `pagelog.G'.
 * DO NOT EDIT BY HAND.
 */

extern Attr_attribute INSTANCE;


typedef struct {
        Xv_opaque    frame;
        Xv_opaque    textsw;
} pagelog_frame_objects;

extern pagelog_frame_objects *pagelog_frame_objects_initialize();

extern Xv_opaque pagelog_frame_frame_create();
extern Xv_opaque pagelog_frame_textsw_create();
#endif
```

pmsg_client.h

```
struct pmsg_hdr {
        char *desc; /* Description of a message */
        char *id;   /* unique identifier of a message */
};
```

```
struct pmsg {
   char *id;      /* Login ID of person writing/receiving message */
   char *caller;  /* Full name of person who called */
   char *time;    /* Time they called */
   char *org;     /* Their organization */
   char *phnum;   /* Their phone number */
   char *text;    /* Any add'l mesg text */
   int  flags;    /* Flags corresponding to checkboxes on message form */
};

struct pmsg_hdr *get_pmsg_headers ();
```

version.h

```
#define PROGRAM_VERSION "1.0-Demo"
```

.C FILES

The following .C files are used by this system:

aboutwin.c	About window
alertwin.c	Alert window
amwin.c	Add/Modify window
find.c	Scanmsg find window
logwin.c	Log window
mainwin.c	Main window
mb_client.c	Client RPC routines
mb_com.c	Common routines
mbtty.c	Bare minimum lister for the msgboard
msgboard_xv.c	XView version of msgboard
nightly.c	Housekeeping routines
outmodwin.c	Abbreviated modify window to record when user is out
outs_menu.c	Outs menu
pagewin.c	Pager-dialing window
pmsg_client.c	Phone message RPC client
pmsg_prt.c	Phone message printer
pmsgwin.c	Phone message window
propswin.c	Property windows
scanwin.c	Scan message window
send_drag.c	Source a drag 'n' drop event
sendwin.c	Send phone message
set_hints.c	Set hints
srv-emulate.c	Server routines
warpme.c	Pointer-warping routines

alertwin.c

```
/*
 * alertwin.c - Notify and event callback function stubs.
 */

#include <stdio.h>
#include <sys/param.h>
#include <sys/types.h>
#include <xview/xview.h>
#include <xview/panel.h>
#include <xview/textsw.h>
#include <xview/xv_xrect.h>
#include <X11/Xutil.h>
#include "alertwin_ui.h"
#include "msgboard.h"
#include "msgboard_xv.h"


/*
 *  Puts up an alert popup announcing that "id" logged in.
 */
void
watch_alert(id)
char *id;
{
#ifdef SCALABLE
    int xpos, ypos;
#endif
    alertwin_frame_objects *ip;
    Panel_item glyph;
    char buf[50];
    Window xid;
    XSizeHints *hints;

    ip = alertwin_frame_objects_initialize(NULL, base_frame);


    /*
     *  Create glyph manually so we can re-use the program's icon
     *  server image.
     */
    glyph = (Panel_item)xv_create(ip->panel, PANEL_MESSAGE,
        XV_KEY_DATA, INSTANCE, ip,
        XV_X, 16,
        XV_Y, 16,
        XV_WIDTH, 64,
        XV_HEIGHT, 64,
        PANEL_LABEL_IMAGE, (Server_image)xv_get(
                (Icon)xv_get(base_frame, FRAME_ICON), ICON_IMAGE),
                NULL);

    sprintf(buf, "%s checked in.", get_fname(id));
    xv_set(ip->text, PANEL_LABEL_STRING, buf, NULL);

#ifdef SCALABLE
    xv_set(glyph, XV_X, wgrid, XV_Y, wgrid, NULL);
    xpos = wgrid * 2 + (int)xv_get(glyph, XV_WIDTH);
    ypos = wgrid + (int)xv_get(glyph, XV_HEIGHT) / 2 -
        (int)xv_get(ip->text, XV_HEIGHT) / 2;
    xv_set(ip->text, XV_X, xpos, XV_Y, ypos, NULL);
    window_fit(ip->panel);
    window_fit(ip->frame);
#endif
```

```
    xid = (Window)xv_get(ip->frame, XV_XID);
    hints = XAllocSizeHints();

    /* This particular window doesn't allow resizing */
/*  hints->flags = PMinSize | PMaxSize;
    hints->min_height = hints->max_height = (int)xv_get(ip->frame,
                                                        XV_HEIGHT);
 */ hints->min_width = hints->max_width = (int)xv_get(ip->frame, XV_WIDTH);
    hints->flags = PBaseSize;
    hints->base_height = (int)xv_get(ip->frame, XV_HEIGHT);
    hints->base_width = (int)xv_get(ip->frame, XV_WIDTH);
    XSetWMNormalHints(dpy, xid, hints);
    XFree(hints);
    xv_set(ip->frame, XV_SHOW, TRUE, NULL);
    window_bell(ip->frame);
}

/*
 * Done callback function for 'frame'.
 */
void
alertwin_done(frame)
Frame frame;
{
    xv_set(frame, XV_SHOW, FALSE, 0);

    free( (char *)xv_get(frame, XV_KEY_DATA, INSTANCE) );
    if ( xv_destroy_safe(frame) != XV_OK )
      pr_msg(NULL, TRUE, "Destroy of popup failed!");
}
```

amwin.c

```
/*
 * amwin.c - Support routines for Message Board add/modify window
 */

#include <stdio.h>
#include <string.h>
#include <sys/param.h>
#include <sys/types.h>
#include <xview/xview.h>
#include <xview/panel.h>
#include <xview/textsw.h>
#include <xview/xv_xrect.h>
#include "amwin_ui.h"
#include "msgboard.h"
#include "msgboard_xv.h"
#include <pwd.h>

amwin_am_frame_objects    *am_ip;
amwin_names_frame_objects *nameswin_p;

int
    am_window_created = FALSE, /* is A/M window created? */
    names_window_created = FALSE, /* is name chooser window created? */
    am_mode = IDLE; /* What's the A/M window being used for? */
void names_panel_event();

void
create_am_window()
```

```
{
#ifdef SCALABLE
    int valx, ypos;
#endif

    am_ip = amwin_am_frame_objects_initialize(NULL, base_frame);

    xv_set(am_ip->pagernum_item, PANEL_NOTIFY_LEVEL, PANEL_ALL, NULL);

#ifdef SCALABLE
    /*
     * sortby has the longest label, so we position it properly from the
     * left edge of the panel.
     */
    xv_set(am_ip->sortby_item, XV_X, wgrid * 2, NULL);
    valx = (int)xv_get(am_ip->sortby_item, PANEL_VALUE_X);

    ypos = wgrid * 2;
    align_values(am_ip->logid_item, valx, ypos);
    xv_set(am_ip->names_item,
        XV_X,          (int)xv_get(am_ip->logid_item, XV_X) +
                       (int)xv_get(am_ip->logid_item, XV_WIDTH) + wgrid,
        XV_Y,          ypos,
        NULL);

    ypos += wgrid + (int)xv_get(am_ip->logid_item, XV_HEIGHT);
    align_values(am_ip->fname_item, valx, ypos);

    ypos += wgrid + (int)xv_get(am_ip->fname_item, XV_HEIGHT);
    align_values(am_ip->status_item, valx, ypos);

    ypos += wgrid + (int)xv_get(am_ip->status_item, XV_HEIGHT);
    align_values(am_ip->until_item, valx, ypos);

    ypos += wgrid + (int)xv_get(am_ip->until_item, XV_HEIGHT);
    align_values(am_ip->comment_item, valx, ypos);

    ypos += wgrid * 2 + (int)xv_get(am_ip->comment_item, XV_HEIGHT);
    align_values(am_ip->cat_item, valx, ypos);

    ypos += wgrid + (int)xv_get(am_ip->cat_item, XV_HEIGHT);
    xv_set(am_ip->sortby_item, XV_Y, ypos, NULL);

    ypos += wgrid + (int)xv_get(am_ip->sortby_item, XV_HEIGHT);
    align_values(am_ip->ext_item, valx, ypos);

    ypos += wgrid + (int)xv_get(am_ip->ext_item, XV_HEIGHT);
    align_values(am_ip->pagernum_item, valx, ypos);
    xv_set(am_ip->pagertype_item,
        XV_X,          (int)xv_get(am_ip->pagernum_item, XV_X) +
                       (int)xv_get(am_ip->pagernum_item, XV_WIDTH) + wgrid,
        XV_Y,          ypos,
        NULL);

    ypos += wgrid * 2 + (int)xv_get(am_ip->pagertype_item, XV_HEIGHT);
    align_values(am_ip->plan_item, valx, ypos);

    ypos += wgrid / 2 + (int)xv_get(am_ip->plan_item, XV_HEIGHT);
    align_values(am_ip->preserve_item, valx, ypos);

    ypos += wgrid / 2 + (int)xv_get(am_ip->preserve_item, XV_HEIGHT);
    align_values(am_ip->via_mail_item, valx, ypos);
```

```
        ypos += wgrid / 2 + (int)xv_get(am_ip->via_mail_item, XV_HEIGHT);
        align_values(am_ip->via_mb_item, valx, ypos);

        ypos += wgrid / 2 + (int)xv_get(am_ip->via_mb_item, XV_HEIGHT);
        align_values(am_ip->admin_item, valx, ypos);

        ypos += wgrid * 2 + (int)xv_get(am_ip->admin_item, XV_HEIGHT);

        xv_set(am_ip->apply_item, XV_Y, ypos, NULL);
        xv_set(am_ip->reset_item, XV_Y, ypos, NULL);

        window_fit(am_ip->am_panel);
        window_fit(am_ip->am_frame);

        position_bot_buttons(am_ip->am_panel, am_ip->apply_item,
                                              am_ip->reset_item);
#endif

    am_window_created = TRUE;
}

/*
 * Prepare A/M window for Add mode
 */
void
prep_add_mode()
{
/*
 * Check to see if we're not already doing something with the window!
 */
    if (!am_window_created) create_am_window();

    xv_set(am_ip->logid_item,
        PANEL_VALUE,                "",
        PANEL_READ_ONLY,FALSE,
        NULL);
    xv_set(am_ip->names_item, XV_SHOW, TRUE, NULL);
    xv_set(am_ip->fname_item, PANEL_VALUE, "", NULL);
    xv_set(am_ip->status_item, PANEL_VALUE, MB_UNK, NULL);
    xv_set(am_ip->until_item, PANEL_VALUE, "", NULL);
    xv_set(am_ip->comment_item, PANEL_VALUE, "", NULL);
    xv_set(am_ip->cat_item, PANEL_VALUE, "", XV_SHOW, TRUE, NULL);
    xv_set(am_ip->sortby_item,
        PANEL_VALUE, "",
        XV_SHOW,        TRUE,
        NULL);
    xv_set(am_ip->ext_item, PANEL_VALUE, "", XV_SHOW, TRUE, NULL);
    xv_set(am_ip->pagernum_item, PANEL_VALUE, "", XV_SHOW, TRUE, NULL);
    xv_set(am_ip->pagertype_item,
        PANEL_VALUE, globrec.pagertype,
        XV_SHOW,        TRUE,
        PANEL_INACTIVE, TRUE,
        NULL);
    xv_set(am_ip->plan_item,
        PANEL_VALUE, (globrec.flags & MB_G_CHG_PLAN) != 0,
        NULL);
    xv_set(am_ip->via_mail_item,
        PANEL_VALUE, (globrec.flags & MB_G_VIA_MAIL) != 0,
        NULL);
    xv_set(am_ip->via_mb_item,
        PANEL_VALUE, (globrec.flags & MB_G_VIA_MB) != 0,
        NULL);
```

```
    xv_set(am_ip->preserve_item,
        PANEL_VALUE, (globrec.flags & MB_G_PRESERVE) != 0,
        NULL);
    xv_set(am_ip->admin_item,
        PANEL_VALUE, FALSE,
        XV_SHOW,     TRUE,
        NULL);

    xv_set(am_ip->am_panel, PANEL_CARET_ITEM, am_ip->logid_item, NULL);

    am_mode = ADDING;
    xv_set(am_ip->am_frame,
        XV_LABEL,    "Message Board: Add Entry",
        XV_SHOW,     TRUE,
        NULL);
}

/*
 *  Prepare A/M window for modify mode
 */
void
prep_modify_mode()
{
    Mem_Rec *rec;

    if (admin)
        rec = &ulist[cur_sel];
    else {
        if (myentry == (struct mem_rec *)NULL) {
            pr_msg(NULL, TRUE, "%s is not currently on the Message Board.",
                    mylogid);
            return;
        }
        rec = myentry;
    }
/*
 *  Check to see if we're not already doing something with the window!
 */
    if (!am_window_created) create_am_window();

    xv_set(am_ip->am_panel, PANEL_CARET_ITEM, am_ip->until_item, NULL);
    xv_set(am_ip->logid_item,
        PANEL_VALUE,            rec->logid,
        PANEL_READ_ONLY,        TRUE,
        NULL);
    xv_set(am_ip->names_item, XV_SHOW, FALSE, NULL);
    xv_set(am_ip->fname_item,
        PANEL_VALUE,            rec->fname,
        PANEL_READ_ONLY, !admin,
        NULL);
    xv_set(am_ip->status_item, PANEL_VALUE, rec->status, NULL);
    xv_set(am_ip->until_item, PANEL_VALUE, rec->until, NULL);
    xv_set(am_ip->comment_item, PANEL_VALUE, rec->comment, NULL);
    xv_set(am_ip->cat_item,
        PANEL_VALUE, rec->cat,
        XV_SHOW, admin,
        NULL);
    xv_set(am_ip->sortby_item,
        PANEL_VALUE, rec->sortby,
        XV_SHOW, admin,
        NULL);
```

```
    xv_set (am_ip->ext_item,
        PANEL_VALUE, rec->ext,
        XV_SHOW, admin,
        NULL);
    xv_set (am_ip->pagernum_item,
        PANEL_VALUE, rec->pagernum,
        XV_SHOW, admin,
        NULL);
    xv_set (am_ip->pagertype_item,
        PANEL_VALUE, rec->pagertype,
        PANEL_INACTIVE, rec->pagernum[0] == '\0',
        XV_SHOW, admin,
        NULL);
    xv_set (am_ip->plan_item,
        PANEL_VALUE, (rec->flags & MB_CHG_PLAN) != 0,
        NULL);
    xv_set (am_ip->preserve_item,
        PANEL_VALUE, (rec->flags & MB_PRESERVE) != 0,
        NULL);
    xv_set (am_ip->via_mail_item,
        PANEL_VALUE, (rec->flags & MB_VIA_MAIL) != 0,
        NULL);
    xv_set (am_ip->via_mb_item,
        PANEL_VALUE, (rec->flags & MB_VIA_MB) != 0,
        NULL);
    xv_set (am_ip->admin_item,
        PANEL_VALUE,                (rec->flags & MB_ADMIN) != 0,
        XV_SHOW,                    admin,
        NULL);

    am_mode = MODIFYING;
    xv_set (am_ip->am_frame,
        XV_LABEL,       "Message Board: Modify Entry",
        XV_SHOW,        TRUE,
        NULL);

    if (names_window_created && (int)xv_get(nameswin_p->names_frame,
                                                    XV_SHOW))
        xv_set (nameswin_p->names_frame,
            FRAME_CMD_PIN_STATE, FRAME_CMD_PIN_OUT,
            XV_SHOW,                              FALSE,
            NULL);
}

void
create_names_window()
{
    int i, x, y;
    struct passwd *pwbuf;
    Rect am_rect;

    nameswin_p = amwin_names_frame_objects_initialize(NULL, base_frame);

#ifdef SCALABLE
    xv_set (nameswin_p->list_item, XV_X, wgrid * 2, XV_Y, wgrid * 2, NULL);
    window_fit (nameswin_p->names_panel);
    window_fit (nameswin_p->names_frame);
#endif
    /*
     * Get the list of possible users
     */
```

```
    setpwent();

    i = 0;
    while ( (pwbuf = getpwent()) != (struct passwd *)NULL) {
        if (pwbuf->pw_uid >= MIN_UID && pwbuf->pw_uid <= MAX_UID) {
            xv_set(nameswin_p->list_item,
                    PANEL_LIST_STRING, i, pwbuf->pw_name,
                    NULL);
            i++;
        }
    }

    xv_set(nameswin_p->list_item,
        PANEL_LIST_SORT, PANEL_FORWARD,
        NULL);

    /*
     * Position the window to initially appear just to the right of the
     * "Names..." button
     */
    frame_get_rect(am_ip->am_frame, &am_rect);
    x = am_rect.r_left +
        (int)xv_get(am_ip->names_item, XV_X) +
        (int)xv_get(am_ip->names_item, XV_WIDTH) +
        (int)xv_get(am_ip->am_panel, PANEL_ITEM_X_GAP);

    y = am_rect.r_top +
        (int)xv_get(am_ip->names_item, XV_Y);

/*
 * Check to make sure we're not moving it off the screen!
 */

    /* i = y + names-frame-height - root_win_height
       if ( i > 0 ) y -= i; */

    if ( y < 0 ) y = 0;

    /* i = x +names-frame-width - root_win_width
       if ( i > 0 ) x -= i; */

    if ( x < 0 ) x = 0;

    xv_set(nameswin_p->names_frame,
        FRAME_CMD_DEFAULT_PIN_STATE,FRAME_CMD_PIN_IN,
        XV_X, x,
        XV_Y, y,
        NULL);

    xv_set(nameswin_p->names_panel,
        WIN_EVENT_PROC, names_panel_event,
        NULL);

    names_window_created = TRUE;
}

/*
 * Fills record pointed to by "r" with values from input window.
 */ void
get_am_data(r)
Mem_Rec *r;
```

```
{
    strcpy(r->logid, (char *)xv_get(am_ip->logid_item, PANEL_VALUE));
    strcpy(r->fname, (char *)xv_get(am_ip->fname_item, PANEL_VALUE));
    strcpy(r->until, (char *)xv_get(am_ip->until_item, PANEL_VALUE));
    strcpy(r->comment, (char *)xv_get(am_ip->comment_item, PANEL_VALUE));
    strcpy(r->cat, (char *)xv_get(am_ip->cat_item, PANEL_VALUE));
    strcpy(r->sortby, (char *)xv_get(am_ip->sortby_item, PANEL_VALUE));
    strcpy(r->ext, (char *)xv_get(am_ip->ext_item, PANEL_VALUE));
    strcpy(r->pagernum, (char *)xv_get(am_ip->pagernum_item, PANEL_VALUE));
    r->status = (int)xv_get(am_ip->status_item, PANEL_VALUE);
    r->flags = 0;
    if ((int)xv_get(am_ip->plan_item, PANEL_VALUE)) r->flags |= MB_CHG_PLAN;
    if ((int)xv_get(am_ip->admin_item, PANEL_VALUE)) r->flags |= MB_ADMIN;
    if ((int)xv_get(am_ip->preserve_item, PANEL_VALUE)) r->flags
                                                    |= MB_PRESERVE;
    if ((int)xv_get(am_ip->via_mail_item, PANEL_VALUE)) r->flags
                                                    |= MB_VIA_MAIL;
    if ((int)xv_get(am_ip->via_mb_item, PANEL_VALUE)) r->flags |= MB_VIA_MB;
    r->pagertype = (int)xv_get(am_ip->pagertype_item, PANEL_VALUE);
}

/*
 * Notify callback function for `names_item'.
 */
void
am_names_notify(item, event)
Panel_item item;
Event *event;
{
    if (!names_window_created) create_names_window();

    xv_set(nameswin_p->names_frame,
        XV_SHOW,                        TRUE,
        NULL);
    /*
     * Keep A/M window from being dismissed by this event,
     * even if it's unpinned:
     */
    xv_set(item, PANEL_NOTIFY_STATUS, XV_ERROR, NULL);
}

/*
 * Notify callback function for `logid_item'.
 */
Panel_setting
am_logid_item_notify(item, event)
Panel_item item;
Event *event;
{
    if (make_default_fname()) {
      clear_msg();
      if (event_shift_is_down(event))
          return PANEL_PREVIOUS;
      else
          return PANEL_NEXT;
    }
    else {
      pr_msg(NULL, TRUE, "Invalid login ID: %s",
          (char *)xv_get(item, PANEL_VALUE));
      return PANEL_NONE;
    }
}
```

```
/*
 * Notify callback function for 'fname_item'.
 */
Panel_setting
am_fname_item_notify(item, event)
Panel_item item;
Event *event;
{
    char sortby[SORTBY_LEN+1];

    strcpy(sortby, (char *)xv_get(am_ip->sortby_item, PANEL_VALUE));
    if (sortby[0] == '\0') {
      make_sort_string((char *)xv_get(am_ip->fname_item, PANEL_VALUE),
          sortby);
      xv_set(am_ip->sortby_item, PANEL_VALUE, sortby, NULL);
    }
    if (event_shift_is_down(event))
      return PANEL_PREVIOUS;
    else
      return PANEL_NEXT;
}


/*
 * Notify callback function for 'status_item'.
 */
void
am_inout_notify(item, value, event)
Panel_item item;
int value;
Event *event;
{
    if (value == MB_OUT)
        xv_set(am_ip->am_panel, PANEL_CARET_ITEM, am_ip->until_item, NULL);
    else if (value == MB_IN) {
        xv_set(am_ip->until_item, PANEL_VALUE, "", NULL);
        if (!(int)xv_get(am_ip->preserve_item, PANEL_VALUE))
            xv_set(am_ip->comment_item, PANEL_VALUE, "", NULL);
    }
}


/*
 * Notify callback function for 'pagernum_item'.
 */
Panel_setting
am_pagernum_item_notify(item, event)
Panel_item item;
Event *event;
{
    xv_set(am_ip->pagertype_item,
        PANEL_INACTIVE, (strlen((char *)xv_get(item, PANEL_VALUE)) == 0),
        NULL);
%STOPPED HERE
    return panel_text_notify(item, event);
}


/*
 * Notify callback function for 'reset_item'.
 */
void
am_reset_notify(item, event)
Panel_item item;
Event *event;
```

```
{
    if ((int)xv_get(am_ip->am_frame, FRAME_CMD_PIN_STATE) ==
      FRAME_CMD_PIN_IN) {
      if (am_mode == ADDING)
          prep_add_mode();
      else if (am_mode == MODIFYING)
          prep_modify_mode();
    }
    else {
      am_mode = IDLE;
      if (names_window_created)
          xv_set(nameswin_p->names_frame,
                  FRAME_CMD_PIN_STATE, FRAME_CMD_PIN_OUT,
                  XV_SHOW, FALSE,
                  NULL);
    }
}

/*
 * Notify callback function for 'apply_item'.
 */
void
am_apply_notify(item, event)
Panel_item item;
Event *event;
{
    Mem_Rec new_rec;

    get_am_data(&new_rec);
    if (am_mode == ADDING) {
      if (add_user_end(&new_rec) == 0) {
          clear_msg();
          if ((int)xv_get(am_ip->am_frame, FRAME_CMD_PIN_STATE) ==
              FRAME_CMD_PIN_IN)
                  prep_add_mode();
          else
                  am_mode = IDLE;
      }
      else
          xv_set(item, PANEL_NOTIFY_STATUS, XV_ERROR, NULL);
    }
    else if (am_mode == MODIFYING) {
      if (modify_user_end(&new_rec) == 0) {
          clear_msg();
          if ((int)xv_get(am_ip->am_frame, FRAME_CMD_PIN_STATE) ==
              FRAME_CMD_PIN_IN)
                  prep_modify_mode();
          else
                  am_mode = IDLE;
      }
      else
          xv_set(item, PANEL_NOTIFY_STATUS, XV_ERROR, NULL);
    }

    if (am_mode == IDLE) {
      if (names_window_created)
      xv_set(nameswin_p->names_frame,
          FRAME_CMD_PIN_STATE, FRAME_CMD_PIN_OUT,
          XV_SHOW, FALSE,
          NULL);
    }
```

```
}

/*
 *  Act on the choice they made from the name chooser.
 */
void
set_name_from_list(string)
char *string;
{
    xv_set(am_ip->logid_item,
        PANEL_VALUE, string,
        NULL);
    if (make_default_fname())
        xv_set(am_ip->am_panel, PANEL_CARET_ITEM, am_ip->fname_item,
            NULL);
    else
        xv_set(am_ip->am_panel, PANEL_CARET_ITEM, am_ip->logid_item,
            NULL);
    xv_set(am_ip->sortby_item, PANEL_VALUE, "", NULL);
}

/*
 * Notify callback function for `list_item'.
 */
int
amwin_list_notify(item, string, client_data, op, event, row)
Panel_item item;
char *string;
Xv_opaque client_data;
Panel_list_op op;
Event *event;
int row;
{
    if (op == PANEL_LIST_OP_SELECT)
        set_name_from_list(string);

    return XV_OK;
}

/*
 *  Uses lookup_user() to get a reasonable full name out of the GECOS field;
 *  also gets the user's group and makes it their default category.
 *
 *  If MB_G_LASTNM1ST (last name first) is set, make a stab at reversing the
 *  name order...
 */
int
make_default_fname()
{
    int len;
    char logid[LOGID_LEN+1], fname[FNAME_LEN+1], cat[CAT_LEN+1],
        buf[FNAME_LEN + 1], *space, *ptr;

    strcpy(logid, (char *)xv_get(am_ip->logid_item, PANEL_VALUE));
    if (logid[0] == '\0' || lookup_user(logid, fname, cat) != 0)
        return FALSE;

    if ((globrec.flags & MB_G_LASTNM1ST) != 0 &&
      (space = strrchr(fname, ' ')) != CNULL) {
        strcpy(buf, space + 1);
        strncat(buf, ", ", FNAME_LEN - strlen(buf));
        for (ptr = fname, len = strlen(buf) ;
        ptr != space && len < FNAME_LEN ; ptr++, len++)
            buf[len] = *ptr;
```

```
        buf[len] = '\0';
        strcpy(fname, buf);
    }
    xv_set(am_ip->fname_item, PANEL_VALUE, fname, NULL);
    xv_set(am_ip->cat_item, PANEL_VALUE, cat, NULL);

    return TRUE;
}

/*
 *  Monitors resize events on the name chooser panel
 */
void
names_panel_event(window, event)
Xv_window window;
Event *event;
{
    /*
     *  Check for a resize event
     */
    if (event_action(event) == WIN_RESIZE) {
      int rh, nrows, nlist_h, xtra;

      /*
       *  "xtra" is the part of the scrolling list height that is not
       *  contributed by the rows themselves
       */
      rh = (int)xv_get(nameswin_p->list_item, PANEL_LIST_ROW_HEIGHT);
      xtra = (int)xv_get(nameswin_p->list_item, XV_HEIGHT) -
          rh * (int)xv_get(nameswin_p->list_item, PANEL_LIST_DISPLAY_ROWS);

      /*
       *  Figure out how long the scrolling list should be now
       */
      nlist_h = (int)xv_get(nameswin_p->names_panel, XV_HEIGHT) -
          (int)xv_get(nameswin_p->list_item, XV_Y) - wgrid * 2;

      nrows = (nlist_h - xtra) / rh;
      nlist_h = nrows * rh  + xtra;

      xv_set(nameswin_p->list_item,
          XV_HEIGHT, nlist_h,
          PANEL_LIST_DISPLAY_ROWS, nrows,
          NULL);
    }
}

/*
 * Done callback function for 'am_frame'.
 */
void
amwin_done(frame)
Frame frame;
{
    if (names_window_created)
      xv_set(nameswin_p->names_frame,
          FRAME_CMD_PIN_STATE, FRAME_CMD_PIN_OUT,
          XV_SHOW,                              FALSE,
          NULL);
    xv_set(frame, XV_SHOW, FALSE, NULL);
}
```

`find.c`

```
/*
 * find.c - routines supporting the scanmsg find window.
 */

#include <stdio.h>
#include <sys/param.h>
#include <sys/types.h>
#include <xview/xview.h>
#include <xview/panel.h>
#include "scanwin_ui.h"
#include "msgboard.h"

/*
 * Global object definitions.
 */
extern scanwin_frame_objects *scan_ip;
extern scanwin_find_frame_objects *find_ip;
extern int cur_msg, num_msgs, num_selected;

/*
 *  Returns TRUE if string is in lowercased version
 *  of line's panel_value.
 *  Convert string to lowercase before calling this routine.
 */
int
scan_find(line, string, clear_msgs)
int line, clear_msgs;
char *string;
{
    char *target, *c;
    int matched;

    target = strdup((char *)xv_get(scan_ip->list_item,
        PANEL_LIST_STRING, line));
    c = target - 1;
    while ( *(++c) != '\0' )
       if ( isupper(*c) ) *c = tolower(*c);

    matched = (strstr(target, string) != CNULL);
    free(target);

    if (matched) {
    if (clear_msgs) select_all_msgs(FALSE);
       cur_msg = line;
       xv_set(scan_ip->list_item, PANEL_LIST_SELECT, cur_msg, TRUE, NULL);
       if (smsg_is_up()) show_smsg_window();
    }
    return matched;
}

/*
 * Notify callback function for 'find_fwd_item'.
 */
void
find_fwd_notify(item, event)
Panel_item item;
Event *event;
```

```
{
    char *ss, *c;
    int temp_msg, failed;

    ss = strdup((char *)xv_get(find_ip->find_text_item, PANEL_VALUE));
    c = ss - 1;
    while ( *(++c) != '\0' )
        if ( isupper(*c) ) *c = tolower(*c);

    failed = FALSE;
    temp_msg = (cur_msg < num_msgs - 1 && cur_msg >= 0) ? cur_msg + 1 : 0;
    while (temp_msg < num_msgs) {
        if (scan_find(temp_msg, ss, TRUE)) break;
        temp_msg++;
    }

    if (temp_msg == num_msgs) {
        if (cur_msg > 0) {
            temp_msg = 0;
            while (temp_msg <= cur_msg) {
                    if (scan_find(temp_msg, ss, TRUE)) break;
                    temp_msg++;
            }
            if (temp_msg > cur_msg) failed = TRUE;
        }
        else
            failed = TRUE;
    }
    if (failed)
        pr_msg(scan_ip->frame, TRUE, "No match.");
    else {
        pr_msg(scan_ip->frame, FALSE, "");
        num_selected = 1;
        set_scanwin_items_status();
    }
}

/*
 * User-defined action for 'find_bkw_item'.
 */
void
find_bkw_notify(item, event)
Panel_item item;
Event *event;
{
    char *ss, *c;
    int temp_msg, failed;

    ss = strdup((char *)xv_get(find_ip->find_text_item, PANEL_VALUE));
    c = ss - 1;
    while ( ++*c != '\0' )
        if ( isupper(*c) ) tolower(*c);

    failed = FALSE;
    temp_msg = (cur_msg > 0 && cur_msg <= num_msgs - 1) ?
        cur_msg - 1 : num_msgs - 1;
    while (temp_msg >= 0) {
        if (scan_find(temp_msg, ss, TRUE))
            break;
        temp_msg--;
    }
```

```
    if ( temp_msg == -1 ) {
        if (cur_msg > 0) {
            temp_msg = num_msgs - 1;
            while (temp_msg >= cur_msg) {
                    if (scan_find(temp_msg, ss, TRUE))
                        break;
                    temp_msg--;
            }
            if (temp_msg < cur_msg) failed = TRUE;
        }
        else
            failed = TRUE;
    }
    if (failed)
        pr_msg(scan_ip->frame, TRUE, "No match.");
    else {
        pr_msg(scan_ip->frame, FALSE, "");
        num_selected = 1;
        set_scanwin_items_status();
    }
}

/*
 * Notify callback function for 'find_all_item'.
 */
void
find_all_notify(item, event)
Panel_item item;
Event *event;
{
    char *ss, *c;
    int i, found;

    ss = strdup((char *)xv_get(find_ip->find_text_item, PANEL_VALUE));
    c = ss - 1;
    while ( ++*c != '\0' )
        if ( isupper(*c) ) tolower(*c);

    found = 0;
    for ( i = 0 ; i < num_msgs; i++)
        if (scan_find(i, ss, found == 0)) found++;

    if (found == 0)
        pr_msg(scan_ip->frame, TRUE, "No match.");
    else {
        pr_msg(scan_ip->frame, FALSE, "");
        num_selected = found;
        set_scanwin_items_status();
    }
}

/*
 * Notify callback function for 'find_text_item'.
 */
Panel_setting
find_text_notify(item, event)
Panel_item item;
Event *event;
{
    if (event_shift_is_down(event))
        find_bkw_notify((Panel_item)NULL, (Event *)NULL);
```

```
        else
            find_fwd_notify((Panel_item)NULL, (Event *)NULL);

        if ((int)xv_get(find_ip->find_frame, FRAME_CMD_PIN_STATE) ==
            FRAME_CMD_PIN_OUT)
            xv_set(find_ip->find_frame, XV_SHOW, FALSE, NULL);
        return PANEL_NONE;
}
```

`logwin.c`

```
/*
 * logwin.c - Notify and event callback function stubs.
 */

#include <stdio.h>
#include <sys/param.h>
#include <sys/types.h>
#include <xview/xview.h>
#include <xview/panel.h>
#include <xview/textsw.h>
#include <xview/xv_xrect.h>
#include "logwin_ui.h"
#include "msgboard_xv.h"

logwin_frame_objects *log_ip;

int log_window_created = FALSE; /* is log window created? */

void
create_log_window()
{
    log_ip = logwin_frame_objects_initialize(NULL, base_frame);

    log_window_created = TRUE;
}

void
show_log_window()
{
    if (!log_window_created) create_log_window();

    xv_set(log_ip->frame, XV_SHOW, TRUE, NULL);
}
```

`mainwin.c`

```
/*
 * mainwin.c - support routines for the Message Board main window.
 */
#include <sys/param.h>
#include <sys/types.h>
#include <stdio.h>
#include <ctype.h>
```

```
#include <string.h>
#include <search.h>
#include <xview/xview.h>
#include <xview/panel.h>
#include <xview/textsw.h>
#include <xview/xv_xrect.h>
#include <xview/notice.h>
#include <xview/scrollbar.h>
#include <xview/font.h>
#include "mainwin_ui.h"
#include "msgboard.h"
#include "msgboard_xv.h"


/*
 *  Warning: the next defines must be changed if you change the order of
 *  items on the View menu.  Note that the pushpin is considered an item,
 *  which is why "Category", the first selectable item on the menu, is
 *  numbered 2.
 */
#define VIEW_CAT_POSITION 2
#define VIEW_STATUS_POSITION 3
#define VIEW_WATCH_POSITION 5


/*
 *  Maximum length of the "display" string for each scrolling list item,
 *  including the null character
 */
#define DISP_LEN FNAME_LEN + EXT_LEN + UNTIL_LEN + COMMENT_LEN + 15

mainwin_frame_objects *main_ip;

void (*msl_event_proc)();

Menu_item ed_delete_mi = (Menu_item)NULL,
                        ed_modify_mi = (Menu_item)NULL,
                        view_watch_mi = (Menu_item)NULL,
                        msl_mod_mi = (Menu_item)NULL,
                        msl_watch_mi = (Menu_item)NULL,
                        msl_send_mi = (Menu_item)NULL,
                        msl_scan_mi = (Menu_item)NULL,
                        msl_page_mi = (Menu_item)NULL,
                        msl_outs_mi = (Menu_item)NULL;


Menu cat_menu = (Menu)NULL;


Scrollbar main_list_bar;

int
    pending_sel = BOGUS, /* Holds last row touched on main scrolling list */

    sb_offset = 0, /* width of panel list scrollbar, iff it's located on the
                      left. */
    display_mode = DISP_TEXT; /* What type of info the list shows */

static char *status[3] = {
    "Out",
    "In",
    "???",
    };

Server_image signs[3];
```

```
short out_bits[] = {
#include "out.icon"
};

short in_bits[] = {
#include "in.icon"
};

short unk_bits[] = {
#include "unk.icon"
};

void
create_signs()
{
    signs[0] = (Server_image)xv_create(NULL, SERVER_IMAGE,
        XV_WIDTH, INOUT_WIDTH,
        XV_HEIGHT, 16,
        SERVER_IMAGE_BITS, out_bits,
        NULL);

    signs[1] = (Server_image)xv_create(NULL, SERVER_IMAGE,
        XV_WIDTH, INOUT_WIDTH,
        XV_HEIGHT, 16,
        SERVER_IMAGE_BITS, in_bits,
        NULL);

    signs[2] = (Server_image)xv_create(NULL, SERVER_IMAGE,
        XV_WIDTH, INOUT_WIDTH,
        XV_HEIGHT, 16,
        SERVER_IMAGE_BITS, unk_bits,
        NULL);
}

/*
 * Call this routine whenever the state of the program changes in some way
 * to require the active/inactive status of main window objects to change.
 *
 * The display status of the various objects is dependent on:
 *  * whether there's a current selection on the main list
 *    * whether the user is currently in admin mode
 *  * whether the connection to the server is active
 * The scan button is also dependent on whether MB_G_TRUSTED
 * ("trusted office" mode) is true for the current server.
 */
void
set_mainwin_items_status()
{
    int no_sel, server_down, state;

    no_sel = (cur_sel == BOGUS);
    server_down = !server_connected();

/*
 * The edit button only depends on the current server status.
 */
    xv_set(main_ip->edit_item, PANEL_INACTIVE, server_down, NULL);
/*
 * If the user is in admin mode, these items are inactive when there's
 * no selection:
 */
```

```
       state = (admin && no_sel) || server_down;
       if ( (globrec.flags & MB_G_TRUSTED) == 0 )
           xv_set(main_ip->scanmsg_item, PANEL_INACTIVE, state, NULL);
       xv_set(main_ip->outs_item, PANEL_INACTIVE, state, NULL);
       if (ed_delete_mi != (Menu_item)NULL)
           xv_set(ed_delete_mi, MENU_INACTIVE, state, NULL);
       if (ed_modify_mi != (Menu_item)NULL)
           xv_set(ed_modify_mi, MENU_INACTIVE, state, NULL);
       if (msl_mod_mi != (Menu_item)NULL)
           xv_set(msl_mod_mi, MENU_INACTIVE, state, NULL);
       if (msl_scan_mi != (Menu_item)NULL)
           xv_set(msl_scan_mi, MENU_INACTIVE, state, NULL);
       if (msl_outs_mi != (Menu_item)NULL)
           xv_set(msl_outs_mi, MENU_INACTIVE, state, NULL);

/*
 * These items are inactive when there's no selection in either mode:
 */
       state = no_sel || server_down;
       if ( view_watch_mi == (Menu_item)NULL) {
         Menu view_menu;

           view_menu = (Menu)xv_get(main_ip->view_item, PANEL_ITEM_MENU);
           view_watch_mi = (Menu_item)xv_get(view_menu, MENU_NTH_ITEM,
               VIEW_WATCH_POSITION);
       }
       xv_set(view_watch_mi, MENU_INACTIVE, state, NULL);
       if ( (globrec.flags & MB_G_TRUSTED) != 0 )
           xv_set(main_ip->scanmsg_item,
               PANEL_INACTIVE, state, NULL);
       xv_set(main_ip->sendmsg_item, PANEL_INACTIVE, state, NULL);
       xv_set(main_ip->page_item, PANEL_INACTIVE, state, NULL);
       if (msl_watch_mi != (Menu_item)NULL)
           xv_set(msl_watch_mi, MENU_INACTIVE, state, NULL);
       if (msl_send_mi != (Menu_item)NULL)
           xv_set(msl_send_mi, MENU_INACTIVE, state, NULL);
       if (msl_page_mi != (Menu_item)NULL)
           xv_set(msl_page_mi, MENU_INACTIVE, state, NULL);

/*
 * Fix up the comment line:
 */
       if (no_sel)
           xv_set(main_ip->comment_item,
               PANEL_INACTIVE, TRUE,
               PANEL_VALUE, "",
               NULL);
       else
           xv_set(main_ip->comment_item,
               PANEL_INACTIVE, FALSE,
               PANEL_VALUE, ulist[cur_sel].comment,
               NULL);

/*
 * Turn the "new messages" glyph on or off.
 */
       xv_set(main_ip->newmsg_item,
           XV_SHOW, myentry != NULL && (myentry->flags & MB_NEWMSGS) != 0,
           NULL);
}
```

```
/*
 *  Displays the site name and message of the day line
 */
void
update_global_display()
{
    int p_wid, m_wid, disconnected;
    char lbuf[SITE_LEN + 19];

    disconnected = !server_connected();

    if (disconnected)
       xv_set(main_ip->motd_item, PANEL_LABEL_STRING,
          "Not connected to a server", NULL);
    else if (admin && globrec.name[0] == '\0' && globrec.motd[0] == '\0')
       xv_set(main_ip->motd_item, PANEL_LABEL_STRING,
           "Press 'Props...' button to set site name and/or message", NULL);
    else
       xv_set(main_ip->motd_item, PANEL_LABEL_STRING, globrec.motd, NULL);

    p_wid = (int)xv_get(main_ip->display_panel, XV_WIDTH);
    m_wid = (int)xv_get(main_ip->motd_item, XV_WIDTH);
    xv_set(main_ip->motd_item, XV_X, (p_wid - m_wid) / 2, NULL);

    /*
     *  Update main frame label:
     */
    if (disconnected)
       strcpy(lbuf, "Message Board");
    else {
       sprintf(lbuf, "Message Board for %s", globrec.name);
       if (admin) strcat(lbuf, " (admin mode)");
       xv_set(base_frame, XV_LABEL, lbuf, NULL);
    }
}


/*
 *  Wrapper to let the scrolling list menu bring up the modify window.
 *  (msl_* : Main Scrolling List)
 */
void
msl_modify_notify(menu, menu_item)
Menu menu;
Menu_item menu_item;
{
    clear_msg();
    prep_modify_mode();
}


/*
 *  Wrapper to let the scrolling list menu bring up the send window
 */
void
msl_send_notify(menu, menu_item)
Menu menu;
Menu_item menu_item;
{
    clear_msg();
    show_sendmsg_window();
}
```

```
/*
 *  Wrapper to let the scrolling list menu bring up the scan window
 */
void
msl_scan_notify(menu, menu_item)
Menu menu;
Menu_item menu_item;
{
    clear_msg();
    show_scan_window();
}

/*
 *  Wrapper to let the scrolling list menu bring up the page window
 */
void
msl_page_notify(menu, menu_item)
Menu menu;
Menu_item menu_item;
{
    clear_msg();
    show_page_window();
}

/*
 *  Monitor resize events on the main display panel.
 */
void
main_display_event(window, event)
Xv_window window;
Event *event;
{
    static int
      list_w, list_h;                          /* list width, height */
    int y, row_h, nrows;

    if (event_action(event) != WIN_RESIZE) return;

    list_h =
        (int)xv_get(main_ip->display_panel, XV_HEIGHT) -
        (int)xv_get(main_ip->list_item, XV_Y) -
        (int)xv_get(main_ip->comment_item, XV_HEIGHT) -
        wgrid * 3;

    /*
     *  20 may or may not be an appropriate constant here
     */
    row_h = (int)xv_get(main_ip->list_item, PANEL_LIST_ROW_HEIGHT);
    nrows = (list_h - 20) / row_h;
    list_h = nrows * row_h  + 20;
    list_w = (int)xv_get(main_ip->display_panel, XV_WIDTH) - wgrid * 4;

    xv_set(main_ip->list_item,
        XV_HEIGHT,                           list_h,
        PANEL_LIST_WIDTH,            list_w,
        PANEL_LIST_DISPLAY_ROWS, nrows,
        NULL);

    y = list_h + (int)xv_get(main_ip->list_item, XV_Y, NULL) + wgrid;
    xv_set(main_ip->comment_item, XV_Y, y, NULL);
    xv_set(main_ip->newmsg_item, XV_Y, y + wgrid, NULL);
```

```
        if (nrows >= users)
            xv_set(main_list_bar, SCROLLBAR_VIEW_START, 0, NULL);
        update_global_display();
}


/*
 * Menu handler for `list_menu'.
 */
Menu
main_list_menu_handler(menu, op)
Menu menu;
Menu_generate op;
{
    static int main_list_menu_updated = FALSE;

    if (op == MENU_DISPLAY && !main_list_menu_updated) {
        Menu pr_menu;

        xv_set(menu, MENU_TITLE_ITEM, "Board Entries", NULL);

        if (admin) {
            msl_mod_mi = (Menu_item)xv_create(NULL, MENUITEM,
                    MENU_STRING,                "Modify Entry...",
                    MENU_NOTIFY_PROC, msl_modify_notify,
                    MENU_INACTIVE,         (cur_sel == BOGUS),
                    NULL);
            xv_set(menu, MENU_APPEND_ITEM, msl_mod_mi, NULL);
        }

        /*
         * Create a "Watch For" entry, using the same menu as the
         * similar entry on the View menu does.
         */
        if ( view_watch_mi == (Menu_item)NULL) {
            pr_menu = (Menu)xv_get(main_ip->view_item, PANEL_ITEM_MENU);
            view_watch_mi = (Menu_item)xv_get(pr_menu, MENU_NTH_ITEM,
                    VIEW_WATCH_POSITION);
        }
        pr_menu = (Menu)xv_get(view_watch_mi, MENU_PULLRIGHT);
        msl_watch_mi = (Menu_item)xv_create(NULL, MENUITEM,
            MENU_STRING, "Watch For",
            MENU_PULLRIGHT, pr_menu,
            MENU_INACTIVE, (cur_sel == BOGUS),
            NULL);
        xv_set(menu, MENU_APPEND_ITEM, msl_watch_mi, NULL);

        msl_send_mi = (Menu_item)xv_create(NULL, MENUITEM,
            MENU_STRING, "Send Pmsg...",
            MENU_NOTIFY_PROC, msl_send_notify,
            MENU_INACTIVE, (cur_sel == BOGUS),
            NULL);
        xv_set(menu, MENU_APPEND_ITEM, msl_send_mi, NULL);

        if (admin) {
            msl_scan_mi = (Menu_item)xv_create(NULL, MENUITEM,
                    MENU_STRING,                "Scan Pmsgs...",
                    MENU_NOTIFY_PROC, msl_scan_notify,
                    MENU_INACTIVE,                (cur_sel == BOGUS),
                    NULL);
            xv_set(menu, MENU_APPEND_ITEM, msl_scan_mi, NULL);
        }
```

```
        msl_page_mi = (Menu_item)xv_create(NULL, MENUITEM,
            MENU_STRING, "Page...",
            MENU_NOTIFY_PROC, msl_page_notify,
            MENU_INACTIVE, (cur_sel == BOGUS),
            NULL);
        xv_set(menu, MENU_APPEND_ITEM, msl_page_mi, NULL);

        if (admin) {
            pr_menu = (Menu)xv_get(main_ip->outs_item, PANEL_ITEM_MENU);
            msl_outs_mi = (Menu_item)xv_create(NULL, MENUITEM,
                    MENU_STRING,  "Outs",
                    MENU_PULLRIGHT,pr_menu,
                    MENU_INACTIVE, (cur_sel == BOGUS),
                    NULL);
            xv_set(menu, MENU_APPEND_ITEM, msl_outs_mi, NULL);
        }

        main_list_menu_updated = TRUE;
    }
    return menu;
}

/*
 * Handles destroy events off of the main window, including the
 * dreaded WM_SAVE_YOURSELF.
 */
Notify_value
save_me(client, status)
Notify_client client;
Destroy_status status;
{
    Destroy_status retval = NOTIFY_DONE;

    switch (status) {
    case DESTROY_CHECKING:
        retval = notify_next_destroy_func(client, status);
    case DESTROY_SAVE_YOURSELF:
        save_params();
        break;
    case DESTROY_CLEANUP:
        retval = notify_next_destroy_func(client, status);
        break;
    case DESTROY_PROCESS_DEATH:
        base_frame = NULL;
        break;
    }
    return NOTIFY_DONE;
}

/*
 * Event callback function for `list_item'.
 * Catches clicks on the "In/Out" column of the scrolling list.
 */
void
main_list_event(item, event)
Panel_item item;
Event *event;
{
    static int
        list_preview = FALSE; /* Is list in preview mode?*/
```

```
/*
 *  First, call the main list's "real? ( event proc:
 */
(*msl_event_proc)(item, event);

/*
 *  Now, do our own processing on the event.
 *  We're only interested in events from the SELECT mouse button.
 */
if (event_action(event) != ACTION_SELECT) return;

/*
 *  A down event in the scrolling list; enter preview mode.
 */
if (event_is_down(event))
   list_preview = TRUE;
/*
 *  A release event when we're in preview mode;
 *  Check whether to complete selection or abort preview.
 */
else if (event_is_up(event) && list_preview) {
   clear_msg(); /* For good housekeeping's sake */
   list_preview = FALSE;

   /*
    *  If there's a good selection pending, act on it.
    */
   if (pending_sel != BOGUS) {
      /*
       *  If the action took place on the glyph column and we have
       *  permission, make this the current selection and toggle its
       *  in/out value.
       */
      if (event_x(event) - (int)xv_get(main_ip->list_item, XV_X) -
             sb_offset < INOUT_WIDTH + 10 &&
             (admin || &(ulist[pending_sel]) == myentry)) {
         int new_status;
         char *new_until, *new_comment, temp_logid[LOGID_LEN + 1];
         Mem_Rec *cur_ent;

         cur_ent = &(ulist[pending_sel]);
         new_status = (cur_ent->status != MB_IN);
         /*
          *  If moving to In: clear the until field;
          *  if preserve isn't set, clear comment field too.
          */
         if (new_status == MB_IN) {
            new_until = strdup("");
            if ((cur_ent->flags & MB_PRESERVE) != 0)
                    new_comment = CNULL;
            else
                    new_comment = strdup("");
         }
         else
            new_until = new_comment = CNULL;

         /*
          *  Save the id so we can relocate this record
          *  after we call get_modified_records()...
          */
         strcpy(temp_logid, cur_ent->logid);
```

```
                    if (modify_status(cur_ent->logid, new_status, new_until,
                        new_comment) == 0 &&
                        get_modified_records() == 0) {
                        /*
                         *  Find this record again.
                         */
                        cur_ent = find_urec(temp_logid);

                        if (cur_ent == (Mem_Rec *)NULL)
                                cur_sel = BOGUS;
                        else {
                                /*
                                 *  If we moved to OUT and pop_mod is set,
                                 *  expose  the "Out modify" window.
                                 */
                                if (cur_ent->status == MB_OUT && pop_mod)
                                    show_outmod_window(cur_ent);

                                /*
                                 *  Clicking on the glyph column of a row
                                 *  that was selected will have
                                 *  deselected it; we want
                                 *  to keep it selected.
                                 */
                                if (!(int)xv_get(main_ip->list_item,
                                    PANEL_LIST_SELECTED, cur_ent->row))
                                    xv_set(main_ip->list_item,
                                            PANEL_LIST_SELECT,
                                        cur_ent->row, TRUE, NULL);
                                cur_sel = cur_ent - ulist;
                        }
                }
        }
        /*
         *  If it took place on the name column, or the glyph column of
         *  a row we don't have permission to toggle: deselect if this
         *  was already the current selection, else move to it.
         */
        else {
                if (cur_sel == pending_sel)
                        cur_sel = BOGUS;
                else
                        cur_sel = pending_sel;
        }

        set_mainwin_items_status();
        pending_sel = BOGUS;
    } /* if (pending_sel != BOGUS) */


    } /* if ( up_event && list_preview ) */

    return;
}

/*
 *  Calls the DevGuide-generated routine to create the various XView
 *  objects, makes the tweaks that DevGuide itself doesn't support yet,
 *  including installing various event handlers.
 */
void
create_main_window()
```

```
{
    Xv_Font font;
    Window_rescale_state scale;
    int xpos, ypos;

    main_ip = mainwin_frame_objects_initialize(NULL, NULL);

    base_frame = main_ip->frame;

    /*
     * What scale is the window at?  We use "wgrid" to lay out panel
     * items all through the rest of the application.
     */
    font = (Xv_Font)xv_get(base_frame, XV_FONT);
    scale = (Window_rescale_state)xv_get(font, FONT_SCALE);
    switch(scale) {
    case WIN_SCALE_SMALL:
        wgrid = 8;
        break;
    case WIN_SCALE_LARGE:
        wgrid = 12;
        break;
    case WIN_SCALE_EXTRALARGE:
        wgrid = 16;
        break;
    default:
        wgrid = 10;
    }

    notify_interpose_destroy_func(base_frame, save_me);

    if (main_params.state != BOGUS)
        frame_set_rect(base_frame, &main_params.rect);

    xv_set(main_ip->display_panel,
        WIN_EVENT_PROC,                 main_display_event,
        PANEL_ACCEPT_KEYSTROKE,TRUE,
        NULL);

    xv_set((Menu)xv_get(main_ip->list_item, PANEL_ITEM_MENU),
        MENU_GEN_PROC, main_list_menu_handler, NULL);

    /*
     * Save the main scrolling list's original event handler, then
     * replace it with our own.
     */
    msl_event_proc = (void (*)())xv_get(main_ip->list_item,PANEL_EVENT_PROC);

    xv_set(main_ip->list_item, PANEL_EVENT_PROC, main_list_event, NULL);

    /*
     * The routine that tracks select events on the panel list needs to
     * know if the scrollbar is on the left side, and if so, how wide it
     * is, so that it can figure out whether or not a mouse event
     * is occurring on the column the "In/Out/???" glyph appears in.
     */
    main_list_bar = (Scrollbar)xv_get(main_ip->list_item,
        PANEL_LIST_SCROLLBAR);
    if ((int)xv_get(main_list_bar, XV_X) ==
        (int)xv_get(main_ip->list_item, XV_X))
        sb_offset = (int)xv_get(main_list_bar, XV_WIDTH);
```

```
    /*
     * Create the outs menu and attach it to the outs button
     */
    outs_menu_create(main_ip->outs_item);

#ifdef SCALABLE
    /*
     * Position panel items in a scalable fashion:
     */
    ypos = wgrid * 0.8;
    xpos = wgrid * 3;
    xv_set(main_ip->view_item,
        XV_X,           xpos,
        XV_Y,           ypos,
        NULL);

    xpos += (int)xv_get(main_ip->view_item, XV_WIDTH) + wgrid;
    xv_set(main_ip->edit_item, XV_X, xpos, XV_Y, ypos, NULL);

    xpos += (int)xv_get(main_ip->edit_item, XV_WIDTH) + wgrid;
    xv_set(main_ip->props_item, XV_X, xpos, XV_Y, ypos, NULL);

    xpos += (int)xv_get(main_ip->props_item, XV_WIDTH) + wgrid * 2;
    xv_set(main_ip->sendmsg_item, XV_X, xpos, XV_Y, ypos, NULL);

    xpos += (int)xv_get(main_ip->sendmsg_item, XV_WIDTH) + wgrid;
    xv_set(main_ip->scanmsg_item, XV_X, xpos, XV_Y, ypos, NULL);

    xpos += (int)xv_get(main_ip->scanmsg_item, XV_WIDTH) + wgrid;
    xv_set(main_ip->page_item, XV_X, xpos, XV_Y, ypos, NULL);

    xpos += (int)xv_get(main_ip->page_item, XV_WIDTH) + wgrid * 2;
    xv_set(main_ip->outs_item, XV_X, xpos, XV_Y, ypos, NULL);

    ypos = wgrid * 1.6 + (int)xv_get(main_ip->view_item, XV_HEIGHT);
    xv_set(main_ip->control_panel, XV_HEIGHT, ypos, NULL);
    window_fit_width(main_ip->control_panel);

    xv_set(main_ip->display_panel,
        XV_Y, ypos,
        XV_WIDTH,       (int)xv_get(main_ip->control_panel, XV_WIDTH),
        NULL);

    ypos = wgrid *.8;
    /*
     * As we set the motd_item, set its value to something, so that it has
     * a usable height.
     */
    xv_set(main_ip->motd_item,
        XV_Y, ypos,
        PANEL_PAINT, PANEL_NONE,
        PANEL_LABEL_STRING, "FOOBAR",
        NULL);

    ypos += (int)xv_get(main_ip->motd_item, XV_HEIGHT) + wgrid *.8;
    xv_set(main_ip->list_item,
        XV_X, wgrid,
        XV_Y, ypos,
        PANEL_LIST_WIDTH, 100,
        NULL);
    /*
     * We don't set the comment or newmsg item's Y position here; that's
     * done in main_display_event().  16 is the width of the newmsg glyph;
```

```
         *  yet another possibly inappropriate thing to hardwire.
         */
        xv_set(main_ip->newmsg_item, XV_X, wgrid, NULL);
        xv_set(main_ip->comment_item, XV_X, wgrid * 2 + 16, NULL);
        window_fit(base_frame);
#endif
}


/*
 *  Creates in "sbuf" the display line for record pointed to by "rp"
 */
void
make_disp_string(sbuf, rp)
char *sbuf;
Mem_Rec *rp;
{
    strcpy(sbuf, rp->fname);
    if (admin && (rp->flags & MB_NEWMSGS) != 0)
      strcat(sbuf, "\266");
    if (display_mode == DISP_TEXT) {
        if (strlen(rp->ext) > 0) {
            strcat(sbuf, ", x");
            strcat(sbuf, rp->ext);
        }
        if (strlen(rp->until) > 0) {
            strcat(sbuf, " - until ");
            strcat(sbuf, rp->until);
        }
      if (strlen(rp->comment) > 0) {
            strcat(sbuf, " - ");
            strcat(sbuf, rp->comment);
        }
    }
    else {
        strcat(sbuf, " - ");
        strcat(sbuf, ctime(&(rp->timestamp)));
    }
}


/*
 *  Updates a currently existing line on the screen
 */
void
update_line(rp)
Mem_Rec *rp;
{
    char sbuf[DISP_LEN];

    make_disp_string(sbuf, rp);

    xv_set(main_ip->list_item,
        PANEL_LIST_STRING, rp->row, sbuf,
        PANEL_LIST_GLYPH, rp->row, signs[rp->status],
        NULL);

    if (rp->row == cur_sel)
        xv_set(main_ip->comment_item,
            PANEL_VALUE, ulist[cur_sel].comment,
            PANEL_INACTIVE, FALSE,
            NULL);
}
```

```
/*
 *  Redoes everything on the main scrolling list.
 */
void
update_screen()
{
    int i, list_size, new_size;
    char fbuf[CAT_LEN + 24], sbuf[DISP_LEN];

    list_size = (int)xv_get(main_ip->list_item, PANEL_LIST_NROWS);

    xv_set(main_ip->list_item, XV_SHOW, FALSE, NULL);

    /*
     *  Turn off select indicator if it's on
     */
    if (cur_sel != BOGUS && ulist[cur_sel].row != BOGUS)
        xv_set(main_ip->list_item,
            PANEL_LIST_SELECT, ulist[cur_sel].row, FALSE, NULL);

    new_size = 0;
    for ( i = 0; i < users; i++) {
        /*
         *  A user is displayed if:
         *          They're in the current category, or the current
         *              category is ALL, AND
         *          Their status is the current one, or the current status
         *              is ALL.
         */
        if ( (cur_cat == MB_ALL || strcmp(cats[cur_cat], ulist[i].cat) == 0)
                                                        &&
            (cur_status == MB_ALL || cur_status == ulist[i].status) ) {

            /*
             *  Create the display string
             */
            make_disp_string(sbuf, &(ulist[i]));

            /*
             *  If the list is large enough to accomodate this user, go
             *  ahead, else create a new slot.  Set client data for each
             *  row to the ulist index for this row.
             */
            if ( new_size < list_size)
                    xv_set(main_ip->list_item,
                        PANEL_LIST_STRING, new_size,sbuf,
                        PANEL_LIST_GLYPH, new_size,signs[ulist[i].status],
                        PANEL_LIST_CLIENT_DATA, new_size,i,
                        NULL);
            else {
                    xv_set(main_ip->list_item,
                        PANEL_LIST_INSERT,                      new_size,
                        PANEL_LIST_STRING, new_size,sbuf,
                        PANEL_LIST_GLYPH, new_size,signs[ulist[i].status],
                        PANEL_LIST_CLIENT_DATA, new_size,i,
                        NULL);
                    ++list_size;
            }
            ulist[i].row = new_size;
            ++new_size;
        }
        else
```

```
                    ulist[i].row = BOGUS;
        }
        /*
         *  See if we have to destroy some list rows:
         */
        if (list_size > new_size) {
            xv_set(main_ip->list_item,
                PANEL_LIST_DELETE_ROWS, new_size, list_size - new_size,
                NULL);
            if (cur_sel >= users) cur_sel = BOGUS;
        }

        /*
         *  Turn indicator back on if appropriate; set comment line.
         */
        if (cur_sel != BOGUS && ulist[cur_sel].row != BOGUS) {
            xv_set(main_ip->list_item,
                PANEL_LIST_SELECT, ulist[cur_sel].row, TRUE, NULL);
            xv_set(main_ip->comment_item,
                PANEL_VALUE,ulist[cur_sel].comment,
                PANEL_INACTIVE,FALSE,
                NULL);
        }
        else
            xv_set(main_ip->comment_item,
                PANEL_VALUE, "",
                PANEL_INACTIVE,TRUE,
                NULL);

        xv_set(main_ip->list_item, XV_SHOW, TRUE, NULL);

        /*
         *  Update the footer:
         */
        if (cur_cat != MB_ALL) {
          sprintf(fbuf, "Category: %s", cats[cur_cat]);
          if (cur_status != MB_ALL)
                        strcat(fbuf, ", ");
        }
        else
            fbuf[0] = '\0';
        if (cur_status != MB_ALL) {
            strcat(fbuf, "Status: ");
            strcat(fbuf, status[cur_status]);
        }
        xv_set(base_frame, FRAME_RIGHT_FOOTER, fbuf, NULL);
}

/*
 *  Handles notify events from the category menu
 */
void
cat_menu_notify(menu, menu_item)
Menu menu;
Menu_item menu_item;
{
    int i, old_cat;

    char mstr[CAT_LEN+1];

    old_cat = cur_cat;
    strcpy(mstr, (char *)xv_get(menu_item, MENU_STRING));
```

```
    /*
     *  If the selected item is "(Next)", cycle the current category to the
     *  next higher item. If we go above the highest available categories,
     *  we cycle back to the first item (MB_ALL).
     */
    if (strcmp(mstr, "(Next)") == 0) {
      cur_cat++;
      if (cur_cat >= numcats) cur_cat = MB_ALL;
    }
    else if ( strcmp(mstr, "All") == 0)
      cur_cat = MB_ALL;
    else
      for (i = 0; i < numcats; i++)
          if ( strcmp(mstr, cats[i]) == 0) {
                  cur_cat = i;
                  break;
          }

    if (cur_cat != old_cat) {
      update_screen();
      xv_set(main_list_bar, SCROLLBAR_VIEW_START, 0, NULL);
    }
}

/*
 *  Handles notify events from the status menu.
 *  This code assumes the menu looks like:
 *    1.    o  -[]=|  (the pushpin)
 *    2.    (Next)
 *    3.    All
 *    4.    "In"
 *    5.    "Out"
 *    6.    ???
 */

#define NUM_STATUS_MENU_ITEMS 6

void
status_menu_notify(menu, menu_item)
Menu menu;
Menu_item menu_item;
{
    int pos, old_status;

    old_status = cur_status;

    for (pos = 2; pos <= NUM_STATUS_MENU_ITEMS; pos++)
      if (menu_item == (Menu_item)xv_get(menu, MENU_NTH_ITEM, pos)) break;

    /*
     *  This should never happen:
     */
    if (pos == NUM_STATUS_MENU_ITEMS + 1) {
      pr_msg(NULL, TRUE, "Couldn't match item on View->Status menu");
      return;
    }

    if (pos == 2) {
      cur_status++;
      if (cur_status > 2) cur_status = MB_ALL;
    }
```

```
        else if (pos == 3)
            cur_status = MB_ALL;
        else
            cur_status = pos - 4;

        if (cur_status != old_status) {
            update_screen();
            xv_set(main_list_bar, SCROLLBAR_VIEW_START, 0, NULL);
        }
}

/*
 * Menu handler for 'edit_menu (Modify Entry...)'.
 */
Menu_item
main_modify_handler(item, op)
Menu_item item;
Menu_generate op;
{
    switch (op) {
    case MENU_DISPLAY:
        if (ed_modify_mi == (Menu_item)NULL)
            ed_modify_mi = item;
        if (admin) xv_set(item, MENU_INACTIVE, cur_sel == BOGUS, NULL);
        break;

    case MENU_NOTIFY:
        prep_modify_mode();
        break;
    }
    return item;
}

/*
 * Menu handler for 'edit_menu (Add Entry...)'.
 */
Menu_item
main_add_handler(item, op)
Menu_item item;
Menu_generate op;
{
    switch (op) {
    case MENU_DISPLAY:
        xv_set(item, MENU_INACTIVE, !admin, NULL);
        break;

    case MENU_DISPLAY_DONE:
        break;

    case MENU_NOTIFY:
        prep_add_mode(base_frame);
        break;

    case MENU_NOTIFY_DONE:
        break;
    }
    return item;
}

/*
 * Menu handler for 'edit_menu (Delete Entry)'.
 */
```

```
Menu_item
main_delete_handler(item, op)
Menu_item item;
Menu_generate op;
{
    char logid[LOGID_LEN + 1], del_string[LOGID_LEN + FNAME_LEN + 4];
    Xv_Notice notice;
    int notice_stat;

    switch (op) {
    case MENU_DISPLAY:
        if (ed_delete_mi == (Menu_item)NULL)
            ed_delete_mi = item;
        xv_set(item, MENU_INACTIVE, !admin || (cur_sel == BOGUS), NULL);
        break;

    case MENU_DISPLAY_DONE:
        break;

    case MENU_NOTIFY:
        /*
         * Save the login ID, in case the user manages somehow to
         * move the current selection before we call delete_user.
         */
        strcpy(logid, ulist[cur_sel].logid);

        /*
         * Generate "Did you really want to do this?" notice
         */
        sprintf(del_string, "%s (%s)", logid, ulist[cur_sel].fname);
        notice = xv_create(base_frame, NOTICE,
            NOTICE_MESSAGE_STRINGS, "Confirm deletion of entry for",
                                                            del_string,
                                                            NULL,
            NOTICE_BUTTON_YES,      "Delete",
            NOTICE_BUTTON_NO,       "Cancel",
            NOTICE_STATUS,           &notice_stat,
            XV_SHOW,                 TRUE,
            NULL);

        if (notice_stat == NOTICE_YES) {
            xv_set(main_ip->list_item,
                    PANEL_LIST_SELECT, ulist[cur_sel].row, FALSE, NULL);
            cur_sel = BOGUS;
            set_mainwin_items_status();
            delete_user(logid);
        }

        xv_destroy_safe(notice);
        break;

    case MENU_NOTIFY_DONE:
        break;
    }
    return item;
}

/*
 * Menu handler for 'view_menu (About Message Board...)'.
 */
Menu_item
about_handler(item, op)
```

```
Menu_item item;
Menu_generate op;
{
    if (op == MENU_NOTIFY) show_about_window();
    return item;
}


/*
 * Menu handler for `display_menu (Until/Comment)'.
 */
Menu_item
disp_text_notify(item, op)
Menu_item item;
Menu_generate op;
{
    if (op == MENU_NOTIFY && display_mode == DISP_DATES) {
      display_mode = DISP_TEXT;
      update_screen();
      }
    return item;
}


/*
 * Menu handler for `display_menu (Modification Times)'.
 */
Menu_item
disp_times_notify(item, op)
Menu_item item;
Menu_generate op;
{
    if (op == MENU_NOTIFY && display_mode == DISP_TEXT) {
        display_mode = DISP_DATES;
        update_screen();
      }
    return item;
}


/*
 * Menu handler for `watch_menu (Add to Watch List)'.
 */
Menu_item
watch_add_handler(item, op)
Menu_item item;
Menu_generate op;
{
    if (op == MENU_NOTIFY) {
      char *u;

      if (cur_sel == BOGUS) return item;
      u = ulist[cur_sel].logid;
      if (watchnum == 0) {
          watchnum = 1;
          watchlist = (char **)malloc(sizeof(char *));
          watchlist[0] = (char *)malloc(strlen(u)+1);
          strcpy(watchlist[0], u);
          pr_msg(NULL, FALSE, "%s added to watch list.",
                  get_fname(ulist[cur_sel].logid));
      }
      else {
          if ( (char *)lfind((char *)&u, (char *)watchlist, &watchnum,
                  sizeof(char *), comp_strings) != CNULL) {
                  pr_msg(NULL, TRUE, "%s already on watch list.",
                  get_fname(ulist[cur_sel].logid));
```

```
                    }
            else {
                        watchnum++;
                        watchlist = (char **)realloc((char *)watchlist,
                            sizeof(char *)*watchnum);
                        watchlist[watchnum - 1] = (char *)malloc(strlen(u)+1);
                        strcpy(watchlist[watchnum - 1], u);
                        pr_msg(NULL, FALSE, "%s added to watch list.",
                            get_fname(ulist[cur_sel].logid));
                    }
                }
            }
        }
    return item;
}


/*
 * Menu handler for `watch_menu (Remove from Watch List)'.
 */
Menu_item
watch_remove_handler(item, op)
Menu_item item;
Menu_generate op;
{
    if (op == MENU_NOTIFY) {
        if (cur_sel == BOGUS) return item;
        if (watch_del(ulist[cur_sel].logid))
            pr_msg(NULL, FALSE, "%s deleted from watch list.",
                    get_fname(ulist[cur_sel].logid));
else
            pr_msg(NULL, TRUE, "%s not on watch list.",
                    get_fname(ulist[cur_sel].logid));
    }
    return item;
}


/*
 * Event callback function for `frame'.
 */
Notify_value
main_frame_event(frame, event, arg, type)
Frame frame;
Event *event;
Notify_arg arg;
Notify_event_type type;
{
    int was_closed, is_closed;
    Notify_value value;

    was_closed = (int)xv_get(frame, FRAME_CLOSED);
    value = notify_next_event_func(frame, (Notify_event) event, arg, type);
    is_closed = (int)xv_get(frame, FRAME_CLOSED);

    if (was_closed != is_closed) {
        if (!is_closed)
            set_timer(TRUE);
        else if (watchnum == 0)
            set_timer(FALSE);
    }

    return value;
}
```

```
/*
 * Notify callback function for 'props_item'.
 */
void
main_props_notify(item, event)
Panel_item item;
Event *event;
{
    clear_msg();
    show_props_window();
}


/*
 * Notify callback function for 'sendmsg_item'.
 */
void
main_sendmsg_notify(item, event)
Panel_item item;
Event *event;
{
    clear_msg();
    show_sendmsg_window();
}


/*
 * Notify callback function for 'scanmsg_item'.
 */
void
main_scanmsg_notify(item, event)
Panel_item item;
Event *event;
{
    clear_msg();
    show_scan_window();
}


/*
 * Notify callback function for 'list_item'.
 */
int
main_list_notify(item, string, client_data, op, event)
Panel_item item;
char *string;
Xv_opaque client_data;
Panel_list_op op;
Event *event;
{
    switch (op) {
    /*
     *  For either SELECT or DESELECT, set pending_sel to the index of the
     *  ulist record for the row they just touched, which will be used in
     *  another routine when a mouse up-event occurs.
     */
    case PANEL_LIST_OP_DESELECT:
    case PANEL_LIST_OP_SELECT:
      pending_sel = (int)client_data;
      break;
    }
    return XV_OK;
}
```

```
/*
 *  Menu handler for `view_menu'.
 */

Menu
view_menu_handler(menu, op)
Menu menu;
Menu_generate op;
{
    static int status_menu_prepped = FALSE;

    /*
     *  cat_menu is NULL on program startup; it is also set to NULL
     *  whenever the cats[] array is modified.
     */
    if (op == MENU_DISPLAY && cat_menu == (Menu)NULL ) {
      Menu_item mi;
      Menu status_menu;
      int i;

      cat_menu = xv_create(NULL, MENU_CHOICE_MENU,
            MENU_STRINGS,             "(Next)", "All", NULL,
            MENU_NOTIFY_PROC,         cat_menu_notify,
            MENU_GEN_PIN_WINDOW, base_frame, "Categories",
            NULL);

      for (i = 0 ; i < numcats ; i++ ) {
          mi = (Menu_item)xv_create(NULL, MENUITEM,
                          MENU_STRING,      cats[i],
                          MENU_RELEASE,
                          NULL);
          xv_set(cat_menu, MENU_APPEND_ITEM, mi, NULL);
      }

      /*
       *  Get the handle to what better be the "Category" item on the
       *  View menu and attach the menu we just created.
       */
      mi = (Menu_item)xv_get(menu, MENU_NTH_ITEM, VIEW_CAT_POSITION);
      xv_set(mi, MENU_PULLRIGHT, cat_menu, NULL);

      /*
       *  Get the handle to what we hope is the "Status" item and
       *  establish its menu's notify proc.
       */
      if ( !status_menu_prepped) {
          mi = (Menu_item)xv_get(menu, MENU_NTH_ITEM, VIEW_STATUS_POSITION);
          status_menu = (Menu)xv_get(mi, MENU_PULLRIGHT);
          xv_set(status_menu, MENU_NOTIFY_PROC, status_menu_notify, NULL);
          status_menu_prepped = TRUE;
          }
    }
    return menu;
}

/*
 * Menu handler for `view_menu (Page Log...)'.
 */
Menu_item
page_log_handler(item, op)
Menu_item item;
Menu_generate op;
{
```

```
        if (op == MENU_NOTIFY) show_log_window();
        return item;
}


/*
 * Event callback function for `display_panel'.
 * Traps for ASCII keystrokes, which we use to select items on the
 * scrolling list by the first character of their last name.
 */
Notify_value
main_display_panel_event(win, event, arg, type)
Xv_window win;
Event *event;
Notify_arg arg;
Notify_event_type type;
{
        if (event_is_down(event) && isascii(event_action(event)) &&
            isalpha(event_action(event))) {
            int c, ri, failed;

            c = tolower(event_action(event));
            failed = FALSE;
            for (ri = (cur_sel == BOGUS ? 0 : cur_sel + 1); ri < users; ri++)
                if (ulist[ri].sortby[0] == c && ulist[ri].row != BOGUS)
                        break;

if (ri == users) {
    if ( cur_sel != BOGUS ) {
                    for (ri = 0; ri <= cur_sel; ri ++)
                      if (ulist[ri].sortby[0] == c && ulist[ri].row != BOGUS)
                                break;
                    if ( ri > cur_sel ) failed = TRUE;
    }
    else
                    failed = TRUE;
}

        if (failed)
            window_bell(base_frame);
        else {
            cur_sel = ri;
            /*
             *  Make sure list is showing the proper selection.
             */
            if (!(int)xv_get(main_ip->list_item, PANEL_LIST_SELECTED,
                            ulist[cur_sel].row))
                            xv_set(main_ip->list_item,
                                    PANEL_LIST_SELECT, ulist[cur_sel].row,
                                                        TRUE, NULL);
        }
        set_mainwin_items_status();
  }
  else
        return notify_next_event_func(win, (Notify_event) event, arg, type);
}

/*
 * Notify callback function for `page_item'.
 */
void
main_page_notify(item, event)
Panel_item item;
Event *event;
{
```

```
    clear_msg();
    show_page_window();
}


/*
 * We "update" the category list (actually the menu built from it) by
 * destroying said menu; this will cause it to be re-created the next
 * time its parent menu is accessed.
 */
void
update_cat_list()
{
    if (cat_menu != (Menu)NULL) {
       xv_destroy(cat_menu);
       cat_menu = (Menu)NULL;
    }
}


/*
 * Gathers all the parameters for this window
 */
void
get_main_params(p)
struct winparams *p;
{
    p->state = FRAME_CMD_PIN_IN; /* Main window is always created */
    frame_get_rect(main_ip->frame, &(p->rect));
}


/*
 * Wrapper to allow routines outside of mainwin to redo the outs
 * menu
 */
void
redo_outs_menu()
{
    Menu omenu;

    if ( (omenu = (Menu)xv_get(main_ip->outs_item, PANEL_ITEM_MENU)) != NULL)
       xv_destroy(omenu);

    outs_menu_create(main_ip->outs_item);
    if (msl_outs_mi != (Menu_item)NULL) {
       omenu = (Menu)xv_get(main_ip->outs_item, PANEL_ITEM_MENU);
       xv_set(msl_outs_mi, MENU_PULLRIGHT, omenu, NULL);
    }
}
```

mb_client.c

```
/*
 * mb_client.c: routines to connect to the RPC server
 */

#include <sys/param.h>
#include <stdio.h>
#include <stdlib.h>
#include <string.h>
```

```
#include "mb_client.h"
#include "msgboard.h"

unsigned int last_seq_no = 0;

char *msgd_err[7] = {
    "what error?",
    "not connected to server",
    "remote procedure call failed",
    "you're not validated for that function",
    "record not found",
    "record already exists",
    "unknown error"
};

/*
 * Establishes a connection to a new RPC server.  Disconnects from the
 * old one if necessary.
 * Returns TRUE if connect succeeds, else FALSE.
 */
int
connect_to_server()
{
    return TRUE;
}

/*
 * Update the given login id's "status" field; update "until" or "comment"
 * unless passed NULL pointers.  Returns 0 on success, error code on
 * fail.
 */
int
modify_status(logid, status, until, comment)
char *logid, *until, *comment;
int status;
{
    unsigned int *result;
    int retval;

/*
    if ( record->retval == 0 ) {
      pr_msg(NULL, TRUE, "Record for %s no longer exists!", logid);
      xdr_free(xdr_get_rec_data, record);
      return MSGD_NOT_FOUND;
    }


    result = put_rec_1(&pr_data, cl);
    xdr_free(xdr_get_rec_data, record);
*/

    return retval;
}
```

`mb_com.c`

```
/*
 * Utility routines common to all versions of the Message Board
 */
```

```
#include <stdio.h>
#include <ctype.h>
#include <pwd.h>
#include <grp.h>
#include <string.h>
#include "msgboard.h"

/*
 *  Used by lsearch/lfind to do lookups in ulist by login ID
 */
int
comp_by_logid(i, j)
Mem_Rec *i, *j;
{
    return strcmp(i->logid, j->logid);
}


/*
 *  Returns pointer to a record in the list, keyed on login ID, or NULL if
 *  not found.
 */
Mem_Rec *
find_urec(id)
char *id;
{
    Mem_Rec temp;

    if (strlen(id) == 0)
        return (Mem_Rec *)NULL;
    else {
        strncpy(temp.logid, id, LOGID_LEN);
        temp.logid[LOGID_LEN] = '\0';
        return (Mem_Rec *)lfind((char *)&temp,
            (char *)ulist, &users, sizeof(Mem_Rec), comp_by_logid);
    }
}


/*
 *  Gets the user's full name.
 *
 *  If MB_G_LASTNM1ST (last name first) is set, make a stab at reversing the
 *  name order...
 */
char *
get_fname(id)
{
    Mem_Rec *mp;
    static char result[FNAME_LEN + 1];
    char *comma;

    if ( ( mp = find_urec(id) ) == (Mem_Rec *)NULL)
        strcpy(result, id);
    else
        strcpy(result, mp->fname);

    if ((globrec.flags & MB_G_LASTNM1ST) != 0 &&
        (comma = strrchr(result, ',')) != CNULL) {
        char buf[FNAME_LEN + 1], *ptr;
        int len;

        if (*(comma + 1) == ' ')
            strcpy(buf, comma + 2);
```

```
            else
                strcpy(buf, comma + 1);
            strncat(buf, " ", FNAME_LEN - strlen(buf)) ;
            for (ptr = result, len = strlen(buf) ;
                ptr != comma && len < FNAME_LEN ; ptr++, len++)
                buf[len] = *ptr;
            buf[len] = '\0';
            strcpy(result, buf);
        }

    return result;
}

/*
 * looks up "logname" in the passwd file/map; fills in the full name,
 * and if passed a non-null pointer, the category name.
 * Returned value is 0 if user lookup is successful, -1 if it fails.
 */
int
lookup_user(logname, fullname, cat)
char *logname, *fullname, *cat;
{
    struct passwd *pwbuf;
    struct group *grpbuf;
    int l;

    pwbuf = getpwnam(logname);
    if ( pwbuf == (struct passwd *)NULL) return -1;

    /*
     * Read in the full name from the GECOS field, accepting a maximum of
     * 20 characters, up to but not including the first character that is
     * not alpha, blank or a period.  Then, trim trailing blanks.
     * WARNING: the constant "20" in the below format should be equal to
     * FNAME_LEN; be sure to change it if you change FNAME_LEN's value!
     *                                              vv             */
    if (sscanf(pwbuf->pw_gecos, "%20[A-Za-z .]%n", fullname, &l) == 1)
        while ( fullname[l-1] == ' ')
            fullname[--l] = '\0';
    else
        fullname[0] = '\0';

    /*
     * If they want it, get the category name.
     */
    if (cat != (char *)NULL) {
        if ( (grpbuf = getgrgid(pwbuf->pw_gid)) == (struct group *)NULL)
            cat[0] = '\0';
        else
            strncpy(cat, grpbuf->gr_name, CAT_LEN+1);
    }
    return 0;
}

/*
 * We want to sort by last name, and a good guess on what their last name
 * is might be "everything past the last space in the full name field."
 */
void
make_sort_string(fname, sortby)
char *fname, *sortby;
{
```

```
    char *pos;

    if ((globrec.flags & MB_G_LASTNM1ST) == 0) {
       if ( (pos = strrchr(fname, ' ')) == CNULL)
          pos = fname;
       else
          ++pos;

       strcpy(sortby, pos);
    }
    else {
       strcpy(sortby, fname);
       if ( (pos = strchr(sortby, ',')) != CNULL)
          *pos = '\0';
    }

    for (pos = sortby; *pos != '\0'; pos++)
       if (isupper(*pos)) *pos = tolower(*pos);
}

/*
 *  Compare user list items by their sort field
 */
int
comp_by_sortby(i, j)
Mem_Rec *i, *j;
{
    return strcmp(i->sortby, j->sortby);
}

/*
 *  Compare strings called by pointer-to-pointer; used to sort category
 *  list, and names list in add/modify window.
 */
int
comp_strings(i, j)
char **i, **j;
{
    return(strcmp(*i, *j));
}
```

mbtty.c

```
/*
 *  mbtty -- Bare minimum lister for the msgboard.
 */

#include <sys/param.h>
#include <stdio.h>
#include "msgboard.h"

Mem_Rec
    *ulist,                        /* Pointer to list of users*/
    *myentry;                      /* Pointer to current user's record in
                                                ulist array          */

char
    mb_server[MAXHOSTNAMELEN+1],
```

```
        **cats,                         /* Pointer to array of category names*/
    mylogid[L_cuserid];/* Current user's login ID*/

int
    users = 0,                          /* Number of users in datalist*/
    numcats = 0,                        /* Number of categories known*/
    cur_cat = MB_ALL,                   /* Category to restrict display to */
    cur_status = MB_ALL,                /* Category to restrict display to */
    admin = FALSE,                      /* Is user in admin mode?*/
    admin_enable = TRUE,
    newmsgs = FALSE;                    /* Did they get new messages? */

Global_Rec
    globrec;                            /* Global data from server*/


void
pr_msg(ignore, bell, format, a1, a2, a3)
int bell;
char *ignore, *format, *a1, *a2, *a3;
{
    if (bell) fputc('\007', stderr);
    fprintf(stderr, format, a1, a2, a3);
    fputc('\n', stderr);
}

main(argc, argv)
int argc;
char **argv;
{
    if (cuserid(mylogid) == CNULL) {
        pr_msg(NULL, TRUE, "System doesn't know who %s is! (cuserid failed)",
            mylogid);
        exit(1);
    }

    if (!connect_to_server()) {
        pr_msg(NULL, TRUE, "Could not connect to server %s.", mb_server);
        exit(1);
    }

    (void)get_modified_records();
}

void
update_screen()
{
    static char *status[3] = {
        "out",
        "in",
        "???"
    };
    int i;

    printf("Message Board for %s:\n", globrec.name);
    if (globrec.motd[0] != '\0') printf("    ** %s **\n", globrec.motd);
    for (i = 0; i < users; i++) {
        printf("%s", ulist[i].fname);
        if (ulist[i].ext[0] !='\0') printf(", x%s", ulist[i].ext);
        printf(": %s", status[ulist[i].status]);
        if (ulist[i].until[0] != '\0') printf(" until %s", ulist[i].until);
```

```
            if (ulist[i].comment[0] != '\0') printf(" - %s", ulist[i].comment);
            printf("\n");
        }
        if (newmsgs) printf("(You have new phone messages)\n");
}

void
set_mainwin_items_status()
{
        if (myentry != NULL && (myentry->flags & MB_NEWMSGS) != 0)
            newmsgs = TRUE;
}

void
update_line(rp)
Mem_Rec *rp;
{
}

void
update_global_display()
{
}

void
update_cat_list()
{
}

void
watch_del()
{
}

void
watch_alert()
{
}

void
server_was_dropped()
{
}
```

msgboard_xv.c

```
/*
 *  msgboard_xv.c - XView version of the Message Board.
 */

#include <stdio.h>
#include <sys/param.h>
#include <sys/types.h>
#include <sys/stat.h>
#include <X11/Xlib.h>
#include <xview/xview.h>
```

```
#include <xview/panel.h>
#include <xview/xv_xrect.h>
#include <pwd.h>
#include "msgboard_xv.h"
#include "msgboard.h"
#include "outs_menu.h"


/*
 * Instance XV_KEY_DATA key.  An instance is a set of related
 * user interface objects.  A pointer to an object's instance
 * is stored under this key in every object.  This must be a
 * global variable.
 */
Attr_attribute INSTANCE;

Notify_func timer_notify();

struct itimerval timer;

Frame base_frame = NULL;
Display *dpy;

int
    cur_sel = BOGUS,                /* Index of currently selected user */
    cur_cat = MB_ALL,               /* current category -- default ALL  */
    cur_status = MB_ALL,            /* current category -- default ALL  */
    delay = CK_INT,                 /* Time between each database check*/
    fmt_msgs = TRUE,                /* Format phone messages?*/
    pop_mod = TRUE,                 /* Popup modify window when a list entry
                                            is toggled to Out?*/
    users = 0,                      /* Number of users in datalist*/
    numcats = 0,                    /* Number of categories    */
    watchnum = 0,                   /* Number of logids on watchlist */
    admin = FALSE,                  /* Does user have admin caps? */
    admin_enable = TRUE,            /* and do they want to use them? */
    prt_dest = TO_PRINTER,          /* print to printer or file?*/
    prt_type = POSTSCRIPT,          /* print postscript or ascii?*/
    wgrid,                          /* spacing for panel items, in pixels */
    dragstyle = BOGUS;              /*  What DnD style should we use? */

char
    mb_server[MAXHOSTNAMELEN+1],    /* Name of the server host*/
    mylogid[L_cuserid],             /* Current user's login ID*/
    **cats,                         /* Pointer to array of category names*/
    **watchlist,                    /* Pointer to array of logids to watch for*/
    prt_name[PRINTERNAME_LEN+1],    /* Name of printer to print msgs to */
    prt_dir[MAXPATHLEN],            /* Name of directory to print msgs to */
    prt_file[81];                   /* Name of file to print msgs to */

struct winparams main_params, send_params, scan_params, page_params,
                                outmod_params;

Mem_Rec
    *ulist,                         /*  Pointer to list of users*/
    *myentry;                       /*  Pointer to current user's record in
                                                ulist array */

Global_Rec
    globrec;                        /*  Global data from the server*/
```

```
/*
 *   Displays an error message in the footer of "frame".  If frame is NULL,
 *   use the main frame.  If we're out of the window system, just print.
 */
void
pr_msg(frame, bell, format, a1, a2, a3)
Frame frame;
int bell;
char *format, *a1, *a2, *a3;
{
    if (base_frame != NULL) {
        char msg[512];

        sprintf(msg, format, a1, a2, a3);
        if ( frame == NULL ) frame = base_frame;
        if (bell) window_bell(frame);
        xv_set(frame, FRAME_LEFT_FOOTER, msg, NULL);
    }
    else {
        if (bell) fputc('\007', stderr);
        fprintf(stderr, format, a1, a2, a3);
    }
}


/*
 *   Initializes/resets the delay between automatic checks of the database
 */
void
set_timer(flag)
int flag;
{
    if (flag) {
        timer.it_value.tv_sec = 1;
        timer.it_value.tv_usec = 0;
        timer.it_interval.tv_sec = delay;
        timer.it_interval.tv_usec = 0;
        (void)notify_set_itimer_func(base_frame, timer_notify, ITIMER_REAL,
            &timer, ITIMER_NULL);
    }
    else
        (void)notify_set_itimer_func(base_frame, NOTIFY_FUNC_NULL,
            ITIMER_REAL, NULL, ITIMER_NULL);
}


void
set_prt_defaults()
{
    char *ptr;

    ptr = getenv("PRINTER");
    if (ptr == CNULL)
      strcpy(prt_name, "lp");
    else {
        strncpy(prt_name, ptr, PRINTERNAME_LEN);
        prt_name[PRINTERNAME_LEN] = '\0';
    }
    getwd(prt_dir);
    strcpy(prt_file, "msgs.ps");
}


/*
 *   Save program parameters out to user parameter file
 */
```

```
void
save_params()
{
    FILE *file;
    char *ptr, filename[MAXPATHLEN + 1];
    struct winparams params;
    int i;

    ptr = getenv("HOME");
    if (ptr == CNULL) {
      pr_msg(NULL, TRUE, "Can't find your home directory!");
      return;
    }

    sprintf(filename, "%s/%s", ptr, PARAMFILE);
    if ( (file = fopen(filename, "w")) == FNULL) {
      pr_msg(NULL, TRUE, "Could not open %s", filename);
      return;
    }

    fprintf(file, "delay: %d\n", delay);
    fprintf(file, "pop_mod: %d\n", pop_mod);
    fprintf(file, "fmt_msgs: %d\n", fmt_msgs);
    fprintf(file, "admin_enable: %d\n", admin_enable);
    get_main_params(&params);
    fprintf(file, "mainwin: %d %d %d %d %d\n", params.state,
        params.rect.r_left, params.rect.r_top, params.rect.r_width,
        params.rect.r_height);
    get_send_params(&params);
    fprintf(file, "sendwin: %d %d %d %d %d\n", params.state,
        params.rect.r_left, params.rect.r_top, params.rect.r_width,
        params.rect.r_height);
    get_scan_params(&params);
    fprintf(file, "scanwin: %d %d %d %d %d\n", params.state,
        params.rect.r_left, params.rect.r_top, params.rect.r_width,
        params.rect.r_height);
    get_page_params(&params);
    fprintf(file, "pagewin: %d %d %d %d %d\n", params.state,
        params.rect.r_left, params.rect.r_top, params.rect.r_width,
        params.rect.r_height);
    get_outmod_params(&params);
    fprintf(file, "outmodwin: %d %d %d %d %d\n", params.state,
        params.rect.r_left, params.rect.r_top, params.rect.r_width,
        params.rect.r_height);

    for ( i = 0 ; i < num_outs ; i++ )
        fprintf(file, "outs: %1s|%1s|%1s|%d\n",
          outlist[i].label, outlist[i].until,
          outlist[i].message, outlist[i].pop);

    fclose(file);
}

/*
 *  Read program parameters in from PARAMFILE
 */
void
load_params()
{
    FILE *file;
    char *ptr, keywd[21], filename[MAXPATHLEN+1], buf[151];
```

```
   ptr = getenv("HOME");
   if (ptr == CNULL)
      return;

send_params.state = BOGUS;
scan_params.state = BOGUS;
page_params.state = BOGUS;
outmod_params.state = BOGUS;
main_params.state = BOGUS;

sprintf(filename, "%s/%s", ptr, PARAMFILE);
if ( (file = fopen(filename, "r")) == FNULL) {
   return;

while (fgets(buf, 150, file) != CNULL) {
   if (sscanf(buf, "%20[^:]", keywd) == 1) {
      if (strcmp("delay", keywd) == 0) {
              sscanf(buf, "%*s %d", &delay);
      }
      else if (strcmp("pop_mod", keywd) == 0) {
              sscanf(buf, "%*s %d", &pop_mod);
      }
      else if (strcmp("fmt_msgs", keywd) == 0) {
              sscanf(buf, "%*s %d", &fmt_msgs);
      }
      else if (strcmp("admin_enable", keywd) == 0) {
              sscanf(buf, "%*s %d", &admin_enable);
      }
      else if (strcmp("outs", keywd) == 0)
              read_outs_line(buf);
      else if (strcmp("mainwin", keywd) == 0) {
              sscanf(buf, "%*s %d %hd %hd %hd %hd",
                  &(main_params.state),
                  &(main_params.rect.r_left),
                  &(main_params.rect.r_top),
                  &(main_params.rect.r_width),
                  &(main_params.rect.r_height));
      }
      else if (strcmp("sendwin", keywd) == 0) {
              sscanf(buf, "%*s %d %hd %hd %hd %hd",
                  &(send_params.state),
                  &(send_params.rect.r_left),
                  &(send_params.rect.r_top),
                  &(send_params.rect.r_width),
                  &(send_params.rect.r_height));
      }
      else if (strcmp("scanwin", keywd) == 0) {
              sscanf(buf, "%*s %d %hd %hd %hd %hd",
                  &(scan_params.state),
                  &(scan_params.rect.r_left),
                  &(scan_params.rect.r_top),
                  &(scan_params.rect.r_width),
                  &(scan_params.rect.r_height));
      }
      else if (strcmp("pagewin", keywd) == 0) {
              sscanf(buf, "%*s %d %hd %hd %hd %hd",
                  &(page_params.state),
                  &(page_params.rect.r_left),
                  &(page_params.rect.r_top),
                  &(page_params.rect.r_width),
                  &(page_params.rect.r_height));
      }
```

```
            else if (strcmp("outmodwin", keywd) == 0) {
                    sscanf(buf, "%*s %d %hd %hd %hd %hd",
                        &(outmod_params.state),
                        &(outmod_params.rect.r_left),
                        &(outmod_params.rect.r_top),
                        &(outmod_params.rect.r_width),
                        &(outmod_params.rect.r_height));
            }
        }
    }
    fclose(file);
}

void
kaboom()
{
    if (base_frame != NULL) {
        xv_destroy_safe(base_frame);
        fprintf(stderr, "Program exited prematurely\n");
        sleep(3);
    }
    exit(1);
}

/****************
 *  Main
 ****************/
void
main(argc, argv)
int argc;
char **argv;
{
    int release;

    if (cuserid(mylogid) == CNULL) {
        pr_msg(NULL, TRUE, "System doesn't know who %s is! (cuserid failed)",
            mylogid);
        kaboom();
    }

    /*
     *  Initialize XView.
     */
    xv_init(XV_INIT_ARGC_PTR_ARGV, &argc, argv, 0);
    INSTANCE = xv_unique_key();

    /*
     *  Read the user's parameter file.
     */
    load_params();

    /*
     *  Initialize user interface components.
     */
    create_main_window();
    dpy = (Display *)xv_get(base_frame, XV_DISPLAY);

    /*
     *  Determine the default drag and drop style.  Use the V2 style only
     *  if we're running on a V2 server.
     */
```

```
    dragstyle = VendorRelease(dpy);
    if (dragstyle >= 2000 && dragstyle < 3000)
        dragstyle = 2;
    else
        dragstyle = 3;

    /*
     * Disable reading of any mail initialization files
     */
    putenv("MAILRC=/dev/null");

    /*
     * More initialization...
     */
    create_signs();
    set_prt_defaults();

    /*
     * Try connecting to the specified server; ask it for info.
     * "Modified records," since we're just firing up, means all
     * records.
     */
    if (connect_to_server()) (void)get_modified_records();

    /*
     * Set the active/inactive status of main panel items to jibe with
     * whether or not any item on the scrolling is selected.
     */
    set_mainwin_items_status();

    /*
     * Turn on the update timer.
     */
    set_timer(TRUE);

    /*
     * Should we bring up any of the popup windows?
     */
    if (send_params.state == FRAME_CMD_PIN_IN)
      show_sendmsg_window();
    if (scan_params.state == FRAME_CMD_PIN_IN)
      show_scan_window();
    if (page_params.state == FRAME_CMD_PIN_IN)
      show_page_window();
    if (outmod_params.state == FRAME_CMD_PIN_IN)
      show_outmod_window((Mem_Rec *)NULL);

    /*
     * Hand control over to XView.
     */
    xv_main_loop(base_frame);
    base_frame = NULL;
    exit(0);
}

/*
 * This should be called whenever a user event is detected, to clear
 * warning-level messages.
 */
void
clear_msg()
{
```

```
            xv_set(base_frame, FRAME_LEFT_FOOTER, "", NULL);
}

void
look_busy(flag)
int flag;
{
    xv_set(base_frame, FRAME_BUSY, flag, NULL);
}

/*
 *  See if there are any changes to the database.  Try to connect to server
 *  if we're disconnected.
 */
Notify_func
timer_notify()
{
    if (get_modified_records() == MSGD_DISCONNECTED) {
        look_busy(TRUE);
        pr_msg(NULL, FALSE, "Attempting to connect to %s...", mb_server);
        if (connect_to_server()) {
            pr_msg(NULL, FALSE, "Connected to %s.", mb_server);
            (void)get_modified_records();
        }
        look_busy(FALSE);
    }

    return NOTIFY_DONE;
}

/*
 *  Positions Apply/Reset type buttons.  Uses: wgrid
 */
void
position_bot_buttons(panel, b1, b2, r)
Panel panel;
Panel_item b1, b2;
int r;
{
    int b1w, b1x;

    b1w = (int)xv_get(b1, XV_WIDTH);
    b1x = ((int)xv_get(panel, XV_WIDTH) - b1w -
        (int)xv_get(b2, XV_WIDTH) - wgrid) / 2;
    xv_set(b1,
        XV_X, b1x,
        NULL);
    xv_set(b2,
        XV_X, b1x + b1w + wgrid,
        NULL);
}

#ifdef SCALABLE
/*
 *  Align items by their values.  Pick your item with the longest label,
 *  position it, and pass its PANEL_VALUE_X as "valx" for all your other
 *  items.
 */
void
align_values(item, valx, ypos)
Panel_item item;
int valx, ypos;
{
```

```
    xv_set(item,
        XV_X, (int)xv_get(item, XV_X) + valx - (int)xv_get(item,
                                                    PANEL_VALUE_X),
        XV_Y, ypos,
        NULL);
}
#endif

/*
 * Deletes a login ID from the watch list.
 */
int
watch_del(u)
char *u;
{
    char **rp;
    int i;

    rp = (char **)lfind((char *)&u, (char *)watchlist, &watchnum,
        sizeof(char *), comp_strings);

    if (rp == (char **)NULL) return FALSE;

    free(*rp);
    watchnum--;
    for ( i = (rp - watchlist); i < watchnum; i++)
        watchlist[i] = watchlist[i+1];

    if ( watchnum == 0 && (int)xv_get(base_frame, FRAME_CLOSED) )
        set_timer(FALSE);

    return TRUE;
}


/*
 * The outs button handler calls this to commit the appropriate values
 * to the database.
 */
void
set_from_out_button(until, comment, pop)
char *until, *comment;
int pop;
{
    Mem_Rec *rec;

    if (admin) {
        if ( cur_sel != BOGUS )
            rec = &ulist[cur_sel];
        else {
            pr_msg(NULL, TRUE, "No one selected on list.");
            return;
        }
    }
    else {
        if (myentry == (Mem_Rec *)NULL) {
            pr_msg(NULL, TRUE, "%s is not currently on the Message board.",
                        mylogid);
            return;
        }
        rec = myentry;
    }
```

```
        modify_status(rec->logid, MB_OUT, until, comment);

        if (get_modified_records() == 0 && pop) show_outmod_window(rec);
}

/*
 *   Called by client library routines whenever server connection is lost.
 */
void
server_was_dropped()
{
    if (users > 0) {
        free(ulist);
        users = 0;
        myentry = NULL;
    }
    globrec.name[0] = '\0';
    globrec.motd[0] = '\0';
    update_screen();
    update_global_display();
}
```

nightly.c

```
/*
 *   nightly -- housekeeping program for the Message Board
 *       Performs the following tasks:
 *                       1.  Finds anyone still marked as "In" and changes their
 *                           status to "Unknown"
 *                       2.  Ages phone messages
 */

#include <sys/param.h>
#include <stdio.h>
#include <time.h>
#include "msgboard.h"
#include "pmsg_client.h"

#define DAYSEC 86400L /*  Number of seconds in a day */

Mem_Rec
    *ulist,           /*  Pointer to list of users*/
    *myentry,         /*  Pointer to current user's record in ulist array */
    tmp_record;       /*  Used when creating/modifying records */

Global_Rec
    globrec;

char
    mb_server[MAXHOSTNAMELEN+1],
    motd[MOTD_LEN+1],/* Message of the day*/
    mylogid[L_cuserid],/* Current user's login ID*/
    sitename[SITE_LEN+1],/* Name of this site */
    **cats;                              /* Pointer to array of category names*/

int
    global_flags,                        /* global flags*/
    users = 0,                                   /* Number of users in datalist*/
```

```
    numcats = 0,                    /* Number of categories  */
    cur_cat = MB_ALL,               /* Category to restrict display to */
    cur_status = MB_ALL,/* Category to restrict display to */
    admin = FALSE,                  /* Is user in admin mode?*/
    admin_enable = TRUE;

void
kaboom()
{
    exit(1);
}


void
pr_msg(ignore, bell, format, a1, a2, a3)
int bell;
char *ignore, *format, *a1, *a2, *a3;
{
    char bellchar;

    if (bell) fputc('\007', stderr);
    fprintf(stderr, format, a1, a2, a3);
}


/*
 * Moves messages older than "date" from from_cat to to_cat. If to_cat is
 * BOGUS, mv_msg_call will just throw the messages out.
 */
void
age_msgs(user, date, from_cat, to_cat)
char *user;
int from_cat, to_cat;
time_t date;
{
    char buf[BUFSIZ], **m_list;
    int dp, size, r_count, m_count, i;
    struct tm tmbuf;
    time_t msgdate;
    struct pmsg_hdr *ph_ptr;

    ph_ptr = get_pmsg_headers(user, from_cat, &size);
    if (size == 0) return;

    r_count = 0;
    for (i = 0; i < size; i++) {
        sscanf(ph_ptr[i].id, "%*s %*s %n", &dp);
        strptime(ph_ptr[i].id + dp, "%a %b %d %T %Y", &tmbuf);
        msgdate = timelocal(&tmbuf);
        if (msgdate < date) {
            r_count++;
            if (r_count == 1)
                    m_list = (char **)malloc(sizeof(char *));
            else
                    m_list = (char **)realloc(m_list, sizeof(char *) *
                                                r_count);
            m_list[r_count - 1] = ph_ptr[i].id;
        }
        else
            free(ph_ptr[i].id);
        free(ph_ptr[i].desc);
    }
```

```c
    if (r_count > 0) {
        m_count = mv_msg_call(user, from_cat, to_cat, r_count, m_list);
        for ( i = 0; i < r_count; i++)
            free(m_list[i]);
        free(m_list);
        if (m_count != r_count)
            fprintf(stderr,
        "Warning: tried to move %d msgs from %s.%d; actually moved %d.\n",
            r_count, user, from_cat, m_count);
    }
}

main(argc, argv)
int argc;
char **argv;
{
    int u;
    time_t now;

    if (cuserid(mylogid) == CNULL) {
        pr_msg(NULL, TRUE, "System doesn't know who %s is! (cuserid failed)",
            mylogid);
        kaboom();
    }

    if (!connect_to_server()) {
        pr_msg(NULL, TRUE, "Could not connect to server %s.", mb_server);
        exit(1);
    }

    (void)get_modified_records();

    time(&now);

    for ( u = 0; u < users; u++) {
        if ( ulist[u].status == MB_IN)
            modify_status(ulist[u].logid, MB_UNK, CNULL, CNULL);

        /*
         *  delete old msgs from trash:
         */
        if (DEL_DAYS > 0)
            age_msgs(ulist[u].logid, now - DAYSEC * DEL_DAYS,
                    SCM_CHOICE_TRA, BOGUS);

        /*
         *  Move complete to trash:
         */
        if (TO_TRASH_DAYS > 0)
            age_msgs(ulist[u].logid, now - DAYSEC * TO_TRASH_DAYS,
                    SCM_CHOICE_COM, SCM_CHOICE_TRA);

        /*
         *  Move pending to complete:
         */
        if (TO_COMPLETE_DAYS > 0)
            age_msgs(ulist[u].logid, now - DAYSEC * TO_COMPLETE_DAYS,
                    SCM_CHOICE_PEN, SCM_CHOICE_COM);

        /*
         *  Move new to pending:
         */
```

```
            if (TO_PENDING_DAYS > 0)
                age_msgs(ulist[u].logid, now - DAYSEC * TO_PENDING_DAYS,
                        SCM_CHOICE_NEW, SCM_CHOICE_PEN);
    }
}

void
update_screen()
{
}

void
set_mainwin_items_status()
{
}

void
update_line(rp)
Mem_Rec *rp;
{
}

void
update_global_display()
{
}

void
update_cat_list()
{
}

void
watch_del()
{
}

void
watch_alert()
{
}

void
server_was_dropped()
{
}
```

outmodwin.c

```
/*
 * outmodwin.c - Notify and event callback function stubs for the abbreviated
 *   modify window that's popped up when a user is marked Out.
 */

#include <stdio.h>
#include <sys/param.h>
#include <sys/types.h>
#include <xview/xview.h>
#include <xview/panel.h>
#include <xview/textsw.h>
#include <xview/xv_xrect.h>
```

```c
#include "outmodwin_ui.h"
#include "msgboard.h"
#include "msgboard_xv.h"


/*
 * Global object definitions.
 */
outmodwin_frame_objects *om_ip;

int
    outmod_window_created = FALSE,
    om_warped = FALSE;

void
create_out_window()
{
#ifdef SCALABLE
    int valx, ypos;
#endif

    om_ip = outmodwin_frame_objects_initialize(NULL, base_frame);

    if (outmod_params.state != BOGUS) {
        frame_set_rect(om_ip->frame, &outmod_params.rect);
        if (outmod_params.state == FRAME_CMD_PIN_IN)
            xv_set(om_ip->frame, FRAME_CMD_PIN_STATE, FRAME_CMD_PIN_IN, NULL);

    }

    xv_set(om_ip->panel,
        PANEL_DEFAULT_ITEM,     om_ip->apply_item,
        PANEL_CLIENT_DATA, CNULL,
        NULL);

#ifdef SCALABLE
    /*
     * comment has the longest label, so we position it properly from the
     * left edge of the panel.
     */
    xv_set(om_ip->comment_item, XV_X, wgrid * 2, NULL);
    valx = (int)xv_get(om_ip->comment_item, PANEL_VALUE_X);

    ypos = wgrid * 2;
    align_values(om_ip->status_item, valx, ypos);

    ypos += wgrid + (int)xv_get(om_ip->status_item, XV_HEIGHT);
    align_values(om_ip->until_item, valx, ypos);

    ypos += wgrid + (int)xv_get(om_ip->until_item, XV_HEIGHT);
    xv_set(om_ip->comment_item, XV_Y, ypos, NULL);

    ypos += wgrid + (int)xv_get(om_ip->comment_item, XV_HEIGHT);
    xv_set(om_ip->apply_item, XV_Y, ypos, NULL);
    xv_set(om_ip->reset_item, XV_Y, ypos, NULL);

    window_fit(om_ip->panel);
    window_fit(om_ip->frame);

    position_bot_buttons(om_ip->panel, om_ip->apply_item, om_ip->reset_item);
#endif
    outmod_window_created = TRUE;
}
```

```
void
show_outmod_window(user)
Mem_Rec *user;
{
    char buf[FNAME_LEN + 25], *old_logid;
    int no_rec_passed;
    Panel_item focus_item;

    if (!outmod_window_created) create_out_window();

    no_rec_passed = (user == (Mem_Rec *)NULL);
    if (no_rec_passed) {
        user = (Mem_Rec *)malloc(sizeof(Mem_Rec));
        user->status = MB_UNK;
        user->logid[0] = user->until[0] = user->comment[0] = '\0';
    }

    xv_set(om_ip->status_item,
        PANEL_VALUE, user->status,
        PANEL_INACTIVE, no_rec_passed,
        NULL);
    xv_set(om_ip->until_item,
        PANEL_VALUE, user->until,
        PANEL_INACTIVE, no_rec_passed,
        NULL);
    xv_set(om_ip->comment_item,
        PANEL_VALUE, user->comment,
        PANEL_INACTIVE, no_rec_passed,
        NULL);

    xv_set(om_ip->apply_item, PANEL_INACTIVE, no_rec_passed, NULL);
    xv_set(om_ip->reset_item, PANEL_INACTIVE, no_rec_passed, NULL);

    old_logid = (char *)xv_get(om_ip->panel, PANEL_CLIENT_DATA);
    if (old_logid != CNULL) {
        free(old_logid);
        xv_set(om_ip->panel, PANEL_CLIENT_DATA, NULL, NULL);
    }

    sprintf(buf, "Message Board: Mark %s" Out", user->fname);

    if (no_rec_passed)
        free(user);
    else {
        xv_set(om_ip->comment_item,
            PANEL_CLIENT_DATA, (user->flags & MB_PRESERVE) != 0, NULL);

        focus_item = (user->until[0] != '\0' && user->comment[0] == '\0') ?
            om_ip->comment_item :
            om_ip->until_item ;

        xv_set(om_ip->panel,
            PANEL_CLIENT_DATA, strdup(user->logid),
            PANEL_CARET_ITEM, focus_item,
            NULL);
    }
    om_warped = FALSE;
    xv_set(om_ip->frame,
        FRAME_LABEL, buf,
        XV_SHOW, TRUE,
        NULL);
}
```

```
void
outmod_done(flag)
int flag;
{
    char *logid;

    logid = (char *)xv_get(om_ip->panel, PANEL_CLIENT_DATA);
    if (flag) {
        modify_status(
            logid,
            (int)xv_get(om_ip->status_item, PANEL_VALUE),
            (char *)xv_get(om_ip->until_item, PANEL_VALUE),
            (char *)xv_get(om_ip->comment_item, PANEL_VALUE)
        );
        (void)get_modified_records();
    }

    if ((int)xv_get(om_ip->frame, FRAME_CMD_PIN_STATE) == FRAME_CMD_PIN_IN)
        show_outmod_window((Mem_Rec *)NULL);
    else
        clear_msg();
}

/*
 * Notify callback function for 'status_item'.
 */
void
out_inout_notify(item, value, event)
Panel_item item;
int value;
Event *event;
{
    if (value == MB_IN) {
        xv_set(om_ip->until_item, PANEL_VALUE, "", NULL);
        if (!(int)xv_get(om_ip->comment_item, PANEL_CLIENT_DATA))
            xv_set(om_ip->comment_item, PANEL_VALUE, "", NULL);
    }
}

/*
 * Notify callback function for 'comment_item'.
 */
Panel_setting
out_comment_notify(item, event)
Panel_item item;
Event *event;
{
    if (event_shift_is_down(event))
        return PANEL_PREVIOUS;
    else {
        outmod_done(TRUE);
        if ((int)xv_get(om_ip->frame, FRAME_CMD_PIN_STATE) ==
                                        FRAME_CMD_PIN_OUT)
            xv_set(om_ip->frame, XV_SHOW, FALSE, NULL);
        return PANEL_NONE;
    }
}
/*
 * Notify callback function for 'apply_item' and 'reset_item'.
 */
```

```
void
out_apply_reset_notify(item, event)
Panel_item item;
Event *event;
{
    char *logid;

    outmod_done(item == om_ip->apply_item);
}


/*
 * Event callback function for 'panel'.
 */
Notify_value
om_panel_event(win, event, arg, type)
Xv_window win;
Event *event;
Notify_arg arg;
Notify_event_type type;
{
    if (!om_warped && event_action(event) == WIN_REPAINT) {
        /*
         *  Conditionally warp the mouse to the apply button
         */
        warpme(om_ip->frame, om_ip->panel, om_ip->apply_item);
        om_warped = TRUE;
    }
    else if (event_action(event) == LOC_WINEXIT)
        /*
         *  If we ever leave the window, cancel any pending dewarp
         */
        no_dewarp();

    return notify_next_event_func(win, (Notify_event) event, arg, type);
}


/*
 * Done callback function for 'frame'.
 */
void
om_done(frame)
Frame              frame;
{
    dewarp();
    xv_set(frame, XV_SHOW, FALSE, NULL);
}


/*
 * Gathers all the parameters for this window
 */
void
get_outmod_params(p)
struct winparams *p;
{
    if (!outmod_window_created)
        *p = outmod_params;
    else {
      p->state = (int)xv_get(om_ip->frame, FRAME_CMD_PIN_STATE);
      frame_get_rect(om_ip->frame, &(p->rect));
    }
}
```

`outs_menu.c`

```
/*
 * outs_menu.c - Code to create "Outs" menu.  Used by msgboard_x,
 * msgboard_sv, msglock_x, msglock_sv
 */

#include <stdio.h>
#include <sys/param.h>
#include <sys/types.h>
#include <sys/time.h>
#include <strings.h>
#include <ctype.h>
#include <xview/xview.h>
#include <xview/panel.h>
#include "outs_menu.h"
#include "msgboard.h"

struct outent *outlist;

int num_outs = 0;

/*
 *  Accepts a line and adds it to the array of entries for the "Outs" menu.
 */
void
read_outs_line(l)
char *l;
{
    char *p;

    if (num_outs == 0) {
      num_outs = 1;
      outlist = (struct outent *)malloc(sizeof(struct outent));
    }
    else {
        num_outs++;
        outlist = (struct outent *)realloc((char *)outlist,
            sizeof(struct outent)*num_outs);
    }

    /*
     *  Scan past the keyword
     */
    (void)strtok(l, ": ");

    p = strtok(NULL, "|\n");
    while ( *p == ' ' || *p == '"' ) p++;
    outlist[num_outs-1].label = strdup(p);
    outlist[num_outs-1].until = strdup(strtok(NULL, "|\n"));
    if ( strcmp(outlist[num_outs-1].until, " ") == 0)
        outlist[num_outs-1].until[0] = '\0';
    outlist[num_outs-1].message = strdup(strtok(NULL, "|\n"));
    if ( strcmp(outlist[num_outs-1].message, " ") == 0)
        outlist[num_outs-1].message[0] = '\0';
    p = strtok(NULL, "|\n");
    outlist[num_outs-1].pop = (p != (char *)NULL) ? atoi(p) : 0;
}

/*
 *  Called when user selects an item from the "Outs" menu
 */
```

```
void
outs_handler(menu, menu_item)
Menu menu;
Menu_item menu_item;
{
    char *menu_choice = (char *)xv_get(menu_item, MENU_STRING),
        until[UNTIL_LEN+1], comment[COMMENT_LEN+1], ubuf[20], *p;
    struct outent *outp;
    int i;

    /*
     *  Find this menu choice in the list of outs options
     */
    outp = NULL;
    for ( i = 0 ; i < num_outs ; i++ )
        if ( strcmp(menu_choice, outlist[i].label) == 0 ) outp =
                                                    &(outlist[i]);


    /*
     *  This should never happen
     */
    if ( outp == NULL ) return;

    strcpy(ubuf, outp->until);
    if (ubuf[0] == '+') {
        struct timeval tp;
        struct tm *tm;
        char tmp[4], *merid;
        int hr, mn;

        for ( i = 1, p = tmp ; isdigit(ubuf[i]) &&
                            i < strlen(ubuf) &&
                            p < tmp + 3 ; i++, p++)
            *p = ubuf[i];

        *(p) = '\0';
        hr = atoi(tmp);

        if ( (p = strchr(ubuf, ':')) != CNULL ) {
            for ( i = p - ubuf + 1, p = tmp ; isdigit(ubuf[i]) &&
                                i < strlen(ubuf) &&
                                p < tmp + 3 ; i++, p++)
                *p = ubuf[i];

            *(p) = '\0';
            mn = atoi(tmp);

        }
        else
            mn = 0;

        gettimeofday(&tp, (struct timezone *)NULL);
        tp.tv_sec += hr * 3600 + mn * 60;

        tm = localtime(&tp.tv_sec);
        hr = tm->tm_hour;
        mn = tm->tm_min;

        if ((mn % 10) > 0) mn += (10 - (mn % 10)); /* Round up to
                                                    nearest 10 */
        if (mn >= 60) {
            mn -= 60;
```

```
            ++hr;
        }

        if (hr > 23) hr -= 24;

        if (hr > 11) {
        merid = "PM";
        if (hr > 12) hr -= 12;
        }
        else {
        merid = "AM";
        if (hr == 0) hr = 12;
        }

        sprintf(ubuf, "%d:%02d %s", hr, mn, merid);
    }

    if ( (p = strchr(ubuf, '%')) != CNULL) {
        if ( *(p + 1) == 'N') {
            struct timeval tp;
            struct tm *tm;
            int nextday, preserve;
            char *p2;

            static char *weekday[7] = {
                    "Sun", "Mon", "Tue", "Wed", "Thu", "Fri", "Sat"
            };

            gettimeofday(&tp, (struct timezone *)NULL);
            tm = localtime(&tp.tv_sec);

            nextday = tm->tm_wday + 1;
            if (nextday > 5) nextday = 1;

            p2 = strlen(ubuf) == 19 ? ubuf + 18 : ubuf + strlen(ubuf) + 1;
            while ( p2 > p + 1 ) {
                *p2 = *(p2 - 1);
                p2--;
            }
            *p = weekday[nextday][0];
            *(++p) = weekday[nextday][1];
            *(++p) = weekday[nextday][2];
        }
    }

    strncpy(until, ubuf, UNTIL_LEN);
    until[UNTIL_LEN] = '\0';
    strncpy(comment, outp->message, COMMENT_LEN+1);
    comment[COMMENT_LEN] = '\0';
    set_from_out_button(until, comment, outp->pop);
}

/*
 * Create object 'outs_menu'
 */
void
outs_menu_create(button)
Panel_item button;
{
    Menu menu;
    Menu_item mi;
    int i;
```

```
    if (num_outs == 0) {
        outlist = (struct outent *)malloc((unsigned)(sizeof(struct
                                                outent)*2));

        outlist[0].label = strdup("Lunch");
        outlist[0].until = strdup("+1:10");
        outlist[0].message = strdup("Lunch");
        outlist[0].pop = FALSE;
        outlist[1].label = strdup("For the Day");
        outlist[1].until = strdup("9 AM %N");
        outlist[1].message = strdup("");
        outlist[1].pop = FALSE;
        num_outs = 2;
    }

    menu = xv_create(XV_NULL, MENU_COMMAND_MENU,
        MENU_NOTIFY_PROC, outs_handler,
        NULL);

    for ( i = 0; i < num_outs; i++ ) {
        mi = xv_create(NULL, MENUITEM,
            MENU_STRING, outlist[i].label,
            MENU_RELEASE,
            NULL);
        xv_set(menu, MENU_APPEND_ITEM, mi, NULL);
    }
    xv_set(button, PANEL_ITEM_MENU, menu, NULL);
}
```

pagewin.c

```
/*
 * pagewin.c - Pager-dialing window for the Message Board.
 */

#include <stdio.h>
#include <sys/param.h>
#include <sys/types.h>
#include <xview/xview.h>
#include <xview/panel.h>
#include <xview/textsw.h>
#include <xview/xv_xrect.h>
#include "pagewin_ui.h"
#include "msgboard.h"
#include "msgboard_xv.h"

/*
 * Compatibility defines to match msgboard code to beeptool's:
 */
#define SelectedType (pagee.pagertype)
#define SelectedLogin (pagee.logid)
#define SelectedName (pagee.fname)

#define MAX_PAGE_STRING 150

char *PagerTypes[] = {
        "alpha",
        "numeric",
        "skypager"
};
```

```
pagewin_frame_objects *page_ip;

/*
 * Info about the person to page (the "pagee"):
 */
Mem_Rec pagee;

int
    page_window_created = FALSE;/* is page window created?*/

void
create_page_window()
{
#ifdef SCALABLE
    int valx, ypos;
#endif

    page_ip = pagewin_frame_objects_initialize(NULL, base_frame);

    if (page_params.state != BOGUS) {
      frame_set_rect(page_ip->frame, &page_params.rect);
      if (page_params.state == TRUE)
          xv_set(page_ip->frame, FRAME_CMD_PIN_STATE, FRAME_CMD_PIN_IN,
                                                         NULL);
    }

#ifdef SCALABLE
    xv_set(page_ip->textfield1, XV_X, wgrid * 2, NULL);
    valx = (int)xv_get(page_ip->textfield1, PANEL_VALUE_X);

    ypos = wgrid * 2;
    align_values(page_ip->to_item, valx, ypos);
    xv_set(page_ip->fname_item,
        XV_X,          (int)xv_get(page_ip->to_item, XV_X) +
                       (int)xv_get(page_ip->to_item, XV_WIDTH) + wgrid,
        XV_Y,          wgrid * 2,
        NULL);
    ypos += (int)xv_get(page_ip->to_item, XV_HEIGHT) + wgrid;
    align_values(page_ip->numeric, valx, ypos);
    align_values(page_ip->textfield1, valx, ypos);
    ypos += (int)xv_get(page_ip->numeric, XV_HEIGHT) + wgrid;
    align_values(page_ip->textfield2, valx, ypos);
    ypos += (int)xv_get(page_ip->textfield2, XV_HEIGHT) + wgrid * 2;
    xv_set(page_ip->send_item, XV_Y, ypos, NULL);
    xv_set(page_ip->cancel_item, XV_Y, ypos, NULL);
    window_fit(page_ip->panel);
    window_fit(page_ip->frame);
    position_bot_buttons(page_ip->panel, page_ip->send_item,
        page_ip->cancel_item);
#endif

    page_window_created = TRUE;
}

/*
 * Gets the necessary info for the person we want to page.
 */
void
set_pagewin_items()
{
    char cbuf[FNAME_LEN+3], typebuf[15];
    Mem_Rec *mp;
```

```
    strncpy(pagee.logid, (char *)xv_get(page_ip->to_item, PANEL_VALUE),
        LOGID_LEN);
    pagee.logid[LOGID_LEN] = '\0';
    mp = find_urec(pagee.logid);
    if (mp == (Mem_Rec *)NULL) {
        xv_set(page_ip->fname_item, PANEL_LABEL_STRING, "(???)", NULL);
        pagee.pagernum[0] = '\0';
    }
    else {
        pagee = *mp;
        sprintf(cbuf, "(%s)", pagee.fname);
        xv_set(page_ip->fname_item, PANEL_LABEL_STRING, cbuf, NULL);
    }

    if (pagee.pagernum[0] == '\0') {
        pr_msg(page_ip->frame, TRUE, "No pager number found for %s.",
            pagee.logid);
        xv_set(page_ip->frame, FRAME_RIGHT_FOOTER, "", NULL);
        xv_set(page_ip->send_item, PANEL_INACTIVE, TRUE, NULL);
        xv_set(page_ip->textfield1, XV_SHOW, FALSE, NULL);
        xv_set(page_ip->textfield2, XV_SHOW, FALSE, NULL);
        xv_set(page_ip->numeric,
            PANEL_VALUE,"",
            PANEL_INACTIVE,TRUE,
            XV_SHOW,                TRUE,
            NULL);
    }
    else {
        sprintf(typebuf, "Type: %s", PagerTypes[pagee.pagertype]);
        xv_set(page_ip->frame, FRAME_RIGHT_FOOTER, typebuf, NULL);
        pr_msg(page_ip->frame, FALSE, "");

        xv_set(page_ip->send_item, PANEL_INACTIVE, FALSE, NULL);

        if (pagee.pagertype != BEEP_ALPHA) {
            xv_set(page_ip->textfield1,
                    XV_SHOW,        FALSE,
                    NULL);
            xv_set(page_ip->textfield2,
                    XV_SHOW,        FALSE,
                    NULL);
            xv_set(page_ip->numeric,
                    PANEL_VALUE,    "",
                    PANEL_INACTIVE,FALSE,
                    XV_SHOW ,       TRUE,
                    NULL);
            xv_set(page_ip->panel,
                    PANEL_CARET_ITEM, page_ip->numeric,
                    NULL);
        }
        else {
            xv_set(page_ip->numeric,
                        XV_SHOW ,       FALSE,
                        NULL);
            xv_set(page_ip->textfield1,
                        PANEL_VALUE,    "",
                        XV_SHOW,        TRUE,
                        NULL);
            xv_set(page_ip->textfield2,
                        PANEL_VALUE,    "",
                        XV_SHOW,        TRUE,
                        NULL);
```

```
            xv_set(page_ip->panel,
                        PANEL_CARET_ITEM, page_ip->textfield1,
                        NULL);
        }
    }
}

void
show_page_window()
{
    if (!page_window_created) create_page_window();

    if (cur_sel != BOGUS)
        xv_set(page_ip->to_item, PANEL_VALUE, ulist[cur_sel].logid, NULL);
    set_pagewin_items();
    xv_set(page_ip->frame, XV_SHOW, TRUE, NULL);
}

/*
 * Notify callback function for 'send_button'.
 */
void
send_message_handler(item, event)
Panel_item item;
Event *event;
{
    char message[MAX_PAGE_STRING];
    char *ptr;

    switch (SelectedType) {
    case BEEP_ALPHA:
        sprintf(message, "%s %s",
            (char *)xv_get(page_ip->textfield1, PANEL_VALUE),
            (char *)xv_get(page_ip->textfield2, PANEL_VALUE));
        break;

    case BEEP_NUM:
    case BEEP_SKY:
        ptr = (char *)xv_get(page_ip->numeric, PANEL_VALUE);
        if (ptr[0] == NULL)
            strcpy(message, MESSAGE);
        else
            strcpy(message, ptr);

        break;

    default:
        pr_msg(page_ip->frame, TRUE, "Unknown pager type defined for %s.",
            SelectedName);
        return;
        break;
    }

    if ( sendpage(SelectedLogin, message) == 0 )
        pr_msg(page_ip->frame, FALSE, "page sent to %s", SelectedName);
}

/*
 * Notify callback function for 'to_item'.
 */
Panel_setting
pagewin_to_notify(item, event)
```

```
Panel_item item;
Event *event;
{
    set_pagewin_items();
    if (event_shift_is_down(event))
        return PANEL_PREVIOUS;
    else
        return PANEL_NEXT;
}


/*
 *  Gathers all the parameters for this window
 */
void
get_page_params(p)
struct winparams *p;
{
    if (!page_window_created)
        *p = page_params;
    else {
        p->state = (int)xv_get(page_ip->frame, FRAME_CMD_PIN_STATE);
        frame_get_rect(page_ip->frame, &(p->rect));
    }
}
```

pmsg_client.c

```
/*
 *  pmsg_client.c: routines for sending and scanning phone messages
 *  to and from the RPC server.
 */

#include <stdio.h>
#include <string.h
#include "msgboard.h"
#include "mb_client.h"
#include "pmsg_client.h"

int
send_msg_to_server(msg)
struct pmsg *msg;
{
    unsigned int *result;
    int retval;

/*      result = send_pmsg_1(&req, cl); */
/*      retval = *result; */

    if (retval != MSGD_OK) {
        pr_msg(NULL, TRUE, "Could not send phone message; reason: %s.",
            msgd_err[retval]);
        return FALSE;
    }
    else
        return TRUE;
}

struct pmsg_hdr *
get_pmsg_headers(user, cat, count)
```

```
char *user;
int cat, *count;
{
    struct pmsg_hdr *ph_ptr;

    *count = 0;
/*    result = scan_pmsg_1(&req, cl); */

#ifdef FIXITINTHEMIX
    if (result->ret_type != MSGD_OK)
        return (struct pmsg_hdr *)NULL;

    for (hl = result->scan_pmsg_data_u.list; hl != NULL; hl = hl->next) {
        if (*count == 0)
            ph_ptr = (struct pmsg_hdr *)malloc(sizeof(struct pmsg_hdr));
        else
            ph_ptr = (struct pmsg_hdr *)realloc(ph_ptr,
                                            sizeof(struct pmsg_hdr) *
                                                (*count + 1));
        ph_ptr[*count].desc = strdup(hl->desc);
        ph_ptr[*count].id = strdup(hl->tag);
        (*count)++;
    }
#endif

    return ph_ptr;
}

/*
 * Passed: user, cat, id, pointer to pmsg struct
 * Modifies: pointers to malloc'ed data in msg struct.
 */
int
get_pmsg(user, cat, id, msg)
char *user, *id;
int cat;
struct pmsg *msg;
{
    struct srv_pmsg *rmsg;
    int retval;

/*    result = read_pmsg_1(&req, cl); */

#ifdef FIXITINTHEMIX
    if (result->ret_type != MSGD_OK)
        return result->ret_type;

    rmsg = &(result->read_pmsg_data_u.msg);
    msg->id = strdup(rmsg->id);
    msg->caller = strdup(rmsg->caller);
    msg->time = strdup(rmsg->time);
    msg->org = strdup(rmsg->org);
    msg->phnum = strdup(rmsg->phnum);
    msg->flags = rmsg->flags;
    msg->text = strdup(rmsg->text);
#endif

    retval = MSGD_OK;
    return retval;
}
```

```
/*
 *  Frees all the malloc'ed items pointed to in the structure pointed
 *  to by mp.
 */
void
free_pmsg(mp)
struct pmsg *mp;
{
    free(mp->id);
    free(mp->caller);
    free(mp->time);
    free(mp->org);
    free(mp->phnum);
    free(mp->text);
}


/*
 *  Passed: current msg category, destination category, number of messages
 *     to move, list of message headers
 *  Returns: number of messages actually moved
 */
int
mv_msg_call(user, src, dest, num, list)
char *user;
int src, dest, num;
char **list;
{
    int *result, i;

/*    result = mv_pmsgs_1(&req, cl); */

    return *result;
}
```

pmsg_prt.c

```
/*
 * pmsg_prt.c - Phone message printing and drag'n'drop preparation routines.
 */

#include <stdio.h>
#include <stdlib.h>
#include <string.h>
#include <sys/param.h>
#include <sys/types.h>
#include <xview/xview.h>
#include <xview/panel.h>
#include "scanwin_ui.h"
#include "pmsg_prolog.h"
#include "msgboard.h"
#include "msgboard_xv.h"
#include "pmsg_client.h"


/*
 *  Pointer to scan window objects:
 */
extern scanwin_frame_objects *scan_ip;
extern scanwin_copy_frame_objects *copy_ip;
extern int num_msgs, msg_cat;
extern char cur_msg_user[];
```

```
/*
 *  These should be the same as the ones declared in pmsg_prt.c !
 */
char *messages[] = {
        "No message",
        "Returned your call",
        "Please call back",
        "Will call again",
        "Left following message"
        };

/*
 * Make sure parentheses and backslashes are escaped in strings heading for
 * PostScript-land.  The passed string MUST be one that has been malloc'ed!
 */
void
prep_string_4_ps(s)
char *s;
{
    char *tmp;
    int i, j, l;

    if (strpbrk(s, "()\") != CNULL) {
        tmp = malloc(strlen(s) * 2);
        j = -1;
        l = strlen(s);
        for (i = 0; i < l; i++) {
            if (s[i] == '(' || s[i] == ')' || s[i] == '\\')
            tmp[++j] = '\\';
            tmp[++j] = s[i];
        }
        tmp[++j] = '\0';
        free(s);
        s = realloc(tmp, strlen(tmp) + 1);
    }
}

/*
 * Print selected messages, in PostScript or pretty crude ASCII format.
 */
void
print_messages()
{
    int msg_to_print, msgs_printed, i;
    char *p, fullname[FNAME_LEN+1];
    FILE *outfile;
    struct pmsg pmsg;

    msg_to_print = (int)xv_get(scan_ip->list_item,PANEL_LIST_FIRST_SELECTED);
    if (msg_to_print == -1) {
      pr_msg(scan_ip->frame, TRUE, "No messages selected for printing");
      return;
    }

    if (prt_dest == TO_PRINTER) {
        p = malloc(strlen(prt_name) + 7);
        sprintf(p, "lpr -P%s", prt_name);
        outfile = popen(p, "w");
    }
    else {
        if (prt_file[0] == '/') {
            p = malloc(strlen(prt_file) + 1);
            strcpy(p, prt_file);
```

```
    }
    else {
        p = malloc(strlen(prt_dir) + strlen(prt_file) + 2);
        sprintf(p, "%s/%s", prt_dir, prt_file);
    }
    outfile = fopen(p, "w");
}
free(p);

if (outfile == FNULL) {
    if (prt_dest == TO_PRINTER)
        pr_msg(scan_ip->frame, TRUE, "Could not open pipe to printer!");
    else
        pr_msg(scan_ip->frame, TRUE, "Could not open print output file!");
    return;
}

if (prt_type == POSTSCRIPT)
    fputs(pmsg_prolog, outfile);

strcpy(fullname, get_fname(cur_msg_user));

msgs_printed = 0;
while (msg_to_print != -1) {
    get_pmsg(cur_msg_user, msg_cat,
        (char *)xv_get(scan_ip->list_item,
                PANEL_LIST_CLIENT_DATA, msg_to_print),
                &pmsg);

    if (prt_type == POSTSCRIPT) {
        fprintf(outfile, "StartMsg\n");
        prep_string_4_ps(pmsg.id);
        fprintf(outfile, "(%s) PrintSig\n", pmsg.id);
        prep_string_4_ps(fullname);
        fprintf(outfile, "(%s) PrintFor\n", fullname);
        prep_string_4_ps(pmsg.caller);
        fprintf(outfile, "(%s) PrintCaller\n", pmsg.caller);
        prep_string_4_ps(pmsg.time);
        fprintf(outfile, "(%s) PrintTime\n", strtok(pmsg.time, " "));
        fprintf(outfile, "(%s) PrintDate\n", strtok(CNULL, "\n"));
        prep_string_4_ps(pmsg.org);
        fprintf(outfile, "(%s) PrintOrg\n", pmsg.org);
        prep_string_4_ps(pmsg.phnum);
        fprintf(outfile, "(%s) PrintPhone\n", pmsg.phnum);
        for (i = 0; i <= SM_MAX_CHOICE; i++)
                if ( (pmsg.flags & (2 << i)) != 0 )
                    fprintf(outfile, "%d MarkMsg\n", i);
        if ((pmsg.flags & SM_CHOICE_LV_MSG) != 0) {
                fprintf(outfile, "(%s) PrintMsg\n", pmsg.text);
        }
        fprintf(outfile, "FinishMsg\n\n");
    }
    else {
        fprintf(outfile, "  Message by: %s\n", pmsg.id);
        fprintf(outfile, "          To: %s\n", fullname);
        fprintf(outfile, "      Caller: %s\n", pmsg.caller);
        fprintf(outfile, "        Time: %s\n", pmsg.time);
        fprintf(outfile, "Organization: %s\n", pmsg.org);
        fprintf(outfile, "       Phone: %s\n", pmsg.phnum);
        for (i = 0; i <= SM_MAX_CHOICE; i++)
                if ( (pmsg.flags & (2 << i)) != 0 )
                    fprintf(outfile, "     Message: %s\n", messages[i]);
```

```
            if ((pmsg.flags & SM_CHOICE_LV_MSG) != 0)
                    fprintf(outfile, "\n%s\n\n", pmsg.text);
        }

        free_pmsg(&pmsg);
        msgs_printed++;
        msg_to_print = (int)xv_get(scan_ip->list_item,
            PANEL_LIST_NEXT_SELECTED, msg_to_print);
    }

    if (prt_type == POSTSCRIPT)
        fprintf(outfile, "EndItAll\n");

    if (prt_dest == TO_PRINTER)
        pclose(outfile);
    else
        fclose(outfile);

    if (msgs_printed == 1)
        pr_msg(scan_ip->frame, FALSE, "One message printed");
    else
        pr_msg(scan_ip->frame, FALSE, "%d messages printed", msgs_printed);
}

/*
 * Prepare a file to drag'n'drop (V2).
 */
void
dnd_messages(outname)
char *outname;
{
    int msg_to_print, msgs_printed;
    FILE *outfile;
    struct pmsg pmsg;

    msg_to_print = (int)xv_get(scan_ip->list_item,
                    PANEL_LIST_FIRST_SELECTED);
    if (msg_to_print == -1) {
        pr_msg(scan_ip->frame, TRUE, "No messages selected for dragging");
        return;
    }

    outfile = fopen(outname, "w");
    if (outfile == FNULL) {
        pr_msg(scan_ip->frame, TRUE, "Could not open output file!");
        return;
    }

    msgs_printed = 0;
    while (msg_to_print != -1) {
        get_pmsg(cur_msg_user, msg_cat,
            (char *)xv_get(scan_ip->list_item,
                    PANEL_LIST_CLIENT_DATA, msg_to_print),
                    &pmsg);

        fprintf(outfile, "%s\n", pmsg.caller);
        fprintf(outfile, "%s\n", pmsg.time);
        fprintf(outfile, "%s\n", pmsg.org);
        fprintf(outfile, "%s\n", pmsg.phnum);
        if ((pmsg.flags & SM_CHOICE_LV_MSG) != 0)
            fprintf(outfile, "\n%s\n", pmsg.text);
        fprintf(outfile, "\n\n");
```

```
            free_pmsg(&pmsg);
            msgs_printed++;
            msg_to_print = (int)xv_get(scan_ip->list_item,
                PANEL_LIST_NEXT_SELECTED, msg_to_print);
        }
        fclose(outfile);

        if (msgs_printed == 1)
            pr_msg(scan_ip->frame, FALSE, "One message copied");
        else
            pr_msg(scan_ip->frame, FALSE, "%d messages copied", msgs_printed);
}


/*
 * Prepare a buffer containing the currently selected messages.  Returns
 * pointer to malloc'ed string, and assigns length of the string to
 * location "length" points to.
 */
char *
copy_messages(length)
unsigned long *length;
{
        int msg_to_print, msgs_printed, buflen, obuflen;
        struct pmsg pmsg;
        char *ptr;

        msg_to_print = (int)xv_get(scan_ip->list_item,PANEL_LIST_FIRST_SELECTED);
        if (msg_to_print == -1) {
            pr_msg(scan_ip->frame, TRUE, "No messages selected for clipboard");
            return;
        }

        ptr = strdup("");
        buflen = 1;

        msgs_printed = 0;
        while (msg_to_print != -1) {
            get_pmsg(cur_msg_user, msg_cat,
                (char *)xv_get(scan_ip->list_item,
                            PANEL_LIST_CLIENT_DATA, msg_to_print),
                            &pmsg);

            obuflen = buflen;
            buflen += strlen(pmsg.caller) + strlen(pmsg.time)
                + strlen(pmsg.org) + strlen(pmsg.phnum) + 6;
            ptr = realloc(ptr, buflen);
            sprintf(ptr + obuflen - 1, "%s\n%s\n%s\n%s\n",
                pmsg.caller, pmsg.time, pmsg.org, pmsg.phnum);

            if ((pmsg.flags & SM_CHOICE_LV_MSG) != 0) {
                obuflen = buflen;
                buflen += strlen(pmsg.text) + 2;
                ptr = realloc(ptr, buflen);
                sprintf(ptr + obuflen - 3, "\n%s\n", pmsg.text);
            }

            sprintf(ptr + buflen - 3, "\014\n");

            free_pmsg(&pmsg);
            msgs_printed++;
            msg_to_print = (int)xv_get(scan_ip->list_item,
                PANEL_LIST_NEXT_SELECTED, msg_to_print);
```

```
        }

    if (msgs_printed == 1)
        pr_msg(scan_ip->frame, FALSE, "One message copied");
    else
        pr_msg(scan_ip->frame, FALSE, "%d messages copied",
            msgs_printed);

    *length = buflen - 1;
    return ptr;
}


/*
 * Copy selected messages to specified file.
 */
void
sc_copy_to_file()
{
    int msg_to_print, msgs_printed, i;
    char fullname[FNAME_LEN+1], outfilename[MAXPATHLEN];
    FILE *outfile;
    struct pmsg pmsg;

    msg_to_print = (int)xv_get(scan_ip->list_item,
                                  PANEL_LIST_FIRST_SELECTED);
    if (msg_to_print == -1) {
        pr_msg(scan_ip->frame, TRUE, "No messages selected for printing");
        return;
    }
    strcpy(outfilename, (char *)xv_get(copy_ip->copy_file_item,
                                  PANEL_VALUE));
    if (outfilename[0] != '/')
        sprintf(outfilename, "%s/%s",
            (char *)xv_get(copy_ip->copy_dir_item, PANEL_VALUE),
            (char *)xv_get(copy_ip->copy_file_item, PANEL_VALUE));
    outfile = fopen(outfilename, "w");

    if (outfile == FNULL) {
        pr_msg(scan_ip->frame, TRUE, "Could not open %s!", outfilename);
        return;
    }

    strcpy(fullname, get_fname(cur_msg_user));

    msgs_printed = 0;
    while (msg_to_print != -1) {
        get_pmsg(cur_msg_user, msg_cat,
            (char *)xv_get(scan_ip->list_item,
                        PANEL_LIST_CLIENT_DATA, msg_to_print), &pmsg);

            fprintf(outfile, "  Message by: %s\n", pmsg.id);
            fprintf(outfile, "          To: %s\n", fullname);
            fprintf(outfile, "      Caller: %s\n", pmsg.caller);
            fprintf(outfile, "        Time: %s\n", pmsg.time);
            fprintf(outfile, "Organization: %s\n", pmsg.org);
            fprintf(outfile, "       Phone: %s\n", pmsg.phnum);
            for (i = 0; i <= SM_MAX_CHOICE; i++)
                    if ( (pmsg.flags & (2 << i)) != 0 )
                        fprintf(outfile, "     Message: %s\n", messages[i]);
        if ((pmsg.flags & SM_CHOICE_LV_MSG) != 0)
                fprintf(outfile, "\n%s\n\n", pmsg.text);
```

```
        free_pmsg(&pmsg);
        msgs_printed++;
        msg_to_print = (int)xv_get(scan_ip->list_item,
            PANEL_LIST_NEXT_SELECTED, msg_to_print);
    }

    fclose(outfile);

    if (msgs_printed == 1)
        pr_msg(scan_ip->frame, FALSE, "One message copied");
    else
        pr_msg(scan_ip->frame, FALSE, "%d messages copied", msgs_printed);
}
```

pmsgwin.c

```
/*
 * pmsgwin.c - Routines to support the phone message display window.
 */

#include <stdio.h>
#include <sys/param.h>
#include <sys/types.h>
#include <X11/Xlib.h>
#include <xview/xview.h>
#include <xview/panel.h>
#include <xview/textsw.h>
#include <xview/xv_xrect.h>
#include "pmsgwin_ui.h"
#include "scanwin_ui.h"
#include "msgboard.h"
#include "msgboard_xv.h"
#include "pmsg_client.h"

/*
 * Global object definitions.
 */
pmsgwin_frame_objects *smsg_ip;

extern char cur_msg_user[];
extern scanwin_frame_objects *scan_ip;
extern int msg_cat, cur_msg;
int
    smsg_window_created = FALSE; /* is message window created? */

void
create_smsg_window()
{
#ifdef SCALABLE
    int valx, ypos;
#endif

    Rect scan_rect, smsg_rect;
    int disp_ht;

    smsg_ip = pmsgwin_frame_objects_initialize(NULL, base_frame);
#ifdef SCALABLE
```

```
    /*
     *  Use "signed" to set the position for all the other text items
     */
    xv_set(smsg_ip->signed_item, XV_X, wgrid * 2, NULL);
    valx = (int)xv_get(smsg_ip->signed_item, PANEL_VALUE_X);

    ypos = wgrid * 2;
    align_values(smsg_ip->caller_item, valx, ypos);

    ypos += wgrid + (int)xv_get(smsg_ip->caller_item, XV_HEIGHT);
    align_values(smsg_ip->of_item, valx, ypos);

    ypos += wgrid + (int)xv_get(smsg_ip->of_item, XV_HEIGHT);
    align_values(smsg_ip->phone_item, valx, ypos);

    xv_set(smsg_ip->flags_item,
        XV_X,           (int)xv_get(smsg_ip->phone_item, XV_X) +
                        (int)xv_get(smsg_ip->phone_item, XV_WIDTH) + wgrid,
        XV_Y,           ypos,
        NULL);

    ypos += wgrid + (int)xv_get(smsg_ip->phone_item, XV_HEIGHT);
    align_values(smsg_ip->time_item, valx, ypos);

    ypos += wgrid * 2 + (int)xv_get(smsg_ip->time_item, XV_HEIGHT);
    xv_set(smsg_ip->signed_item, XV_Y, ypos, NULL);

    window_fit(smsg_ip->panel);

    xv_set(smsg_ip->textsw,
        XV_Y,           (int)xv_get(smsg_ip->panel, XV_HEIGHT),
        XV_WIDTH,       (int)xv_get(smsg_ip->panel, XV_WIDTH),
        NULL);

    xv_set(smsg_ip->frame,
        XV_HEIGHT, (int)xv_get(smsg_ip->panel, XV_HEIGHT) + wgrid * 6,
        NULL);

    window_fit_width(smsg_ip->frame);
#endif

    xv_set(smsg_ip->textsw,
        TEXTSW_BROWSING,        TRUE,
        TEXTSW_IGNORE_LIMIT, TEXTSW_INFINITY,   /* Turn off quit warning */
        TEXTSW_LOWER_CONTEXT,   -1,                 /* Turn off autoscroll */
        TEXTSW_UPPER_CONTEXT,   -1,
        TEXTSW_MEMORY_MAXIMUM, 100000,
        NULL);

    xv_set(smsg_ip->frame,
        FRAME_CMD_DEFAULT_PIN_STATE, FRAME_CMD_PIN_IN,
        NULL);

    /*
     *  Position frame immediately below scan window
     */
    disp_ht = DisplayHeight(dpy, DefaultScreen(dpy));

    frame_get_rect(scan_ip->frame, &scan_rect);
    frame_get_rect(smsg_ip->frame, &smsg_rect);
    smsg_rect.r_top = scan_rect.r_top + scan_rect.r_height;
    if ((smsg_rect.r_top + smsg_rect.r_height) > disp_ht)
```

```
        smsg_rect.r_top = disp_ht - smsg_rect.r_height;
    smsg_rect.r_left = scan_rect.r_left;
    frame_set_rect(smsg_ip->frame, &smsg_rect);

    smsg_window_created = TRUE;
}

/*
 *  Bring the message window up, showing the current message.
 *  Returns 0 if successful, error number if not.
 */
int
show_smsg_window()
{
    struct pmsg msg;
    int retval;
    char label[FNAME_LEN + 40];

    retval = get_pmsg(cur_msg_user, msg_cat,
        (char *)xv_get(scan_ip->list_item, PANEL_LIST_CLIENT_DATA,
        cur_msg), &msg);
    if (retval != MSGD_OK) return retval;

    if (!smsg_window_created) create_smsg_window();

    textsw_reset(smsg_ip->textsw, 0, 0);
    if ((msg.flags & SM_CHOICE_LV_MSG) != 0) {
        textsw_insert(smsg_ip->textsw, msg.text, strlen(msg.text));
        textsw_normalize_view(smsg_ip->textsw, 0);
    }

    xv_set(smsg_ip->signed_item, PANEL_VALUE, msg.id, NULL);
    xv_set(smsg_ip->caller_item, PANEL_VALUE, msg.caller, NULL);
    xv_set(smsg_ip->time_item, PANEL_VALUE, msg.time, NULL);
    xv_set(smsg_ip->of_item, PANEL_VALUE, msg.org, NULL);
    xv_set(smsg_ip->phone_item, PANEL_VALUE, msg.phnum, NULL);
    xv_set(smsg_ip->flags_item, PANEL_VALUE, msg.flags >> 1, NULL);
    free_pmsg(&msg);

    sprintf(label, "Message Board: Message %d for %s", cur_msg + 1,
        get_fname(cur_msg_user));
    xv_set(smsg_ip->frame,
        XV_SHOW,   TRUE,
        XV_LABEL, label,
        NULL);
    return retval;
}

/*
 *  Returns true if showmsg window is created and currently visible
 */
int
smsg_is_up()
{
    return (smsg_window_created && (int)xv_get(smsg_ip->frame, XV_SHOW));
}

/*
 *  Clears the message display window
 */
void
clear_smsg_window()
```

```
{
    if (!smsg_window_created) return;

    xv_set(smsg_ip->caller_item, PANEL_VALUE, "", NULL);
    xv_set(smsg_ip->of_item, PANEL_VALUE, "", NULL);
    xv_set(smsg_ip->phone_item, PANEL_VALUE, "", NULL);
    xv_set(smsg_ip->time_item, PANEL_VALUE, "", NULL);
    xv_set(smsg_ip->signed_item, PANEL_VALUE, "", NULL);
    xv_set(smsg_ip->flags_item, PANEL_VALUE, 0, NULL);
    textsw_reset(smsg_ip->textsw, 0, 0);
    xv_set(smsg_ip->frame, FRAME_LABEL, "Message Board: No Message Selected",
                                                        NULL);
}

void
dismiss_smsg_window()
{
    if (smsg_window_created)
        xv_set(smsg_ip->frame,
            FRAME_CMD_PIN_STATE, FRAME_CMD_PIN_OUT,
            XV_SHOW, FALSE,
            NULL);
}

/*
 * Event callback function for 'flags_item'.
 *  This function's purpose in life is silently to consume SELECT actions
 *  on the checkboxes, causing them to be effectively read-only.
 */
void
scm_flags_event(item, event)
Panel_item item;
Event *event;
{
    if (event_action(event) != ACTION_SELECT && event_action(event) !=
        LOC_DRAG)
        panel_default_handle_event(item, event);
}

/*
 * Done callback function for 'frame'.
 */
void
pmsg_done_proc(frame)
Frame frame;
{
    pr_msg(scan_ip->frame, FALSE, "");
    xv_set(frame, XV_SHOW, FALSE, NULL);
}
```

`propswin.c`

```
/*
 * propswin.c - Support for Message Board properties window.
 *   There are currently three property sheets defined: user, outs and
 *   global.  User contains general properties, outs allows definition of
 *   entries on the "Outs" button, and global defines global
 *   properties, which may only be altered by users in admin mode.
 */
```

```c
#include <stdio.h>
#include <sys/param.h>
#include <sys/types.h>
#include <xview/xview.h>
#include <xview/panel.h>
#include <xview/textsw.h>
#include <xview/notice.h>
#include "propswin_ui.h"
#include "msgboard.h"
#include "msgboard_xv.h"
#include "outs_menu.h"

#define PROPS_CAT_GENERAL 0
#define PROPS_CAT_OUTS 1
#define PROPS_CAT_GLOBAL 2

#define ADD_BEFORE 43
#define ADD_AFTER 44

propswin_frame_objects *props_ip;

int
    props_window_created = FALSE,/* is props window created?*/
    outs_changes_pending = FALSE,
    temp_num_outs = 0;

struct outent *temp_outlist = NULL;

/*
 * Configures the print-related items, based on current panel settings.
 */
void
set_prt_items(dest, type)
int dest, type;
{
    if (dest == TO_PRINTER) {
        xv_set(props_ip->prt_dir_item,
            PANEL_LABEL_STRING,"Printer:",
            PANEL_VALUE,prt_name,
            NULL);
        xv_set(props_ip->prt_file_item,
            XV_SHOW, FALSE,
            NULL);
    }
    else {
        xv_set(props_ip->prt_dir_item,
            PANEL_LABEL_STRING,"Directory:",
            PANEL_VALUE,prt_dir,
            NULL);

        if ((type == POSTSCRIPT) && (strcmp(prt_file, "msgs.txt") == 0))
            xv_set(props_ip->prt_file_item,
                    PANEL_VALUE,   "msgs.ps",
                    XV_SHOW, TRUE,
                    NULL);
        else if ((type == ASCII) && (strcmp(prt_file, "msgs.ps") == 0))
            xv_set(props_ip->prt_file_item,
                    PANEL_VALUE, "msgs.txt",
                    XV_SHOW,        TRUE,
                    NULL);
```

```
            else
                xv_set(props_ip->prt_file_item,
                        PANEL_VALUE, prt_file,
                        XV_SHOW,        TRUE,
                        NULL);
    }
}

/*
 *  Checks to see whether cat_item should be modified to have the "global"
 *  entry added or removed.
 */
void
modify_cat_item(needs_global)
int needs_global;
{
    static int has_global = BOGUS;   /* Initialized to neither true nor
                                          false */

    if (needs_global == has_global) return;

    if (has_global == BOGUS) {
        has_global = ((int)xv_get(props_ip->cat_item, PANEL_NCHOICES) >
            PROPS_CAT_GLOBAL);
        if (needs_global == has_global) return;
    }

    if (needs_global)
        xv_set(props_ip->cat_item,
            PANEL_CHOICE_STRING,PROPS_CAT_GLOBAL, "Global",
            NULL);
    else {
        xv_destroy(props_ip->cat_item);
        props_ip->cat_item =
            propswin_frame_cat_item_create(props_ip, props_ip->cat_panel);
    }
    has_global = needs_global;
}

/*
 *  Exposes the proper panel for the properties category they've selected.
 */
void
show_props_cat(cat)
int cat;
{
    xv_set(props_ip->general_panel, XV_SHOW, cat == PROPS_CAT_GENERAL, NULL);
    xv_set(props_ip->outs_panel, XV_SHOW, cat == PROPS_CAT_OUTS, NULL);
    xv_set(props_ip->global_panel, XV_SHOW, cat == PROPS_CAT_GLOBAL, NULL);
}

/*
 *  Makes a temporary duplicate of the list of "outs" options for us to
 *  work with.
 */
void
make_temp_outlist()
{
    int i;

    temp_outlist =
        (struct outent *)malloc((unsigned)(sizeof(struct outent)*num_outs));
```

```
    for ( i = 0 ; i < num_outs ; i++ ) {
        temp_outlist[i].label = strdup(outlist[i].label);
        temp_outlist[i].until = strdup(outlist[i].until);
        temp_outlist[i].message = strdup(outlist[i].message);
        temp_outlist[i].pop = outlist[i].pop;
    }
    temp_num_outs = num_outs;
}


/*
 *  Destroys the list of "outs" options passed to it
 */
void
destroy_outlist(lp, n)
struct outent **lp;
int *n;
{
    int i;
    struct outent *l;

    l = *lp;
    for ( i = 0 ; i < *n ; i++ ) {
        free(l[i].label);
        free(l[i].until);
        free(l[i].message);
    }
    *n = 0;
    free(l);
    *lp = (struct outent *)NULL;
}

void
prep_props_window()
{
    int i, flags;

    if (!admin &&
        (int)xv_get(props_ip->cat_item, PANEL_VALUE) == PROPS_CAT_GLOBAL)
        xv_set(props_ip->cat_item, PANEL_VALUE, PROPS_CAT_GENERAL, NULL);
    modify_cat_item(admin);
    xv_set(props_ip->intvl_item, PANEL_VALUE, delay, NULL);
    xv_set(props_ip->server_item, PANEL_VALUE, mb_server, NULL);
    xv_set(props_ip->prt_type_item, PANEL_VALUE, prt_type, NULL);
    xv_set(props_ip->prt_dest_item, PANEL_VALUE, prt_dest, NULL);
    set_prt_items(prt_dest, prt_type);
    xv_set(props_ip->dragstyle_item, PANEL_VALUE, dragstyle - 2, NULL);
    xv_set(props_ip->pop_mod_item, PANEL_VALUE, pop_mod, NULL);
    xv_set(props_ip->fmt_item, PANEL_VALUE, fmt_msgs, NULL);
    xv_set(props_ip->admin_item,
        PANEL_VALUE, admin_enable,
        XV_SHOW, myentry != (struct mem_rec *)NULL &&
                            (myentry->flags & MB_ADMIN) != 0,
        NULL);
    xv_set(props_ip->site_item,
        PANEL_VALUE, globrec.name,
        NULL);
    xv_set(props_ip->motd_item,
        PANEL_VALUE, globrec.motd,
        NULL);
    xv_set(props_ip->fname_fmt_item,
        PANEL_VALUE, (globrec.flags & MB_G_LASTNM1ST) != 0,
        NULL);
```

```
        flags =((globrec.flags & MB_G_CHG_PLAN) != 0) +
                      ((globrec.flags & MB_G_PRESERVE) != 0) * 2 +
                      ((globrec.flags & MB_G_VIA_MAIL) != 0) * 4 +
                      ((globrec.flags & MB_G_VIA_MB) != 0) * 8;
    xv_set(props_ip->flags_item,
       PANEL_VALUE, flags,
       NULL);

    xv_set(props_ip->pgr_type_item,
       PANEL_VALUE, globrec.pagertype,
       NULL);

    /*
     *  Prepare the "outs" panel
     */
    i = (int)xv_get(props_ip->outs_list, PANEL_LIST_NROWS);
    if ( i > 0 )
        xv_set(props_ip->outs_list, PANEL_LIST_DELETE_ROWS, 0, i, NULL);
    for ( i = 0 ; i < num_outs ; i++ )
      xv_set(props_ip->outs_list,
          PANEL_LIST_INSERT,i,
          PANEL_LIST_STRING,i, outlist[i].label,
          NULL);
    xv_set(props_ip->outs_label_item, PANEL_VALUE, "", NULL);
    xv_set(props_ip->outs_until_item,
       PANEL_VALUE, "",
       PANEL_INACTIVE, TRUE,
       NULL);
    xv_set(props_ip->outs_msg_item,
       PANEL_VALUE, "",
       PANEL_INACTIVE, TRUE,
       NULL);
    xv_set(props_ip->outs_pop_item,
       PANEL_VALUE, FALSE,
       PANEL_INACTIVE, TRUE,
       NULL);
    xv_set(props_ip->outs_add_item, PANEL_INACTIVE, TRUE, NULL);
    xv_set(props_ip->outs_change_item, PANEL_INACTIVE, TRUE, NULL);
    xv_set(props_ip->outs_delete_item, PANEL_INACTIVE, TRUE, NULL);
    if (temp_outlist != NULL) {
        destroy_outlist(&temp_outlist, &temp_num_outs);
        temp_outlist = NULL;
    }
    outs_changes_pending = FALSE;

    show_props_cat((int)xv_get(props_ip->cat_item, PANEL_VALUE));
}

void outs_add_menu_notify();

void
create_props_window()
{
#ifdef SCALABLE
    int valx, ypos;
#endif

    props_ip = propswin_frame_objects_initialize(NULL, base_frame);

    xv_set((Menu)xv_get(props_ip->outs_add_item, PANEL_ITEM_MENU),
       MENU_NOTIFY_PROC, outs_add_menu_notify, NULL);
```

```
        xv_set(props_ip->outs_label_item, PANEL_NOTIFY_LEVEL, PANEL_ALL, NULL);

#ifdef SCALABLE
    /*
     *  Position the category item on the category panel...
     */
    xv_set(props_ip->cat_item,
        XV_X,           wgrid * 2,
        XV_Y,           wgrid * 2,
        NULL);
    window_fit_height(props_ip->cat_panel);

    /*
     *  Position the general, outs and global panels just under the category
     *  panel...
     */
    ypos = xv_get(props_ip->cat_panel, XV_HEIGHT);
    xv_set(props_ip->general_panel, XV_Y, ypos, NULL);
    xv_set(props_ip->outs_panel, XV_Y, ypos, NULL);
    xv_set(props_ip->global_panel, XV_Y, ypos, NULL);

    /*
     *  Position items on the general panel.
     *  message1 is the word "seconds", which is a label to be placed
     *  immediately after the interval item.
     */
    ypos = wgrid * 2;
    xv_set(props_ip->intvl_item,
        XV_X,           wgrid * 2,
        XV_Y,           ypos,
        NULL);
    valx = (int)xv_get(props_ip->intvl_item, PANEL_VALUE_X);
    xv_set(props_ip->message1,
        XV_X,           wgrid * 3 + (int)xv_get(props_ip->intvl_item, XV_WIDTH),
        XV_Y,           wgrid * 2,
        NULL);

    ypos += wgrid + (int)xv_get(props_ip->intvl_item, XV_HEIGHT);
    align_values(props_ip->server_item, valx, ypos);

    ypos += wgrid * 2 + (int)xv_get(props_ip->server_item, XV_HEIGHT);
    align_values(props_ip->prt_type_item, valx, ypos);

    ypos += wgrid + (int)xv_get(props_ip->prt_type_item, XV_HEIGHT);
    align_values(props_ip->prt_dest_item, valx, ypos);

    ypos += wgrid + (int)xv_get(props_ip->prt_dest_item, XV_HEIGHT);
    align_values(props_ip->prt_dir_item, valx, ypos);

    ypos += wgrid + (int)xv_get(props_ip->prt_dir_item, XV_HEIGHT);
    align_values(props_ip->prt_file_item, valx, ypos);

    ypos += wgrid * 2 + (int)xv_get(props_ip->prt_file_item, XV_HEIGHT);
    align_values(props_ip->dragstyle_item, valx, ypos);

    ypos += wgrid * 2 + (int)xv_get(props_ip->dragstyle_item, XV_HEIGHT);
    xv_set(props_ip->pop_mod_item, XV_X, wgrid * 2, XV_Y, ypos, NULL);

    ypos += wgrid / 2 + (int)xv_get(props_ip->pop_mod_item, XV_HEIGHT);
    xv_set(props_ip->fmt_item, XV_X, wgrid * 2, XV_Y, ypos, NULL);
    ypos += wgrid / 2 + (int)xv_get(props_ip->fmt_item, XV_HEIGHT);
```

```
    xv_set(props_ip->admin_item, XV_X, wgrid * 2, XV_Y, ypos, NULL);
    window_fit(props_ip->general_panel);

    /*
     *  Position items on the outs panel.
     *  "Outs List" is the widest text item label on this list...
     */
    xv_set(props_ip->outs_list,
        XV_X, wgrid * 2,
        XV_Y, wgrid * 2,
        NULL);
    valx = (int)xv_get(props_ip->outs_list, PANEL_VALUE_X);

    ypos = wgrid * 3 + (int)xv_get(props_ip->outs_list, XV_HEIGHT);
    align_values(props_ip->outs_label_item, valx, ypos);

    ypos += wgrid + (int)xv_get(props_ip->outs_label_item, XV_HEIGHT);
    align_values(props_ip->outs_until_item, valx, ypos);

    ypos += wgrid + (int)xv_get(props_ip->outs_until_item, XV_HEIGHT);
    align_values(props_ip->outs_msg_item, valx, ypos);

    ypos += wgrid + (int)xv_get(props_ip->outs_msg_item, XV_HEIGHT);
    align_values(props_ip->outs_pop_item, valx, ypos);

    valx = (int)xv_get(props_ip->outs_change_item, XV_WIDTH);
    xv_set(props_ip->outs_add_item, PANEL_LABEL_WIDTH,
        (int)xv_get(props_ip->outs_add_item, PANEL_LABEL_WIDTH) + valx -
        (int)xv_get(props_ip->outs_add_item, XV_WIDTH), NULL);
    xv_set(props_ip->outs_delete_item, PANEL_LABEL_WIDTH,
        (int)xv_get(props_ip->outs_delete_item, PANEL_LABEL_WIDTH) + valx -
        (int)xv_get(props_ip->outs_delete_item, XV_WIDTH), NULL);

    valx = wgrid * 3 + (int)xv_get(props_ip->outs_list, XV_WIDTH);
    ypos = wgrid * 2 + (int)xv_get(props_ip->outs_list, XV_HEIGHT) / 2 -
        (int)xv_get(props_ip->outs_delete_item, XV_HEIGHT) / 2;
    xv_set(props_ip->outs_delete_item,
        XV_X, valx,
        XV_Y, ypos,
        NULL);

    xv_set(props_ip->outs_add_item,
        XV_X, valx,
        XV_Y, ypos - wgrid - (int)xv_get(props_ip->outs_add_item, XV_HEIGHT),
        NULL);

    xv_set(props_ip->outs_change_item,
        XV_X, valx,
        XV_Y, ypos + wgrid + (int)xv_get(props_ip->outs_delete_item,
                                            XV_HEIGHT),
        NULL);
    window_fit(props_ip->outs_panel);

    /*
     *  Position items on the global panel.
     *  First group is sitename and motd:
     */
    xv_set(props_ip->site_item,
        XV_X, wgrid * 2,
        XV_Y, wgrid * 2,
        NULL);
```

```
    ypos = wgrid * 3 + (int)xv_get(props_ip->site_item, XV_HEIGHT);
    valx = (int)xv_get(props_ip->site_item, PANEL_VALUE_X);
    align_values(props_ip->motd_item, valx, ypos);

    /*
     * Remainder are grouped together.  "Defaults Pager Type" is longest
     * label:
     */
    xv_set(props_ip->pgr_type_item, XV_X, wgrid * 2, NULL);
    valx = (int)xv_get(props_ip->pgr_type_item, PANEL_VALUE_X);

    ypos += wgrid * 2 + (int)xv_get(props_ip->motd_item, XV_HEIGHT);
    align_values(props_ip->fname_fmt_item, valx, ypos);

    ypos += wgrid + (int)xv_get(props_ip->fname_fmt_item, XV_HEIGHT);
    align_values(props_ip->flags_item, valx, ypos);

    ypos += wgrid + (int)xv_get(props_ip->flags_item, XV_HEIGHT);
    align_values(props_ip->pgr_type_item, valx, ypos);

    window_fit(props_ip->global_panel);

    /*
     * Final sizing of the middle panels.  Assumes global panel
     * is the widest, general panel is the tallest.
     */
    valx = (int)xv_get(props_ip->global_panel, XV_WIDTH, NULL);
    ypos = (int)xv_get(props_ip->general_panel, XV_HEIGHT, NULL);
    xv_set(props_ip->general_panel,
        XV_WIDTH, valx,
        NULL);
    xv_set(props_ip->outs_panel,
        XV_WIDTH, valx,
        XV_HEIGHT, ypos,
        NULL);
    xv_set(props_ip->global_panel,
        XV_HEIGHT, ypos,
        NULL);
    xv_set(props_ip->apply_panel,
        XV_Y,          (int)xv_get(props_ip->general_panel, XV_Y) + ypos,
        NULL);

    /*
     * Position items in the apply panel
     */
    xv_set(props_ip->apply_item, XV_Y, wgrid, NULL);
    xv_set(props_ip->reset_item, XV_Y, wgrid, NULL);
    window_fit_height(props_ip->apply_panel);

    window_fit(props_ip->frame);
    position_bot_buttons(props_ip->apply_panel, props_ip->apply_item,
        props_ip->reset_item);
#endif

    props_window_created = TRUE;
}

void
show_props_window()
{
    if (!props_window_created) create_props_window();
```

```
        prep_props_window();
        xv_set(props_ip->frame, XV_SHOW, TRUE, NULL);
}

void
props_apply_changes()
{
    int has_admin_caps;

    /*
     *  If they changed the delay value, process accordingly
     */
    if (delay != (int)xv_get(props_ip->intvl_item, PANEL_VALUE)) {
        delay = (int)xv_get(props_ip->intvl_item, PANEL_VALUE);
        set_timer(TRUE);
    }

    prt_type = (int)xv_get(props_ip->prt_type_item, PANEL_VALUE);
    prt_dest = (int)xv_get(props_ip->prt_dest_item, PANEL_VALUE);
    if (prt_dest == TO_PRINTER) {
        strncpy(prt_name, (char *)xv_get(props_ip->prt_dir_item, PANEL_VALUE),
            PRINTERNAME_LEN);
        prt_name[PRINTERNAME_LEN] = '\0';
    }
    else {
        strncpy(prt_dir, (char *)xv_get(props_ip->prt_dir_item, PANEL_VALUE),
            MAXPATHLEN);
        prt_dir[MAXPATHLEN - 1] = '\0';
        strncpy(prt_file, (char *)xv_get(props_ip->prt_file_item,
            PANEL_VALUE), 81);
        prt_file[80] = '\0';
    }

    /*
     *  Did they change the outs list?
     */
    if ( temp_outlist != NULL ) {
        destroy_outlist(&outlist, &num_outs);
        outlist = temp_outlist;
        temp_outlist = NULL;
        num_outs = temp_num_outs;
        redo_outs_menu();
    }

    if ((int)xv_get(props_ip->dragstyle_item, PANEL_VALUE) != dragstyle - 2){
        if ( (int)xv_get(props_ip->dragstyle_item, PANEL_VALUE) == 0 )
            dragstyle = 2;
        else
            dragstyle = 3;
        set_scanwin_items_status();
    }

    pop_mod = (int)xv_get(props_ip->pop_mod_item, PANEL_VALUE);

    /*
     *  Did they change message formatting?
     */
    if (fmt_msgs != (int)xv_get(props_ip->fmt_item, PANEL_VALUE)) {
        fmt_msgs = !fmt_msgs;
        set_sendwin_items_status();
    }
    admin_enable = (int)xv_get(props_ip->admin_item, PANEL_VALUE);
```

```
   /*
    *  Are they allowed to go into admin mode?
    */
   has_admin_caps = myentry != (Mem_Rec *)NULL &&
                               (myentry->flags & MB_ADMIN) != 0;


   /*
    *  Did they ask to go into or out of admin mode?
    */
   if ( admin != (has_admin_caps && admin_enable) ) {
     admin = (has_admin_caps && admin_enable);
     update_global_display();
     set_mainwin_items_status();
   }


   /*
    *  saves global variables
    */
   if (has_admin_caps) {
     Global_Rec new_glob;
     int flags;

     strcpy(new_glob.name, (char *)xv_get(props_ip->site_item,
                                          PANEL_VALUE));
     strcpy(new_glob.motd, (char *)xv_get(props_ip->motd_item,
                                          PANEL_VALUE));
     new_glob.flags = 0;
     if ((int)xv_get(props_ip->fname_fmt_item, PANEL_VALUE))
         new_glob.flags |= MB_G_LASTNM1ST;
     flags = (int)xv_get(props_ip->flags_item, PANEL_VALUE);
     if ((flags & 1) != 0) new_glob.flags |= MB_G_CHG_PLAN;
     if ((flags & 2) != 0) new_glob.flags |= MB_G_PRESERVE;
     if ((flags & 4) != 0) new_glob.flags |= MB_G_VIA_MAIL;
     if ((flags & 8) != 0) new_glob.flags |= MB_G_VIA_MB;
     new_glob.pagertype = (int)xv_get(props_ip->pgr_type_item,
                                      PANEL_VALUE);

     modify_global_values(&new_glob);
   }


   /*
    *  Save user-specific program parameters to PARAMFILE:
    */
   save_params();


   /*
    *  If they asked to change servers, do it last.
    */

   if ( strcmp(mb_server, (char *)xv_get(props_ip->server_item,
       PANEL_VALUE)) != 0 ) {
       strcpy(mb_server, (char *)xv_get(props_ip->server_item, PANEL_VALUE));
       if(connect_to_server()) (void)get_modified_records();
   }

   prep_props_window();
}
/*
 *  Called whenever we change categories or dismiss the window; checks
 *  whether there are pending changes for this category.
 */
```

```c
int
props_ok_to_leave()
{
    int cat = (int)xv_get(props_ip->cat_item, PANEL_VALUE);
    int retval = TRUE;
    Xv_Notice notice;

    if ( cat == PROPS_CAT_GENERAL ) {
        /*
         *  This is a real knot.  Apologies to anyone who has to figure it
         *  out...all we're trying to do is see if anything was changed.
         */
        if ( (int)xv_get(props_ip->intvl_item, PANEL_VALUE) != delay ||
            strcmp((char *)xv_get(props_ip->server_item, PANEL_VALUE),
                    mb_server) != 0 ||
            (int)xv_get(props_ip->prt_type_item, PANEL_VALUE) != prt_type ||
            (int)xv_get(props_ip->prt_dest_item, PANEL_VALUE) != prt_dest ||
            (int)xv_get(props_ip->dragstyle_item, PANEL_VALUE) !=
                    (dragstyle - 2) ||
            (int)xv_get(props_ip->pop_mod_item, PANEL_VALUE) != pop_mod ||
            (int)xv_get(props_ip->fmt_item, PANEL_VALUE) != fmt_msgs ||
            (int)xv_get(props_ip->admin_item, PANEL_VALUE) != admin_enable )
            retval = FALSE;
        else {
            if ( (int)xv_get(props_ip->prt_dest_item, PANEL_VALUE ) ==
                TO_PRINTER ) {
                if ( strcmp((char *)xv_get(props_ip->prt_dir_item,
                                    PANEL_VALUE),
                            prt_name) != 0 )
                            retval = FALSE;
            }
            else {
                    if ( strcmp((char *)xv_get(props_ip->prt_dir_item,
                                        PANEL_VALUE),
                        prt_dir) != 0 ||
                                strcmp((char*)xv_get
                                (props_ip->prt_file_item,
                        PANEL_VALUE), prt_file)
                                != 0 )
                                retval = FALSE;
                }
            }
        }
    }
    else if (cat == PROPS_CAT_OUTS ) {
        if ( outs_changes_pending ||
            strlen((char *)xv_get(props_ip->outs_label_item, PANEL_VALUE)) >0)
            retval = FALSE;
    }
    else if (cat == PROPS_CAT_GLOBAL ) {
        int flags = ((globrec.flags & MB_G_CHG_PLAN) != 0) +
            ((globrec.flags & MB_G_PRESERVE) != 0) * 2 +
            ((globrec.flags & MB_G_VIA_MAIL) != 0) * 4 +
            ((globrec.flags & MB_G_VIA_MB) != 0) * 8;

        if ( strcmp((char *)xv_get(props_ip->site_item, PANEL_VALUE),
                globrec.name) != 0 ||
            strcmp((char *)xv_get(props_ip->motd_item, PANEL_VALUE),
                globrec.motd) != 0 ||
            (int)xv_get(props_ip->fname_fmt_item, PANEL_VALUE) !=
                ((globrec.flags & MB_G_LASTNM1ST) != 0) ||
```

```
                (int)xv_get(props_ip->flags_item, PANEL_VALUE) != flags )
            retval = FALSE;
    }

    if ( retval == FALSE ) {
        notice = xv_create(props_ip->frame, NOTICE,
            NOTICE_MESSAGE_STRINGS,
                "Changes to this category have not been applied.",
                                        NULL,
            NOTICE_BUTTON, "Apply Changes", 42,
            NOTICE_BUTTON, "Discard Changes", TRUE,
            NOTICE_BUTTON, "Cancel", FALSE,
            NOTICE_STATUS, &retval,
            XV_SHOW, TRUE,
            NULL);

        xv_destroy_safe(notice);
    }

    if (retval == 42) {
        props_apply_changes();
        retval = TRUE;
    }

    return retval;
}

void
props_out_add(where)
int where;
{
    int i, new_row;

    if (temp_outlist == NULL) make_temp_outlist();

    new_row = (int)xv_get(props_ip->outs_list, PANEL_LIST_FIRST_SELECTED);
    if (where == ADD_AFTER) {
        if (new_row == -1)
            new_row = (int)xv_get(props_ip->outs_list, PANEL_LIST_NROWS);
        else
            new_row++;
    }
    else if (new_row == -1)
        new_row = 0;

    temp_num_outs++;
    temp_outlist = (struct outent *)realloc((char *)temp_outlist,
        (unsigned)(sizeof(struct outent)*temp_num_outs));
        for ( i = temp_num_outs - 1 ; i > new_row ; i--) {
            temp_outlist[i].label = temp_outlist[i-1].label;
            temp_outlist[i].until = temp_outlist[i-1].until;
            temp_outlist[i].message = temp_outlist[i-1].message;
            temp_outlist[i].pop = temp_outlist[i-1].pop;
    }
    temp_outlist[new_row].label =
            strdup((char *)xv_get(props_ip->outs_label_item, PANEL_VALUE));
    temp_outlist[new_row].until =
            strdup((char *)xv_get(props_ip->outs_until_item, PANEL_VALUE));
    temp_outlist[new_row].message =
            strdup((char *)xv_get(props_ip->outs_msg_item, PANEL_VALUE));
    temp_outlist[new_row].pop =
            (int)xv_get(props_ip->outs_pop_item, PANEL_VALUE);
```

```c
    xv_set(props_ip->outs_list,
        PANEL_LIST_INSERT, new_row,
        PANEL_LIST_STRING, new_row, temp_outlist[new_row].label,
        PANEL_LIST_SELECT, new_row, TRUE,
        NULL);

    xv_set(props_ip->outs_change_item, PANEL_INACTIVE, FALSE, NULL);
    xv_set(props_ip->outs_delete_item, PANEL_INACTIVE, FALSE, NULL);

    outs_changes_pending = TRUE;
}

void
props_out_change()
{
    int drow;

    drow = (int)xv_get(props_ip->outs_list, PANEL_LIST_FIRST_SELECTED);

    if (temp_outlist == NULL) make_temp_outlist();

    free(temp_outlist[drow].label);
    free(temp_outlist[drow].until);
    free(temp_outlist[drow].message);
    temp_outlist[drow].label =
        strdup((char *)xv_get(props_ip->outs_label_item, PANEL_VALUE));
    temp_outlist[drow].until =
        strdup((char *)xv_get(props_ip->outs_until_item, PANEL_VALUE));
    temp_outlist[drow].message =
        strdup((char *)xv_get(props_ip->outs_msg_item, PANEL_VALUE));
    temp_outlist[drow].pop =
        (int)xv_get(props_ip->outs_pop_item, PANEL_VALUE);
    xv_set(props_ip->outs_list,
        PANEL_LIST_STRING, drow, temp_outlist[drow].label,
        NULL);

    outs_changes_pending = TRUE;
}


/*
 * Notify callback function for 'outs_label_item'.
 */
Panel_setting
props_outs_label_notify(item, event)
Panel_item item;
Event *event;
{
    int flag;

    flag = strlen((char *)xv_get(item, PANEL_VALUE)) == 0;

    xv_set(props_ip->outs_until_item, PANEL_INACTIVE, flag, NULL);
    xv_set(props_ip->outs_msg_item, PANEL_INACTIVE, flag, NULL);
    xv_set(props_ip->outs_pop_item, PANEL_INACTIVE, flag, NULL);
    xv_set(props_ip->outs_add_item, PANEL_INACTIVE, flag, NULL);

    return panel_text_notify(item, event);
}

/*
 * Notify callback function for 'reset_item'.
 */
```

```
void
props_reset_notify(item, event)
Panel_item item;
Event *event;
{
    prep_props_window();
}


/*
 * Notify callback function for 'cat_item'.
 */
void
props_cat_notify(item, value, event)
Panel_item item;
int value;
Event *event;
{
    show_props_cat(value);
}


/*
 * Notify callback function for 'prt_dest_item' and 'prt_type_item'.
 */
void
props_prt_settings_notify(item, value, event)
Panel_item item;
int value;
Event *event;
{
    int dest, type;

    if (item == props_ip->prt_dest_item) {
        dest = value;
        type = (int)xv_get(props_ip->prt_type_item, PANEL_VALUE);
    }
    else {
        type = value;
        dest = (int)xv_get(props_ip->prt_dest_item, PANEL_VALUE);
    }
    set_prt_items(dest, type);
}


/*
 * Notify callback function for 'apply_item'.
 */
void
props_apply_notify(item, event)
Panel_item item;
Event *event;
{
    int s, retval = TRUE;
    Xv_Notice notice;

    /*
     * The Outs category requires special treatment, as it is possible to
     * have started to make changes but not have completed them.
     */
    if ( (int)xv_get(props_ip->cat_item, PANEL_VALUE) != PROPS_CAT_OUTS)
      props_apply_changes();

    if ( ( s = (int)xv_get(props_ip->outs_list, PANEL_LIST_FIRST_SELECTED))
        == -1 ) {
```

```
        if ( strlen((char *)xv_get(props_ip->outs_label_item, PANEL_VALUE))
                                                            > 0 ) {
            notice = xv_create(props_ip->frame, NOTICE,
                    NOTICE_MESSAGE_STRINGS,
                    "You have not finished adding this item.",
                    "You may add it to the list, discard it, or",
                    "cancel the Apply:",
                    NULL,
                    NOTICE_BUTTON, "Add to Top", ADD_BEFORE,
                    NOTICE_BUTTON, "Add to Bottom", ADD_AFTER,
                    NOTICE_BUTTON, "Discard", TRUE,
                    NOTICE_BUTTON, "Cancel", FALSE,
                    NOTICE_STATUS, &retval,
                    XV_SHOW, TRUE,
                    NULL);
            xv_destroy_safe(notice);
        }
    }
    else {
        if (temp_outlist == NULL) make_temp_outlist();

        if ( strcmp(temp_outlist[s].label,
            (char *)xv_get(props_ip->outs_label_item, PANEL_VALUE))
                                                        != 0 ||
            strcmp(temp_outlist[s].until,
            (char *)xv_get(props_ip->outs_until_item, PANEL_VALUE))
                                                        != 0 ||
            strcmp(temp_outlist[s].message,
            (char *)xv_get(props_ip->outs_msg_item, PANEL_VALUE)) != 0 ||
            temp_outlist[s].pop !=
            (int)xv_get(props_ip->outs_pop_item, PANEL_VALUE)) {
            notice = xv_create(props_ip->frame, NOTICE,
                    NOTICE_MESSAGE_STRINGS,
                                        "You have not finished adding or
                                            changing this",
                                        "item.  You may change the
                                            selected item on the",
                                        "list, add a new item, discard
                                            your changes, or",
                                        "cancel the Apply:",
                                        NULL,
                    NOTICE_BUTTON, "Change Selected Item", 42,
                    NOTICE_BUTTON, "Add Before Selected Item", ADD_BEFORE,
                    NOTICE_BUTTON, "Add After Selected Item", ADD_AFTER,
                    NOTICE_BUTTON, "Discard", TRUE,
                    NOTICE_BUTTON, "Cancel", FALSE,
                    NOTICE_STATUS, &retval,
                    XV_SHOW, TRUE,
                    NULL);
            xv_destroy_safe(notice);
        }
    }

    if (retval == TRUE)
        props_apply_changes();
    else if (retval == FALSE)
        xv_set(item, PANEL_NOTIFY_STATUS, XV_ERROR, NULL);
    else if (retval == 42) {
        props_out_change();
        props_apply_changes();
    }
    else if (retval == ADD_BEFORE || retval == ADD_AFTER) {
```

```
            props_out_add(retval);
            props_apply_changes();
        }
}

/*
 *  Notify callback from the outs panel's Add button menu
 */
void
outs_add_menu_notify(menu, menu_item)
Menu menu;
Menu_item menu_item;
{
    if (strcmp((char *)xv_get(menu_item, MENU_STRING), "After") == 0)
        props_out_add(ADD_AFTER);
    else
        props_out_add(ADD_BEFORE);

    /*
     *  Keep window from being dismissed.
     */
    xv_set(menu, MENU_NOTIFY_STATUS, XV_ERROR, NULL);
}

/*
 * Notify callback function for 'outs_delete_item'.
 */
void
outs_delete_notify(item, event)
Panel_item item;
Event *event;
{
    int drow, i;

    drow = (int)xv_get(props_ip->outs_list, PANEL_LIST_FIRST_SELECTED);

    if (temp_outlist == NULL) make_temp_outlist();
    xv_set(props_ip->outs_list, PANEL_LIST_DELETE, drow, NULL);
    free(temp_outlist[drow].label);
    free(temp_outlist[drow].until);
    free(temp_outlist[drow].message);
    for ( i = drow ; i < temp_num_outs - 1 ; i++ ) {
        temp_outlist[i].label = temp_outlist[i+1].label;
        temp_outlist[i].until = temp_outlist[i+1].until;
        temp_outlist[i].message = temp_outlist[i+1].message;
        temp_outlist[i].pop = temp_outlist[i+1].pop;
    }
    temp_num_outs--;

    xv_set(props_ip->outs_change_item, PANEL_INACTIVE, TRUE, NULL);
    xv_set(props_ip->outs_delete_item, PANEL_INACTIVE, TRUE, NULL);

    outs_changes_pending = TRUE;

    /*
     *  Keep the window from being dismissed
     */
    xv_set(item, PANEL_NOTIFY_STATUS, XV_ERROR, NULL);
}

/*
 * Notify callback function for 'outs_change_item'.
 */
```

```
void
outs_change_notify(item, event)
Panel_item item;
Event *event;
{
    props_out_change();

    /*
     *  Keep the window from being dismissed
     */
    xv_set(item, PANEL_NOTIFY_STATUS, XV_ERROR, NULL);
}

/*
 * Notify callback function for 'outs_list'.
 */
int
outs_list_notify(item, string, client_data, op, event, row)
Panel_item item;
char *string;
Xv_opaque client_data;
Panel_list_op op;
Event *event;
int row;
{
    int selected;

    selected = (op == PANEL_LIST_OP_SELECT);
    if (selected) {
        if (temp_outlist == NULL) make_temp_outlist();
        xv_set(props_ip->outs_label_item,
            PANEL_VALUE, temp_outlist[row].label, NULL);
        xv_set(props_ip->outs_until_item,
            PANEL_VALUE, temp_outlist[row].until,
            PANEL_INACTIVE, FALSE,
            NULL);
        xv_set(props_ip->outs_msg_item,
            PANEL_VALUE, temp_outlist[row].message,
            PANEL_INACTIVE, FALSE,
            NULL);
        xv_set(props_ip->outs_pop_item,
            PANEL_VALUE, temp_outlist[row].pop,
            PANEL_INACTIVE, FALSE,
            NULL);
    }
    else {
        xv_set(props_ip->outs_label_item,
            PANEL_VALUE, "",
            NULL);
        xv_set(props_ip->outs_until_item,
            PANEL_VALUE, "",
            PANEL_INACTIVE, TRUE,
            NULL);
        xv_set(props_ip->outs_msg_item,
            PANEL_VALUE, "",
            PANEL_INACTIVE, TRUE,
            NULL);
        xv_set(props_ip->outs_pop_item,
            PANEL_VALUE, FALSE,
            PANEL_INACTIVE, TRUE,
            NULL);
    }
```

```
        xv_set(props_ip->outs_add_item, PANEL_INACTIVE, !selected, NULL);
        xv_set(props_ip->outs_change_item, PANEL_INACTIVE, !selected, NULL);
        xv_set(props_ip->outs_delete_item, PANEL_INACTIVE, !selected, NULL);
        return XV_OK;
}


/*
 * Done callback function for 'frame'.
 */
void
props_done_proc(frame)
Frame frame;
{
    if (props_ok_to_leave()) {
        if (temp_outlist != NULL) destroy_outlist(temp_outlist,
                                                    &temp_num_outs);

        xv_set(frame, XV_SHOW, FALSE, NULL);
    }
}
```

scanwin.c

```
/*
 *  scanwin.c --  support for the msgboard "scan message" window.
 */

#include <stdio.h>
#include <string.h>
#include <sys/param.h>
#include <sys/types.h>
#include <xview/xview.h>
#include <xview/panel.h>
#include <xview/xv_xrect.h>
#include <xview/scrollbar.h>
#include <xview/cursor.h>
#include <xview/sel_pkg.h>
#include <xview/dragdrop.h>
#include <X11/Xlib.h>
#include "scanwin_ui.h"
#include "msgboard.h"
#include "msgboard_xv.h"
#include "pmsg_client.h"


Atom targ_atom = NULL, len_atom, dragdone_atom;

#define TARGETS targ_atom
#define LENGTH len_atom
#define _SUN_DRAGDROP_DONE dragdone_atom

short rolo_bits[] = {
#include "rolo_cursor.icon"
};

short mrolo_bits[] = {
#include "mrolo_cursor.icon"
};

short r_accept_bits[] = {
#include "r_accept_cursor.icon"
};
```

```
static char
        *scan_categories[] = {"new", "pending", "complete", "trash"};

Scrollbar scan_list_bar;
Server_image rolo_image, mrolo_image, r_accept_image;
Xv_Cursor rolo_cursor, mrolo_cursor, r_accept_cursor;

scanwin_frame_objects *scan_ip;
scanwin_find_frame_objects *find_ip;
scanwin_copy_frame_objects *copy_ip;

Menu_item
        /*
         *  Items added to the scrolling list's menu:
         */
        scsl_select_item = (Menu_item)NULL,
        scsl_show_item = (Menu_item)NULL,
        scsl_move_item = (Menu_item)NULL,
        scsl_print_item = (Menu_item)NULL,
        /*
         *  Items on the move menu:
         */
        scmm_next_item = (Menu_item)NULL,
        scmm_new_item = (Menu_item)NULL,
        scmm_pending_item = (Menu_item)NULL,
        scmm_complete_item = (Menu_item)NULL,
        scmm_trash_item = (Menu_item)NULL,
        scmm_clip_item = (Menu_item)NULL,
        scmm_file_item = (Menu_item)NULL;

char
    cur_msg_user[LOGID_LEN+1], /* Name of the person whose msgs are
                                           currently displayed */
    *clip_buf = CNULL;              /* Pointer to buffer for CLIPBOARD
                                           transfers */

int
    scan_window_created = FALSE,      /* is scan window created?*/
    find_window_created = FALSE,      /* is find window created?*/
    copy_window_created = FALSE,      /* is copy window created?*/
    scan_list_menu_updated = FALSE,   /* has menu for the scroll_list been
                                           customized yet? */
    num_msgs,                         /* How many items in list? */
    num_selected,                     /* How many items are selected? */
    cur_msg = BOGUS,                  /* Current message */
    not_my_msgs,                      /* TRUE if we're not showing the */
                                      /* user's own messages */
    msg_cat,                          /* current message category*/
    clip_len;                         /* Length of clip_buf string*/

/*
 * Sets the fullname string for the scanmsg popup
 */
void
set_scm_fname_item()
{
    char cbuf[FNAME_LEN+3];

    sprintf(cbuf, "(%s)",
        get_fname((char *)xv_get(scan_ip->user_item, PANEL_VALUE)));
    xv_set(scan_ip->fname_item, PANEL_LABEL_STRING, cbuf, NULL);
}
```

```
/*
 *  Updates the status of various objects on the window
 */
void
set_scanwin_items_status()
{
    char msgs[15], buf[32];
    int no_sel;

    if (!scan_window_created) return;

    if (num_msgs == 0)
        sprintf(msgs, "No messages");
    else if (num_msgs == 1)
        sprintf(msgs, "One message", num_msgs);
    else
        sprintf(msgs, "%d messages", num_msgs);
    if (num_selected > 0)
        sprintf(buf, "%s (%d selected)", msgs, num_selected);
    else
        strcpy(buf, msgs);

    xv_set(scan_ip->frame, FRAME_RIGHT_FOOTER, buf, NULL);

    no_sel = (num_selected == 0);

    xv_set(scan_ip->show_item, PANEL_INACTIVE, no_sel, NULL);
    xv_set(scan_ip->move_item, PANEL_INACTIVE, no_sel, NULL);
    xv_set(scan_ip->print_item, PANEL_INACTIVE, no_sel, NULL);

    xv_set(scan_ip->find_item,
        PANEL_INACTIVE, num_msgs == 0,
        NULL);

    xv_set(scan_ip->torolo_item,
        PANEL_INACTIVE, no_sel,
        XV_SHOW, dragstyle == 2,
        NULL);

    xv_set(scan_ip->drop_target1,
        PANEL_DROP_FULL, !no_sel,
        XV_SHOW, dragstyle == 3,
        NULL);

    xv_set(scan_ip->select_all_item,
        PANEL_INACTIVE, num_msgs == num_selected,
        NULL);
    xv_set(scan_ip->clear_all_item,
        PANEL_INACTIVE, num_selected == 0,
        NULL);

    if (scsl_select_item != (Menu_item)NULL)
        xv_set(scsl_select_item, MENU_INACTIVE, num_msgs == num_selected,
                                                    NULL);
    if (scsl_show_item != (Menu_item)NULL)
        xv_set(scsl_show_item, MENU_INACTIVE, no_sel, NULL);
    if (scsl_move_item != (Menu_item)NULL)
        xv_set(scsl_move_item, MENU_INACTIVE, no_sel, NULL);
    if (scsl_print_item != (Menu_item)NULL)
        xv_set(scsl_print_item, MENU_INACTIVE, no_sel, NULL);

}
```

```
/*
 *  Chooses or clears all items on the list.
 */
void
select_all_msgs(flag)
int flag;
{
    int i;

    xv_set(scan_ip->list_item, XV_SHOW, FALSE, NULL);
    num_selected = 0;
    for ( i = 0; i < num_msgs; i++) {
        xv_set(scan_ip->list_item, PANEL_LIST_SELECT, i, flag, NULL);
        if (flag) num_selected++;
    }
    set_scanwin_items_status();
    xv_set(scan_ip->list_item, XV_SHOW, TRUE, NULL);
}

/*
 * Displays message selected on the list.
 */
void
display_message()
{
    int ret;

    cur_msg = (int)xv_get(scan_ip->list_item,
        PANEL_LIST_NEXT_SELECTED, cur_msg);
    if (cur_msg == -1)
        cur_msg = (int)xv_get(scan_ip->list_item, PANEL_LIST_FIRST_SELECTED);
    if (cur_msg == -1) {
        cur_msg = BOGUS;
        return;
    }

    ret = show_smsg_window();
    if ( ret != MSGD_OK)
        pr_msg(scan_ip->frame, TRUE, "Error %d retrieving message", ret);
    else
        pr_msg(scan_ip->frame, FALSE, "Showing message %d", cur_msg + 1);
}

/*
 *  Gets a summary line of each message.
 */
void
scm_get_messages()
{
    int new_size, i;
    struct pmsg_hdr *ph_ptr;

    strcpy(cur_msg_user, (char *)xv_get(scan_ip->user_item, PANEL_VALUE));
    if (strlen(cur_msg_user) == 0) {
        set_scanwin_items_status();
        return;
    }

    if (myentry == (struct mem_rec *)NULL)
        not_my_msgs = TRUE;
    else
        not_my_msgs = (strcmp(cur_msg_user, myentry->logid) != 0);
```

```
        xv_set(scan_ip->choice_item, PANEL_INACTIVE, not_my_msgs, NULL);

    /*
     *  The "From" header for the message associated with each list row
     *  is stored in a string pointed to by PANEL_CLIENT_DATA; free all
     *  these strings:
     */
    num_msgs = (int)xv_get(scan_ip->list_item, PANEL_LIST_NROWS);
    if (num_msgs > 0)
        for (i = 0 ; i < num_msgs ; i ++)
            free((char *)xv_get(scan_ip->list_item, PANEL_LIST_CLIENT_DATA,
                                                      i));

    msg_cat = (int)xv_get(scan_ip->choice_item, PANEL_VALUE);
    /*
     *  get_pmsg_headers returns a pointer to a list of structs; each
     *  of these structs contains a pointer to a string we'll display
     *  on the scrolling list, and a pointer to a string we'll store as
     *  the list item's PANEL_CLIENT_DATA.  The display string and the
     *  list of structs itself should be freed immediately after we
     *  put everything on the list; the client data will be freed the
     *  next time the list is redone.
     */
    ph_ptr = get_pmsg_headers(cur_msg_user, msg_cat, &new_size);

    for (i = 0; i < new_size; i++) {
        xv_set(scan_ip->list_item,
            PANEL_LIST_STRING,      i, ph_ptr[i].desc,
            PANEL_LIST_CLIENT_DATA, i, ph_ptr[i].id,
            NULL);
        free(ph_ptr[i].desc);
    }

    if (ph_ptr != NULL) free(ph_ptr);

    /*
     *  See if we have to destroy some list rows:
     *
     */
    if (num_msgs > new_size)
        xv_set(scan_ip->list_item,
            PANEL_LIST_DELETE_ROWS, new_size, num_msgs - new_size,
            NULL);
        for (i = num_msgs - 1; i >= new_size; i--)
            xv_set(scan_ip->list_item, PANEL_LIST_DELETE, i, NULL);

    num_msgs = new_size;
    num_selected = 0;
    cur_msg = BOGUS;

    pr_msg(scan_ip->frame, FALSE, "");
    if (num_msgs > 1)
        xv_set(scan_list_bar, SCROLLBAR_VIEW_START, 0, NULL);
    select_all_msgs(msg_cat == SCM_CHOICE_NEW);
    set_scanwin_items_status();
    xv_set(scan_ip->list_item, XV_SHOW, TRUE, NULL);
    if (msg_cat == SCM_CHOICE_NEW && smsg_is_up())
        display_message();
    else
        clear_smsg_window();
}
```

```
/*
 *  Move messages from one message category to another
 */
void
mv_msgs(dest_cat)
int dest_cat;
{
    int r_count, m_count, smsg;
    char **m_list;

    smsg = (int)xv_get(scan_ip->list_item, PANEL_LIST_FIRST_SELECTED);
    if ( smsg != -1 ) {
        m_list = (char **)malloc(sizeof(char *));
        m_list[0] = (char *)xv_get(scan_ip->list_item,
            PANEL_LIST_CLIENT_DATA, smsg);
        r_count = 1;
        while ( (smsg = (int)xv_get(scan_ip->list_item,
            PANEL_LIST_NEXT_SELECTED, smsg)) != -1) {
            r_count++;
            m_list = (char **)realloc(m_list, sizeof(char *) * r_count);
            m_list[r_count - 1] = (char *)xv_get(scan_ip->list_item,
                    PANEL_LIST_CLIENT_DATA, smsg);
        }

        m_count = mv_msg_call(cur_msg_user, msg_cat, dest_cat, r_count,
                                                                m_list);
        free(m_list);
    }

    scm_get_messages();
    if (m_count == 1)
        pr_msg(scan_ip->frame, FALSE, "One message moved.");
    else if (m_count > 1)
        pr_msg(scan_ip->frame, FALSE, "%d messages moved.", m_count);
}

/*
 *  Wrapper to let the scrolling list menu execute the Select function
 */
void
scsl_select_notify(menu, menu_item)
Menu menu;
Menu_item menu_item;
{
    select_all_msgs(TRUE);
}

/*
 *  Wrapper to let the scrolling list menu execute the Show function
 */
void
scsl_show_notify(menu, menu_item)
Menu menu;
Menu_item menu_item;
{
    display_message();
}

/*
 *  Wrapper to let the scrolling list menu execute the Print function
 */
void
scsl_print_notify(menu, menu_item)
```

```
Menu menu;
Menu_item menu_item;
{
    print_messages();
}


/*
 * Menu handler for 'list_menu'.
 */
Menu
scan_list_menu_handler(menu, op)
Menu menu;
Menu_generate op;
{
    if (op == MENU_DISPLAY && !scan_list_menu_updated) {
        Menu pr_menu;

        xv_set(menu, MENU_TITLE_ITEM, "Messages", NULL);

        scsl_select_item = (Menu_item)xv_create(NULL, MENUITEM,
            MENU_STRING,"Select All Msgs",
            MENU_NOTIFY_PROC,scsl_select_notify,
            MENU_INACTIVE, (num_msgs == num_selected),
            NULL);
        xv_set(menu, MENU_APPEND_ITEM, scsl_select_item, NULL);

        scsl_show_item = (Menu_item)xv_create(NULL, MENUITEM,
            MENU_STRING,"Show...",
            MENU_NOTIFY_PROC,scsl_show_notify,
            MENU_INACTIVE, (num_msgs == 0),
            NULL);
        xv_set(menu, MENU_APPEND_ITEM, scsl_show_item, NULL);

        pr_menu = (Menu)xv_get(scan_ip->move_item, PANEL_ITEM_MENU);
        scsl_move_item = (Menu_item)xv_create(NULL, MENUITEM,
            MENU_STRING,"Move",
            MENU_PULLRIGHT,pr_menu,
            MENU_INACTIVE, (num_msgs == 0),
            NULL);
        xv_set(menu, MENU_APPEND_ITEM, scsl_move_item, NULL);

        scsl_print_item = (Menu_item)xv_create(NULL, MENUITEM,
            MENU_STRING,"Print",
            MENU_NOTIFY_PROC,scsl_print_notify,
            MENU_INACTIVE, (num_msgs == 0),
            NULL);
        xv_set(menu, MENU_APPEND_ITEM, scsl_print_item, NULL);

        scan_list_menu_updated = TRUE;
    }
    return menu;
}


/*
 * Initializes atoms we use locally
 */
void
init_atoms()
{
    TARGETS = XInternAtom(dpy, "TARGETS", False);
    LENGTH = XInternAtom(dpy, "LENGTH", False);
```

```
        _SUN_DRAGDROP_DONE = XInternAtom(dpy, "_SUN_DRAGDROP_DONE", False);
}
/*
 *   Respond to drag
 */
static int
drag_conv_proc(sel_owner, sel_type, replyBuff, length, format)
Selection_owner sel_owner;
Atom *sel_type;
Xv_opaque *replyBuff;
unsigned long *length;
int *format;
{
    static Atom targs[3] = { NULL, NULL, NULL };
    static char *drag_buf;
    static int drag_len;

    /*
     *   Initialize list of atoms we will respond to
     */
    if ( TARGETS == NULL ) init_atoms();
    if (targs[0] == NULL ) {
       targs[0] = TARGETS;
       targs[1] = XA_STRING;
       targs[2] = _SUN_DRAGDROP_DONE;
    }

    if ( *sel_type == TARGETS ) {
       *format = 32;
       *length = 4;
       *sel_type = XA_ATOM;
       *replyBuff = (Xv_opaque)targs;
       return TRUE;
    }
    else if ( *sel_type == XA_STRING ) {
        if (drag_buf == CNULL) drag_buf = (char *)copy_messages(&drag_len);
        *format = 8;
        *length = drag_len;
        *replyBuff = (Xv_opaque)drag_buf;
        return TRUE;
    }
    else if ( *sel_type == _SUN_DRAGDROP_DONE ) {
        if (drag_buf != CNULL) {
            free(drag_buf);
            drag_buf = CNULL;
        }
        *format = 32;
        *length = 0;
        *replyBuff = NULL;
        *sel_type = XInternAtom(dpy, "NULL", False);
        return TRUE;
    }
    else
        return FALSE;
}

void
create_scan_window()
{
#ifdef SCALABLE
    int xpos, ypos;
#endif
```

```
    scan_ip = scanwin_frame_objects_initialize(NULL, base_frame);
    if (scan_params.state != BOGUS)
        frame_set_rect(scan_ip->frame, &scan_params.rect);

#ifdef SCALABLE
    xv_set(scan_ip->show_item, XV_X, wgrid * 2, XV_Y, wgrid, NULL);

    xpos = wgrid * 3 + (int)xv_get(scan_ip->show_item, XV_WIDTH);
    xv_set(scan_ip->move_item, XV_X, xpos, XV_Y, wgrid, NULL);

    xpos += (int)xv_get(scan_ip->move_item, XV_WIDTH) + wgrid;
    xv_set(scan_ip->print_item, XV_X, xpos, XV_Y, wgrid, NULL);

    xpos += (int)xv_get(scan_ip->print_item, XV_WIDTH) + wgrid;
    xv_set(scan_ip->find_item, XV_X, xpos, XV_Y, wgrid, NULL);

    xpos += (int)xv_get(scan_ip->find_item, XV_WIDTH) + wgrid * 2;
    xv_set(scan_ip->torolo_item, XV_X, xpos, XV_Y, wgrid, NULL);


    ypos = wgrid * 2 + (int)xv_get(scan_ip->torolo_item, XV_HEIGHT);
    xv_set(scan_ip->user_item, XV_X, wgrid * 2, XV_Y, ypos, NULL);
    xv_set(scan_ip->fname_item,
        XV_X, wgrid * 3 + (int)xv_get(scan_ip->user_item, XV_WIDTH),
        XV_Y, ypos,
        NULL);

    ypos += wgrid + (int)xv_get(scan_ip->user_item, XV_HEIGHT);
    xv_set(scan_ip->choice_item, XV_X, wgrid * 2, XV_Y, ypos, NULL);

    ypos += wgrid + (int)xv_get(scan_ip->choice_item, XV_HEIGHT);
    xv_set(scan_ip->clear_all_item, XV_X, wgrid * 2, XV_Y, ypos, NULL);

    xpos = wgrid * 3 + (int)xv_get(scan_ip->clear_all_item, XV_WIDTH);
    xv_set(scan_ip->select_all_item, XV_X, xpos, XV_Y, ypos, NULL);

    ypos += wgrid + (int)xv_get(scan_ip->clear_all_item, XV_HEIGHT);
    xv_set(scan_ip->list_item, XV_X, wgrid * 2, XV_Y, ypos, NULL);
    window_fit(scan_ip->panel);

    window_fit(scan_ip->frame);
#endif

    scan_list_bar = (Scrollbar)xv_get(scan_ip->list_item,
        PANEL_LIST_SCROLLBAR);

    xv_set((Menu)xv_get(scan_ip->list_item, PANEL_ITEM_MENU),
        MENU_GEN_PROC, scan_list_menu_handler, NULL);
    xv_set(scan_ip->select_all_item, PANEL_INACTIVE, TRUE, NULL);

    rolo_image = (Server_image)xv_create(NULL, SERVER_IMAGE,
        XV_WIDTH, 48,
        XV_HEIGHT, 48,
        SERVER_IMAGE_BITS, rolo_bits,
        NULL);
    rolo_cursor = (Xv_Cursor)xv_create(NULL, CURSOR,
        CURSOR_IMAGE, rolo_image,
        CURSOR_XHOT, 32,
        CURSOR_YHOT, 32,
        NULL);
```

```
        mrolo_image = (Server_image)xv_create(NULL, SERVER_IMAGE,
            XV_WIDTH, 48,
            XV_HEIGHT, 48,
            SERVER_IMAGE_BITS, mrolo_bits,
            NULL);
        mrolo_cursor = (Xv_Cursor)xv_create(NULL, CURSOR,
            CURSOR_IMAGE, mrolo_image,
            CURSOR_XHOT, 32,
            CURSOR_YHOT, 32,
            NULL);
        r_accept_image = (Server_image)xv_create(NULL, SERVER_IMAGE,
            XV_WIDTH, 48,
            XV_HEIGHT, 48,
            SERVER_IMAGE_BITS, r_accept_bits,
            NULL);
        r_accept_cursor = (Xv_Cursor)xv_create(NULL, CURSOR,
            CURSOR_IMAGE, r_accept_image,
            CURSOR_XHOT, 32,
            CURSOR_YHOT, 32,
            NULL);

    xv_set(scan_ip->drop_target1,
        PANEL_DROP_DND, (Drag_drop)xv_create(scan_ip->panel, DRAGDROP,
            DND_TYPE, DND_COPY,
            SEL_CONVERT_PROC, drag_conv_proc,
            DND_CURSOR, rolo_cursor,
            DND_ACCEPT_CURSOR, r_accept_cursor,
            NULL),
        NULL);

    scan_window_created = TRUE;
}

void
show_scan_window()
{
    if (!scan_window_created) create_scan_window();

    if ( admin || ((globrec.flags & MB_G_TRUSTED) != 0 && cur_sel != BOGUS))
        xv_set(scan_ip->user_item,
            PANEL_VALUE,ulist[cur_sel].logid,
            PANEL_READ_ONLY,FALSE,
            NULL);
    else if ((globrec.flags & MB_G_TRUSTED) == 0) {
        if (myentry == (struct mem_rec *)NULL) {
            pr_msg(scan_ip->frame, TRUE,
                    "%s is not currently on the Message Board.", mylogid);
            return;
        }
        xv_set(scan_ip->user_item,
            PANEL_VALUE,myentry->logid,
            PANEL_READ_ONLY,TRUE,
            NULL);
    }

    xv_set(scan_ip->choice_item,
        PANEL_VALUE, SCM_CHOICE_DEFAULT,
        NULL);
    scm_get_messages();
    set_scm_fname_item();
    xv_set(scan_ip->frame, XV_SHOW, TRUE, NULL);
}
```

```
void
create_find_window()
{
    find_ip = scanwin_find_frame_objects_initialize(NULL, base_frame);

    xv_set(find_ip->find_panel,
        PANEL_DEFAULT_ITEM, find_ip->find_fwd_item,
        NULL);

    find_window_created = TRUE;
}

void
show_find_window()
{
    if (!find_window_created) create_find_window();
    xv_set(find_ip->find_frame, XV_SHOW, TRUE, NULL);
}

void
create_copy_window()
{
    copy_ip = scanwin_copy_frame_objects_initialize(NULL, base_frame);

    xv_set(copy_ip->copy_panel,
        PANEL_DEFAULT_ITEM, copy_ip->copy_copy_item,
        NULL);

    copy_window_created = TRUE;
}

void
show_copy_window()
{
    if (!copy_window_created) create_copy_window();

    if ( strlen((char *)xv_get(copy_ip->copy_dir_item, PANEL_VALUE)) == 0){
        char wd[MAXPATHLEN];

        getwd(wd);
        xv_set(copy_ip->copy_dir_item, PANEL_VALUE, wd, NULL);
        xv_set(copy_ip->copy_panel, PANEL_CARET_ITEM,
            copy_ip->copy_file_item, NULL);
    }
    xv_set(copy_ip->copy_frame, XV_SHOW, TRUE, NULL);
}

/******************************************
 * The following routines handle the initial request to copy messages
 * to the clipboard, as well as the request from another application
 * for the clipboard data.
 *
 * Respond to a request for the contents of the CLIPBOARD selection
 */
static int
clip_conv_proc(sel_owner, sel_type, replyBuff, length, format)
Selection_owner sel_owner;
Atom *sel_type;
Xv_opaque *replyBuff;
unsigned long *length;
int *format;
{
```

```
    static Atom targs[3] = { NULL, NULL, NULL };

    /*
     *  Initialize list of atoms we will respond to
     */
    if ( TARGETS == NULL ) init_atoms();
    if (targs[0] == NULL ) {
       targs[0] = TARGETS;
       targs[1] = LENGTH;
       targs[2] = XA_STRING;
    }

    if ( *sel_type == TARGETS ) {
       *format = 32;
       *length = 4;
       *sel_type = XA_ATOM;
       *replyBuff = (Xv_opaque)targs;
       return TRUE;
    }
    else if ( *sel_type == LENGTH ) {
      if (clip_buf == CNULL) clip_buf = (char *)copy_messages(&clip_len);
      *format = 32;
      *length = 1;
      *sel_type = XA_INTEGER;
      *replyBuff = (Xv_opaque)&clip_len;
      return TRUE;
    }
    else if ( *sel_type == XA_STRING ) {
      if (clip_buf == CNULL) clip_buf = (char *)copy_messages(&clip_len);
      *format = 8;
      *length = clip_len;
      *replyBuff = (Xv_opaque)clip_buf;
      return TRUE;
    }
    else
      return FALSE;
}

/*
 *  Handle loss of the selection
 */
void
sel_lose_proc(sel)
Selection_ownersel;
{
    pr_msg(scan_ip->frame, FALSE, "(clipboard relinquished)");

    if ( clip_buf != CNULL ) {
       free(clip_buf);
       clip_buf = CNULL;
    }
}

/*
 *  Become the owner of the CLIPBOARD selection
 */
void
sc_own_clipboard()
{
    static Selection_owner sel_owner = NULL;
    if (sel_owner == NULL)
        sel_owner = xv_create(scan_ip->frame, SELECTION_OWNER,
```

```
            SEL_CONVERT_PROC,clip_conv_proc,
            SEL_LOSE_PROC,sel_lose_proc,
            NULL);

    if ( clip_buf != CNULL ) {
        free(clip_buf);
        clip_buf = CNULL;
    }

    clip_buf = (char *)copy_messages(&clip_len);

    xv_set(sel_owner,
        SEL_OWN,       TRUE,
        SEL_RANK_NAME,"CLIPBOARD",
        NULL);
}

/*
 * Notify callback function for 'find_item'.
 */
void
sc_find_notify(item, event)
Panel_item item;
Event *event;
{
    show_find_window();
}

/*
 * Event callback function for 'torolo_item'.
 */
void
sc_torolo_event(item, event)
Panel_item item;
Event *event;
{
    if ( event_action(event) == ACTION_SELECT &&
        !(int)xv_get(item, PANEL_INACTIVE)) {
        Xv_Cursor c;
        char *tf;

        if (num_selected > 1)
            c = mrolo_cursor;
        else
            c = rolo_cursor;

        tf = tempnam("/tmp", "mb.");
        dnd_messages(tf);
        xview_send_drag_event(base_frame, c, tf);
        look_busy(TRUE);
        sleep(1);
        unlink(tf);
        free(tf);
        look_busy(FALSE);
    }
    else
        panel_default_handle_event(item, event);
}

/*
 * Notify callback function for 'user_item'.
 */
```

```
Panel_setting
sc_user_notify(item, event)
Panel_item item;
Event *event;
{
    set_scm_fname_item();
    xv_set(scan_ip->choice_item, PANEL_VALUE, SCM_CHOICE_DEFAULT, NULL);
    scm_get_messages();
    return PANEL_NONE;/* Freeze focus on this item */
}


/*
 * Notify callback function for 'choice_item'.
 */
void
sc_choice_notify(item, value, event)
Panel_item item;
int value;
Event *event;
{
    set_scm_fname_item();
    strcpy(cur_msg_user, (char *)xv_get(scan_ip->user_item, PANEL_VALUE));

    /*
     *  If this isn't the current user's messages, don't let them choose any
     *  category other than NEW.
     */
    if (myentry == (struct mem_rec *)NULL ||
       (strcmp(cur_msg_user, myentry->logid) != 0 &&
       value != SCM_CHOICE_NEW))
       xv_set(item, PANEL_VALUE, SCM_CHOICE_NEW, NULL);
    scm_get_messages();
}


/*
 * Notify callback function for 'copy_file_item'.
 */
Panel_setting
copy_file_notify(item, event)
Panel_item item;
Event *event;
{
    if (event_shift_is_down(event))
        return PANEL_PREVIOUS;
    else {
        sc_copy_to_file();
        if ((int)xv_get(copy_ip->copy_frame, FRAME_CMD_PIN_STATE) ==
            FRAME_CMD_PIN_OUT)
            xv_set(copy_ip->copy_frame, XV_SHOW, FALSE, NULL);
        return PANEL_NONE;
    }
}


/*
 * Notify callback function for 'copy_copy_item'.
 */
void
copy_copy_notify(item, event)
Panel_item item;
Event *event;
{
    sc_copy_to_file();
}
```

```
/*
 * Menu handler for `move_menu (to Next Category)'.
 */
Menu_item
sc_to_next_handler(item, op)
Menu_item item;
Menu_generate op;
{
    switch (op) {
    case MENU_DISPLAY:
        if (scmm_next_item == (Menu_item)NULL)
            scmm_next_item = item;
        xv_set(item,
            MENU_INACTIVE, (msg_cat == SCM_MAX_CHOICE) ||
                    (not_my_msgs && (msg_cat != SCM_CHOICE_NEW)),
            NULL);
        break;

    case MENU_NOTIFY:
        if (msg_cat < SCM_MAX_CHOICE)
            mv_msgs(msg_cat + 1);
        break;
    }
    return item;
}


/*
 * Menu handler for `move_menu (to New)'.
 */
Menu_item
sc_to_new_handler(item, op)
Menu_item item;
Menu_generate op;
{
    switch (op) {
    case MENU_DISPLAY:
        if (scmm_new_item == (Menu_item)NULL)
            scmm_new_item = item;
        xv_set(item,
            MENU_INACTIVE, not_my_msgs || (msg_cat == SCM_CHOICE_NEW),
            NULL);
        break;

    case MENU_NOTIFY:
        mv_msgs(SCM_CHOICE_NEW);
        break;
    }
    return item;
}

/*
 * Menu handler for `move_menu (to Pending)'.
 */
Menu_item
sc_to_pending_handler(item, op)
Menu_item item;
Menu_generate op;
{
    switch (op) {
    case MENU_DISPLAY:
        if (scmm_pending_item == (Menu_item)NULL)
            scmm_pending_item = item;
```

```
          xv_set(item,
              MENU_INACTIVE, not_my_msgs || (msg_cat == SCM_CHOICE_PEN),
              NULL);
          break;

      case MENU_NOTIFY:
          mv_msgs(SCM_CHOICE_PEN);
          break;
      }
      return item;
}

/*
 * Menu handler for 'move_menu (to Complete)'.
 */
Menu_item
sc_to_complete_handler(item, op)
Menu_item item;
Menu_generate op;
{
      switch (op) {
      case MENU_DISPLAY:
          if (scmm_complete_item == (Menu_item)NULL)
              scmm_complete_item = item;
          xv_set(item,
              MENU_INACTIVE, not_my_msgs || msg_cat == (SCM_CHOICE_COM),
              NULL);
          break;

      case MENU_NOTIFY:
          mv_msgs(SCM_CHOICE_COM);
          break;
      }
      return item;
}

/*
 * Menu handler for 'move_menu (to Trash)'.
 */
Menu_item
sc_to_trash_handler(item, op)
Menu_item item;
Menu_generate op;
{
      switch (op) {
      case MENU_DISPLAY:
          if (scmm_trash_item == (Menu_item)NULL)
              scmm_trash_item = item;
          xv_set(item,
          MENU_INACTIVE, not_my_msgs || msg_cat == (SCM_CHOICE_TRA),
          NULL);
          break;

      case MENU_NOTIFY:
          mv_msgs(SCM_CHOICE_TRA);
          break;
      }
      return item;
}

/*
 * Menu handler for 'move_menu (Copy to Clipboard)'.
 */
```

```
Menu_item
sc_to_clip_handler(item, op)
Menu_item item;
Menu_generate op;
{
    switch (op) {
    case MENU_DISPLAY:
        if (scmm_clip_item == (Menu_item)NULL)
            scmm_clip_item = item;
        xv_set(item, MENU_INACTIVE, not_my_msgs, NULL);
        break;

    case MENU_NOTIFY:
        sc_own_clipboard();
        break;
    }
    return item;
}

/*
 * Menu handler for 'move_menu (Copy to File...)'.
 */
Menu_item
sc_to_file_handler(item, op)
Menu_item item;
Menu_generate op;
{
    switch (op) {
    case MENU_DISPLAY:
        if (scmm_file_item == (Menu_item)NULL)
            scmm_file_item = item;
        xv_set(item, MENU_INACTIVE, not_my_msgs, NULL);
        break;

    case MENU_NOTIFY:
        show_copy_window();
        break;
    }
    return item;
}

/*
 * Notify callback function for 'show_item'.
 */
void
sc_show_notify(item, event)
Panel_item item;
Event *event;
{
    display_message();
}

/*
 * Notify callback function for 'print_item'.
 */
void
sc_print_notify(item, event)
Panel_item item;
Event *event;
{
    print_messages();
}
```

```
/*
 * Notify callback function for 'clear_all_item'.
 */
void
sc_clear_all_notify(item, event)
Panel_item item;
Event *event;
{
    select_all_msgs(FALSE);
}

/*
 * Notify callback function for 'select_all_item'.
 */
void
sc_select_all_notify(item, event)
Panel_item item;
Event *event;
{
    select_all_msgs(TRUE);
}

/*
 * Notify callback function for 'list_item'.
 */
int
sc_list_notify(item, string, client_data, op, event)
Panel_item item;
char *string;
Xv_opaque client_data;
Panel_list_op op;
Event *event;
{
    switch(op) {
    case PANEL_LIST_OP_DESELECT:
        num_selected--;
        set_scanwin_items_status();
        break;
    case PANEL_LIST_OP_SELECT:
        num_selected++;
        set_scanwin_items_status();
        break;
    }
    return XV_OK;
}

/*
 * Done callback function for 'frame'.
 */
void
scanwin_done(frame)
Frame frame;
{
    xv_set(frame, XV_SHOW, FALSE, NULL);
    if (find_window_created)
        xv_set(find_ip->find_frame,
            FRAME_CMD_PIN_STATE,FRAME_CMD_PIN_OUT,
            XV_SHOW, FALSE,
            NULL);
    if (copy_window_created)
        xv_set(copy_ip->copy_frame,
            FRAME_CMD_PIN_STATE,FRAME_CMD_PIN_OUT,
```

```
                    XV_SHOW,FALSE,
                    NULL);
            dismiss_smsg_window();
}

/*
 * Gathers all the parameters for this window
 */
void
get_scan_params(p)
struct winparams *p;
{
    if (!scan_window_created)
        *p = scan_params;
    else {
        p->state = (int)xv_get(scan_ip->frame, FRAME_CMD_PIN_STATE);
        frame_get_rect(scan_ip->frame, &(p->rect));
    }
}

/*
 * Event callback function for 'frame'.
 */
Notify_value
sc_frame_event(win, event, arg, type)
Xv_window win;
Event *event;
Notify_arg arg;
Notify_event_type type;
{
    /*
     * Check for a resize event
     */
    if (event_action(event) == WIN_RESIZE) {
        int rh, nrows, list_h, xtra;

        /*
         * "xtra" is the part of the scrolling list height that is not
         * contributed by the rows themselves
         */
        rh = (int)xv_get(scan_ip->list_item, PANEL_LIST_ROW_HEIGHT);
        xtra = (int)xv_get(scan_ip->list_item, XV_HEIGHT) -
            rh * (int)xv_get(scan_ip->list_item, PANEL_LIST_DISPLAY_ROWS);
        /*
         * Figure out how long the scrolling list should be now
         */
        list_h = (int)xv_get(scan_ip->panel, XV_HEIGHT) -
            (int)xv_get(scan_ip->list_item, XV_Y) - wgrid * 2;
        nrows = (list_h - xtra) / rh;
        list_h = nrows * rh  + xtra;

        xv_set(scan_ip->list_item,
            PANEL_LIST_WIDTH, (int)xv_get(scan_ip->frame, XV_WIDTH) - wgrid *
                        4,
            XV_HEIGHT, list_h,
            PANEL_LIST_DISPLAY_ROWS, nrows,
            NULL);
    }
    return notify_next_event_func(win, (Notify_event) event, arg, type);
}
```

send_drag.c

```
/*
 * From: sdo@soliado.East.Sun.COM (Scott Oaks - Sun Consulting NYC)
 *
 * Call this function when you get the mouse down event that
 * initiates the drag event, passing it the cursor you want displayed
 * and the filename that the receiving tool should get as the d-n-d
 * event.
 */

#include <xview/xview.h>
#include <xview/fullscreen.h>
#include <X11/X.h>
#include <X11/Xatom.h>

xview_send_drag_event(src_win, cursor, fname)
    Xv_opaque src_win, cursor;
    char *fname;

{
Xv_opaque fullscreen, dest_win_xid;
Inputmask im;
Event event;
int data[5];
Atom drop_atom;

    fullscreen = xv_create(0, FULLSCREEN,
        FULLSCREEN_INPUT_WINDOW, src_win,
        FULLSCREEN_SYNC, TRUE,
        WIN_CURSOR, cursor,
        WIN_CONSUME_EVENTS, WIN_MOUSE_BUTTONS, NULL,
        NULL);
    input_imnull(&im);
    win_setinputcodebit(&im, MS_LEFT);
    win_setinputcodebit(&im, LOC_DRAG);
    im.im_flags = IM_NEGEVENT;

    XAllowEvents(xv_get(src_win, XV_DISPLAY), SyncPointer, CurrentTime);
    do {
        xv_input_readevent(src_win, &event, TRUE, TRUE, &im);
    } while (!(win_inputnegevent(&event) && event_action(&event) ==
                                        ACTION_SELECT));

    fullscreen_destroy(fullscreen);

    dest_win_xid = win_pointer_under(src_win, event_x(&event),
                                        event_y(&event));

    drop_atom = XInternAtom(xv_get(src_win, XV_DISPLAY), "FOOBAR", FALSE);
    XChangeProperty(xv_get(src_win, XV_DISPLAY),
                        xv_get(src_win, XV_XID), drop_atom,
                        XA_STRING, 8, PropModeReplace,
                        (Xv_opaque) fname, strlen(fname) + 1);
    data[0] = XV_POINTER_WINDOW;
    data[1] = event_x(&event);
    data[2] = event_y(&event);
    data[3] = xv_get(src_win, XV_XID);
    data[4] = drop_atom;

    xv_send_message(src_win, dest_win_xid, "XV_DO_DRAG_LOAD", 32, data, 20);
}
```

sendwin.c

```
/*
 *  sendwin.c -- Routines to support the msgboard "Send Pmsg" window.
 */

#include <stdio.h>
#include <sys/param.h>
#include <sys/types.h>
#include <xview/xview.h>
#include <xview/panel.h>
#include <xview/textsw.h>
#include <xview/xv_xrect.h>
#include "sendwin_ui.h"
#include "msgboard.h"
#include "msgboard_xv.h"
#include "pmsg_client.h"

sendwin_frame_objects *send_ip;

int
    send_window_created = FALSE,        /* is sendmsg window created? */
    to_is_wide = FALSE,                 /* is the to item in "wide mode"? */
    old_choice,                         /* Previous state of choice item */
    bot_panel_ht;

char default_to[LOGID_LEN+1]; /* "To" value that we go back to */
                              /* if the Reset button is pressed */

void
create_sendmsg_window()
{
#ifdef SCALABLE
    int valx, ypos;
#endif

    send_ip = sendwin_frame_objects_initialize(NULL, base_frame);

#ifdef SCALABLE
    /*
     *  Phone number text item has the widest label on this panel, so use
     *  it to set the X positioning for all the other ones.
     */
    xv_set(send_ip->phnum_item, XV_X, wgrid * 2, NULL);
    valx = (int)xv_get(send_ip->phnum_item, PANEL_VALUE_X);

    ypos = wgrid * 2;
    align_values(send_ip->to_item, valx, ypos);
    xv_set(send_ip->fname_item,
        XV_Y,           ypos,
        XV_X,           (int)xv_get(send_ip->to_item, XV_X) +
            (int)xv_get(send_ip->to_item, XV_WIDTH) + wgrid,
        NULL);

    ypos += wgrid + (int)xv_get(send_ip->to_item, XV_HEIGHT);
    align_values(send_ip->time_item, valx, ypos);

    ypos += wgrid + (int)xv_get(send_ip->time_item, XV_HEIGHT);
    align_values(send_ip->caller_item, valx, ypos);
```

```
        ypos += wgrid + (int)xv_get(send_ip->caller_item, XV_HEIGHT);
        align_values(send_ip->org_item, valx, ypos);

        ypos += wgrid + (int)xv_get(send_ip->org_item, XV_HEIGHT);
        align_values(send_ip->phnum_item, valx, ypos);

        ypos += wgrid + (int)xv_get(send_ip->phnum_item, XV_HEIGHT);
        align_values(send_ip->choice_item, valx, ypos);

        window_fit(send_ip->panel);

        xv_set(send_ip->textsw,
            XV_Y, (int)xv_get(send_ip->panel, XV_HEIGHT),
            XV_WIDTH,      (int)xv_get(send_ip->panel, XV_WIDTH),
            XV_HEIGHT,   wgrid * 6,
            NULL);
        xv_set(send_ip->fmt_item,
            XV_X, wgrid * 2,
            XV_Y, wgrid,
            NULL);
        xv_set(send_ip->send_item, XV_Y, wgrid * 2, NULL);
        xv_set(send_ip->reset_item, XV_Y, wgrid * 2, NULL);
        window_fit_height(send_ip->bot_panel);
        xv_set(send_ip->bot_panel,
            XV_Y, (int)xv_get(send_ip->textsw, XV_Y) +
                    (int)xv_get(send_ip->textsw, XV_HEIGHT),
            XV_WIDTH, (int)xv_get(send_ip->panel, XV_WIDTH),
            NULL);
        window_fit(send_ip->frame);
#endif
        bot_panel_ht = (int)xv_get(send_ip->bot_panel, XV_HEIGHT);

        if (send_params.state != BOGUS) {
            frame_set_rect(send_ip->frame, &send_params.rect);
            if (send_params.state == TRUE)
                xv_set(send_ip->frame, FRAME_CMD_PIN_STATE, FRAME_CMD_PIN_IN,
                                                        NULL);
        }

        xv_set(send_ip->textsw,
            TEXTSW_IGNORE_LIMIT, TEXTSW_INFINITY,
            NULL);

        xv_set(send_ip->to_item,
            PANEL_NOTIFY_STRING, "\n\r\t@, !",
            NULL);

        send_window_created = TRUE;
}

/*
 * Sets the fullname string for the sendmsg popup
 */
void
set_sm_fname_item()
{
    char cbuf[FNAME_LEN+3];

    sprintf(cbuf, "(%s)",
        get_fname((char *)xv_get(send_ip->to_item, PANEL_VALUE)));
```

```
        xv_set(send_ip->fname_item, PANEL_LABEL_STRING, cbuf, NULL);
}

void
set_sm_time()
{
    time_t now;
    char timebuf[17];

    if (strlen((char *)xv_get(send_ip->to_item, PANEL_VALUE)) == 0)
        timebuf[0] = '\0';
    else {
        time(&now);
        strftime(timebuf, 17, "%k:%M %a %b %e", localtime(&now));
    }
    xv_set(send_ip->time_item, PANEL_VALUE, timebuf, NULL);
}

/*
 * Change width of "to" display to extra-wide if flag is TRUE, or
 * normal if FALSE.
 */
void
set_to_wide(flag)
int flag;
{
    if (to_is_wide == flag) return;

    to_is_wide = flag;
    if (to_is_wide)
        xv_set(send_ip->to_item,
            PANEL_VALUE_DISPLAY_LENGTH, 40,
            NULL);
    else
        xv_set(send_ip->to_item,
            PANEL_VALUE_DISPLAY_LENGTH, LOGID_LEN,
            NULL);

    xv_set(send_ip->fname_item,
            XV_X, (int)xv_get(send_ip->to_item, XV_X) +
                            (int)xv_get(send_ip->to_item, XV_WIDTH) +
                                                            wgrid,
            NULL);
}

/*
 * Makes sure those panel items whose active or visible status can vary
 * are set properly.
 */
void
set_sendwin_items_status()
{
    int no_text;

    if (!send_window_created) return;

    no_text = ((int)xv_get(send_ip->choice_item, PANEL_VALUE) &
        SM_CHOICE_LV_MSG) == 0;
```

```
    if (fmt_msgs)
        xv_set(send_ip->fmt_item, XV_SHOW, FALSE, NULL);
    else
        xv_set(send_ip->fmt_item,
            PANEL_INACTIVE, no_text,
            XV_SHOW, TRUE,
            NULL);

    xv_set(send_ip->textsw,
        TEXTSW_BROWSING, no_text,
        TEXTSW_READ_ONLY, no_text,
        NULL);
}

void
prep_sendmsg_window()
{
    xv_set(send_ip->to_item, PANEL_VALUE, default_to, NULL);
    set_to_wide(FALSE);
    set_sm_fname_item();
    set_sm_time();
    xv_set(send_ip->caller_item, PANEL_VALUE, "", NULL);
    xv_set(send_ip->org_item, PANEL_VALUE, "", NULL);
    xv_set(send_ip->phnum_item, PANEL_VALUE, "", NULL);
    xv_set(send_ip->choice_item, PANEL_VALUE, SM_CHOICE_DEFAULT, NULL);
    old_choice = SM_CHOICE_DEFAULT;
    textsw_reset(send_ip->textsw, 0, 0);
    if (default_to[0] == '\0')
        xv_set(send_ip->panel, PANEL_CARET_ITEM, send_ip->to_item, NULL);
    else
        xv_set(send_ip->panel,
            PANEL_CARET_ITEM, send_ip->caller_item,
            NULL);
    set_sendwin_items_status();
}

void
show_sendmsg_window()
{
    if (!send_window_created) create_sendmsg_window();

    if (cur_sel != BOGUS)
        strcpy(default_to, ulist[cur_sel].logid);
    prep_sendmsg_window();
    xv_set(send_ip->frame, XV_SHOW, TRUE, NULL);
}

/*
 * Formats the text in the send text subwindow
 */
void
fmt_sendwin()
{
    char buf[100], tmpname[20];
    FILE *pipe;

    sprintf(tmpname, "/tmp/msgb_%d", getpid());
    textsw_store_file(send_ip->textsw, tmpname, 0, 0);
    sprintf(buf, "fmt %s", tmpname);
```

```
    if ((pipe = popen(buf, "r")) == FNULL) {
        pr_msg(NULL, TRUE, "Couldn't open pipe!");
        return;
    }
    textsw_reset(send_ip->textsw, 0, 0);

    while (fgets(buf, 100, pipe) != CNULL)
        textsw_insert(send_ip->textsw, buf, strlen(buf));
    pclose(pipe);
    textsw_normalize_view(send_ip->textsw, 0);
    unlink(tmpname);
}

/*
 * Does the actual sending stuff.  Returns TRUE if successful, FALSE if not.
 */
int
send_pmsg()
{
    int buf_len, retval;
    struct pmsg msg;
    char caller[CALLER_LEN + 1];

    msg.id = strdup((char *)xv_get(send_ip->to_item, PANEL_VALUE));
    if (msg.id[0] == '\0') {
        pr_msg(NULL, TRUE, "No recipient specified.");
        free(msg.id);
        return FALSE;
    }

    msg.caller = strdup((char *)xv_get(send_ip->caller_item, PANEL_VALUE));
    if (msg.caller[0] == '\0') {
        pr_msg(NULL, TRUE, "No caller specified.");
        free(msg.id);
        free(msg.caller);
        return FALSE;
    }

    msg.flags = (int)xv_get(send_ip->choice_item, PANEL_VALUE);
    if ( (msg.flags & SM_CHOICE_LV_MSG) != 0 ) {
        buf_len = (int)xv_get(send_ip->textsw, TEXTSW_LENGTH);
        if ( buf_len == 0 ) {
            pr_msg(NULL, TRUE, "No text in message.");
            free(msg.id);
            free(msg.caller);
            return FALSE;
        }
        if (fmt_msgs) {
            fmt_sendwin();
            buf_len = (int)xv_get(send_ip->textsw, TEXTSW_LENGTH);
        }
        msg.text = malloc(buf_len + 1);
        (void)xv_get(send_ip->textsw, TEXTSW_CONTENTS, 0, msg.text, buf_len);
        msg.text[buf_len] = '\0';
    }
    else
        msg.text = strdup("");

    msg.org = strdup((char *)xv_get(send_ip->org_item, PANEL_VALUE));
    msg.phnum = strdup((char *)xv_get(send_ip->phnum_item, PANEL_VALUE));
    msg.time = strdup((char *)xv_get(send_ip->time_item, PANEL_VALUE));
```

```
        retval = send_msg_to_server(&msg);
        free_pmsg(msg);
        return retval;
}


/*
 *  Gathers all the parameters for this window
 */
void
get_send_params(p)
struct winparams *p;
{
    if (!send_window_created)
        *p = send_params;
    else {
        p->state = (int)xv_get(send_ip->frame, FRAME_CMD_PIN_STATE);
        frame_get_rect(send_ip->frame, &(p->rect));
    }
}


/*
 * Event callback function for 'frame'.
 */
Notify_value
sm_frame_event(win, event, arg, type)
Xv_window win;
Event *event;
Notify_arg arg;
Notify_event_type type;
{
    /*
     *  Check for a resize event
     */
    if (event_action(event) == WIN_RESIZE) {
        int text_ht, top_panel_ht;

        /*
         *  Make the textsw the pane that consumes any additional height
         *  on a resize.  Textsw will always be at least wgrid * 6
         *  pixels high; this means the bottom panel may disappear if
         *  the window is made too short.  C'est la vie, caveat resizer
         *  and all that.
         */
        top_panel_ht = (int)xv_get(send_ip->panel, XV_HEIGHT);
        text_ht = (int)xv_get(send_ip->frame, XV_HEIGHT) - top_panel_ht -
            bot_panel_ht;
        if (text_ht < wgrid * 6) text_ht = wgrid * 6;
        xv_set(send_ip->textsw, XV_HEIGHT, text_ht, NULL);
        xv_set(send_ip->bot_panel,
            XV_Y, top_panel_ht + text_ht,
            XV_HEIGHT, bot_panel_ht,
            NULL);
        position_bot_buttons(send_ip->bot_panel, send_ip->send_item,
            send_ip->reset_item);
    }
    return notify_next_event_func(win, (Notify_event) event, arg, type);
}


/*
 * Notify callback function for 'to_item'.
 */
```

```
Panel_setting
sm_to_notify(item, event)
Panel_item item;
Event *event;
{
    /*
     *  Process special chars
     */
    if (event_action(event) == '@' || event_action(event) == '!') {
        set_to_wide(TRUE);
        xv_set(send_ip->fname_item,
            PANEL_LABEL_STRING, "(OFFSITE)",
            NULL);
        return PANEL_INSERT;
    }
    else if (event_action(event) == ' ' || event_action(event) == ',') {
        set_to_wide(TRUE);
        xv_set(send_ip->fname_item,
            PANEL_LABEL_STRING, "(MULTIPLE)",
            NULL);
        return PANEL_INSERT;
    }
    /*
     *  Normal completion chars (NL, TAB, etc.)
     */
    else {
        if (to_is_wide) {
            char tmpbuf[TO_LEN + 1];

            strcpy(tmpbuf, (char *)xv_get(send_ip->to_item, PANEL_VALUE));
            if (strchr(tmpbuf, '@') == 0 && strchr(tmpbuf, '!') == 0 &&
                    strchr(tmpbuf, ' ') == 0 && strchr(tmpbuf, ',') == 0)
                    set_to_wide(FALSE);
        }
        if (!to_is_wide)
            set_sm_fname_item();
        set_sm_time();
        if (event_shift_is_down(event))
            return PANEL_PREVIOUS;
        else
            return PANEL_NEXT;
    }
}

/*
 * Notify callback function for `phnum_item'.
 */
Panel_setting
sm_phnum_notify(item, event)
Panel_item item;
Event *event;
{
    if (event_shift_is_down(event))
        return PANEL_PREVIOUS;
    else {
        int msg_flags;

        xv_set(send_ip->panel,
            PANEL_CARET_ITEM, send_ip->caller_item,
            NULL);
        msg_flags= (int)xv_get(send_ip->choice_item, PANEL_VALUE);
        if ( (msg_flags & SM_CHOICE_LV_MSG) !=0 )
```

```
            win_set_kbd_focus(textsw_first(send_ip->textsw),
            xv_get(textsw_first(send_ip->textsw), XV_XID));
        return PANEL_NONE;
    }
}

/*
 * Notify callback function for 'choice_item'.
 */
void
sm_choice_notify(item, value, event)
Panel_item item;
int value;
Event *event;
{
    if ( (value & SM_CHOICE_DEFAULT) == SM_CHOICE_DEFAULT ) {
        if ( (old_choice & SM_CHOICE_DEFAULT) != SM_CHOICE_DEFAULT )
            value = SM_CHOICE_DEFAULT;
        else
            value -= SM_CHOICE_DEFAULT;
        xv_set(send_ip->choice_item, PANEL_VALUE, value, NULL);
    }
    if ( value == 0 ) {
        value = SM_CHOICE_DEFAULT;
        xv_set(send_ip->choice_item, PANEL_VALUE, value, NULL);
    }
    if ( (value & SM_CHOICE_LV_MSG) != 0 )
        win_set_kbd_focus(textsw_first(send_ip->textsw),
            xv_get(textsw_first(send_ip->textsw), XV_XID));
    else
        xv_set(send_ip->panel,
            PANEL_CARET_ITEM, send_ip->caller_item,
            NULL);

    set_sendwin_items_status();
    old_choice = value;
}

/*
 * Notify callback function for 'fmt_item'.
 */
void
sm_fmt_notify(item, event)
Panel_item item;
Event *event;
{
    fmt_sendwin();
    xv_set(item, PANEL_NOTIFY_STATUS, XV_ERROR, NULL);
}

/*
 * Notify callback function for 'send_item'.
 */
void
sm_send_notify(item, event)
Panel_item item;
Event *event;
{
    clear_msg();
    if(send_pmsg()) {
        default_to[0] = '\0';
        prep_sendmsg_window();
```

```
        }
    else
        xv_set(item, PANEL_NOTIFY_STATUS, XV_ERROR, NULL);
}


/*
 * Notify callback function for `reset_item'.
 */
void
sm_reset_notify(item, event)
Panel_item item;
Event *event;
{
    prep_sendmsg_window();
}
```

set_hints.c

```
#include <sys/param.h>
#include <string.h>
#include <xview/xview.h>
/* #include <xview/panel.h> */
#include <X11/Xutil.h>
#include "msgboard_xv.h"

set_hints(frame, progname)
Frame frame;
char *progname;
{
    Window xid;
    XSizeHints *hints;
    XClassHint c_hint;
    XTextProperty text;
    char buf[MAXHOSTNAMELEN + 1], *list = buf, *p;

    xid = (Window)xv_get(frame, XV_XID);
    hints = XAllocSizeHints();

    /* This particular window doesn't allow resizing */
    hints->flags = PMinSize | PMaxSize;
    hints->min_height = hints->max_height = (int)xv_get(frame, XV_HEIGHT);
    hints->min_width = hints->max_width = (int)xv_get(frame, XV_WIDTH);
    XSetWMNormalHints(dpy, xid, hints);
    XFree(hints);

    p = strrchr(progname, '/') + 1;
    if ( p == (char *)1 ) p = progname;
    c_hint.res_name = p;
    c_hint.res_class = CLASS_NAME;
    XSetClassHint(dpy, xid, &c_hint);

    (void)gethostname(buf, sizeof buf);
    (void)XStringListToTextProperty(&list, 1, &text);
    XSetWMClientMachine(dpy, xid, &text);
}
```

srv-emulate.c

```
#include <stdio.h>
#include <sys/time.h>
#include <sys/stat.h>
#include "msgboard.h"
#include "mb_client.h"

/*
 *  Determined by the max size of a record; needs to be recomputed each
 *  time we change what's stored in the datafile
 */
#define DFINBUFSIZE 161

#define DF_COOKIE "msgdata"
#define DF_VERSION 3
#define SEP '\034'

int
    initialized = FALSE;/* Have we read the data file yet? */

unsigned int
    globals_seq_no,                   /* Header sequence number*/
    highest_seq_no = 0,               /* last sequence number issued*/
    *seq_no;

#ifdef FIXITINMIX

#include <sys/param.h>
#include <sys/limits.h>
#include <string.h>
#include <pwd.h>
#include <signal.h>
#include "msgd.h"
#include "mb_server.h"

#ifdef DEBUG
#include <errno.h>
extern int sys_nerr;
extern char *sys_errlist[];
#endif


#define DFNAME "msgdata"
#define PMSGDIRNAME "msgs"
#define LOGNAME "errlog"

/*
 *  Number of seconds that we wait before flushing modifications
 *  to the checkpoint file.
 */
#define CACHE_TIME 30

/*
 *  OFF =      No timer running
 *  RUNNING = timer running, not blocked
 *  BLOCKED = function that modifies data in progress
 *  EXPIRED = alarm went off while blocked
 *  KILLED  = terminate signal received while blocked
 */
#define TIMER_OFF 0
#define TIMER_RUNNING 1
```

```
#define TIMER_BLOCKED 2
#define TIMER_EXPIRED 3
#define TIMER_KILLED 4

char
#ifdef DEBUG
    remhost[MAXHOSTNAMELEN + 1], /* Remote host, for debugging */
#endif
    *mb_datafile = CNULL,/* Name of the data file */
    *pmsg_dir = CNULL,   /* Directory phone messages are in */
    *logfilename = CNULL;/* Name of logfile. */

int
    users = 0,              /* Number of users in datalist*/
    timer_status = TIMER_OFF,
    init_client_cnt,        /* counters for usage stats*/
    get_rec_cnt,
    put_rec_cnt,
    get_mod_rec_cnt, gmr_null_cnt,
    send_page_cnt,
    send_pmsg_cnt,
    scan_pmsg_cnt,
    read_pmsg_cnt,
    mv_pmsgs_cnt;

Server_Data *s_list;    /* The server's list of users*/

Global_Rec globrec;     /* Global data */

init_data srvinfo;      /*  Initial server info, such as required
                        /*  authorization levels and start time */


#endif
/*
 * "cstok" stands for "Character-Separator TOKen" -- it works the same way
 * "strtok" does except that the second argument is a single character
 *  rather than a string, and the token separator in the input string is
 *  always assumed to be exactly one character long, rather than one or
 *  more  characters long.
 */
char *
cstok(start, sep)
char *start, sep;
{
    static char *p = CNULL;

    if (start == CNULL)
        start = p;
    else
        p = start;
    if (p == CNULL || *p == '\0') return CNULL;

    while (*p != sep && *p != '\0') ++p;

    if (*p != '\0')
        *p++ = '\0';

    return start;
}
#ifdef FIXITINTHEMIX
```

```
/*
 *  Look up a user on this machine's UID.  If "logid" is not a valid
 *  UNIX login ID on this machine, return BOGUS.
 */
int
get_uid_by_logid(logid)
char *logid;
{
    struct passwd *pwbuf;

    pwbuf = getpwnam(logid);
    if ( pwbuf != (struct passwd *)NULL)
        return pwbuf->pw_uid;
    else
        return BOGUS;
}


/*
 *  Makes sure a string does not contain the field separator character.
 */
void
strclean(s)
char *s;
{
    char *p;

    while( (p = strchr(s, SEP)) != CNULL )
        *p = '!';
}

void
logmsg(fmt, s1, s2, s3)
char *fmt, *s1, *s2, *s3;
{
    struct stat statbuf;
    time_t now;
    FILE *logfile;
    char timestr[26];

    if (logfilename == CNULL) find_files();
    if (stat(logfilename, &statbuf) != 0 ||
        (logfile = fopen(logfilename, "a")) == FNULL) return;

    now = time(NULL);
    strcpy(timestr, ctime(&now));
    timestr[19] = '\0';
    fprintf(logfile, "%s ", timestr + 4);
    fprintf(logfile, fmt, s1, s2, s3);
    fputc('\n', logfile);
    fclose(logfile);
}

/*
 *  Flushes the data to a checkpoint file.
 */
void
write_cpfile()
{
    int i;
    FILE *dbfile;

    if ( (dbfile = fopen(mb_datafile, "w")) == FNULL) {
```

```
#ifdef DEBUG
        logmsg("Checkpoint failed!");
#endif
        return;
    }

    strclean(globrec.name);
    strclean(globrec.motd);
    fprintf(dbfile, "%s\034%d\034%s\034%s\034%d\034%d\n",
        DF_COOKIE, DF_VERSION, globrec.name, globrec.motd, globrec.flags,
        globrec.pagertype);
    for (i = 0; i < users; i++) {
        /*
         *  Don't write deleted records to the checkpoint file.
         */
        if (s_list[i].status != BOGUS) {
            strclean(s_list[i].logid);
            strclean(s_list[i].fname);
            strclean(s_list[i].until);
            strclean(s_list[i].comment);
            strclean(s_list[i].cat);
            strclean(s_list[i].sortby);
            strclean(s_list[i].ext);
            strclean(s_list[i].pagernum);
            fprintf(dbfile, "%s\034%s\034%s\034%s\034%s\034%s\034%s\034%s",
                        s_list[i].logid,
                        s_list[i].fname,
                        s_list[i].until,
                        s_list[i].comment,
                        s_list[i].cat,
                        s_list[i].sortby,
                        s_list[i].ext,
                        s_list[i].pagernum);
            fprintf(dbfile, "\034%d\034%d\034%d\034%ld\n",
                        s_list[i].status,
                        s_list[i].flags,
                        s_list[i].pagertype,
                        s_list[i].timestamp);
        }
    }

    fclose(dbfile);
#ifdef DEBUG
    logmsg("Checkpointed.");
#endif
}
#endif

void
init_server()
{
    char inline[DFINBUFSIZE];
    Mem_Rec *cur_rec;
    FILE *dbfile;
    struct stat statbuf;
    int i;
    struct timeval now;

    if ( (dbfile = fopen("msgdata", "r")) == FNULL) {
        exit(1);
    }
```

```
    /*
     *  Read header
     */
    if ( fgets(inline, DFINBUFSIZE, dbfile) == CNULL) exit(1);
    if (inline[strlen(inline)] == '\n') inline[strlen(inline)] = '\0';
    if (strcmp(cstok(inline, SEP), DF_COOKIE) != 0) {
       exit(1);
    }
    if (atoi(cstok(NULL, SEP)) != DF_VERSION) {
       exit(1);
    }

    strncpy(globrec.name, cstok(NULL, SEP), SITE_LEN+1);
    strncpy(globrec.motd, cstok(NULL, SEP), MOTD_LEN+1);
    globrec.flags = atoi(cstok(NULL, SEP));
    globrec.pagertype = atoi(cstok(NULL, SEP));
    globals_seq_no = ++highest_seq_no;

    /*
     *  Loop to read in remaining lines
     */
    users = 0;
    while ( fgets(inline, DFINBUFSIZE, dbfile) != CNULL) {
      if (inline[strlen(inline)] == '\n') inline[strlen(inline)] = '\0';
      /*
       * Allocate a slot
       */
      if (++users == 1) {
          ulist = (Mem_Rec *)malloc(
                        (unsigned)sizeof(Mem_Rec) );
          seq_no = (unsigned int *)malloc(sizeof(unsigned int));
      }
      else {
          ulist = (Mem_Rec *)realloc( (char *)ulist,
                        (unsigned)( sizeof(Mem_Rec) * users ) );
          seq_no = (unsigned int *)realloc( (char *)seq_no, sizeof(unsigned
                                                            int));
      }

      cur_rec = &ulist[users-1];

      strncpy(cur_rec->logid, cstok(inline, SEP), LOGID_LEN+1);
      strncpy(cur_rec->fname, cstok(NULL, SEP), FNAME_LEN+1);
      strncpy(cur_rec->until, cstok(NULL, SEP), UNTIL_LEN+1);
      strncpy(cur_rec->comment, cstok(NULL, SEP), COMMENT_LEN+1);
      strncpy(cur_rec->cat, cstok(NULL, SEP), CAT_LEN+1);
      strncpy(cur_rec->sortby, cstok(NULL, SEP), SORTBY_LEN+1);
      strncpy(cur_rec->ext, cstok(NULL, SEP), EXT_LEN+1);
      strncpy(cur_rec->pagernum, cstok(NULL, SEP), PAGERNUM_LEN+1);
      cur_rec->status = atoi(cstok(NULL, SEP));
      cur_rec->flags = atoi(cstok(NULL, SEP));
      cur_rec->pagertype = atoi(cstok(NULL, SEP));
          cur_rec->timestamp = atol(cstok(NULL, SEP));
      seq_no[users-1] = ++highest_seq_no;
      }

    fclose(dbfile);

    initialized = TRUE;
}
#ifdef FIXITINMIX
```

```
/*
 *  Used by lsearch/lfind to do lookups in s_list by login ID
 */
int
comp_by_logid(i, j)
Server_Data *i, *j;
{
    return strcmp(i->logid, j->logid);
}


/*
 *  Used by lsearch/lfind to do lookups in s_list by user ID
 */
int
comp_by_uid(i, j)
Server_Data *i, *j;
{
    return (i->uid == j->uid) ? 0 : 1;
}


/*
 *  Validate the calling host; if the user ID pointer uidp is non-NULL,
 *  return the validated user ID.
 *
 *  Currently, the host is only validated if the authorization level is
 *  AUTH_DES, and then only to the extent of "is this host in our NIS
 *  domain?"  User validation works for both AUTH_UNIX and
 *  AUTH_DES, but AUTH_UNIX is trivially easy to spoof.
 *
 *  TO DO: read a file of additional trusted hosts beyond the current NIS
 *  domain.  These hosts should also be notified via init_client() that
 *  their allowed validation level is AUTH_UNIX instead of AUTH_DES.
 */
int
ok_user(rqstp, uidp, level)
struct svc_req *rqstp;
int *uidp, level;
{
    struct sockaddr_in *sockaddr;
    u_long addr;
    int retval;

    /*
     * Get the caller's host address.  (This is where we should verify it
     * against list of allowed/disallowed hosts.)
     */
    sockaddr = svc_getcaller(rqstp->rq_xprt);
    addr = sockaddr->sin_addr.s_addr;
    /*
     *  If no authentication required for this service, return immediately.
     *  If they asked for UID authentication, they're out of luck.
     */
    if (level == AUTH_NONE) {
       if (uidp != (int *)NULL) *uidp = BOGUS;
       return TRUE;
    }

    /*
     *  For UNIX and DES authentication, use the intrinsic checks for
     *  validation.  Also, return FALSE if they're using the wrong level
     *  of authentication.
     */
```

```
        if (uidp != (int *)NULL) {
            switch (rqstp->rq_cred.oa_flavor) {
            case AUTH_UNIX:
                {
                            struct authunix_parms *aup;

                            aup = (struct authunix_parms *)rqstp->rq_clntcred;
                            *uidp = aup->aup_uid;
                            retval = (level == AUTH_UNIX);
                }
                break;
            case AUTH_DES:
                {
                            struct authdes_cred *des_cred;
                            int gid, gidlen, gidlist[10];
                            char host[MAXHOSTNAMELEN];
                            des_cred = (struct authdes_cred *)rqstp->rq_clntcred;
                            if ( ! netname2user(des_cred->adc_fullname.name,
                                uidp, &gid, &gidlen, gidlist))
                                return FALSE;
                            retval = (level == AUTH_DES);
                }
                break;
            }
        }
        return retval;
}

/*
 *  gets record based on UID.
 */
Server_Data *
get_rec_by_uid(uid)
int uid;
{
    Server_Data tmp_record;

    tmp_record.uid = uid;
    return (Server_Data *)lfind((char *)&tmp_record,
        (char *)s_list, &users, sizeof(Server_Data), comp_by_uid);
}

/*
 *  Does this UID have admin privs?
 */
int
is_admin(uid)
int uid;
{
    Server_Data *recp;

    recp = get_rec_by_uid(uid);
    if (recp == (Server_Data *)NULL)
        return FALSE;

    return (recp->flags & MB_ADMIN) != 0;
}

/*
 *  Part of the routine to caches writes.  After we update any of the server
 *  data, we start a timer; actual flush to disk is deferred until the
```

```
 *    timer expires.  If the timer is already running, this call does
 *    nothing.
 */
void
start_timer()
{
    struct itimerval ntime, otime;

    switch (timer_status) {
    case TIMER_EXPIRED:
        /*
         *    Timer went off in between the time we set the block and now.
         *    Perform the flush now.
         */
        write_cpfile();
        timer_status == TIMER_OFF;
        break;
    case TIMER_OFF:
        /*
         *    No timer in effect -- start it.
         */
        timerclear(&(ntime.it_interval));
        ntime.it_value.tv_sec = CACHE_TIME;
        ntime.it_value.tv_usec = 0;

        setitimer(ITIMER_REAL, &ntime, &otime);
        timer_status = TIMER_RUNNING;
        break;
    case TIMER_BLOCKED:
        /*
         *    Timer was running when we started our update, so we blocked it;
         *    unblock it.
         */
        timer_status = TIMER_RUNNING;
        break;
    case TIMER_KILLED:
        /*
         *    Got a quit signal while we were doing our update.  Flush and exit.
         */
        write_cpfile();
        exit(0);
    }
}


/*
 *    Copies incoming data to server record pointed to by "rec"; increments
 *    sequence number; updates timestamp.
 *
 *    Does not copy logid; also does not assign value to uid.
 */
void
copy_data_to_rec(rec_p, data_p)
Server_Data *rec_p;
user_data *data_p;
{
    struct timeval now;

    strcpy(rec_p->fname, data_p->fname);
    strcpy(rec_p->until, data_p->until);
    strcpy(rec_p->comment, data_p->comment);
    strcpy(rec_p->cat, data_p->cat);
    strcpy(rec_p->sortby, data_p->sortby);
    strcpy(rec_p->ext, data_p->ext);
```

```
      strcpy(rec_p->pagernum, data_p->pagernum);
      rec_p->status = data_p->status;
      rec_p->flags = data_p->flags;
      rec_p->pagertype = data_p->pagertype;
      rec_p->seq_no = ++highest_seq_no;
      gettimeofday(&now, (struct timezone *)NULL);
      rec_p->timestamp = now.tv_sec;
}


/*
 *  Copies a server record to the RPC data struct
 */
void
copy_rec_to_data(data_p, rec_p)
user_data *data_p;
Server_Data *rec_p;
{
      data_p->logid = rec_p->logid;
      data_p->fname = rec_p->fname;
      data_p->until = rec_p->until;
      data_p->comment = rec_p->comment;
      data_p->cat = rec_p->cat;
      data_p->sortby = rec_p->sortby;
      data_p->ext = rec_p->ext;
      data_p->pagernum = rec_p->pagernum;
      data_p->status = rec_p->status;
      data_p->flags = rec_p->flags;
      data_p->pagertype = rec_p->pagertype;
      data_p->seq_no = rec_p->seq_no;
      data_p->timestamp = rec_p->timestamp;
}

/*****************************************
 *  The actual remotely called procedures:
 *****************************************/

/*
 *  Returns initialization information to a client.  Since the clients need
 *  to call this to find out what auth levels they need, no authorization
 *  is needed to make this call.
 */
init_data *
init_client_1()
{

      init_client_cnt++;

      if (!initialized) init_server();

      return &srvinfo;
}

/*
 *  Returns either a user record (keyed on login ID), or the global record.
 */
get_rec_data *
get_rec_1(req, rqstp)
get_rec_req *req;
struct svc_req *rqstp;
{
      static get_rec_data result;
      Server_Data *rec_ptr, tmp_record;
```

```
        get_rec_cnt++;

        if (!ok_user(rqstp, (int *)NULL, srvinfo.get_auth)) {
            result.retval = MSGD_VOID;
            return &result;
        }

        if (!initialized) init_server();

        if ( req->req_type == MSGD_GREC ) {
            result.retval = MSGD_GREC;
            result.get_rec_data.u.g_dat.site = globrec.name;
            result.get_rec_data.u.g_dat.motd = globrec.motd;
            result.get_rec_data.u.g_dat.flags = globrec.flags;
            result.get_rec_data.u.g_dat.pagertype = globrec.pagertype;
            result.get_rec_data.u.g_dat.seq_no = globals_seq_no;
        }
        else {
            strcpy(tmp_record.logid, req->get_rec_req.u.u_rec.logid);
            rec_ptr = (Server_Data *)lfind((char *)&tmp_record,
                (char *)s_list, &users, sizeof(Server_Data), comp_by_logid);
            if (rec_ptr == (Server_Data *)NULL || rec_ptr->status == BOGUS) {
                result.retval = MSGD_VOID;
            }
            else {
                result.retval = MSGD_UREC;
                copy_rec_to_data(&(result.get_rec_data.u.u_dat), rec_ptr);
            }
        }
        return &result;
}

/*
 * Modifies, adds or deletes a record.  Returns MSGD_OK on success, error
 * code on fail.  If srvinfo.put_auth is AUTH_NONE,
 * then anyone can perform this operation on any record, which is probably
 * not the greatest idea.
 */
unsigned int *
put_rec_1(data, rqstp)
put_rec_data *data;
struct svc_req *rqstp;
{
    static unsigned int result;
    Server_Data *rec_ptr, tmp_record;
    int r_uid, no_auth_reqd;
    user_data *dptr;


    put_rec_cnt++;

    if (!ok_user(rqstp, &r_uid, srvinfo.put_auth)) {
        result = MSGD_VALID_FAIL;
        return &result;
    }
    no_auth_reqd = (srvinfo.put_auth == AUTH_NONE);

    if (!initialized) init_server();

    if (timer_status == TIMER_RUNNING) timer_status = TIMER_BLOCKED;
```

```
/*
 *  Handle a global record
 */
if ( data->req_type == MSGD_GREC ) {
    global_data *g_rec = &(data->put_rec_data_u.g_rec);

    strcpy(globrec.name, g_rec->site);
    strcpy(globrec.motd, g_rec->motd);
    /*
     *  We don't want MB_G_TRUSTED to be set from clients.  Mask it
     *  out and add it back in from the current setting.
     */
    globrec.flags = (g_rec->flags & ~MB_G_TRUSTED) |
    (globrec.flags & MB_G_TRUSTED);
    globrec.pagertype = g_rec->pagertype;
    globals_seq_no = ++highest_seq_no;

    result = MSGD_OK;
    start_timer();
    return &result;
}

/*
 *  For remaining operations, try to find a record matching the request
 */
if ( data->req_type == MSGD_DREC )
    strcpy(tmp_record.logid, data->put_rec_data_u.d_rec.logid);
else if ( data->req_type == MSGD_AREC )
    strcpy(tmp_record.logid, data->put_rec_data_u.a_rec.logid);
else if ( data->req_type == MSGD_UREC )
    strcpy(tmp_record.logid, data->put_rec_data_u.u_rec.logid);
rec_ptr = (Server_Data *)lfind((char *)&tmp_record,
    (char *)s_list, &users, sizeof(Server_Data), comp_by_logid);

/*
 *  Handle a delete request
 */
if ( data->req_type == MSGD_DREC ) {
    if (rec_ptr == (Server_Data *)NULL || rec_ptr->status == BOGUS)
        result = MSGD_NOT_FOUND;
    else if (no_auth_reqd || is_admin(r_uid)) {
        rec_ptr->status = BOGUS;
        rec_ptr->seq_no = ++highest_seq_no;
        result = MSGD_OK;
    }
    else
        result = MSGD_VALID_FAIL;
}

/*
 *  Handle an ADD request
 */
else if ( data->req_type == MSGD_AREC ) {
    if (rec_ptr == (Server_Data *)NULL || rec_ptr->status == BOGUS) {
        if (no_auth_reqd || is_admin(r_uid)) {
            dptr = &(data->put_rec_data_u.a_rec);
            if ( rec_ptr == (Server_Data *)NULL ) {
                if (++users == 1)
                    s_list = (Server_Data *)malloc
                    ( sizeof(Server_Data) );
                else
                    s_list = (Server_Data *)realloc( (char *)s_list,
```

```
                                        (unsigned)( sizeof(Server_Data) * users
                                                 ) );
                        rec_ptr = &s_list[users-1];
                        strcpy(rec_ptr->logid, dptr->logid);
                }
                rec_ptr->uid = get_uid_by_logid(rec_ptr->logid);
                copy_data_to_rec(rec_ptr, dptr);
                result = MSGD_OK;
        }
        else
                result = MSGD_VALID_FAIL;
    }
    else
        result = MSGD_ALREADY_EXISTS;
    }

    /*
     *  Handle a modify request
     */
    else {
        if (rec_ptr == (Server_Data *)NULL || rec_ptr->status == BOGUS)
            result = MSGD_NOT_FOUND;
        else if (no_auth_reqd || (r_uid == rec_ptr->uid || is_admin(r_uid))){
            dptr = &(data->put_rec_data.u.u_rec);
            /*
             *  If this user does not have admin caps, strip out any attempt
             *  to set the admin bit.
             */
            if (!no_auth_reqd && !is_admin(r_uid))
                    dptr->flags &= (~MB_ADMIN | (rec_ptr->flags &
                                                MB_ADMIN));
            copy_data_to_rec(rec_ptr, dptr);
            result = MSGD_OK;
        }
        else
            result = MSGD_VALID_FAIL;
    }
    if (result == MSGD_OK) start_timer();
    return &result;
}
#endif

/*
 *  Looks for a record with a sequence number higher than the one passed
 *  and returns it if found.  Returns error number + 1000 on errors.
 */
struct bogosity {
    enum msgd_types ret_type;
    unsigned int seq_no;
    Mem_Rec *rec;
};

struct bogosity *
get_mod_rec_1()
{
    int i;
    unsigned int found_seq_no;
    Mem_Rec *p, *found_rec;
    static struct bogosity result;

    result.ret_type = MSGD_VOID;
    if ( last_seq_no < globals_seq_no ) {
```

```
        result.ret_type = MSGD_GREC;
        result.seq_no = globals_seq_no;
    }
    else
        for ( i = 0 ; i < users ; i++ )
            if ( seq_no[i] > last_seq_no ) {
                    result.ret_type = MSGD_UREC;
                    result.seq_no = seq_no[i];
                    result.rec = &ulist[i];
                    break;
            }

    return &result;
}
```

warpme.c

```
/*
 * warpme.c -- warp the pointer to the center of a button -- ONLY if the
 * user wants us to!
 */

#include <xview/xview.h>
#include <xview/panel.h>
#include <xview/defaults.h>

static Display *dewarp_dpy;
static Window dewarp_win;
static int dewarp_x, dewarp_y, dewarp_pending = FALSE;

void
warpme(frame, panel, button)
Frame frame;
Panel panel;
Panel_item button;
{
    int mouse_x, mouse_y;
    Window junk, win;

    if ( ! defaults_get_boolean("openwindows.popupjumpcursor",
        "OpenWindows.PopupJumpCursor", TRUE) )
        return;

    mouse_x = (int)xv_get(button, XV_X) + (int)xv_get(button, XV_WIDTH) / 2;
    mouse_y = (int)xv_get(button, XV_Y) + (int)xv_get(button, XV_HEIGHT) / 2;

    dewarp_dpy = (Display *)xv_get(frame, XV_DISPLAY);
    win = (int)xv_get(panel, XV_XID);

    (void)XQueryPointer(
        dewarp_dpy,    /* Display */
        win,           /* Pass it a real window to keep it happy, but we
                          don't really care */
        &dewarp_win,   /* Save root window for dewarp function */
        &junk,         /* child window -- don't care */
        &dewarp_x,     /* Mouse x location relative to root window */
        &dewarp_y,     /* Mouse y "                                 */
        &junk,         /* x relative to child window -- don't care  */
```

```
        &junk,          /* y "                                    */
        &junk);         /* modifier key status -- don't care    */

    XWarpPointer(
        dewarp_dpy,     /* display */
        None,           /* src_w      */
        win,            /* dest_w     */
        None,           /* src_x      */
        None,           /* src_y      */
        None,           /* src_width  */
        None,           /* src_height */
        mouse_x,        /* dest_x     */
        mouse_y         /* dest_y     */
        );
    dewarp_pending = TRUE;
}


/*
 * Call this function when any criterion for doing the dewarp is violated
 */
void
no_dewarp()
{
    dewarp_pending = FALSE;
}


/*
 * Returns the mouse to its rightful place, but only if we never called
 * no_dewarp() .
 */
void
dewarp()
{
    if (!dewarp_pending) return;

    XWarpPointer(
        dewarp_dpy,                     /* display    */
        None,                           /* src_w      */
        dewarp_win,                     /* dest_w     */
        None,                           /* src_x      */
        None,                           /* src_y      */
        None,                           /* src_width  */
        None,                           /* src_height */
        dewarp_x,                       /* dest_x     */
        dewarp_y                        /* dest_y     */
        );
    dewarp_pending = FALSE;
}
```

How to Use archie

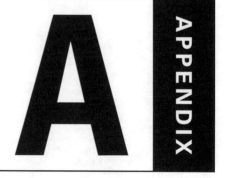

The **archie** is the Internet archive server–listing service. Through **archie**, you can locate files that are available on a large number of anonymous FTP sites. There are three interfaces to **archie**:

- telnet
- archie client
- email

TELNET ACCESS TO archie

To access **archie** via telnet, telnet to one of the following hosts:

`archie.ans.net`	Elmsford, New York, USA
`archie.au`	Geelong, Australia
`archie.funet.fi`	Helsinki, Finland
`archie.mcgill.ca`	Montreal, Quebec, Canada
`archie.rutgers.edu`	Piscataway, New Jersey, USA
`archie.sura.net`	College Park, Maryland, USA
`archie.unl.edu`	Lincoln, Nebraska, USA

with a command like

```
host% telnet archie.unl.edu
```

Then, when prompted for **login:**, say **archie**:

```
Login: archie
```

At this point, you should be logged onto the system. Type **help** for more information.

archie CLIENT

The **archie** clients are available via anonymous FTP on the **archie** servers (and other anonymous FTP sites). They are stored in the directory **archie/clients** or **pub/archie/clients**. Instructions on the use of each client are provided with the source code.

EMAIL ACCESS

Email access is available through the following addresses:

`archie@ans.net`	Elmsford, New York, USA
`archie@au`	Geelong, Australia
`archie@funet.fi`	Helsinki, Finland
`archie@mcgill.ca`	Montreal, Quebec, Canada
`archie@rutgers.edu`	Piscataway, New Jersey, USA
`archie@sura.net`	College Park, Maryland, USA
`archie@unl.edu`	Lincoln, Nebraska, USA

To get help via email, you would use an exchange like the following:

```
host% mail archie@unl.edu
Subject:
help
quit
```

To find the XView source via the email interface, you would use an exchange like the following:

```
host% mail archie@unl.edu
Subject:
prog xview
compress
path my-return-address@host
quit
```

The **prog** command does a search of the database using regular expressions. The **compress** command will compress and **uu-encode** the list of found files. The **path** command overrides the mail address in your mailer. Finally, the **quit** command tells **archie** to stop processing (so it won't process your **.signature**).

FTPMAIL

Once you know where the file is, you can retrieve the file via anonymous FTP. If you don't have FTP access, you can use ftpmail. To find out more about ftpmail, do the following:

```
host% ftpmail@decwrl.dec.com
Subject: help
```

and you'll receive a description of the ftpmail server.

Icon Listings

B

T he following icons are used by the icon demo programs.

state0.icon

```
/* Format_version=1, Width=64, Height=64, Depth=1, Valid_bits_per_item=16
 */
        0x0000,      0x0000,      0x0000,      0x0000,
        0x0000,      0x0000,      0x0000,      0x0000,
        0x0000,      0x0000,      0x0000,      0x0000,
        0x0000,      0x0000,      0x0000,      0x0000,
        0x0000,      0x0003,      0xE000,      0x0000,
        0x0000,      0x003E,      0x3E00,      0x0000,
        0x0000,      0x0027,      0xFB00,      0x0000,
        0x0000,      0x0014,      0x1700,      0x0000,
        0x0000,      0x0008,      0x0E00,      0x0000,
        0x0000,      0x0037,      0x3C00,      0x0000,
        0x0000,      0x0010,      0xE400,      0x0000,
        0x0000,      0x0012,      0x2400,      0x0000,
        0x0000,      0x0010,      0x0400,      0x0000,
        0x0000,      0x0013,      0xE400,      0x0000,
        0x0000,      0x0009,      0xC800,      0x0000,
        0x0000,      0x0004,      0x1000,      0x0000,
        0x0000,      0x0003,      0xE000,      0x0000,
        0x0000,      0x0001,      0xC000,      0x0000,
        0x0000,      0x0007,      0xF000,      0x0000,
        0x0000,      0x0038,      0x8800,      0x0000,
        0x0000,      0x0020,      0x0400,      0x0000,
        0x0000,      0x00C0,      0x0180,      0x0000,
        0x0000,      0x0080,      0x8000,      0x0000,
        0x0000,      0x0100,      0x0040,      0x0000,
        0x0000,      0x0100,      0x0040,      0x0000,
        0x0000,      0x0200,      0x8030,      0x0000,
        0x0000,      0x0620,      0x0810,      0x0000,
        0x0000,      0x0C60,      0x0C10,      0x0000,
        0x0000,      0x0820,      0x84F0,      0x0000,
        0x0000,      0x0F20,      0x0480,      0x0000,
```

```
        0x0000,     0x05D0,     0x0D00,     0x0000,
        0x0000,     0x0050,     0x0600,     0x0000,
        0x0000,     0x003F,     0xFE00,     0x0000,
        0x0000,     0x003F,     0xFC00,     0x0000,
        0x0000,     0x0040,     0x0A00,     0x0000,
        0x0000,     0x0041,     0x0200,     0x0000,
        0x0000,     0x0081,     0x8100,     0x0000,
        0x0000,     0x0081,     0x8080,     0x0000,
        0x0000,     0x0082,     0x8080,     0x0000,
        0x0000,     0x0082,     0xC000,     0x0000,
        0x0000,     0x0082,     0x4040,     0x0000,
        0x0000,     0x0084,     0x2020,     0x0000,
        0x0000,     0x0104,     0x2020,     0x0000,
        0x0000,     0x0104,     0x1020,     0x0000,
        0x0000,     0x0104,     0x1010,     0x0000,
        0x0000,     0x0104,     0x1000,     0x0000,
        0x0000,     0x0208,     0x1010,     0x0000,
        0x0000,     0x0608,     0x0808,     0x0000,
        0x0000,     0x0410,     0x0808,     0x0000,
        0x0000,     0x0410,     0x0408,     0x0000,
        0x0000,     0x0410,     0x0408,     0x0000,
        0x0000,     0x0420,     0x0404,     0x0000,
        0x0000,     0x0420,     0x0404,     0x0000,
        0x0000,     0x0420,     0x0204,     0x0000,
        0x0000,     0x1C20,     0x0107,     0x0000,
        0x0000,     0x6060,     0x01C0,     0xC000,
        0x0000,     0xC040,     0x0140,     0x2000,
        0x0001,     0x0040,     0x0100,     0x1000,
        0x0001,     0x7F00,     0x00FF,     0xE000,
        0x0000,     0x0000,     0x0000,     0x0000,
        0x0000,     0x0000,     0x0000,     0x0000,
        0x0000,     0x0000,     0x0000,     0x0000,
        0x0000,     0x0000,     0x0000,     0x0000,
        0x0000,     0x0000,     0x0000,     0x0000
```

state1.icon

```
/* Format_version=1, Width=64, Height=64, Depth=1, Valid_bits_per_item=16
 */
        0x0000,     0x0000,     0x0000,     0x0000,
        0x0000,     0x0000,     0x0000,     0x0000,
        0x0000,     0x0000,     0x0000,     0x0000,
        0x0000,     0x0000,     0x0000,     0x0000,
        0x0000,     0x0000,     0x0000,     0x0000,
        0x0000,     0x0000,     0x0000,     0x0000,
        0x0000,     0x0000,     0x0000,     0x0000,
        0x0000,     0x0001,     0xC000,     0x0000,
        0x0000,     0x0007,     0xF000,     0x0000,
        0x0000,     0x0038,     0x8800,     0x0000,
        0x0000,     0x0020,     0x0400,     0x0000,
        0x0000,     0x00C0,     0x0100,     0x0000,
        0x0000,     0x0080,     0x8080,     0x0000,
        0x0000,     0x0100,     0x0040,     0x0000,
        0x0000,     0x0100,     0x0020,     0x0000,
        0x0000,     0x0200,     0x8010,     0x0000,
        0x0000,     0x0620,     0x0C10,     0x0000,
        0x0000,     0x0C60,     0x0E10,     0x0000,
        0x0000,     0x0820,     0x8420,     0x0000,
        0x0000,     0x0F20,     0x04C0,     0x0000,
```

```
        0x0000,        0x05D0,        0x0D00,        0x0000,
        0x0000,        0x0050,        0x0600,        0x0000,
        0x0000,        0x003F,        0xFE00,        0x0000,
        0x0000,        0x003F,        0xFC00,        0x0000,
        0x0000,        0x0040,        0x0A00,        0x0000,
        0x0000,        0x0041,        0x0200,        0x0000,
        0x0000,        0x0081,        0x8180,        0x0000,
        0x0000,        0x0081,        0x8080,        0x0000,
        0x0000,        0x0082,        0x8080,        0x0000,
        0x0000,        0x0082,        0xC000,        0x0000,
        0x0000,        0x0082,        0x4040,        0x0000,
        0x0000,        0x0184,        0x2020,        0x0000,
        0x0000,        0x0104,        0x2020,        0x0000,
        0x0000,        0x0104,        0x1020,        0x0000,
        0x0000,        0x0104,        0x1010,        0x0000,
        0x0000,        0x0104,        0x1000,        0x0000,
        0x0000,        0x0208,        0x1010,        0x0000,
        0x0000,        0x0608,        0x0808,        0x0000,
        0x0000,        0x0410,        0x0808,        0x0000,
        0x0F00,        0x0410,        0x0408,        0x0000,
        0x1080,        0x0410,        0x0408,        0x0000,
        0x2440,        0x0420,        0x0404,        0x0000,
        0x4220,        0x0420,        0x0404,        0x0000,
        0x49A0,        0x0420,        0x0206,        0x0000,
        0x4020,        0x1FA0,        0x010F,        0x0000,
        0x4220,        0x60E0,        0x01F0,        0xC000,
        0x2040,        0xC040,        0x0140,        0x2000,
        0x5081,        0x0040,        0x0100,        0x1000,
        0x2F01,        0x7F00,        0x00FF,        0xE000,
        0x1000,        0x0000,        0x0000,        0x0000,
        0x0000,        0x0000,        0x0000,        0x0000,
        0x0000,        0x0000,        0x0000,        0x0000,
        0x0000,        0x0000,        0x0000,        0x0000,
        0x0000,        0x0000,        0x0000,        0x0000,
        0x0000,        0x0000,        0x0000,        0x0000,
        0x0000,        0x0000,        0x0000,        0x0000,
        0x0000,        0x0000,        0x0000,        0x0000,
        0x0000,        0x0000,        0x0000,        0x0000,
        0x0000,        0x0000,        0x0000,        0x0000,
        0x0000,        0x0000,        0x0000,        0x0000,
        0x0000,        0x0000,        0x0000,        0x0000,
        0x0000,        0x0000,        0x0000,        0x0000,
        0x0000,        0x0000,        0x0000,        0x0000
```

a0.icon

```
/* Format_version=1, Width=64, Height=64, Depth=1, Valid_bits_per_item=16
 */

        0x0000,        0x0000,        0x0000,        0x0000,
        0x0000,        0x0000,        0x0000,        0x0000,
        0x0000,        0x0000,        0x0000,        0x0000,
        0x0000,        0x0000,        0x0000,        0x0000,
        0x0000,        0x0000,        0x0000,        0x0000,
        0x0000,        0x0000,        0x0000,        0x0000,
        0x0000,        0x0000,        0x0000,        0x0000,
```

```
0x0000,    0x0000,    0x0000,    0x0000,
0x0000,    0x0000,    0x0000,    0x0000,
0x0000,    0x0000,    0x0000,    0x0000,
0x0000,    0x0000,    0x0000,    0x0000,
0x0000,    0x0000,    0x0000,    0x0000,
0x0000,    0x0000,    0x0000,    0x0000,
0x0000,    0x0000,    0x0000,    0x0000,
0x0000,    0x0000,    0x0000,    0x0000,
0x0000,    0x0000,    0x0000,    0x0000,
0x0000,    0x0100,    0x0000,    0x0000,
0x0000,    0x01C0,    0x0000,    0x0000,
0x0000,    0x01C0,    0x6000,    0x0000,
0x0000,    0x03E0,    0xC000,    0x0000,
0x0000,    0x01A1,    0xB000,    0x0000,
0x0000,    0x01FF,    0xF000,    0x0000,
0x0000,    0x0340,    0x3000,    0x2000,
0x0000,    0x0400,    0xE003,    0xA000,
0x0000,    0x0C00,    0x3004,    0x0000,
0x0000,    0x0444,    0x0808,    0x0000,
0x0000,    0x0C00,    0x0408,    0x0000,
0x0000,    0x3800,    0x0210,    0x0000,
0x0001,    0xFC00,    0xDF08,    0x0000,
0x0000,    0x1238,    0xD518,    0x0000,
0x0000,    0x3F00,    0x9818,    0x0000,
0x0000,    0x0282,    0x1210,    0x0000,
0x0000,    0x07EF,    0x8208,    0x0000,
0x0000,    0x0780,    0x8130,    0x0000,
0x0000,    0x0500,    0x81B0,    0x0000,
0x0000,    0x0100,    0x00C0,    0x0000,
0x0000,    0x0340,    0x6050,    0x0000,
0x0000,    0x0600,    0x2060,    0x0000,
0x0000,    0x0641,    0x2818,    0x0000,
0x0000,    0x0201,    0x2604,    0x0000,
0x0000,    0x0210,    0x2204,    0x0000,
0x0000,    0x0201,    0x1424,    0x0000,
0x0000,    0x0628,    0x9604,    0x0000,
0x0000,    0x08C2,    0x96EC,    0x0000,
0x0000,    0x0080,    0x9830,    0x0000,
0x0000,    0x0F00,    0x7000,    0x0000,
0x0000,    0x0000,    0x6000,    0x0000,
0x0000,    0x0000,    0x0000,    0x0000,
0x0000,    0x0000,    0x0000,    0x0000,
0x0000,    0x0000,    0x0000,    0x0000,
0x0000,    0x0000,    0x0000,    0x0000,
0x0000,    0x0000,    0x0000,    0x0000,
0x0000,    0x0000,    0x0000,    0x0000,
0x0000,    0x0000,    0x0000,    0x0000,
0x0000,    0x0000,    0x0000,    0x0000,
0x0000,    0x0000,    0x0000,    0x0000,
0x0000,    0x0000,    0x0000,    0x0000,
0x0000,    0x0000,    0x0000,    0x0000,
0x0000,    0x0000,    0x0000,    0x0000,
0x0000,    0x0000,    0x0000,    0x0000,
0x0000,    0x0000,    0x0000,    0x0000,
0x0000,    0x0000,    0x0000,    0x0000,
0x0000,    0x0000,    0x0000,    0x0000
```

a1.icon

```
/* Format_version=1, Width=64, Height=64, Depth=1, Valid_bits_per_item=16
*/
        0x0000,         0x0000,         0x0000,         0x007F,
        0x0000,         0x0000,         0x0000,         0x003E,
        0x0000,         0x0000,         0x0000,         0x001C,
        0x0000,         0x0000,         0x0000,         0x0000,
        0x0000,         0x0000,         0x0000,         0x0000,
        0x0000,         0x0000,         0x0000,         0x0000,
        0x0000,         0x0000,         0x0000,         0x0000,
        0x0000,         0x0000,         0x0000,         0x0000,
        0x0000,         0x0000,         0x0000,         0x0000,
        0x0000,         0x0000,         0x0000,         0x0000,
        0x0000,         0x0000,         0x0000,         0x0000,
        0x0000,         0x0000,         0x0000,         0x0000,
        0x0000,         0x0000,         0x0000,         0x0000,
        0x0000,         0x0000,         0x0000,         0x0000,
        0x0000,         0x0000,         0x0000,         0x0000,
        0x0000,         0x0000,         0x0000,         0x0000,
        0x0000,         0x0100,         0x0000,         0x0000,
        0x0000,         0x01C0,         0x0000,         0x0000,
        0x0000,         0x01C0,         0x6000,         0x0000,
        0x0000,         0x03E0,         0xC000,         0x0000,
        0x0000,         0x01A1,         0xB000,         0x0000,
        0x0000,         0x01FF,         0xF000,         0x0000,
        0x0000,         0x0340,         0x3000,         0x2000,
        0x0000,         0x0400,         0xE003,         0xA000,
        0x0000,         0x0C00,         0x3004,         0x0000,
        0x0000,         0x0444,         0x0808,         0x0000,
        0x0000,         0x0C00,         0x0408,         0x0000,
        0x0000,         0x3800,         0x0210,         0x0000,
        0x0001,         0xFC00,         0xDF08,         0x0000,
        0x0000,         0x1238,         0xD518,         0x0000,
        0x0000,         0x3F00,         0x9818,         0x0000,
        0x0000,         0x0282,         0x1210,         0x0000,
        0x0000,         0x07EF,         0x8208,         0x0000,
        0x0000,         0x0780,         0x8130,         0x0000,
        0x0000,         0x0500,         0x81B0,         0x0000,
        0x0000,         0x0100,         0x00C0,         0x0000,
        0x0000,         0x0340,         0x6050,         0x0000,
        0x0000,         0x0600,         0x2060,         0x0000,
        0x0000,         0x0641,         0x2818,         0x0000,
        0x0000,         0x0201,         0x2604,         0x0000,
        0x0000,         0x0210,         0x2204,         0x0000,
        0x0000,         0x0201,         0x1424,         0x0000,
        0x0000,         0x0628,         0x9604,         0x0000,
        0x0000,         0x08C2,         0x96EC,         0x0000,
        0x0000,         0x0080,         0x9830,         0x0000,
        0x0000,         0x0F00,         0x7000,         0x0000,
        0x0000,         0x0000,         0x6000,         0x0000,
        0x0000,         0x0000,         0x0000,         0x0000,
        0x0000,         0x0000,         0x0000,         0x0000,
        0x0000,         0x0000,         0x0000,         0x0000,
        0x0000,         0x0000,         0x0000,         0x0000,
        0x0000,         0x0000,         0x0000,         0x0000,
        0x0000,         0x0000,         0x0000,         0x0000,
        0x0000,         0x0000,         0x0000,         0x0000,
        0x0000,         0x0000,         0x0000,         0x0000,
```

```
      0x0000,       0x0000,       0x0000,       0x0000,
      0x0000,       0x0000,       0x0000,       0x0000,
      0x0000,       0x0000,       0x0000,       0x0000,
      0x0000,       0x0000,       0x0000,       0x0000,
      0x0000,       0x0000,       0x0000,       0x0000,
      0x0000,       0x0000,       0x0000,       0x0000,
      0x0000,       0x0000,       0x0000,       0x0000,
      0x0000,       0x0000,       0x0000,       0x0000
```

a2.icon

```
/* Format_version=1, Width=64, Height=64, Depth=1, Valid_bits_per_item=16
*/
      0x0000,       0x0000,       0x0000,       0x0000,
      0x0000,       0x0000,       0x0000,       0x0000,
      0x0000,       0x0000,       0x0000,       0x0000,
      0x0000,       0x0000,       0x0000,       0x0000,
      0x0000,       0x0000,       0x0000,       0xE000,
      0x0000,       0x0000,       0x0001,       0xF000,
      0x0000,       0x0000,       0x0003,       0xD800,
      0x0000,       0x0000,       0x0003,       0xF800,
      0x0000,       0x0000,       0x0003,       0xF800,
      0x0000,       0x0000,       0x0001,       0xF000,
      0x0000,       0x0000,       0x0000,       0xE000,
      0x0000,       0x0000,       0x0000,       0x0000,
      0x0000,       0x0000,       0x0000,       0x0000,
      0x0000,       0x0000,       0x0000,       0x0000,
      0x0000,       0x0000,       0x0000,       0x0000,
      0x0000,       0x0000,       0x0000,       0x0000,
      0x0000,       0x0100,       0x0000,       0x0000,
      0x0000,       0x01C0,       0x0000,       0x0000,
      0x0000,       0x01C0,       0x6000,       0x0000,
      0x0000,       0x03E0,       0xC000,       0x0000,
      0x0000,       0x01A1,       0xB000,       0x0000,
      0x0000,       0x01FF,       0xF000,       0x0000,
      0x0000,       0x0340,       0x3000,       0x2000,
      0x0000,       0x0400,       0xE003,       0xA000,
      0x0000,       0x0C00,       0x3004,       0x0000,
      0x0000,       0x0444,       0x0808,       0x0000,
      0x0000,       0x0C00,       0x0408,       0x0000,
      0x0000,       0x3800,       0x0210,       0x0000,
      0x0001,       0xFC00,       0xDF08,       0x0000,
      0x0000,       0x1238,       0xD518,       0x0000,
      0x0000,       0x3F00,       0x9818,       0x0000,
      0x0000,       0x0282,       0x1210,       0x0000,
      0x0000,       0x07EF,       0x8208,       0x0000,
      0x0000,       0x0780,       0x8130,       0x0000,
      0x0000,       0x0500,       0x81B0,       0x0000,
      0x0000,       0x0100,       0x00C0,       0x0000,
      0x0000,       0x0340,       0x6050,       0x0000,
      0x0000,       0x0600,       0x2060,       0x0000,
      0x0000,       0x0641,       0x2818,       0x0000,
      0x0000,       0x0201,       0x2604,       0x0000,
      0x0000,       0x0210,       0x2204,       0x0000,
      0x0000,       0x0201,       0x1424,       0x0000,
      0x0000,       0x0628,       0x9604,       0x0000,
      0x0000,       0x08C2,       0x96EC,       0x0000,
      0x0000,       0x0080,       0x9830,       0x0000,
```

```
        0x0000,        0x0F00,        0x7000,        0x0000,
        0x0000,        0x0000,        0x6000,        0x0000,
        0x0000,        0x0000,        0x0000,        0x0000,
        0x0000,        0x0000,        0x0000,        0x0000,
        0x0000,        0x0000,        0x0000,        0x0000,
        0x0000,        0x0000,        0x0000,        0x0000,
        0x0000,        0x0000,        0x0000,        0x0000,
        0x0000,        0x0000,        0x0000,        0x0000,
        0x0000,        0x0000,        0x0000,        0x0000,
        0x0000,        0x0000,        0x0000,        0x0000,
        0x0000,        0x0000,        0x0000,        0x0000,
        0x0000,        0x0000,        0x0000,        0x0000,
        0x0000,        0x0000,        0x0000,        0x0000,
        0x0000,        0x0000,        0x0000,        0x0000,
        0x0000,        0x0000,        0x0000,        0x0000,
        0x0000,        0x0000,        0x0000,        0x0000,
        0x0000,        0x0000,        0x0000,        0x0000,
        0x0000,        0x0000,        0x0000,        0x0000
```

a3.icon

```
/* Format_version=1, Width=64, Height=64, Depth=1, Valid_bits_per_item=16
*/
        0x0000,        0x0000,        0x0000,        0x0000,
        0x0000,        0x0000,        0x0000,        0x0000,
        0x0000,        0x0000,        0x0000,        0x0000,
        0x0000,        0x0000,        0x0000,        0x0000,
        0x0000,        0x0000,        0x0000,        0x0000,
        0x0000,        0x0000,        0x0000,        0x0000,
        0x0000,        0x0000,        0x0000,        0x0000,
        0x0000,        0x0000,        0x0000,        0x0000,
        0x0000,        0x0000,        0x0000,        0x0000,
        0x0000,        0x0000,        0x0000,        0x0000,
        0x0000,        0x0000,        0x0000,        0x0000,
        0x0000,        0x0000,        0x0000,        0x0000,
        0x0000,        0x0000,        0x0000,        0x0000,
        0x0000,        0x0000,        0x0700,        0x0000,
        0x0000,        0x0000,        0x0F80,        0x0000,
        0x0000,        0x0000,        0x1EC0,        0x0000,
        0x0000,        0x0100,        0x1FC0,        0x0000,
        0x0000,        0x01C0,        0x1FC0,        0x0000,
        0x0000,        0x01C0,        0x6F80,        0x0000,
        0x0000,        0x03E0,        0xC700,        0x0000,
        0x0000,        0x01A1,        0xB000,        0x0000,
        0x0000,        0x01FF,        0xF000,        0x0000,
        0x0000,        0x0340,        0x3000,        0x2000,
        0x0000,        0x0400,        0xE003,        0xA000,
        0x0000,        0x0C00,        0x3004,        0x0000,
        0x0000,        0x0444,        0x0808,        0x0000,
        0x0000,        0x0C00,        0x0408,        0x0000,
        0x0000,        0x3800,        0x0210,        0x0000,
        0x0001,        0xFC00,        0xDF08,        0x0000,
        0x0000,        0x1238,        0xD518,        0x0000,
        0x0000,        0x3F00,        0x9818,        0x0000,
        0x0000,        0x0282,        0x1210,        0x0000,
        0x0000,        0x07EF,        0x8208,        0x0000,
        0x0000,        0x0780,        0x8130,        0x0000,
        0x0000,        0x0500,        0x81B0,        0x0000,
        0x0000,        0x0100,        0x00C0,        0x0000,
```

```
    0x0000,        0x0340,        0x6050,        0x0000,
    0x0000,        0x0600,        0x2060,        0x0000,
    0x0000,        0x0641,        0x2818,        0x0000,
    0x0000,        0x0201,        0x2604,        0x0000,
    0x0000,        0x0210,        0x2204,        0x0000,
    0x0000,        0x0201,        0x1424,        0x0000,
    0x0000,        0x0628,        0x9604,        0x0000,
    0x0000,        0x08C2,        0x96EC,        0x0000,
    0x0000,        0x0080,        0x9830,        0x0000,
    0x0000,        0x0F00,        0x7000,        0x0000,
    0x0000,        0x0000,        0x6000,        0x0000,
    0x0000,        0x0000,        0x0000,        0x0000,
    0x0000,        0x0000,        0x0000,        0x0000,
    0x0000,        0x0000,        0x0000,        0x0000,
    0x0000,        0x0000,        0x0000,        0x0000,
    0x0000,        0x0000,        0x0000,        0x0000,
    0x0000,        0x0000,        0x0000,        0x0000,
    0x0000,        0x0000,        0x0000,        0x0000,
    0x0000,        0x0000,        0x0000,        0x0000,
    0x0000,        0x0000,        0x0000,        0x0000,
    0x0000,        0x0000,        0x0000,        0x0000,
    0x0000,        0x0000,        0x0000,        0x0000,
    0x0000,        0x0000,        0x0000,        0x0000,
    0x0000,        0x0000,        0x0000,        0x0000,
    0x0000,        0x0000,        0x0000,        0x0000,
    0x0000,        0x0000,        0x0000,        0x0000,
    0x0000,        0x0000,        0x0000,        0x0000
```

▉▉▉▉▉ a4.icon

```
/* Format_version=1, Width=64, Height=64, Depth=1, Valid_bits_per_item=16
*/
    0x0000,        0x0000,        0x0000,        0x0000,
    0x0000,        0x0000,        0x0000,        0x0000,
    0x0000,        0x0000,        0x0000,        0x0000,
    0x0000,        0x0000,        0x0000,        0x0000,
    0x0000,        0x0000,        0x0000,        0x0000,
    0x0000,        0x0000,        0x0000,        0x0000,
    0x0000,        0x0000,        0x0000,        0x0000,
    0x0000,        0x0000,        0x0000,        0x0000,
    0x0000,        0x0000,        0x0000,        0x0000,
    0x0000,        0x0000,        0x0002,        0x0000,
    0x0000,        0x0000,        0x0002,        0x0000,
    0x0000,        0x0000,        0x0006,        0x0000,
    0x0000,        0x0000,        0x0004,        0x0000,
    0x0000,        0x0000,        0x000A,        0x0000,
    0x0000,        0x0000,        0x000C,        0x0000,
    0x0000,        0x0000,        0x0014,        0x0000,
    0x0000,        0x0000,        0x0004,        0x0000,
    0x0000,        0x0040,        0x0008,        0x0000,
    0x0000,        0x0040,        0x0018,        0x0000,
    0x0000,        0x0020,        0x0018,        0x0000,
    0x0000,        0x0100,        0x0010,        0x0000,
    0x0000,        0x01C7,        0x0030,        0x0000,
    0x0000,        0x01CF,        0x80A0,        0x0000,
    0x0000,        0x03FE,        0xC020,        0x0000,
    0x0000,        0x01BF,        0xC060,        0x0000,
```

```
      0x0000,      0x01FF,      0xC060,      0x0000,
      0x0000,      0x034F,      0xC140,      0x0000,
      0x0000,      0x0407,      0xA240,      0x0000,
      0x0000,      0x0C44,      0x2240,      0x0000,
      0x0000,      0x04AA,      0x1240,      0x0000,
      0x0000,      0x0C40,      0x9640,      0x0000,
      0x0000,      0x3800,      0x30C0,      0x0000,
      0x0001,      0xFC10,      0x8080,      0x0000,
      0x0000,      0x1238,      0x9840,      0x0000,
      0x0000,      0x3F38,      0xD860,      0x0000,
      0x0000,      0x0282,      0x9210,      0x0000,
      0x0000,      0x07EF,      0xD208,      0x0000,
      0x0000,      0x07C0,      0xA106,      0x0000,
      0x0000,      0x0500,      0x9183,      0x0000,
      0x0000,      0x0300,      0x00C1,      0x8000,
      0x0000,      0x0E40,      0x6050,      0xC000,
      0x0000,      0x7040,      0x207C,      0x1C00,
      0x0000,      0xC0C1,      0x280C,      0x7000,
      0x0000,      0xFF01,      0x260E,      0x8000,
      0x0000,      0x0000,      0x2000,      0x0000,
      0x0000,      0x0000,      0x0000,      0x0000,
      0x0000,      0x0000,      0x0000,      0x0000,
      0x0000,      0x0000,      0x0000,      0x0000,
      0x0000,      0x0000,      0x0000,      0x0000,
      0x0000,      0x0000,      0x0000,      0x0000,
      0x0000,      0x0000,      0x0000,      0x0000,
      0x0000,      0x0000,      0x0000,      0x0000,
      0x0000,      0x0000,      0x0000,      0x0000,
      0x0000,      0x0000,      0x0000,      0x0000,
      0x0000,      0x0000,      0x0000,      0x0000,
      0x0000,      0x0000,      0x0000,      0x0000,
      0x0000,      0x0000,      0x0000,      0x0000,
      0x0000,      0x0000,      0x0000,      0x0000,
      0x0000,      0x0000,      0x0000,      0x0000,
      0x0000,      0x0000,      0x0000,      0x0000,
      0x0000,      0x0000,      0x0000,      0x0000
```

a5.icon

```
/* Format_version=1, Width=64, Height=64, Depth=1, Valid_bits_per_item=16
*/
      0x0000,      0x0000,      0x0000,      0x0000,
      0x0000,      0x0000,      0x0000,      0x0000,
      0x0000,      0x0000,      0x0000,      0x0000,
      0x0000,      0x0000,      0x0000,      0x0000,
      0x0000,      0x0000,      0x0000,      0x0000,
      0x0000,      0x0000,      0x0000,      0x0000,
      0x0000,      0x0000,      0x0000,      0x0000,
      0x0000,      0x0000,      0x0000,      0x0000,
      0x0000,      0x0300,      0x0000,      0x0000,
      0x0000,      0x0100,      0x0000,      0x0000,
      0x0000,      0xE100,      0x0000,      0x0000,
      0x0001,      0xF080,      0x0000,      0x0000,
      0x0003,      0xD800,      0x0000,      0x0000,
```

```
0x0003,     0xF800,     0x0000,     0x0000,
0x0003,     0xF800,     0x0000,     0x0000,
0x0001,     0xF000,     0x0000,     0x0000,
0x0000,     0xE000,     0x0000,     0x0000,
0x0000,     0x0000,     0x0000,     0x0000,
0x0000,     0x0000,     0x0200,     0x0000,
0x0000,     0x0000,     0xC100,     0x0000,
0x0000,     0x0100,     0x0000,     0x0000,
0x0000,     0x0104,     0x0400,     0x0000,
0x0000,     0x0100,     0x8040,     0x0000,
0x0000,     0x03C0,     0x0000,     0x0000,
0x0000,     0xF5A0,     0x0000,     0x0000,
0x0000,     0x83F8,     0x8000,     0x03FE,
0x0000,     0xFF4B,     0xF805,     0x686C,
0x0000,     0x4407,     0xA7D0,     0x1FC0,
0x0000,     0x0C47,     0xFF07,     0xF000,
0x0000,     0x04E7,     0x901C,     0x0000,
0x0000,     0x0C43,     0x9670,     0x0000,
0x0000,     0x3803,     0x30C0,     0x0000,
0x0001,     0xFC11,     0x00EF,     0xFD00,
0x0000,     0x123C,     0x1840,     0x0100,
0x0000,     0x3F38,     0x5860,     0x0100,
0x0003,     0xC3B3,     0x8FF0,     0x0600,
0x0006,     0x0FFF,     0x841F,     0xFE00,
0x0008,     0x19D0,     0xC100,     0x0000,
0x0030,     0x30F0,     0x2080,     0x0000,
0x0000,     0xC1B0,     0x1840,     0x0000,
0x001F,     0x81B8,     0x0660,     0x0000,
0x0000,     0x01F8,     0x0320,     0x0000,
0x0000,     0x0140,     0x01E0,     0x0000,
0x0000,     0x01F0,     0x0020,     0x0000,
0x0000,     0x00C0,     0x0000,     0x0000,
0x0000,     0x0000,     0x0000,     0x0000,
0x0000,     0x0000,     0x0000,     0x0000,
0x0000,     0x0000,     0x0000,     0x0000,
0x0000,     0x0000,     0x0000,     0x0000,
0x0000,     0x0000,     0x0000,     0x0000,
0x0000,     0x0000,     0x0000,     0x0000,
0x0000,     0x0000,     0x0000,     0x0000,
0x0000,     0x0000,     0x0000,     0x0000,
0x0000,     0x0000,     0x0000,     0x0000,
0x0000,     0x0000,     0x0000,     0x0000,
0x0000,     0x0000,     0x0000,     0x0000,
0x0000,     0x0000,     0x0000,     0x0000,
0x0000,     0x0000,     0x0000,     0x0000,
0x0000,     0x0000,     0x0000,     0x0000,
0x0000,     0x0000,     0x0000,     0x0000,
0x0000,     0x0000,     0x0000,     0x0000,
0x0000,     0x0000,     0x0000,     0x0000
```

a6.icon

```
/* Format_version=1, Width=64, Height=64, Depth=1, Valid_bits_per_item=16
*/
0x0000,     0x0000,     0x0000,     0x0000,
0x0000,     0x0000,     0x0000,     0x0000,
```

```
0x0000,    0x0000,    0x0000,    0x0000,
0x0000,    0x0000,    0x0000,    0x0000,
0x0000,    0x0000,    0x0000,    0x0000,
0x0000,    0x0000,    0x0000,    0x0000,
0x0000,    0x0000,    0x0000,    0x0000,
0x0000,    0x0000,    0x0000,    0x0000,
0x0000,    0x0000,    0x0000,    0x0000,
0x0000,    0x0000,    0x0000,    0x0000,
0x0000,    0x0000,    0x0000,    0x0000,
0x0000,    0x0000,    0x0000,    0x0000,
0x0000,    0x0000,    0x0000,    0x0000,
0x0000,    0x0000,    0x0000,    0x0000,
0x0000,    0x0000,    0x0000,    0x0000,
0x0000,    0x0000,    0x0000,    0x0000,
0x0000,    0x0000,    0x0000,    0x0000,
0x0000,    0x0000,    0x0000,    0x0000,
0x0000,    0x0000,    0x0000,    0x0000,
0x0000,    0x0000,    0x0000,    0x0000,
0x0000,    0x0100,    0x0000,    0x0000,
0x0000,    0x0100,    0x0000,    0x0000,
0x0000,    0x0100,    0x0000,    0x0000,
0x0000,    0x03C0,    0x0000,    0x0000,
0x0000,    0xF5A0,    0x0000,    0x0000,
0x0000,    0x83F8,    0x8000,    0x03FE,
0x0000,    0xFF4B,    0xF805,    0x686C,
0x0000,    0x4407,    0xA7D0,    0x1FC0,
0x0000,    0x0C47,    0xFF07,    0xF000,
0x0000,    0x04E7,    0x901C,    0x0000,
0x0000,    0x0C43,    0x9670,    0x0000,
0x0000,    0x3803,    0x30C0,    0x0000,
0x0001,    0xFC11,    0x00EF,    0xFD00,
0x0000,    0x123C,    0x1840,    0x0100,
0x0000,    0x3F38,    0x5860,    0x0100,
0x0003,    0xC3B3,    0x8FF0,    0x0600,
0x0006,    0x0FFF,    0x841F,    0xFE00,
0x0008,    0x19D0,    0xC100,    0x0000,
0x0030,    0x30F0,    0x2080,    0x0000,
0x0000,    0xC1B0,    0x1840,    0x0000,
0x001F,    0x81B8,    0x0660,    0x0000,
0x0000,    0x01F8,    0x0320,    0x0000,
0x0000,    0x0140,    0x01E0,    0x0000,
0x0000,    0x01F0,    0x0020,    0x0000,
0x0000,    0x00C0,    0x0000,    0x0000,
0x0000,    0x0000,    0x0000,    0x0000,
0x0000,    0x0000,    0x0000,    0x0000,
0x0000,    0x0000,    0x0000,    0x0000,
0x0000,    0x0000,    0x0000,    0x0000,
0x0000,    0x0000,    0x0000,    0x0000,
0x0000,    0x0000,    0x0000,    0x0000,
0x0000,    0x0000,    0x0000,    0x0000,
0x0000,    0x0000,    0x0000,    0x0000,
0x0000,    0x0000,    0x0000,    0x0000,
0x0000,    0x0000,    0x0000,    0x0000,
0x0000,    0x0000,    0x0000,    0x0000,
0x0000,    0x0000,    0x0000,    0x0000,
0x0000,    0x0000,    0x0000,    0x0000,
0x0000,    0x0000,    0x0000,    0x0000,
0x0000,    0x0000,    0x0000,    0x0000,
0x0000,    0x0000,    0x0000,    0x0000,
0x0000,    0x0000,    0x0000,    0x0000
```

a7.icon

```
/* Format_version=1, Width=64, Height=64, Depth=1, Valid_bits_per_item=16
*/
        0x0000,        0x0000,        0x0000,        0x0000,
        0x0000,        0x0000,        0x0000,        0x0000,
        0x0000,        0x0000,        0x0000,        0x0000,
        0x0000,        0x0000,        0x0000,        0x0000,
        0x0000,        0x0000,        0x0000,        0x0000,
        0x0000,        0x0000,        0x0000,        0x0000,
        0x0000,        0x0000,        0x0000,        0x0000,
        0x0000,        0x0000,        0x0000,        0x0000,
        0x0000,        0x0000,        0x0000,        0x0000,
        0x0000,        0x0000,        0x0000,        0x0000,
        0x0000,        0x0000,        0x0000,        0x0000,
        0x0000,        0x0000,        0x0000,        0x0000,
        0x0000,        0x0000,        0x0000,        0x0000,
        0x0000,        0x0000,        0x0000,        0x0000,
        0x0000,        0x0000,        0x0000,        0x0000,
        0x0000,        0x0000,        0x0000,        0x0000,
        0x0000,        0x0000,        0x0000,        0x0000,
        0x0000,        0x0000,        0x0000,        0x0000,
        0x0000,        0x0000,        0x0000,        0x0500,
        0x0000,        0x0100,        0x0000,        0x3F00,
        0x0000,        0x0100,        0x0001,        0xF000,
        0x0000,        0x0100,        0x0003,        0xC000,
        0x0000,        0x03C0,        0x000E,        0x0000,
        0x0000,        0xF5A0,        0x0012,        0x0000,
        0x0000,        0x83F8,        0x8064,        0x0000,
        0x0000,        0xFF4B,        0xF89C,        0x0000,
        0x0000,        0x4407,        0xA7F0,        0x0000,
        0x0000,        0x0C47,        0xFFC0,        0x0000,
        0x0000,        0x04E7,        0x9000,        0x0000,
        0x0000,        0x0C43,        0x9640,        0x0000,
        0x0000,        0x3803,        0x30C0,        0x0000,
        0x0001,        0xFC11,        0x00EF,        0xFD00,
        0x0000,        0x123C,        0x1840,        0x0100,
        0x0000,        0x3F38,        0x5860,        0x0100,
        0x0003,        0xC3B3,        0x8FF0,        0x0600,
        0x0006,        0x0FFF,        0x841F,        0xFE00,
        0x0008,        0x19D0,        0xC100,        0x0000,
        0x0030,        0x30F0,        0x2080,        0x0000,
        0x0000,        0xC1B0,        0x1840,        0x0000,
        0x001F,        0x81B8,        0x0660,        0x0000,
        0x0000,        0x01F8,        0x0320,        0x0000,
        0x0000,        0x0140,        0x01E0,        0x0000,
        0x0000,        0x01F0,        0x0020,        0x0000,
        0x0000,        0x00C0,        0x0000,        0x0000,
        0x0000,        0x0000,        0x0000,        0x0000,
        0x0000,        0x0000,        0x0000,        0x0000,
        0x0000,        0x0000,        0x0000,        0x0000,
        0x0000,        0x0000,        0x0000,        0x0000,
        0x0000,        0x0000,        0x0000,        0x0000,
        0x0000,        0x0000,        0x0000,        0x0000,
        0x0000,        0x0000,        0x0000,        0x0000,
        0x0000,        0x0000,        0x0000,        0x0000,
        0x0000,        0x0000,        0x0000,        0x0000,
        0x0000,        0x0000,        0x0000,        0x0000,
        0x0000,        0x0000,        0x0000,        0x0000,
        0x0000,        0x0000,        0x0000,        0x0000,
```

```
        0x0000,       0x0000,       0x0000,       0x0000,
        0x0000,       0x0000,       0x0000,       0x0000,
        0x0000,       0x0000,       0x0000,       0x0000,
        0x0000,       0x0000,       0x0000,       0x0000,
        0x0000,       0x0000,       0x0000,       0x0000
```

a8.icon

```
/* Format_version=1, Width=64, Height=64, Depth=1,  Valid_bits_per_item=16
*/
        0x0000,       0x0000,       0x0000,       0x0000,
        0x0000,       0x0000,       0x0000,       0x0000,
        0x0000,       0x0000,       0x0000,       0x0000,
        0x0000,       0x0000,       0x0000,       0x0000,
        0x0000,       0x0000,       0x0000,       0x0000,
        0x0000,       0x0000,       0x0000,       0x0000,
        0x0000,       0x0000,       0x0000,       0x0000,
        0x0000,       0x0000,       0x0000,       0x0000,
        0x0000,       0x0000,       0x0000,       0x0000,
        0x0000,       0x0000,       0x0000,       0x0000,
        0x0000,       0x0000,       0x0000,       0x0000,
        0x0000,       0x0000,       0x0000,       0x0000,
        0x0000,       0x0000,       0x0000,       0x0000,
        0x0000,       0x0000,       0x0000,       0x0000,
        0x0000,       0x0000,       0x0000,       0x0000,
        0x0000,       0x0000,       0x0000,       0x0000,
        0x0000,       0x0100,       0x0000,       0x0000,
        0x0000,       0x01C0,       0x0000,       0x0000,
        0x0000,       0x01C0,       0x6000,       0x0000,
        0x0000,       0x03E0,       0xC000,       0x0000,
        0x0000,       0x01A1,       0xB004,       0x0000,
        0x0000,       0x01FF,       0xF000,       0x0000,
        0x0000,       0x0340,       0x3004,       0x0000,
        0x0000,       0x0400,       0xE002,       0x0000,
        0x0000,       0x0C00,       0x3002,       0x0000,
        0x0000,       0x0444,       0x0803,       0x0000,
        0x0000,       0x0C00,       0x0401,       0x8000,
        0x0000,       0x3800,       0x0200,       0x4000,
        0x0001,       0xFC00,       0xDF00,       0x8000,
        0x0000,       0x1238,       0xD500,       0x4000,
        0x0000,       0x3F00,       0x9801,       0x4000,
        0x0000,       0x0282,       0x1202,       0x8000,
        0x0000,       0x07EF,       0x820A,       0x0000,
        0x0000,       0x0780,       0x811C,       0x0000,
        0x0000,       0x0500,       0x81B0,       0x0000,
        0x0000,       0x0100,       0x00E0,       0x0000,
        0x0000,       0x0340,       0x6050,       0x0000,
        0x0000,       0x0600,       0x2060,       0x0000,
        0x0000,       0x0641,       0x2818,       0x0000,
        0x0000,       0x0201,       0x2604,       0x0000,
        0x0000,       0x0210,       0x2204,       0x0000,
        0x0000,       0x0201,       0x1424,       0x0000,
        0x0000,       0x0628,       0x9604,       0x0000,
        0x0000,       0x08C2,       0x96EC,       0x0000,
        0x0000,       0x0080,       0x9830,       0x0000,
        0x0000,       0x0F00,       0x7000,       0x0000,
        0x0000,       0x0000,       0x6000,       0x0000,
        0x0000,       0x0000,       0x0000,       0x0000,
        0x0000,       0x0000,       0x0000,       0x0000,
        0x0000,       0x0000,       0x0000,       0x0000,
```

```
0x0000,     0x0000,     0x0000,     0x0000,
0x0000,     0x0000,     0x0000,     0x0000,
0x0000,     0x0000,     0x0000,     0x0000,
0x0000,     0x0000,     0x0000,     0x0000,
0x0000,     0x0000,     0x0000,     0x0000,
0x0000,     0x0000,     0x0000,     0x0000,
0x0000,     0x0000,     0x0000,     0x0000,
0x0000,     0x0000,     0x0000,     0x0000,
0x0000,     0x0000,     0x0000,     0x0000,
0x0000,     0x0000,     0x0000,     0x0000,
0x0000,     0x0000,     0x0000,     0x0000,
0x0000,     0x0000,     0x0000,     0x0000,
0x0000,     0x0000,     0x0000,     0x0000,
0x0000,     0x0000,     0x0000,     0x0000,
```

Index